Childhood Aggression and Violence

Sources of Influence, Prevention, and Control

APPLIED CLINICAL PSYCHOLOGY

Series Editors:
Alan S. Bellack, *Medical College of Pennsylvania at EPPI, Philadelphia, Pennsylvania,*
and Michel Hersen, *University of Pittsburgh, Pittsburgh, Pennsylvania*

Current Volumes in this Series

CHILDHOOD AGGRESSION AND VIOLENCE
Sources of Influence, Prevention, and Control
   Edited by David H. Crowell, Ian M. Evans, and Clifford R. O'Donnell

HANDBOOK OF ASSESSMENT IN CHILDHOOD PSYCHOPATHOLOGY
Applied Issues in Differential Diagnosis and Treatment Evaluation
   Edited by Cynthia L. Frame and Johnny L. Matson

HANDBOOK OF BEHAVIORAL GROUP THERAPY
   Edited by Dennis Upper and Steven M. Ross

ISSUES IN PSYCHOTHERAPY RESEARCH
   Edited by Michel Hersen, Larry Michelson, and Alan S. Bellack

A PRIMER OF HUMAN BEHAVIORAL PHARMACOLOGY
   Alan Poling

THE PRIVATE PRACTICE OF BEHAVIOR THERAPY
   Sheldon J. Kaplan

RESEARCH METHODS IN APPLIED BEHAVIOR ANALYSIS
Issues and Advances
   Edited by Alan Poling and R. Wayne Fuqua

SEVERE BEHAVIOR DISORDERS IN THE MENTALLY RETARDED
Nondrug Approaches to Treatment
   Edited by Rowland P. Barrett

SUBSTANCE ABUSE AND PSYCHOPATHOLOGY
   Edited by Arthur I. Alterman

TREATING ADDICTIVE BEHAVIORS
Processes of Change
   Edited by William R. Miller and·Nick Heather

A Continuation Order Plan is available for this series. A continuation order will bring delivery
of each new volume immediately upon publication. Volumes are billed only upon actual ship-
ment. For further information please contact the publisher.

Childhood Aggression and Violence
Sources of Influence, Prevention, and Control

Edited by
David H. Crowell
University of Hawaii at Manoa
Honolulu, Hawaii

Ian M. Evans
State University of New York at Binghamton
Binghamton, New York

and
Clifford R. O'Donnell
University of Hawaii at Manoa
Honolulu, Hawaii

Plenum Press • New York and London

Library of Congress Cataloging in Publication Data

Childhood aggression and violence.
  (Applied clinical psychology)
  Based on one of a series of symposia initiated by the Dept. of Psychology, University of Hawaii at Manoa.
  Includes bibliographies and index.
  1. Aggressiveness in children—Congresses. 2. Violence in children—Congresses. 3. Child psychopathology—Congresses. I. Crowell, David Harrison. II. Evans, Ian M. III. O'Donnell, Clifford R. IV. University of Hawaii at Manoa. Dept. of Psychology. V. Series. [DNLM: 1. Aggression—in infancy & childhood—congresses. 2. Child Behavior Disorders—congresses. 3. Social Behavior Disorders—in infancy and childhood—congresses. WS 350.8.A4 C536]
RJ506.A35C48   1986   618.92′8582   86-30359
ISBN 0-306-42355-3

© 1987 Plenum Press, New York
A Division of Plenum Publishing Corporation
233 Spring Street, New York, N.Y. 10013

Printed in the United States of America

To Doris, Michael, Sandra, Shannon, and Megan
D. H. C.

To my spouse, Luanna Meyer, colleague and friend
I. M. E.

To Barbara, my wife, lover, and favorite person
C. R. O.

Contributors

Jay Belsky
College of Human Development, Department of Individual and Family Studies, Pennsylvania State University, University Park, Pennsylvania

Meda Chesney-Lind
Youth Development and Research Center, University of Hawaii at Manoa, Honolulu, Hawaii

David H. Crowell
Department of Psychology, University of Hawaii at Manoa, Honolulu, Hawaii

Eric Dubow
Department of Psychology, University of Illinois at Chicago, Chicago, Illinois

Leonard Eron
Department of Psychology, University of Illinois at Chicago, Chicago, Illinois

Ian M. Evans
Department of Psychology, State University of New York at Binghamton, Binghamton, New York

J. David Hawkins
School of Social Work, University of Washington, Seattle, Washington

L. Rowell Huesmann
Department of Psychology, University of Illinois at Chicago, Chicago, Illinois

Denise Lishner
School of Social Work, University of Washington, Seattle, Washington

Teru Morton
Department of Psychology, University of Hawaii, Honolulu, Hawaii

Deane Neubauer
Dean, Faculty of Social Sciences, University of Hawaii at Manoa, Honolulu, Hawaii

Clifford R. O'Donnell
Department of Psychology, University of Hawaii at Manoa, Honolulu, Hawaii

David Pearl
Chief, Behavioral Sciences Research Branch, Alcohol, Drug Abuse, and Mental Health Administration, Rockville, Maryland

Jonathan H. Pincus
Department of Neurology, Yale University School of Medicine, New Haven, Connecticut

Richard Romanoff
Department of Psychology, University of Illinois at Chicago, Chicago, Illinois

Alice D. Scheuer
Department of Psychology, University of Hawaii at Manoa, Honolulu, Hawaii

Elliot Turiel
Division of Educational Psychology, Department of Education, University of California, Berkeley, California

Joan Vondra
College of Human Development, Department of Individual and Family Studies, Pennsylvania State University, University Park, Pennsylvania

Patty Warnick Yarmel
Department of Psychology, University of Illinois at Chicago, Chicago, Illinois

Preface

The conference on which this volume is based was one of a series of symposia initiated by the Department of Psychology at the University of Hawaii at Manoa on the theory and research surrounding topics of interest to the faculty and germane to the Hawaiian community. In order to encourage interaction around specific themes, the symposium series has assembled a small, select group of scholars to exchange knowledge, ideas, and enthusiasm with the resident faculty, students, and the community at large.

The first two symposia concentrated on cross-cultural themes (Marsella, Tharp, & Ciborowski, 1979; Marsella, DeVos, & Hsu, 1985). The third one addressed a significant social problem: aggression and violence in children. At the time that our plan was being developed, Hawaii, along with mainland states, was experiencing or at least expressing widespread alarm over the involvement of children and youth in violent crime, in belligerence at school, as perpetrators of aggression at home, and as victims of physical abuse.

This symposium was planned around a major area within the department, the Clinical Studies Program. The Clinical Studies Program has developed along two interrelated lines of concentration: one emphasized the foundation of clincical psychology in basic science and the other expanded its purview into the broader community, covering prevention, systems change, and social networks. It was in this spirit that we tried to link the traditions of a psychobiologist, a developmental psychologist, a clinical psychologist, and a community psychologist with participants who were leading aggression and behavioral researchers with clinical and applied orientations. To this blend of local and national expertise, we extend our warmest aloha and appreciation.

To reflect further our focus on sources of influence and social change, each participant was asked to contribute a practical workshop in addition to a formal presentation. This concern for application was especially appreciated by various service providers in the community.

The involvement of these groups and individuals—many of them concerned largely with direct service—typified the intent of the symposium, which was to reveal the *practical implications* of behavioral research in childhood aggression. Many of the speakers commented on the fact that aggressive behavior is "multiply determined"—it became almost the catchphrase of the conference. Multiply determined, but not mysteriously determined. When reading these chapters, one cannot help but be struck by the extent of our basic understanding in behavioral science of a social issue such as aggression. In an address given in Honolulu some years ago, Theodore Blau, then president of the American Psychological Association, commented on how much we really do know as psychologists (a position of stark contrast to our usual academic stance bemoaning our great ignorance). This general optimism—that significant understanding is attainable even when we refuse to oversimplify the cause of social ills—is a dominant theme of the remarks made by Deane Neubauer, dean of the Faculty of Social Sciences in the University of Hawaii at Manoa. Dean Neubauer gave us his wholehearted administrative support and graciously agreed to write the introduction to this volume. We thank him heartily for both.

This conference is the result of the efforts of the organizing committee: Robert J. Blanchard, psychobiologist and a nationally and internationally recognized researcher on aggression; David H. Crowell, a developmental psychologist, whose involvement was a continuation of interests developed early in his clinical career as a consultant to the Minimum Sentence Board, Oahu State Prison, and to the Juvenile Court, First Judicial District, State of Hawaii; Ian M. Evans, a clinical psychologist, who contributed a broad theoretical and applied behavioral orientation toward childhood aggression; and Clifford R. O'Donnell, a researcher with the Youth Development and Research Center, whose interests in community psychology insured an interdisciplinary focus on aggression in children.

Our department has a number of members who have themselves made notable contributions to aggression research, particularly Carolyn Blanchard, whose national and international reputation is well known, and to developmental and educational research, particularly Richard Dubanoski and Roland Tharp. They provided important input and suggestions for which we express our sincere appreciation. Our student clerical support also must not go unmentioned and appreciation is expressed to Cecilia Valdez and Carol Sulfelix.

A number of agencies extended substantial material support to make the symposium possible. We are particularly grateful to the director, Jack T. Nagoshi, and the staff members of the Youth Development and Research Center of the School of Social Work at the University of Hawaii, especially Joyce Tanji and Lanette Yoshioka.

Finally, special thanks and credit must go to Alice Scheuer, who is a doctoral student in clinical psychology. Her assistance made a major contribution to the editing of this collection, tackling both style and content with authority. We are greatly indebted to her and her outstanding work.

DAVID H. CROWELL
IAN M. EVANS
CLIFFORD R. O'DONNELL

REFERENCES

Marsella, A. J., Tharp, R., & Ciborowski, T. (Eds.). (1979). *Perspectives on cross-cultural psychology*. New York: Academic Press.

Marsella, A. J., DeVos, G., & Hsu, F. L. K. (Eds.). (1985). *Culture and self: Asian and western perspectives*. New York: Tavistock.

Conference Sponsors

The organizing committee gratefully appreciates the support of the following groups:

Public Health Fund of the Chamber of Commerce of Hawaii

President's Advisory Funding Committee of the University of Hawaii Foundation

Division of Social Sciences, University of Hawaii at Manoa

Department of Psychology, University of Hawaii at Manoa

Youth Development and Research Center, School of Social Work, University of Hawaii at Manoa

Department of Psychiatry, John F. Burns School of Medicine, University of Hawaii at Manoa

Department of Education, State of Hawaii

Contents

Clifford R. O'Donnell

PART **I**

PERSPECTIVE

CHAPTER 1

Childhood Aggression and Violence
Introduction

DEANE NEUBAUER

Violence, especially that committed upon, by, and within the young, has become a primary issue in American culture over the past decade. The 1960s, with their political manifestations of violence, including the assassinations of three important political leaders and the maiming of a fourth, civil demonstrations in the name of racial and social equality, and massive protests against governmental policies of conscription and foreign military intervention, provided the nation with a focus on its native traditions of violence and social upheaval which the superficial quietude of the 1950s had obscured.

Social critics and historians were quick to remind us of our collective violent past, a history that includes such salient chains of events as the century-long struggle to claim a continent against the protests of its native inhabitants; the equally long struggle to impose social order along the frontier; the epic battles of capital and labor to establish the conditions of wealth creation and distribution; the lengthy struggle to adapt and assimilate immigrant populations from all parts of the globe; a racial history of oppression, liberation, subsequent suppression, and yet another struggle for liberation; a long and costly civil war of brother against brother, family against family; and an expansionist political history that witnessed the direct intervention of the United States in the affairs of other nations 59 times during the period 1898 to 1941 alone (Williams, 1980).

Enumerating such events does little more, of course, than highlight the social landscape of the two centuries of American society since nationhood, but this litany of social strife alerts us to how the collective memory functions to create a base-line for what we regard as normal in society. The dominant institu-

DEANE NEUBAUER • Dean, College of Social Sciences, University of Hawaii at Manoa, Honolulu, Hawaii 96822.

tions for opinion formation in the United States, including the symbol–creating and sustaining apparatus of government at all levels, operate to develop what the political scientist Murray Edelman calls a sense of "quiescence" within a population, a sense that "all is well" and that informed and potent leaders are in charge of the public weal (Edelman, 1964).

Within this framework disturbances of the social peace are viewed as episodic disruptions to be responded to by discrete actions. These mechanisms for the creation of a public perspective are embodied in the opinion-generating sectors of society including the private media. They lead to a view within the population about society at large that is unhistorical, segmented, nonstructural with respect to ideas of social causation, and heavily focused on explanatory modes that are personalistic and situationally specific. As many commentators have pointed out, this way of viewing social life supports the interests of the institutional status quo because individuals (citizens) are not encouraged to develop longitudinal structural explanations of social events, but rather see them as part of an endless stream of relatively isolated social problems that arise from time to time and require discrete solutions.

It was against this background that the experiences of the 1960s and their manifestations of political and social violence gave rise to the growing interest in violence in a variety of social settings. As scholars and commentators searched to understand the mechanisms and the meanings of civil disorder in the 1960s, they began to ask important questions about violence in American society (Graham & Gurr, 1969). Foremost of these was how American society compares in violence with other, especially other modern, industrial societies. As stated in the *Report Submitted to the National Commission on the Causes and Prevention of Violence,* edited by Hugh Davis Graham and Ted Robert Gurr (1969):

> Many unique aspects of our society and politics have contributed to the individual and collective violence that troubles contemporary America, among them the psychological residues of slavery, the coexistence of mass consumption with pockets and strata of sullen poverty, the conflict among competing ethics that leaves many men without clear guides to social action. Other sources of violence in our national life are inheritances of our own past: a celebration of violence in good causes by our revolutionary progenitors, frontiersmen, and vigilantes; immigrant expectations of an earthly paradise only partly fulfilled; the unresolved tensions of rapid and unregulated urban and industrial growth. Yet many societies as well as our own have experienced violent times in their national development, in some cases disintegrating in a welter of blood and shattered institutions, in others emerging as stronger and more satisfying communities. Examination of our development as a nation provides a sense of understanding of the historical genesis of our present situation. Comparison with the historical experience of other societies helps identify the points at which our cultural experience differed from that of more—and less—orderly societies. Contemporary comparisons provide a mirror that can tell us, *without favor or rancor,* how far we have fallen from our self-anointed status as the most favored of nations. By these comparisons we also begin to identify some of the general conditions, processes, and outcomes of violence, and ultimately to anticipate the effects of what we do now and tomorrow on the

creation, maintenance, and destruction of political community. (emphasis added, pp. xxvii–xxviii)

Judged by a variety of indicators then, it appears that Americans accept a higher level of "normal" violence than citizens of comparable industrial societies (Graham & Gurr, 1969, pp. 572–632). On another level, scholars began to look across the range of transformative factors in American society to comprehend how these changes affect social life, including tendencies toward instances of violence. Here one found an appreciation that the dynamics of post-war prosperity in America had set in motion fundamental changes in the way Americans interacted, lived, worked, communicated, sought leisure, enjoyed health, suffered sickness, and died, all of which signaled a dramatic change in the *kinds* of behavior which might be regarded as relevant to making judgments about the *content* of social relations within this changing pattern of society. These understandings were embodied in widely ranging studies of social relations and their implications for individual behavior.

The conference that gave rise to this volume took form, it seems to me, from this renewed interest in the social sciences in the phenomenon of violence in American culture, and especially its manifestations in the young. The focus of many of the articles, but by no means all, is individual behavior. These chapters express an almost equal concern with comprehension, explanation, and intervention. Their data focus tends to be that cluster of events surrounding the individual, especially the violent and aggressive individual. The apparent hope is that by further study of the primary associations, contacts, and relationships that define the experiences of youth we can come to a better understanding of why some children become aggressive and violent and stay that way. Most of these studies search for the markers of aggression and violence, whether they be in minimal brain damage, in family structure, or in the pattern of socialization institutions. Finding such markers enhances our social power by permitting us early identification of potential cases of violence and aggression, by framing our strategies for intervention, and ultimately by transforming social institutions in order to alter social conditions that impact upon predispositions for violent behavior.

This important and valuable work has achieved successes and will continue to do so. Fueled by the concern of the Surgeon General, the National Institutes of Health, and other major spokespersons for the United States research community, the kind of research presented by this volume will doubtlessly increase in importance during the coming years and continue to make valuable contributions to our understanding of the phenomena at hand.

CAVEATS ON THEORY AND METHOD

Our current preoccupation with violence and aggression in American culture and society has framed it as a classic *social problem*. By this I mean that on the one hand we appreciate and document the long, complex, multifactored etiology of the phenomenon while on the other we are led by our values, beliefs, and professional training to seek resolution of the problem by locating it within the individual and searching for means of effective individual intervention. This dynamic is present in our understanding and treatment of most health issues and is a familiar dilemma in the history of mental health policy in the United States and associated efforts to establish effective means of prevention. As George Albee has repeatedly pointed out, no matter how effective our intervention may be in individual pathologies, this does nothing to affect the incidence of the disease (Albee & Joffe, 1977).

Our continued focus on individual intervention reflects both the dynamics of clinical treatment and the bias of our policy system, which by locating disease and illness within the individual (the patient) glosses over both the difficult issues of identifying and assigning causation (however that is understood) and of having to work directly upon the social forces producing the pathology that we seek to eliminate. This is familiarly understood as the "upstream/downstream" problem in medical care (McKinney, 1974) and is often expressed in terms of the framing that problems receive from medicalizing them (Fox, 1977) or expressing them within the limited boundaries of a medical model (Engel, 1977; Powles, 1973).

Simply expressed, the social problem lies significantly in our collective appreciation of the problem itself and our sense of what to do about it once we are agreed that it is there. Thus, as social historians we can agree that this is indeed a society with a long tradition of violence and aggression. However, as policy makers or clinicians, or as researchers into the causes of violence and aggression as it is located in and expressed through individual behavior, we are far less agreed on what to do about it. And, equally difficult, we are increasingly faced with the problem of doing something about it, the more clearly it is focused for us as a social problem demanding some response. It is at this level that the problem enters the policy realm. It is also at this level that our various understandings of the problem provide importantly different inputs into our policy recommendations or our preferences for a particular form of intervention. It is for this reason that I choose to make use of the remaining pages of this preface to comment briefly on how some of these understandings of the problem come to be held and how they influence our work.

THE SEARCH FOR THE PURE MEASURE OF EFFECT

Current debates within the field of epidemiology illustrate the interaction of methodology and policy. Epidemiologists regard the past decade as one of upheaval and use various terms to dramatize the scope and depth of their reexamination of epidemiological principles, but the root of the problem is conceptually simple. The methods of classical epidemiology grew out of the biological revolution of the late nineteenth and early twentieth centuries. They focused on the relation of discrete agents to discrete pathologies with the goal of discovering interventions that could disrupt that relationship and either protect the affected individual or return him to health. The spectacular successes in the control of bacterial infections and immunization against viral infection resulted in deserved status for the method.

This method has proved less apt, however, in the struggle to understand the complex etiologies of the noninfectious diseases, especially the so-called diseases of civilization, those of the heart, strokes, other cardiovascular complications, diabetes, cancer, and a host of ailments assigned in one way or another to stress. What appears to be common to these diseases, illnesses, or ailments is their development over a long period of time, the fact that they appear to impact differentially along diverse genetic pathways, and the fact that they are sensitive to differences in life-style (U.S. Surgeon General Report, 1979). In the struggle to understand and treat these diseases, the health field has been torn between those who, on one hand, remain close to the traditional medical model and the classical methods of epidemiology that continue to search for discrete interventions directed against discrete pathologies—to gain, as it were, the pure measure of effect—and those who, on the other hand, have opted for a more inclusive model of illness and disease, often called the biopsychosocial model, and a related theory of disease causation. The former have been most often identified with curative medicine, the latter with primary prevention. It is compellingly instructive that the primary arena in which these contrasting models of disease and cure have been played against each other is mental illness, wherein the very nature of disease is itself in question (Engel, 1977). For example, as Albee and Joffe (1977) have expressed it:

> What are primary prevention measures in the field of psychopathology? Treating primary syphilis prevents the appearance, twenty or thirty years later, of general paresis. Where the mental illness is a genuine illness and has an organic cause, things can be done to prevent the occurrence of disease. But what about mental and emotional problems that are not 'diseases' but learned patterns of social maladjustment and emotional distress? Here we get into issues involving less clear-cut empirical relationships between early experiences and later disturbance. Clearly, efforts at primary prevention of psychopathology engage a more amorphous problem and involve a much wider range of actions than public health prevention of disease. (p. xiii)

The tensions present in these debates about theories of disease and appropriate therapies are more than just differences of opinion about styles of research or treatment, they embody differences in regard to epistemology, social theory, and fundamental social values. Proponents of the classical medical model are most closely identified with the status quo and its authoritative position on disease and illness questions; proponents of a more broadly based model which emphasizes the salience of various social and psychological factors are more likely to be proponents of change ranging from moderate to great, depending on the amount of importance they ascribe to social factors in disease etiology. A critical factor for advocates of change appears to be whether one locates interventions within the individual or extends them to social relationships, including political and economic relationships (Powles, 1973; Neubauer & Pratt, 1981).

THE MEDICALIZATION OF VIOLENCE

The current attention being given to the importance of violence in America tends to follow a similar pattern and to employ similar dynamics. The tension is demonstrated in a recent major statement about violence by C. Everett Koop, the United States Surgeon General and Deputy Assistant Secretary for Health, entitled "Violence and Public Health" (1982).

In his address Koop summarizes a number of well-known facts about violence including the distressingly high incidences of motor vehicle accidents, homicide, and suicide. He draws attention to the increased incidence of family violence, noting that violence within the family tends to escalate during periods of economic stress. (Recognition of this fact alone by such a major governmental health official makes the address a significant statement.) Further, he points to the role of television in promoting a culture of accepted violence and extends the observation to include video games. Acknowledging the concern expressed in a recent workshop in which physicians were asked to become increasingly concerned with the identification and treatment of violence, especially within the family, Koop, at first, asks if this might be an unwanted instance of further medicalization—the "medicalization of violence." In the end, however, he advocates this greater awareness of the importance of social factors in the creation of violence and early identification of markers of violence *within a clinical setting*. Thus ultimately, the problem is individualized and professionalized.

Violence and aggression are transformed through this analysis into yet another medical problem to be dealt with by treatment. In the process the language of prevention comes to be constrained to the application of individual treatment in a clinical setting. It seems to me that two important admissions are being advanced here. One is the recognition that the etiology of violence in our society is complex and to a significant extent social in its construction. This means, therefore, that a significant degree of violence is also political in its origins, since irreducibly it is political authority that legitimizes many of the structural conditions of the society within which syndromes of violence are nurtured. And yet, despite the impressive evidence supporting this conclusion, as a society we tend to lack both an effective language for developing discourse on the social and political nature of violence and political institutions for doing something about it. Because of this we are, secondly, driven yet again to the medicalization of a social problem even as we collectively admit the severe limitations that attend clinical intervention on an individual basis, no matter how early the markers of violence are recognized within the clinical setting.

That this significant statement on violence in our society is given by its most important public health officer is a comment both on the general extent to which public health in the United States as a whole has adopted the medical model as the dominant public health perspective and on the extent to which the individualization of health problems is woven deeply within the fabric of the policy process.

HEALTH AND BEHAVIOR

The dilemma articulated in the bold statement on violence by the surgeon general is a familiar one in modern public health. We have observed similar statements of the problem in governmental efforts to define effective health promotion (U.S. Surgeon General, 1979), to limit smoking behavior, and to attack the society-wide problem of alcoholism. The political structure of our society makes government both the recipient of intense and effective pressure from the powerful and the agent responsible for the protection of the victimized (Lowi, 1979). Our society has struggled with dilemmas of this kind since the emergence of corporate capitalism in America and its attendant national consumption system. In the early years, partly as a result of the extravagant excesses of corporate capitalism, the burden of governmental regulation in public health lay on transforming corporate behavior. In the more recent treatment of public health policy, in part because the problems are more complex and in part because corporate power is so great and so much a part of the governmental system itself, the burden has shifted to transforming individual behavior as the vehicle for dealing with acute social and health problems.

That this is so should not be surprising, given the political influence that the tobacco, alcohol, automotive, media, and other industries have within the policy process. Because many of these health problems are so obviously behaviorally related, it is both a sensible and ultimately futile effort for the Surgeon General and others to focus on inducing behavior change as an effective solution to the problem. The evidence of the effectiveness of behavior change in reducing disease incidence is irrefutable in many important health areas and deserves further application. For example, lung cancer among women, now the leading kind of female cancer, from which 29,000 women will die in 1985, is often described by leading cancer researchers as a "completely preventable disease." But one must ask, with sympathy for the dilemma it represents, what are the

effects of emphasizing individual-focused behavior change as the *primary* vehicle for intervention in such areas?

The consequences are, I think, at least these:

- The locus of responsibility for disease clearly related to social pathology
  is shifted from collective entities, including economic firms in the private
  sector, onto individuals, in what is classic victim blaming.
- By stating the nature of the problem so clearly—as Koop does in his
  address on violence—and then focusing on individual intervention and
  medicalization as the remedy, the impression is left that although something must be done, nothing much can be done to affect these problems at
  the level of social causation.
- Thus, medicalization and professionalization of the problem become the
  means for the depoliticization of the issue. Ignoring the structure of social
  relations is responsible in some important sense for the perpetuation of the
  problem and dramatically shifts the locus for action on the problem.
- Individualization of intervention creates a pattern of intervention that
  closely parallels the existing class structure: behavior change is most
  successful within those groups predisposed by education and other factors
  related to socioeconomic status to change in a self-interested direction.
  For example, the Stanford University Heart Study found positive class
  correlates with all at-risk factors. Those who are least able by virtue of
  their personal resources to make key behavior choices—the poor—are
  most dependent on social structures, such as the media, in which the
  negative behavior messages are the strongest (Greenberg, Dervin, Dominick, & Bowers, 1970).

Medicalization and professionalization of the problem also contribute to the
creation of a research context favoring the search for non–socially intrusive
"magic bullets," thereby promoting reductionist biological models of behavior
to the exclusion of others. This tactic is reinforced by politically conservative
regimes such as the Reagan administration, which has favored what it calls basic
biological research into health problems over socially based preventive programs. At the human subject level, this tendency reinforces efforts to discern the
pure measure of effect in complex behavior problems, such as violence or aggression. The result is often an inability to demonstrate with conventional scientific rigor that which appears to others to be manifestly apparent—for example,
that network television and video games provide a context in which violence is
detached from actual social interaction, and to develop social policy accordingly.

THE CULTURE OF THE SOCIAL PROBLEM

In a recent book, *The Culture of the Social Problem* (1981), sociologist
Joseph Gusfield has examined the issue of drinking and driving, usually con-

strued in American society as "drunk driving." His interest is in the characteristic ways in which problems are given definition in society and thus by extension the range of solutions deemed appropriate to the problem are determined. Noting that the locus of various problems in American life has shifted from the private to the public arena and that such a shift involves a corresponding relocation of responsibility, he says:

> The problem of responsibility has both a cultural and a structural dimension. At the cultural level it implies a way of seeing phenomena. Fixing responsibility for preventing accidents by laws against drinking–driving involves seeing drinking–driving as a choice by a willful person. Seeing it as a medical problem involves an attribution of compulsion and illness. At the structural level, however, fixing responsibility implies different institutions and different personnel who are charged with obligations and opportunities to attack the problem. Here, too, change from one set of causal definitions, of cognitive conceptualizations, to another carries implications for institutions. The relation of causal responsibility to political responsibility is then a central question in understanding how public problems take shape and change. (p. 6)

Further discussing the structure of the drinking-driving problem in terms of the social processes by which it is produced in society, he observes:

> Two things struck me as especially significant by their absence: the lack of involvement of alcohol beverage distributors—bartenders, sellers, manufacturers—and the inability or unwillingness of people to see the problem of drinking-driving as a problem of transportation. The producers and distributors of liquor and beer were almost never represented in the conferences, meetings, classes, and committees which fill the organizational agenda of local alcohol agencies. But so, too, was there little representation from medicine, government, planning or other possibly interested groups. In speaking to audiences throughout the country as a presumed "alcohol studies expert" I often pointed out that the city of San Diego had developed an area of hotels alongside a major interstate highway. The hotels all had public bars which provided part of their income and depended on more than their temporary residents for clientele. Autos were almost the only means of transportation to or from such bars in a part of the United States where the spatial spread made taxis expensive. Research on drinking-drivers was similarly silent on alternative means and possibilities of transportation. (pp. 7–8)

Gusfield's study suggests that problems rise to prominance because for various reasons we, collectively, choose to render private behavior public. By doing this we both heighten the issue of responsibility and transform it. The meaning we collectively give to it—and that outcome is a result of value struggle within the collectivity—involves important decisions about doing something and about what that something will be. How we collectively choose to solve the problem depends greatly on how we collectively make decisions about assigning responsibility.

The study of drinking-driving demonstrates the radical segmentation of behavior that attends our highly individualistic, liberal, and yet highly interdependent society. Many of the values that underlie our culture, such as our moralistic construction of responsibility with respect to alcohol consumption, fit poorly into the modern complex fabric of social interaction. In many cases, drinking-driving being one, we as individuals are being held *accountable* to a set of compelling yet contradictory outcomes (social success expressed as conviviality, responsibility for the exercise of self-control, and a transportation system at variance with that context) in a way that leads to tragic but predictable results of individual failure.

Some current efforts at legal reform in this area suggest a growing awareness of the need to reconceptualize drinking-driving as a social problem rather than one of merely the authority of the public (law) in application to a pattern of individual variation. These include laws that expand the realm of legal responsibility to include the alcohol-dispensing agent, the development of social patterns such as the nondrinking driver serving the drinking group, the judicial sentencing that expands legal purviews from simple penalty for transgression (a fine and a jail sentence) to education about the problem—for instance, assigning defendants to Alcoholics Anonymous sessions. Although these measures are still far from recognizing the full extent to which drinking-driving lies within its problem structure as defined by the dominant culture, they are steps toward acknowledging the broader structural nature of drinking-driving as a social act and to treating it beyond the level of individual occurrence and responsibility.

I hope this is the direction in which our thinking on violence and aggression among the young can go. For the reasons indicated above it seems clear that whereas efforts to discover the markers of aggression and violence and to intervene at an early level are vitally important, they are also insufficient. It is right to put our efforts into this activity, just as it is right to work toward answering the riddles of other pathologies attending our clinical reality. But it will be insufficient to do only this, or to do it to the extent that efforts to expand the social understanding and treatment of violence and aggression are shunted aside as important but somehow insufficiently demanding problems.

REFERENCES

Albee, G. W., & Joffe, J. M. (1977). *Primary prevention of psychopathology*. Hanover, NH: University Press of New England.

Edelman, M. (1964). *The symbolic uses of politics*. Urbana, IL: University of Illinois Press.

Engel, G. (1977). The need for a new medical model: A challenge for biomedicine. *Science, 196,* 129–136.

Fox, R. C. (1977). The medicalization and remedicalization of American society. In J. H. Knowles (Ed.), *Doing better and feeling worse*. New York: Norton.

Graham, H. D., & Gurr, T. R. (1969). *The history of violence in America: Historical and comparative perspective*. New York: Prager.

Greenberg, B., Dervin, B., Dominick, J., & Bowers, J. (1970). *Uses of the mass media by the urban poor*. New York: Prager.

Gusfield, J. (1981). *The culture of social problems*. Chicago: University of Chicago Press.

Koop, C. E. (1982). *Violence and public health.* Address to the American Academy of Pediatrics. New York, October 26.

Lowi, T. J. (1979). *The end of liberalism: The second republic of the United States* (2nd ed.). New York: W.W. Norton.

McKinlay, J. B. (June, 1974). The case for refocussing upstream: The political economy of illness. *Behavioral Science Research Data Review, 7*–17.

Neubauer, D. E., & Pratt, R. (1981). The second public health revolution: A critical appraisal. *Journal of Health Politics, Policy and Law, 6,* 205–227.

Powles, J. (1973). On the limitations of modern medicine. *Science, Medicine and Man, 1,* 1–50.

U.S. Surgeon General. (1979). *Healthy people: Report on health promotion and disease prevention.* Promotion and disease prevention. Washington, D.C.: Department of Health, Education, and Welfare.

Williams, W. A. (1980). *Empire as a way of life: An essay on the causes and character of America's present predicament along with a few thoughts about an alternative.* New York: Oxford University Press.

PART **II**

CONTEMPORARY THEMES

CHAPTER 2

Childhood Aggression and Violence
Contemporary Issues

DAVID H. CROWELL

Childhood aggression in our society is generally considered to be behavior that has intentionally led to injury or damage to another individual or their property. Since this definition implies that the aggressive actions of these children are a form of "motivated aggression" (Sears, Maccoby, & Levin, 1957), it raises a number of questions: Was the child aware of his actions, and did he know that they would hurt someone or destroy something? Did this child have sufficient ability to completely control or at least to regulate the intensity of his actions?

Feshbach (1970) has recognized the concerns of many others about these types of questions and suggests that the idea of intentional or motivated aggression "should not be interpreted to imply that the child is aware of or is consciously directing his aggressive behavior; it means only that the aggressive component of this behavior is an essential part of its function" (p. 161). Describing childhood aggression in this manner places no theoretical or practical limitations on studying the problems in the area; aggressive acts are open to inquiry in terms of both the antecedents and consequent events that surround them.

In spite of the universality of aggressive activity by children in all societies, the public often is not aware of the range of behavior which violates their society's agreed upon patterns of acceptable conduct. The *Uniform Crime Reports for the United States* (1983; see Table 1) gives a comprehensive picture of this spectrum. It reveals that children under 15 years of age are legally charged, that is, arrested in our society, for a wide variety of aggressive acts against people and property. Whether these are adjudicated, that is, formally settled through court proceedings, is another question.

DAVID H. CROWELL • Department of Psychology, University of Hawaii at Manoa, Honolulu, Hawaii 96822.

Table 1
Arrests for Index Offenses by Age[a]

	Ages			
Offense charged	<15	<10	10–12	13–14
Total	564,983	47,067	142,304	375,612
Percentage distribution	5.5[b]	.08[c]	.25[c]	.66[c]
Murder and nonnegligent				
manslaughter	157	8	20	129
Forcible rape	1,332	64	274	994
Robbery	9,203	317	1,891	6,995
Aggravated assault	10,148	703	2,570	6,875
Burglary	59,400	4,738	15,503	39,159
Larceny–theft	168,095	15,376	50,660	102,059
Motor vehicle theft	8,628	169	1,132	7,327
Arson	4,113	1,155	1,195	1,763
Violent crime	20,840	1,092	4,755	14,993
Percentage distribution	4.7	.05	.23	.72
Property crime	240,236	21,438	68,490	150,308
Percentage distribution	14.1	.09	.28	.63
Crime Index total	261,076	22,530	73,245	165,301
Percentage distribution	12.1	.09	.28	.63

[a]Abstracted from *Uniform Crime Reports for the United States*, 1983, based on estimated population of 200,692,000.
[b]Percentage of total arrests of 10,287.309 for persons under 25 years of age, 1983.
[c]Percentage of total arrests of 564,983 for persons under 15 years of age, 1983.

What the *Uniform Crime Report for the United States* demonstrates is that childhood aggressive behavior occurs at a number of levels; these can be considered as acts which are qualitatively more serious in scope. Table 1 indicates that children under age 15 were arrested for 5.5% of the Index offenses committed by all persons under 25 years of age. Index offenses consist of *violent personal crimes,* including murder, rape, and robbery, and *property crimes,* such as burglary, larceny, and vehicle theft. They were committed not only by children under 10 years of age but also appeared to increase incrementally through age 14. According to Table 1 these children accounted for approximately one-eighth of the arrests for Index offenses producing a Crime Index percentage of 12.1.

Though less serious in scope, non–Index offenses also were present in the under-15 age group. Again, as illustrated in Table 2, these cover a large array of violations. Non-Index offenses include forgery and counterfeiting, fraud, embezzlement, stolen property, vandalism, carrying and possessing weapons, prostitution and commercialized vice, sex offenses, drug abuse violations, gambling, driving under the influence of alcohol, drunkenness, and disorderly conduct.

Table 2
Arrests for Non-Index Offenses by Age[a]

Offense charged	Ages			
	<15	<10	10–12	13–14
Other assaults	29,817	2,586	7,945	19,286
Forgery and counterfeiting	1,191	32	221	938
Fraud	9,205	383	1,762	7,060
Embezzlement	78	8	13	57
Stolen property: buying, receiving, possessing	7,740	338	1,715	5,687
Vandalism	47,949	7,167	15,673	25,109
Weapons; carrying, possessing, etc.	6,110	252	1,261	4,597
Prostitution and commercialized vice	270	13	24	233
Sex offenses (except forcible rape and prostitution)	5,323	421	1,325	3,577
Drug abuse violations	11,819	173	1,313	10,333
Gambling	127	8	9	110
Offenses against family and children	476	189	84	203
Driving under the influence	522	113	55	354
Liquor laws	8,990	107	572	8,311
Drunkenness	3,191	409	223	2,559
Disorderly conduct	27,262	2,092	6,591	18,579
Vagrancy	617	27	102	488
All other offenses (except traffic)	74,661	7,408	17,451	49,802
Suspicion	1,004	149	241	614
Curfew and loitering law violations	18,721	686	3,556	14,479
Runaways	48,834	1,976	8,923	37,935

[a]Abstracted from *Uniform Crime Reports for the United States,* 1983, based on estimated population of 200,692,000.

Regardless of the type of non–Index offense, there also appeared in 1983 to be a three to fivefold increase for the interval less than 10 years of age up through 12 years. The only exceptions to this general picture were offenses against family and children and driving under the influence of alcohol. *The Uniform Crime Report for the United States* does more than provide data that children are involved in crime. It is substantial evidence that these offenses reflect a failure in adjusting to societal standards and thus represent a form of child maladjustment.

The purpose of this chapter is to review some of the current thinking on questions that have been the basis of much of the continuing research on childhood aggression and violence. Among these substantive issues are the following questions:

- Can childhood aggression be considered as a syndrome of developmental psychopathology and, if so, what are some of the factors that appear to be associated with this type of childhood maladjustment?
- To what extent does evidence support the notion of genetic influences, apart from sex differences, in the occurrence of aggressive activity?
- What is the status of the controversy on gender differences relative to acts of overt aggression?
- Is there a relationship between childhood hyperactivity and aggression?
- Are there developmental precursors of specific types of violence?

CHILDHOOD AGGRESSION AS A SYNDROME OF DEVELOPMENTAL PSYCHOPATHOLOGY

Childhood aggression as a type of behavioral maladjustment is appropriately discussed within the framework of developmental psychopathology. Developmental psychopathology in its broadest sense is concerned with "the origins and time course of a given disorder, its varying manifestation with development, [and] its precursors and sequelae" (Sroufe & Rutter, 1984, p. 18).

Placing childhood aggression within such a conceptual framework suggests that the acts of aggression we shall discuss not only are maladaptive patterns but also are outside the limits usually described for behavior problems seen in the course of early development. Campbell's (1983) conclusion, in her extensive review on behavior problems occurring during the course of early development, provides one way of looking at the relationship between childhood aggression and childhood behavior problems. In terms of her perspective, developmental problems may appear as

> exaggerations of age-appropriate behaviors, as reflections of difficult transitions from one developmental stage to the next, or as age-related but maladaptive reactions to environmental, particularly family, stress . . . . Common developmental problems are indeed transient or are precursors of more severe and persistent difficulties. (Campbell, 1983, p. 34)

In this context, overt childhood aggressive activity may be conceived of as an emerging set of behaviors reflecting an adjustment to a changing environment and also as an early index of potential maladjustment. If, however, the child's behavior reflects a persistent and consistent inability to show age-appropriate behavior that is customarily associated with developing maturity, then an evaluative judgment of "abnormal or maladjusted" is appropriately made. Often this is the time at which this child appears before the principal or the social worker, psychiatrist or psychologist in a mental health service, or possibly a representative of the judicial system. This also is the time when the child's maladaptive behavior is defined or classified.

A number of epidemiology studies (Achenbach, 1978; Gersten, Langner, Eisenberg, Simcha-Fagan, & McCarthy, 1976; MacFarlane, Allen, & Honzik, 1954; Werry & Quay, 1971) have focused on the prevalence rates of childhood behavior problems. The frequency, intensity, and clustering of isolated symptomatic behavior have been plotted as a function of age, sex, ethnic and racial background, and socioeconomic status. There is, however, little evidence for the prognostic significance of behavior problems involving aggressive activity occurring during the preschool or school-age period.

One study, however, has addressed this issue: Working from the premise that the prognostic significance of problem behavior of children may be age-related, Gersten et al. (1976) examined the stability of behavioral disturbances with changing age. In other words, they sought to determine whether children tended to "grow out of" or "show more of" certain types of behavioral disturbances over time. The study included 732 children who had been initially assessed five years earlier when they were 6 to 18 years of age. Data for the dimensions of behavior were obtained through questionnaire interviews that were subsequently rated by psychiatrists. These ratings estimated the extent of impairment that could be inferred from the questionnaire's responses.

Factor analysis of the data obtained in this study produced 16 dimensions of behavioral disturbance, and 6 factors were most highly correlated with total impairment: mentation problems, fighting, conflict with parents, regressive anxiety, isolation, and delinquency. For three of the dimensions which were related to the domain of aggression (fighting, conflict, and delinquency), greater or constant levels of psychopathology were apparent over the five-year interval. In discussing their results, Gersten et al. (1976) conclude that both the longitudinal changes and the stability or constancy of these changes determined the prognostic significance of behavioral disturbances. The relationship between stability and change indicates whether a disturbance is transient or reflects some pattern of continuity in the disturbed activity by a child.

For the triad associated with aggression, the investigators concluded that delinquency or antisocial behavior appeared as a stable behavior pattern at or after 10 years of age. As a result, the prognostic significance for predicting adult antisocial behavior should be possible at this time, but maximal if assessed in middle adolescence. Relative to the intrafamilial aggression dimension, that is, conflict with parents, the data showed high stability and increasing levels of psychopathology very early. The prognostic significance of intrafamilial conflicts was evident during early childhood, that is, before age 6. On the other hand, fighting or aggressive behavior toward others showed a moderate and steady level of stability throughout childhood and early adolescence. Therefore, Gersten *et al.* (1976) concluded that these patterns of aggression have clear prognostic importance when seen at any age.

The attempt to weave a comprehensive scheme for the classification of childhood aggressive behavior or problems in which aggression is a major component has been fraught with semantic and statistical controversies. (Achenbach & Edelbrock, 1978, 1983; Quay, 1979). The efforts at resolving some of the related issues have appeared in systems proposed by the Group for the Advancement of Psychiatry (1966); the Diagnostic and Statistical Manuals of Mental Disorders (DSM-II, 1968; DSM-III, 1980) of the American Psychiatric Association; and the World Health Organization Multiaxial Classification (Rutter, Lebovici, Eisenberg, Sneznevskij, Sadoun, Brooke, & Lin, 1969; Rutter, Shaffer, & Shepherd, 1975). Such schemes are described as clinically derived classification systems; that is, the diagnostic category applied to the child is the clinicians' "label" for behaviors that they have regularly associated with certain disorders. By consensus, DSM-III (1980) is the clinical approach that currently represents the official classification system within the United States. Here,

> The essential feature [of conduct disorder] is a repetitive and persistent pattern of conduct in which either the basic rights of others or major age-appropriate societal norms or rules are violated. The conduct is more serious than the ordinary mischief and pranks of children and adolescents. (p. 45)

DSM-III lists four subtypes of conduct disorder: *undersocialized, aggressive; undersocialized, nonaggressive; socialized, aggressive;* and *socialized, nonaggressive.* In contrast to the aggressive subtypes, which are of prime interest to us, the nonaggressive diagnoses focus on status-offense behaviors such as running away, truancy, stealing, and drug and substance abuse, which typically do not involve confrontation with individuals. In distinction to the conduct disorder syndrome, DSM-III also provides the category of oppositional disorder; in this case the basic rights and major age-appropriate societal norms or rules are not violated. This category is not discussed in this chapter.

In contrast to the clinically derived systems are what may be described as empirically derived criteria for classifying childhood behavior disorders. In this approach statistical techniques have been used to group characteristics of children associated with child psychopathology. Quay (1979), for example, reported four major factors or dimensions that account for the largest amount of variance in children's problems: conduct disorder, anxiety–withdrawal, immaturity, and socialized-aggressive. On the basis of similar statistical processes, Achenbach and Edelbrock (1978) reported that two categories of childhood behavior disorders can be identified: one is a broad-band *undercontrolled* syndrome that is synonymous with characteristics such as aggressiveness, externalizing, acting out, and conduct disorder. This can be distinguished from a narrow-band *over-controlled* syndrome that is synonymous with inhibited, internalizing, shy-anxious behavior, and personality disorder. Further analyses suggested several more narrow-band syndromes identified as aggressive, delinquency, and hyperactive behavior.

There is some basis for rapprochement between the clinically and empirically derived points of view, and as a result a workable system for the diagnosis and classification of children's problems can be constructed. Achenbach (1980), for example, agrees that there is an approximate relation between the DSM-III conduct disorder subcategories of undersocialized aggression and socialized aggression and the narrow-band categories of aggressive and delinquent behaviors (boys). There is also a similarity in description relative to the attention deficit syndrome with hyperactivity (DSM-III) and the narrow-band syndrome of hyperactive behavior. In other words, there is some consensual agreement that (a) disturbed behavior with either an aggressive or hyperactive component can be identified in children and that (b) these dimensions are logical grounds for the classification of maladaptive behavior in children.

In light of this evidence, the problem behavior of children associated with aggression can be appropriately considered as representative of the conduct disorder category. This encompassing category embraces a plethora of terms such as antisocial behavior, fighting, stealing, and threatening people, which are often used when referring to aggressiveness in children. In spite of the arguments against labeling a child in the categorical fashion of DSM-III, the advantages are manifold. As Achenbach (1980) has pointed out, the "categorization of children may nevertheless be necessary to form homogeneous groups in which differences in etiology, treatment effects, and outcome can be identified for purposes of teaching, communication, clinical decisions, epidemiology, and recordkeeping" (pp. 406–407).

Whatever classifications are used, the published literature is replete with well-documented studies of childhood aggressive activity. As we shall see, these studies now enable us to develop a highly reliable perspective on (a) the relationship between early conduct disorder (antisocial behavior) and later delinquent and criminal behavior, (b) the identification of children who are more likely to be chronic offenders, and (c) the possible prediction of later maladjustment for select groups of children.

In terms of the narrow-band aggressive syndrome, the review of Olweus (1979) is among the earliest which called attention to the stability of male aggressive patterns. Using a definition comparable to ours, that is, the "inflicting of injury or discomfort," Olweus concluded that there are marked individual differences in levels of habitual aggression and that these levels are stable reaction tendencies. As a result, these levels can be used to explain as well as predict aggressive behavior.

Studies cited by Olweus (1979) of preschool and school-age groups indicate that marked individual levels of habitual aggression may appear as early as age 3. Other studies show that aggressive reaction patterns are related to similar patterns seen 10 to 14 years later. The correlation between the initial assessment of aggression at time one and the subsequent measurement at time two was +0.63 and averaged +0.49 for the intervals that ranged from 10 to 18 years. An aggressive pattern at ages 12 and 13 accounted for 50% to 90% of the variance for periods of one to five years. For a period of up to 10 years, the stability was similarly high and predictive of later antisocial actions.

As if to doubly emphasize the remarkable stability of male aggressiveness, Olweus (1979) stated that the reviewed studies demonstrate that ''the behavior of highly aggressive boys of these ages is often maintained irrespective of considerable environmental variation and in opposition to forces acting to change this behavior'' (p. 871).

In terms of the conduct disorder or undercontrolled syndrome, there also are studies that have investigated (a) the stability as well as the continuity of childhood antisocial behavior, (b) the prediction of antisocial behavior at later ages, and (c) the etiological factors underlying childhood antisocial behavior.

Loeber (1982) has extensively analyzed and summarized the results of many studies as they relate to children with a background of extensive antisocial behavior. His definition of antisocial emphasizes inflicting pain or loss and is in line with our point of view regarding childhood aggressive behavior. However, he appears to evaluate antisocial behavior qualitatively and conceives of this as including a dimension of extreme antisocial behavior. It is this extreme form that has import for later maladjustment. Loeber's primary thesis is that children who show extreme antisocial behavior are more likely to persist in their antisocial activity over time. Extreme antisocial activity is recognized in some children because it begins early, is continuous, occurs at a high rate, and is present in many situations.

Loeber's (1982) primary thesis is delineated in terms of a number of hypotheses. The first of these, the Density hypothesis, proposes that children who are reported to be involved in conduct disorders at a young age are very likely to show a continued high rate of antisocial offenses. Among the examples in line with this proposition is the finding of Osborn and West (1978) that 39% of their study group who were troublesome at ages 8 or 10 were persistent recidivists before the age of 19. Similarly, Moore, Chamberlain, and Mukai (1979) report that a group of children who were involved in at least four stealing offenses at about an average age of 10 were practically all (84%) arrested by age 17. Later, 67% of this group of stealers were considered to be chronic offenders. The relative prognostic significance of stealing also was supported by evidence from a comparison group which showed that only 15% of the children considered to be aggressive later became delinquent.

Loeber's (1982) second hypothesis, the Multiple Setting hypothesis, proposes that those children whose antisocial behavior appeared in a variety of settings were more likely to show continued antisocial behavior than those whose conduct disorders occurred only in one setting. In support of this hypothesis are the data of Mitchell and Rosa (1981), who found that approximately 71% of the children identified by both teachers and parents as stealers later became recidivists. The figures for parents or teachers alone were 14% and 46% respectively. A similar result was noted for the combined identification of lying; 50% were recidivists compared to 12% and 25% identified only by parents or teachers respectively.

A third hypothesis of Loeber's (1982) addresses the continuity of antisocial behavior in terms of the types of offenses involved in the delinquent's career. This variety hypothesis states that children who display a variety of antisocial activity at an early age are more likely to develop delinquent careers at later ages.

There is, however, questionable support for this proposal. On the one hand, Robins and Ratcliff (1979) have shown that children with three or more types of antisocial acts showed a higher rate of delinquency (39%) than children with one type (6%). On the other hand, data from the Cambridge Study in Delinquent Development (Farrington & West, 1981; Farrington, 1983) suggest a different view of the likelihood that specific aggressive patterns or specialization in delinquent activity at one age will predict later antisocial activity. The Cambridge study, a longitudinal survey using official records and self-reports, was based on a sample of 411 males and began when they were about 8 years of age and ended when the youngest one was aged 25. In regard to the study, Farrington (1983) states quite clearly that with

> official statistics, it is impossible to know the extent to which offending is specialized (as opposed to generalized), or to determine key information about official criminal careers (when they begin, when they end, and how long they last). . . . The available evidence suggests that, with law-violating behavior, there is a small amount of specificity superimposed on a large amount of generality. (p. 18)

However, the evidence is overwhelmingly supportive of Loeber's (1982) fourth hypothesis, the Early Onset hypothesis: Children are at higher risk for a chronic delinquent career if they show an early onset of antisocial behavior. Robins (1966) reported that children whose conduct disorders were observed from 7 years to 11 years appeared to be twice as much at risk for adult antisocial problems than those observed after age 11. Rutter, Tizard, and Whitmore (1970) found that 60% of their cases with later antisocial or psychiatric problems had shown onset of their problem before age 8. Farrington (1983) also concluded that there was definitely a strong relationship between early and later convictions: more than 75% of those with four or more early convictions had four or more adult convictions. On the other hand, more than 83% with no early convictions had no adult convictions. Analysis of the probability of one conviction's being followed by another revealed that the youths convicted at the earliest ages (10–12) were the most persistent offenders, averaging more convictions than any other of the groups. Similarly, Wolfgang, Figlio, and Sellin (1972) noted that police contacts between the ages of 7 years and 12 years were associated with more serious offenses than contacts which occurred between the ages of 13 years and 16 years. Data by Hamparian, Schuster, Dinitz, and Conrad (1978) show a negative relationship between the age of first arrest and the average number of arrests: the average number of arrests decreased from approximately 7.3 (first arrest ≤ 10) to 6.1 (first arrest at age 11) to 5.3 (first arrest at age 12) to 4.1 (first arrest at age 13).

The foregoing material offers substantial evidence that there is considerable stability and continuity over time in the antisocial behavior of children. These data give rise to a number of questions for future research. Among these questions is one that has been pursued vigorously by a number of investigators: What are the variables present during childhood that predict antisocial and delinquent behavior in adolescence and adulthood?

Loeber and Dishion (1983) have summarized and provided an overview of much of the past work dealing with this topic. They began by developing a measure of *predictive* efficiency to identify factors that would improve predictive ability. This measure was designed to select variables quantitatively which would function as a predictor of those children who eventually become delinquent (valid positive) and those who do not become delinquent (valid negative). This *index of relative improvement over chance* was applied to previously published studies. These were prospective and retrospective studies which (a) included both male and female cases, (b) used objective firsthand predictors of subsequent delinquency, (c) referred to an increased or decreased probability of delinquency over time, and (d) were based on police contacts, arrests, and reconviction rates as well as self-reported delinquency. All the reviewed studies contained data that permitted the investigators to reconstruct prediction tables from raw scores. In terms of Loeber and Dishion's index, the most predictive measures of delinquency were (1) parental family management techniques; (2) the child's problem behavior; (3) reports of stealing, lying, or truancy; (4) antisocial (criminal) behavior within the family; and (5) poor educational achievement. Socioeconomic level and separation from parents were among the lowest ranking predictors. Relative to recidivism, the best predictors were childhood involvement in lying, stealing, or truancy. The next best predictors were problem behavior or previous delinquency. The earliest age at which these predictors of delinquency were most effectively measured appeared to be (a) family functioning when the child was 6 (Craig & Glick, 1963), (b) referrals for antisocial behavior (West & Farrington, 1973), aggressiveness (Havighurst, Bowman, Liddle, Matthews, & Pierce, 1962), and predelinquency (Mitchell & Rosa, 1981; Robins, 1966; Scarpitti, 1964) beginning at about 9 years, and (c) parental criminality (Robins, 1978) at 10 years. Grade point average was predictive at age 15.

The practical application of the preceding information clearly lies in developing a procedure for the early identification of children who are at high risk for delinquency. The most recently reported venture of Loeber, Dishion, and Patterson (1984) appears promising. They propose a multiple-stage screening device for achieving early identification. This "multiple-gating" approach uses three sequential assessments: first, teachers rate the boys' problem behavior; second, a risk group culled from the first stage is assessed by parents who evaluate the boys' conduct at home; and third, the children and parents are interviewed about their family-management practices. A sample of 102 boys 12–16 years old, revealed that these three gates improved the predictive accuracy of valid positives in the risk group from about 25.4% to 56%. The three gates produced an overall false positive error rate of about 44% and a false negative error rate of about 6%. The procedure correctly classified 86% of the recidivists.

GENETIC INFLUENCES

The answer to the question about genetic influences on aggressive behavior is succinctly summarized in Lush's (1937) classic but seldom cited statement, "every characteristic is both hereditary and environmental, since it is the end result of a long chain of interactions of the genes with each other, with the environment and with the intermediate products at each stage of development" (p. 77).

This point of view recognizes the legitimacy of adopting an interactional view relative to the influence of genetic factors on antisocial behavior. It also provides a background for recognizing that there is a

> continuum of indirectness along which are found all degrees of remoteness of causal links . . . . Geneticists have sometimes used the term *norm of reaction* to designate the range of variation of possible outcomes of gene properties . . . . Thus heredity sets the norm or limits within which environmental differences determine the eventual outcome. (Anastasi, 1958, pp. 199–200)

When the question of examining genetic influences on antisocial behavior is looked at in this way, the task is realistically described as insurmountable. At best only a global view can be presented.

The genetic component in aggression has been investigated in terms of chromosomal and biochemical abnormalities. Sex chromosomes and the subsequent gonadal production of testosterone or testosterone-like substances (androgens) and estrogen and progesterone have been identified as critical for both brain development and also behavioral functioning (Reinisch, 1974). Analyses of karyotypes have been fairly extensive and have produced data in which karyotypes reveal aberrations in numbers of sex chromosomes. In particular, males with a karyotype of 47 XYY chromosomes instead of the normal 46 XY chromosomes have been intensively studied to determine whether there is a causal tie between the extra Y chromosome and aggressive behavior. For example, prevalence data showed that XYY males constituted about 2% of the inmates in one maximum security prison (Jacobs, Brunton, Melville, Brittain, & McClement, 1965). Other surveys have revealed that both XYY and XXY appear to be present in prison populations and that the intelligence quotients of both XXY (Klinefelter's Syndrome) and XYY groups averaged lower than the population mean (Baker, Teifer, Richardson, & Clark, 1970; Hook, 1973; Nielsen, 1970; Nielsen & Christensen, 1974; Noel, Dupont, Revil, Dussuyer, & Quack, 1974; Owen, 1972). These studies have had definite limitations and consequently have provided no generalizations relevant to linking specific genetic characteristics to aggressiveness. Among the limitations are small sample size, selection of the XYY samples not only in environments likely to contain them—that is, prisons—but also with full knowledge of their genotypes, and, finally, an absence of adequate controls and of prevalence data for the general adult population.

Witkin et al. (1976) attempted to rectify many of these shortcomings. Their study was designed to determine whether men with the XYY pattern have an elevated crime rate and to identify variables that enter into the relation between the XYY karyotype and antisocial activity. Aggressiveness, intelligence, and height were particularly analyzed. Witkin et al. selected a target population of 31,436 male Danish citizens who were residents of Copenhagen between January 1944 and December 1947. From this group the top 15% of the height distribution was selected for intensive individual study. Results suggested a prevalence figure of 2.9/1,000 XYY and 3.9/1,000 XXY among the group of tall men. A higher mean rate of criminal convictions was found among the XYY group than among the XY controls; their hypothesis that height might be a correlate of the elevated XYY crime rate was not confirmed. The XYY sample had a lower level of intellectual functioning, and this appeared to confirm the intellectual dysfunction hypothesis as an explanation for more involvement in criminal activity.

Even though impaired intellectual functioning was implicated, however, Witkin et al. (1976) suggest that this may represent only less adeptness at escaping detection. Further, their aggression hypothesis was not supported. The elevated crime rate which was observed reflected property offenses and not acts against people. Of special note is their conclusion that

> the data from the documentary records we have examined speak on society's legitimate concern about aggression among XYY and XXY men. No evidence has been found that men with either of these sex chromosome complements are especially aggressive. Because such men do not appear to contribute particularly to society's problem with aggressive crimes, their identification would not serve to ameliorate this problem. (p. 187)

As a result of the earlier adult male findings, infant populations also have been examined. The most recent screening of 4,400 consecutive live-borns revealed 11 sex chromosome abnormalities, 3 XXX's, 1 XO, 4 XXY's, and 3 XYY's (Leonard, Landy, Ruddle, & Lubs, 1974). At ages 1–2½ years, however, no distinctive features were associated with these karyotypes. Other studies of sex chromosomal aberrations among newborns suggest an incidence of XYY of 1 to 1,000 live-born males. Hook (1973), Owen (1972), and Borgaononkar and Shah (1974) report a range of 1/1,500 to 1/3,000.

In turning to the literature on gonadal hormone influences, the caveat of Meyer-Bahlburg and Erhardt (1982) provides a significant perspective. As they point out in these studies, aggressive behavior is not consistently defined and may vary from combative activity to incidents surrounding competitive activity.

Research on the early effects of gonadal hormones on development and aggressive behavior has followed two lines. One track has examined cases wherein abnormal sex hormone levels were present at or before the time of birth. The studies here involved prenatal androgen deficiency (hypoandrogenized) in genetic males and prenatal androgen excess or congenital adrenal hyperplasia (CAH) in genetic females. Several studies (Erhardt & Baker, 1974; Money & Erhardt, 1972) have examined CAH and report no significant difference in activities associated with fighting during childhood; one study (Money & Schwartz, 1976) suggests an increased participation in body-contact sports. For CAH genetic males, Ehrhardt and Baker (1974) report no significant amount of activity relative to the initiation of fighting.

The significance of these studies for understanding the influence of endocrine disorders on aggressive behavior is difficult to evaluate. Again the well-founded critique of Meyer-Bahlburg and Ehrhardt (1982) serves as a background for assessment:

> Even if it were well established, however, that prenatal androgen deficiency or excess does influence the development of aggressive behavior in humans, the interpretation would not be simple, and one would have to consider at least several potential mediating factors or modes of action of such hormone effects: (1) genital status, which usually determines the sex of assignment, the sex-typing of a child by parents and others, and the resulting gender identity and self-image; (2) physical activity level, which influences the choice of playmates and may change the probability of accidental aggression provoking encounters in the peer group; (3) muscle development, which is likely to affect the outcome of aggressive encounters with peers and thereby influence future aggressive behavior; (4) direct organizational effects of hormones on brain systems that are involved in the regulation of aggression and may, for instance, change the threshold for aggression arousal. (p. 43)

The literature (Hines, 1982) on prenatal exposure to exogenous hormones is more extensive and primarily reflects hormonal treatment with combined estrogens or progestins for threatened abortions or miscarriages. The administered estrogens have included estradiol and diethystilbestrol. The progestins may have been natural progesterone and/or synthetic progestins. These progestin exposures may have been androgenic, antiandrogenic, estrogenic, or progestational. Among the described effects are a slight increase in aggression in females with genital masculinization associated with androgen therapy (Erhardt & Money, 1967) and synthetic progestins (Reinisch, 1981). Reinisch (1981) has demonstrated that human fetuses exposed during gestation to synthetic progestins showed significantly higher potential for physical aggression than their sex-matched nonexposed sibs. The potential for aggression was assessed with a measure dealing with interpersonal conflict. Subjects were 17 females and sibs, mean age 11 years, 6 months, and 8 males and sibs, mean age 11 years, 4 months. They were exposed during the first trimester, before the seventh week of gestation, a critical interval for central nervous system and genital morphological differentiation.

Increases in aggression-related activities have been noted for both males and females treated with synthetic progesterones and decreases in aggression for males with diethylstilbestrol–progesterone treatment (Yalom, Green, & Fisk, 1973). Meyer-Bahlburg and Ehrhardt (1982) examined the effects of medroxy-progesterone acetate (MPA), a drug related to progesterone used in pregnancy (Provera). In this study 13 boys and 15 girls exposed during gestation and 28 matched controls were compared in a double-blind design. Results showed consistent though "weak" differences with the MPA group showing lower self-reported and mother-reported aggression.

Two methods of human behavioral genetics (Dixon & Johnson, 1980) have been of value in examining inheritance effects relative to aggression; these are twin and adopted-child studies. Comparisons of identical or monozygous (MZ) twins and fraternal or dizygous (DZ) twins provide one technique for isolating the effects of the genotype versus the effects of the environment on behavioral traits. Table 3 provides a summary of the twin data which have been reported to date relative to the impact of genetic factors on aggressive behavior.

In Table 3, the concordance measure reflects the likelihood that both twins will manifest the same condition, in this case antisocial activity, when one twin already shows the aggressive behavior. Although there is considerable variation in concordance rates (MZ twins from 26% to 100% and DZ twins from 11% to 100%), the MZ rates show less dispersion and are generally greater than the DZ rates. Christiansen's (1977) report based on a total of 3,586 twin pairs is particularly striking and buttresses considerably the claim that the biological heritage of identical twins influences their antisocial behavior.

As a partial resolution of the problems associated with full acceptance of the twin research, adopted-child studies have evolved. This variant of the animal cross-fostering studies is purported to be the most powerful technique for assessing the impact of heredity and environment on behavior (DeFries & Plomin, 1978). Mednick, Gabrielli, and Hutchings (1983) argue as follows:

Table 3
Concordance in Twin Criminality Studies

		Monozygotic		Dizygotic	
		Number of pairs	Pairwise concordance percent	Number of pairs	Pairwise concordance percent
Lange (1929)		13	76.9	17	11.8
Legras		4	100.0	5	0.0
Rosanoff, Handy, & Plessett (1941)					
Predelinquent types	(m)	8	100.0	9	56
	(f)	14	100.0	19	42
Juvenile delinquency	(m)	29	100.0	17	71
	(f)	12	92	9	100
Adult criminality	(m)	38	76	23	22
	(f)	7	86	4	25
Stumpfl (1936)		18	64.5	19	36.8
Kranz (1936)		32	65.6	43	53.5
Borgstrom (1939)		4	75.0	5	40.0
Yoshimasu (1962)		28	60.6	18	11.1
Dalgard & Kringlen (1976)		31	25.8	54	14.9
Christiansen (1977a,b)	(m)	325	52	611	22
	(f)	328	35	593	14

Note. Adapted from "A review of studies of criminality among twins" and "A preliminary study of criminality among twins" by K. O. Christiansen, 1977, in S. A. Mednick & K. O. Christiansen (Eds.), *Biosocial Bases of Criminal Behavior*, pp. 45–108. New York: Gardner Press.

> The study of adoptions better separates environmental and genetic effects; if criminal adoptees have disproportionately high numbers of criminal biological fathers (given appropriate controls), this would suggest a genetic factor in criminal behavior. This conclusion is especially supported by the fact that almost none of the adoptees know their biological parents; the adoptee often does not even realize he has been adopted. (p. 40)

A few adopted-child studies have been published. Crowe (1972) examined 52 children of female criminals matched with a control sample on age, sex, race, and age of adoption. The progeny of the offenders showed increased rates of criminality compared to the controls. Mednick *et al.* (1983) selected information on all nonfamilial adoptions in Denmark between 1924 and 1947 ($N=14,427$). Court convictions were used as an index of criminal behavior. From these data Mednick *et al.* (1983) concluded:

> In a total population of adoptions we have noted a relationship between biological parent criminal convictions and criminal convictions in their adopted children. The relationship is particularly strong for chronic adoptee and biological parent crime was

related to type of adoptee crime. A number of potentially confounding variables were considered (subjects not fully identified by name, birthday or birth place; age of adoption, and labeling of the adoptee); none of these proved sufficient to explain the genetic relationship. We conclude that some factor is transmitted by criminal parents which increases the likelihood that their children will engage in criminal behavior. This is especially true for chronic criminality. Since the factor transmitted must be biological this implies that biological factors are involved in the etiology of at least some criminal behavior. (pp. 54–55)

It is difficult to assert that no inroads have been made on the relation of genetic influences and antisocial activity. Even though there is an unquestionable influence by virtue of the hierarchical interplay between the genotype and phenotype, the relationship seen in the data presented here is weak. The Danish data of Mednick *et al.* (1983) are by far the more convincing but still reflect only a particular set of circumstances and lead to one conclusion: environmental homogeneity enhances the expression of genetic qualities.

GENDER DIFFERENCES

The general conclusions emerging from Eme's (1979) review on sex differences in childhood psychopathology provide an appropriate introduction to the topic of gender differences in the expression of aggression. The most clearly reliable finding from this evaluation was the greater prevalence during childhood of males with syndromes involving adjustment reactions, neurotic and psychotic disorder, gender identity, antisocial behavior, and learning disabilities. There were, however, some noticeable changes in adulthood; the sex ratios were different for some of the disorders that had been observed during childhood. The male predominance in aggressive behavior, however, remained consistently stable. Eme concluded that socialization practices and differential stresses related to sex role did not appear to account for these discrepancies in sex ratios, especially for aggressive behavior. As a result he maintained that "biological factors play an important role and need to be given far more attention than they have been given in the recent past" (p. 591).

The question of gender differences in aggression has been comprehensively reviewed by Maccoby and Jacklin (1974). There have appeared a variety of critiques and opposing contentions as to the implications of their findings (Block, 1976; Hyde, 1984; Tieger, 1980). Maccoby and Jacklin's (1974) initial review was based on 94 studies dealing with sex differences in expressing aggression. These covered the range from age 2 through adulthood. In the majority of the studies males were more aggressive than females, but 37 showed no sex difference, and in 5 cases females were more aggressive than males. From these results it was concluded that not only were males more aggressive than females, but also that the observed sex difference was evident as early as the preschool period. The increased levels of male aggressiveness were assumed to stem from sex hormone levels and their related effects on bodily structure and physical strength. Maccoby and Jacklin (1974) rejected all possible counterarguments to their biological hypothesis. Among these were a learned fear of aggression among girls, or a tendency for girls to reinforce the aggressive acts of males, or adult reinforcement of aggression to a greater degree in males than in females.

Tieger (1980) in turn disputed the Maccoby and Jacklin (1974) thesis of a biological predisposition for enhanced male aggression. He argued that the reliance on hormonal level as a basis for the male predominance in aggression was unsubstantiated. He proposed instead that cross-cultural differences support a social environmental hypothesis. In line with this, Tieger contended that differential sex-related aggression is not observed under 6 years of age and that patterns of male aggressive behavior develop in line with culturally appropriate standards and expectations.

In response to Tieger's arguments, Maccoby and Jacklin (1980) provided additional evidence that peer-directed aggression is consistently present earlier than 6 years of age. Their meta-analysis of 32 studies showed highly significant male aggression in 24, no difference in 8, and no evidence of higher female aggression in any of the results. They again concluded that the observed sex difference is not a direct function of male activity or social interaction involving same-sex partners. However, they did explicitly state that the human evidence for a hormonal base underlying male aggression was inconclusive.

The gender difference issue also has been pursued by Hyde (1984), who raised the question as to how large these gender differences are in aggression. On the basis of her metaanalysis, she found that the difference in 143 studies was not large; in fact, within-gender variation was larger than between-gender variation. Her data indicated that gender differences decreased with age, appearing larger among younger children and smaller among older (college) students. Hyde (1984) concluded that neither Tieger's (1980) notion that gender differences are smaller during the preschool years nor Maccoby and Jacklin's (1980) position that gender differences are "well established" could be substantiated.

HYPERACTIVITY AND AGGRESSION

Hyperactivity appears to be a behavioral as well as a medical enigma, and there are innumerable hypotheses posited to account for the child's excessive motoric activity (Ross & Ross, 1976). Historically the initial emphasis in child hyperactivity was on organic factors and was associated with a diagnosis of minimal brain damage to account for the behavior (Doll, Phelps, & Melcher, 1932; Dela Cruz, Fox, & Roberts, 1973). A shift to an emphasis on behavior patterns first appeared with the use of the label "hyperkinetic reaction of child-hood" (DSM-II, 1968). This was reemphasized in the definition of an attention deficit disorder (ADD) syndrome in DSM-III (1980). The ADD was characterized by "developmentally inappropriate inattention, impulsivity, and hyperactivity."

In DSM-III (1980) there is a summary based on systematic longitudinal studies of groups of children characterized as hyperactive. It outlines the types of outcomes which have been observed and is an appropriate introduction to this section on aggression and hyperactivity. One observed pattern shows that the child's later behavior adjustment appears to be a type of compensation for what initially may have been delayed maturation or physiological immaturity (Oettinger, Majorski, Limbeck, & Gauch, 1974). In contrast to this, a second behavioral pattern appears simply to be a persistence of the hyperactivity syndrome, that is, the attention deficit with impulsivity and excessive activity. The sequelae of the third adjustment pattern is most pertinent to the scope of this chapter. Here the developmental pattern observed as the child grew older was characterized by antisocial behavior and maladjustment. The clinical literature is replete with studies which also have associated high levels of activity with increased aggressive activity. As a result of this presumed interaction, a general interest has developed in determining whether childhood hyperactivity is linked to later antisocial behavior and, if so, what the factors or predictors are that have entered into this pattern of maladjustment.

There are only a few studies that have identified possible etiological factors that appear to be associated with both hyperactivity and aggression. Principal among these are investigations that have looked at the relationship among hyperactivity, aggression, and minor physical anomalies. Customarily, minor anomalies have been considered to be "unusual morphological features that are of no serious medical or cosmetic consequence" (Smith, 1976, p. 434). Nonetheless, several investigators have reported a prevalence of minor physical anomalies in hyperactive children (Firestone, Lewy, & Douglas, 1976; Halverson & Victor, 1976; Rapoport, Quinn, & Lamprecht, 1974; Steg & Rapoport, 1975; Waldrop & Goering, 1971; Waldrop & Halverson, 1972; Waldrop, Pederson, & Bell, 1968).

Clinical evidence suggests that minor anomalies may appear more often in individuals with major defects which are apparent at birth than in cases without such abnormalities (Marden, Smith, & McDonald, 1964). Minor anomalies also may accompany other types of defects which are not diagnosed until after birth. In this sense minor physical anomalies may signal "cryptic" congenital defects in normal newborns (Hook, Marden, Reiss, & Smith, 1976). These anomalies are assumed to be due to genetic factors or early prenatal insults. The factors responsible for these anomalies are also presumed to influence structures of the central nervous system that may be associated with hyperactive behavior.

A number of minor anomalies have been described and used in hyperactivity studies (Waldrop & Halverson, 1971). Characteristics observed for the head include size, hypertelorism, hair line, hair whorls, electric hair, low set ears with adherent lobes, and malformed pinnas. Absence of epicanthal folds, mishappen palates, and furrowed tongues in the mouth also have been noted. In the hands, a single transverse palmar crease and inward curved fifth finger have been observed. Differential length of the third toe relative to the second, partial syndactylism between the second and the third toes, and a gap between first and second toe have been found in the feet. Many of these characteristics also are associated with the Down Syndrome.

In an early study, Waldrop, Pedersen, and Bell (1968) reported that hyperactivity was related to the number of anomalies observed in normal preschool children. This finding was confirmed in a series of later studies with males 3 to 12 years of age, in nursery school (Waldrop & Halverson, 1972), and at the elementary school level (Firestone, Lewy, & Douglas, 1976; Halverson & Victor, 1976; Waldrop & Goering, 1971). The accumulated findings from these studies indicated that the relationship between the anomaly score and hyperactivity was stable from ages 2.5 years to 7.5 years and the anomaly score at 2.5 predicted hyperactivity at 7.5.

In their most recent study, Waldrop, Bell, McLaughlin, and Halverson (1978) examined the relationship between the minor anomalies of male newborns, short attention-span, and peer-aggression impulsivity. The infants were assessed during the newborn period ($N=23$) and again at age 3 ($N=59$). The number of minor signs was significantly related to a cluster of behaviors reflecting short attention span, peer aggression, and impulsivity. The authors inferred from their study that "there was an undefined, but nevertheless, a clear indicator of a congenital contributor to some frequently occurring behavior problems in their general population of young boys" (p. 564). In other research newborn anomaly scores have been shown to be a reliable index of high motor activity and emotional irritability at one year of age (Quinn, Renfield, Burg, & Rapoport, 1977). Burg, Hart, Quinn, and Rapoport (1978) reported that their newborn and one-year anomaly scores were significantly correlated with each other and furthermore also correlated significantly with negativistic and problem behaviors of these infants at one and two years of age. Quinn and Rapoport (1974) noted that hyperactive elementary school boys with high anomaly scores seemed to have had an earlier onset of hyperactivity than those with low anomaly scores.

The recognition that aggressive activity might be a significant part of the behavior repertoire of the hyperactive child has emerged rather haltingly over the past 25 years. A number of investigators (Chess, 1960; Marwit & Stenner, 1972; Ney, 1974), looking at the behavior of hyperactive children in response to stimulant medication, concluded that there was considerable heterogeneity within this disorder. They stressed the need to identify homogeneous subgroups.

Some of the early efforts in this direction called attention only to symptoms that differentiated some of the children from others within the hyperactive group. For example, Stewart, Pitts, Craig, and Dieruf (1966) analyzed and compared the life histories of 37 hyperactive children of normal intelligence, age 5–11, to a similar group of control children. The average number of symptoms among the patients was 22, compared to 3 for the control group. Even though stealing (27%), vandalism (22%), fire setting (11%), and cruelty (11%) were present, the relative significance of these symptoms was dismissed for a number of reasons. Only 6 out of 37 of the hyperactive children had a larger number of symptoms than the average number seen in their peers. In light of this, Stewart *et al.* concluded that this group with marked antisocial behavior showed the hyperactive syndrome only in its severe form and did not comprise a discrete subgroup.

Mendelson, Johnson, and Stewart (1971) assessed 83 children between the ages of 12 years and 16 years who had been diagnosed as hyperactive two to five years earlier. They noted that a "significant minority," approximately one in four, were involved in antisocial activities to an extent that raised questions about their future adjustment. The antisocial symptoms included stealing (51%), fighting (51%), destructiveness (52%), and threatening to kill their parents (34%). In closing their report, Mendelson *et al.* stated that "the general picture is . . . [of] children who do not conform to the rules of their families and of society" (p. 275).

An important step in considering aggression as a significant component of the hyperactive syndrome was the recognition that the observed behavior might include both primary and secondary symptoms (Loney, 1974; Wender, 1971). Primary symptoms include those customarily used to diagnose hyperactivity, namely, extreme activity, distractibility, excitability, and impulsivity. Secondary symptoms, on the other hand, are responses or reactions of the child to situations resulting from the interaction between the child's hyperactivity and environmental factors, such as the child's reaction to strict parental control. For example, the child's secondary symptom or reaction might be some form of overt aggression, such as beating a brother.

Milich and Loney (1979) have raised the question as to why secondary symptoms, such as aggression, have not been extensively studied in children diagnosed as hyperactive. Although a number of reasons may account for this, Milich and Loney think that one of the more important is that there is a basic question in the minds of many researchers as to whether hyperactivity is a syndrome in itself or simply a symptom of other disorders.

As previously noted, there has been considerable debate over this issue (Quay, 1979), and only currently is there some resolution and consensus, in recognition that both empirical and clinical evidence support the identification of not only one but several narrow-band syndromes in hyperactivity, namely, aggressive, delinquent and hyperactivity categories. In light of this, Milich and Loney (1979) reasoned:

Is valuable information being lost by lumping the two categories together? . . . Greater predictive precision can be obtained by examining the dimensions of hyperactivity and aggression separately, since they appear to have different antecedents and consequences for hyperactive youngsters. (p. 108)

A case in support of this argument is Morrison's (1980) analysis of the social factors that were etiologically important in the behavior of members of an adult psychiatric group who had had an earlier diagnosis of hyperactive child syndrome (HACS). This group ($N=48$) was compared with a non-HACS control group with which it was matched for age, sex, and economic status. Violent antisocial behavior typified three times as many HACS patients as the non-HACS controls. Two-thirds of the HACS had a history of crime and/or violence, compared to one-third of the non-HACS ($p<.002$). Morrison concluded that hyperkinesis alone could not account for the results but that an environmental factor interacting with the constitutional hyperactivity probably accounted for the observed social pathology. His postulated hypothesis was failure of parental control.

This push to delineate the correlates of hyperactivity and aggression and the interaction among them appears in a number of investigations. For example, Langhorne, Loney, Paternite, and Bechtoldt (1976) proposed that the behavior of the hyperactive children was related to a particular environment surrounding the child. On the basis of this hypothesis they argued that the identification of subgroups would be facilitated if the child's hyperactive behavior were analyzed in terms of its origin or source in a particular environment. Behavioral patterns resulting from assessments made by teachers and parents of 94 hyperkinetic boys, using the Conners (1970) scale, were subjected to factor analysis. The results demonstrated that the behavioral patterns were related to variables within the particular environment (home or school) in which they occurred. In light of this, Langhorne *et al.* concluded that identification of subgroups in their hyperactive children could indeed be more easily made if the child's hyperactive behavior were analyzed in terms of the source.

Loney, Langhorne, and Paternite (1978) went one step further toward defining subgroups by analyzing the ratings of primary and secondary symptoms in 135 hyperkinetic boys. Their analysis of medical charts, as a single source, was based on ratings by judges of the frequency and/or severity of six primary, four secondary, and five unclassified marker symptoms. The six primary symptoms were hyperactivity, inattention, fidgetiness, judgment deficits or impulsivity, negative affect, and lack of coordination. The four secondary symptoms were compulsivity, aggressive interpersonal behavior, control deficits, and self-esteem deficits. The five unclassified marker symptoms were anxiety, depression, mood lability, speech disturbance, and sleep disturbance. Principal-axis factor analysis defined two relatively independent dimensions: aggression and hyperactivity accounted for about 45% and 23% of the variances respectively. Loney *et al.* (1978) therefore concluded that their data suggested four possible distinct subgroups of boys: (1) exclusively hyperactives (high hyperactivity and low aggression), (2) exclusively aggressives (high aggression and low hyperactivity), (3) aggressive hyperactives (high aggression and high hyperactivity), and (4) residuals (low aggression and low hyperactive).

The distinction between two relatively definable behavioral patterns, that is, aggression and hyperactivity, has been validated by Milich, Loney, & Landau (1982). Following the procedures used in the earlier study of Loney *et al.* (1978), data based on ratings from the Conners (1970) scale and playroom observations for 90 consecutive male referrals were evaluated. The notion of two separate externalizing dimensions, that is, aggression and hyperactivity, was supported. As a result, Milich *et al.* concluded:

> The results of both the current study and earlier investigations by the present research group suggest that it is both clinically and empirically desirable to differentiate between hyperactive and aggressive dimensions when evaluating a clinic-referred boy. . . . These results suggest that although both hyperactivity and aggression are constituents of a broad-band externalizing dimension, valuable information regarding current and future functioning may be lost by collapsing these two dimensions into a single broad-band measure. (pp. 196–197)

Subsequent work on defining distinct subgroups within the hyperactive group has approached the problem from several different perspectives. Sandberg, Wieselberg, and Shaffer (1980) attempted to ascertain whether conduct disturbances and hyperkinesis as measured by behavior questionnaires were related to biological and psychosocial factors. The behavior ratings were obtained from parent and teacher questionnaires (Conners, 1969, 1973; Rutter, 1967). Their results showed that parents distinguished between the two conditions and that parents and teachers selected separate behavior patterns of these children as representative of either hyperactive or conduct disturbances. Interestingly enough, there was a lack of association between the measures of hyperactivity and other possible causal influences, for example, minor physical anomalies. In another approach, Schleifer *et al.* (1975) used their observations and teachers ratings on preschool hyperactive children to define two groups. Members of one were situational hyperactives, moderately active children whose high activity levels were specific to the situation, usually the home environment. Members of the other group were seen as true hyperactives, very active children whose behavior appeared in many situations and was accompanied by aggressive acts toward their peers. Not surprisingly, the children who were referred to clinics during the school-age period for inattention and disruptive behavior came from this latter group.

Campbell, Edman, and Benfield (1977) have confirmed this distinction between true and situational hyperactives. Their evidence was based on hyperactive ($N=15$) and control preschool children ($N=16$) who were initially observed at age 4 in nursery school and then followed up at 6½ and again at 7½. Campbell *et al.* interpret their findings as an indication of the presence of distinct hyperactive subgroups which they classified as evidencing reactive hyperactivity or constitutional hyperactivity.

Schacher, Rutter, and Smith (1981) approached this problem by attempting to determine whether the categories of situationally hyperactive, pervasively hyperactive, and nonhyperactive have diagnostic significance. The study group was composed of 1,536 children who were 10–11 years of age at the time of data collection and who were followed up when they were 14–15 years old. In terms of the Rutter parent and teacher scales, the situational hyperactive group was not outstanding relative to emotional and behavioral maladjustment. In contrast, the pervasive hyperactives were outstanding: their rate of behavioral disturbance was high and generally they had a poor prognosis. These data were in accord with the general findings reported by Sandberg, Rutter, and Taylor (1978), Schleifer *et al.* (1975), and Campbell *et al.* (1977).

The emerging evidence supporting the existence of subgroups within what was formerly considered a homogeneous hyperactive population has several implications. For example, one implication is the necessity for further defining the relationship between hyperactivity as a syndrome and the DSM-III category of conduct disorder. Stewart, Cummings, Singer, and DeBlois (1981) were specifically concerned with describing the clinical picture of the child with only hyperactivity and the child with only conduct disorder. Structured interview data were collected from mothers. A sample of 175 cases, of whom 90% ranged between ages 5–14, was classified into diagnostic categories. The results showed that 49% of the children were diagnosed as hyperactive, 46% as unsocialized aggressive, and 34% as having both syndromes. Furthermore, the findings indicated that children with hyperactivity and conduct disorders were more like children with only conduct disorders than they were like children who were "pure" hyperactives.

The presumed relationship between aggression and hyperactivity has also been examined in detail by Prinz, Connor, and Wilson (1981). The unique features of this study were, first, a restriction of ages to 6–8 years for the beginning elementary first, second, and third grades and, second, an assessment when these children were beginning to show hyperactive problems. The Conners Abbreviated Teacher Rating Scale (Conners, 1973) and a behavioral checklist were used as assessment devices. For a selected group of hyperactive children (103 boys and 33 girls) relative to a comparison group of the same size, the results showed that children rated as having the highest rates of hyperactivity also showed higher rates of interpersonal aggression and that hyperactive children with daily hyperactivity scores above 70% were involved in aggressive acts at rates higher than 98% of their comparison classmates.

Loney, Kramer, and Milich (1981) set out to identify and evaluate the relative importance of the variables present at the time of referral and during treatment that might account for the variations seen in the adolescent behavior of formerly diagnosed hyperkinetic/minimal brain dysfunction (HK/MBD) children. The study group was composed of 84 boys from an ongoing longitudinal study of the HK/MBD syndrome. These boys were 6–12 years old at the time of the initial intake evaluation and living with their parents or parental surrogates. They were placed on Ritalin stimulant treatment within 6 weeks of the outpatient evaluation. At the time of the follow-up assessment, they were 12–18 years of age. In their multiple regression analyses, Loney et al. used as independent or predictor variables three environmental categories (ecological, familial, and treatment), two child categories (symptoms and treatment), and miscellaneous variables (age at onset of symptoms, age at time of the psychiatric examination, neurological status, and perinatal complications).

Within the ecological category, the specific variables were socioeconomic status and rural or urban residence. The familial variables were intactness of the biological family, length of time the biological triad had been intact, number of intervening changes in the living situation, and number of children in the family. Four measures of parenting style also were included: maternal and paternal estimates of love and hostility, and maternal and paternal autonomy to control. Treatment variables were response to the methylphenidate stimulant medication and the duration of the CNS stimulant treatment. The child variables were defined in terms of two dimensions, aggression and hyperactivity. Postacademic functioning and current reading and arithmetic achievement constituted the child achievement variables.

The most significant results of multivariate analyses were that childhood aggression and hyperactivity appeared to have different correlates at both the time of referral and the follow-up period. Loney et al. (1981) concluded that "although drug treatment affects childhood hyperactivity, behavioral outcome and subsequent delinquency are determined instead by childhood aggression and by its ecological antecedents—child hyperactivity is not the first link in a chain that leads to teen-age symptoms and delinquency" (p. 412).

As a sequel to their earlier research, Loney, Whaley-Klahn, Kosier, and Konboy (1983) focused on identifying the predictors of antisocial behavior in 65 adults previously diagnosed as HK/MBD children who also had been treated for an average of three years with CNS stimulant medication. The objectives were twofold: first, to determine whether the identified predictors of aggressiveness in adolescence are also associated with adult aggressiveness and, second, to decide whether the symptoms from the attention deficit syndrome (inattention, impulsivity, and hyperactivity) were related to adult antisocial behavior. The subjects were 65 young adults, aged 4–12 at referral, who had no apparent neurological impairment, and none of whom had an IQ below 70. All had been recommended for CNS stimulant treatment. A group of non-HK/MBD full brothers also were evaluated. Loney *et al.* (1983) arrived at a number of substantial conclusions in this study, including the following: The chief predictors of adult aggressive and antisocial outcomes were primarily related to a lower level of intellectual functioning during childhood and, to a lesser degree, to childhood aggression. Parental style and psychopathological behavior, large families, and urban residence were also decidedly negative factors that affected the functioning of these adult probands. In summary, the ADD syndrome triad was rejected as "a sufficient basis for the diagnostic model of childhood disorders" (p. 205)— that is, it is not one with known precursors and describable antecedents across reasonable periods of time.

CHILDHOOD VIOLENCE

The spectrum of childhood violence recorded in the *Uniform Crime Reports for the United States* (1983) is probably not different from that seen in other annual reports. It ranges from first and second degree murder (voluntary and first degree manslaughter along with negligent homocide) to sex offenses (rape, sexual molesting, incest, and sodomy), robbery (unarmed to armed robbery, purse snatching), and assault (assault and battery, assault with deadly weapon, assault with intent to rob and intentional stabbing). Although the Crime Index for children was only 12.1%, the fact that it exists is justification for examining the problem. Unfortunately there is a lack of published literature: this confirms the truism stated by Hamparian *et al.* (1978) that "juvenile violence is a phenomenon that has received relatively little empirical attention" (p. 4).

The research of Hamparian *et al.* (1978), along with that of Wolfgang (1983) and Wolfgang, Figlio, and Sellin (1972), has been instrumental in providing some perspective on childhood violence. Hamparian *et al.* have looked at a number of important variables and their relative effect on subsequent severe aggressive acts; specifically, they have looked at (a) chronic recidivism offenses, (b) the age of onset of antisocial behavior, (c) status offenses, (d) the severity of crimes and the intractability of the offender, and (e) "desistance." Their analysis was based on birth cohorts in Columbus, Ohio, for the years 1956–1960. They selected 1,138 youngsters who were charged with a total of 4,499 offenses, of which 1,504 were crimes of violence and 904 were crimes against persons. In the whole cohort, only about 10% began their careers with a status offense: only 22 were destructive enough to be considered a threat to others. Hamparian *et al.* (1978) note:

The quality of the offenses committed by the cohort ranged from murder, the most serious crime of all, to street corner and schoolyard fist fights that somehow became matters of police record. Less than a third of the offenses could be classified as major crimes against the person. Throughout our report we have stressed the incidental quality of the violence in the delinquent careers making up our cohort. Except for those who committed only 1 offense, necessarily a violent offence, nearly all the cohort members committed far more nonviolent offenses than violent ones. Very few committed more than 1 major crime against the person, and only a handful committed more than 2. If there is a substantial number of youths who are repetitively committing violent acts, their delinquencies have not come to the attention of the police. (p. 128)

About one-third of the cohort were chronic offenders in the sense of the Wolfgang *et al.* (1972) criterion, which defined the chronic recidivist as one who had committed five or more offenses. These chronic offenders were primarily male (34% male, 13% female) from the lower socioeconomic level. More than 81 (7%) of the cohort were chronic recidivists by age 14, and they continued to commit about 9.3% of the aggravated offenses. This group also had committed 44.8% of the Index crimes against persons.

The data dealing with the age of onset of antisocial behavior indicated that a total of 411 were delinquent before age 14, but only 169 or 41% of this group were still committing crimes during their 17th year. This meant that for this particular group, 59% had desisted from any offense before their 17th birthdays. Hamparian *et al.* (1978) suggest that juvenile violent offenders are a minor problem in that only 2% committed the violent offenses. Further, juvenile offenders did not appear to move from less to more serious crimes. More than half of the longer delinquent careers were extinguished before the latter part of adolescence.

The occurrence of violent behavior has been examined relative to psychosocial variables (Pfeffer, Plutchik, & Mizruchi, 1983a). In their studies a child was rated as assaultive if he or she demonstrated any assaultive idea, threat, or attempted homicide during the six months preceding evaluation. In addition, similar measures of parental assaultiveness, as well as the concept of death, the severity of any suicidal behavior, precipitating events, family background, and ego and defense mechanisms were assessed. Analyses showed the assaultiveness of these children to be significantly related to their recent and past acts of aggression, their absence of anxiety and depression, and the assaultive behavior of their parents. Pfeffer *et al.* (1983a) concluded that the appearance of parental assaultive behavior increases the probability of childhood assaultiveness. They also hypothesized that there is an interrelationship between suicidal and assaultive behavior in children and their parents: the child is acting out the fantasies of identification with violent parents and the parents' wish to get rid of them. Subsequent follow-up observations also suggested that the severity of suicidal behavior in the child was significantly correlated with the severity of parental assaultive behavior.

In a subsequent investigation, Pfeffer *et al.* (1983b) focused on why some children express only assaultive as opposed to only suicidal or neither suicidal or assaultive behavior. The subjects ($N=102$), ages 6–12, were evaluated with measures used in the previous study and supplemented with a Spectrum of Suicidal Behavior Scale. The most common diagnoses were borderline personality disorder (39%), specific developmental disorder (34%), conduct disorder (32%), and affective disorder (25%). Aggression was significantly greater for the assaultive only and for the assaultive-suicidal than for either the nonassaultive or suicidal only groups. Antisocial lying, stealing, and truancy were also more common among the assaultive only children than for the nonassaultive and nonsuicidal children. Depression was significantly greater in the suicidal than in the assaultive only children. The assaultive and the assaultive-suicidal children were exposed to more parental violence than the other groups of children. Parents of the assaultive-suicidal and the suicidal had more suicidal behavior present in their histories. On the basis of these data, Pfeffer *et al.* (1983b) inferred that assaultive and suicidal behavior reflect two independent sets of variables. If they occur in isolation, one set of variables may result in suicidal behavior as opposed to assaultive behavior in the child. Pfeffer *et al.* in this study also indicated that two patterns of assaultive-suicidal behavior may be seen in children. One type is uniquely characterized by the presence of assaultive and suicidal behavior among the parents; the other type is not so characterized.

In fact, between groups overall the greatest contrast was between the suicidal only and the assaultive only children. In the former, environmental stresses were clearly present. In the latter, psychobiological factors were more evident. These groups also expressed aggression and depression differently. Finally, Pfeffer *et al.* (1983b) stated that two types of suicidal children can be identified: the first, those in whom extreme environmental pressure induced depression in a fairly well integrated personality structure and the second, those in whom personality deficits were already apparent along with a tendency to identify with parental expressions of suicidal behaviors.

To look at another kind of violent behavior in children, fire setting may be considered a form of violence. The material relevant to children appears to be for the most part in case studies and is limited to articles published by Bempass, Fagelman, and Brix (1983), Gruber, Heck, and Mintzer (1981), and Stewart and Culver (1982). As these last two investigators have appropriately stated, the principal need in this area is for detailed information on the child's motivation, the fire-setting context, and the persistence of fire-setting behavior. Stewart and Culver have compiled some information based on two groups of 46 children (43 boys and 3 girls), ranging from 4 years to 14 years of age. Among these, 34 were age 10 or younger; and 36 were diagnosed as having unsocialized aggressive conduct disorder, 2 as having attention deficit disorder with hyperactivity, and 1 as having an adjustment reaction. The clinical data indicated that (a) most of the referrals of these children who set fires are for other problems; (b) most of the group who set their fires at home tend to be alone, younger, and intellectually dull; (c) the older children set their fires with other children away from their homes but for the most part ended up involved in more serious trouble; (d) 23% (7 of 30 subjects followed for 1–7 years) were still setting fires; and (e) the short-term progress was only fair. At best, the ability to predict whether the fire-setting activity would or would not continue was limited. Stewart and Culver concluded that psychiatric disorders in the parental background of the children were more closely related to the occurrence of unsocialized aggressive conduct disorders than to the problem of fire setting.

The Gruber *et al.* (1981) observations on 90 children identified as fire setters revealed that these offenders were referred primarily because the parents were unable to handle the children and because the children had learning difficulties. Among these children, 55% were labeled as hyperactive, 62% were involved in destroying property in other ways than by fire setting, and about 29% apparently had endangered other children. The social background was poor: 35% had been abandoned, 54% showed parental neglect, and 35% had suffered parental physical abuse.

As with studies relevant to violence in general, there is little empirical evidence on childhood attributes and characteristics associated with sexual violence. Knight, Prentky, Schneider, and Rosenberg (1983) have attempted to outline the developmental precursors of specific acts of sexual violence, namely, patterns associated with rapists and child molesters. In their words, they have focused on examining specific factors that appear to predispose the individual to act in this particular manner. Underlying their investigation is the hypothesis that individuals involved in repetitive and violent sexual offenses are a distinctive group. The object of their study was to develop an explanatory causal model for sexual violence and determine the paths that exist between the variables involved. Data were derived from 125 convicted male sexual offenders committed under provisions of the law (in Massachusetts) as a sexually dangerous person

> whose misconduct in sexual matters indicates a general lack of power to control his sexual impulses, as evidenced by repetitive or compulsive behavior and either violence or aggression by an adult against a victim under the age of sixteen years, and who as a result is likely to attack or otherwise inflict injury on the objects of his uncontrolled or uncontrollable desires. (Knight *et al.*, 1983, p. 208)

Their approach was based on a model involving three data sets of antecedent variables: family and parental pathology, child and juvenile (prior to age 17) pathology, and adult noncriminal incompetence and pathology. Sexual offense was the dependent or outcome variable. Through principal-components analysis these subsets were reduced to a smaller number of factor scores, and with these factor scores a series of simultaneous multiple regression or path analyses were conducted. The final groups of variables which were entered into two linear-structural analysis were considered to represent variables most highly predictive of delinquent and adult antisocial behavior.

Two majors paths were associated with rapists. The first reflected *family instability* and progressed to *juvenile acting out,* then to *adult antisocial behavior,* and then to an increased *frequency in criminal offenses.* The second also emerged from family instability but led to juvenile psychiatric-system contact and then an increased frequency of criminal offenses. Knight *et al.* (1983) interpreted these data as suggesting:

> There is direct evidence for at least two types of rapist in this model. One might be described as an impulsive, antisocial character disorder, while the other might be described as a low impulse, incompetent individual with no evidence of early conduct disorder. An obverse type, while not directly observed in the model, may be inferred from the pattern of correlations. This type of rapist is characterized by no apparent history of family instability, few childhood or juvenile problems, and a low frequency of criminal offenses. (Knight *et al.*, 1983, p. 333)

Four paths appeared for the molesters. The first led from family sexual deviation to criminal offenses. This pattern was considered to typify an individual who was an aggressive and exploitative person. The second path began with family instability, led to psychiatric-system contact in the juvenile period, and to interpersonal and academic and/or vocational incompetence during adulthood, with an increased frequency in criminal offenses. This path was considered to describe an aggression-fixated child molester with a history of general incompetence. The third pattern similarly emerged from family instability and proceeded to alcohol abuse and impulsivity in sexual offenses. The fourth path started with childhood acting-out behaviors, then continued with adult antisocial behavior and an increased number of criminal offenses.

In summary, the evidence from the causal modeling in the Knight *et al.* (1983) study makes one important contribution to our understanding of one pattern of severe aggression against others: it highlights the significant role of the family setting in the etiology of violent sex offenses.

CONCLUSION

This chapter demonstrates that research on childhood aggression has focused on many issues of clinical interest. These efforts appear to have shifted away from concerns with mere descriptive correlates of aggression toward understanding the etiology and the course of antisocial behavior. A major objective has been to define the predictor of childhood and subsequent adolescent aggressive acts against people and property.

This section examines the findings of these investigations as they relate to five questions:

1. Can childhood aggression be considered to be a syndrome of developmental psychopathology and, if so, what are some of the factors that appear to be associated with this type of childhood maladjustment?
2. To what extent does evidence support the idea of genetic influences, apart from sex differences, in the occurrence of aggressive activity?
3. What is the status of the controversy on gender differences relative to acts of overt aggression?
4. Is there a relationship between childhood hyperactivity and aggression?
5. Are there developmental precursors of specific patterns of violence?

The evidence suggest that for a few of these issues substantial progress has been made and for others a partial understanding of the problems involved may be evolving. The nature of the questions may defy a straightforward rational answer and may at best give rise to a set of circumscribed partial equations.

In the matter of the first question, it is clear that the patterns of aggression that are called antisocial transcend the actions associated with the problem behaviors often appearing during early development. Childhood aggression, whether classified in terms of a conduct disorder broad-band externalizing syndrome or a specific narrow-band syndrome, is a pattern of childhood maladjustment. It is legitimately considered to be a form of developmental psychopathology with a level of stability and continuity that warrants monitoring. A survey of the relevant literature indicates that it may be feasible to identify and predict which children are at high risk for antisocial behavior in adolescence and adulthood. In light of this, it is socially expedient to focus on developing campaigns for primary prevention.

In regard to the second question, the examination of possible etiological factors in conduct disorders has defined sociodemographic and psychosocial correlates, and some research has looked at the biological substrate. Within the context of behavioral genetics, there is some evidence suggesting that antisocial behavior might be associated with polygenic factors. Currently the chromosomal, hormonal, twin, and adoption studies provide only a weak link. None of the evidence currently appears likely to define specific genetic factors that directly or indirectly influence aggressive behavior. Although the interaction hypothesis linking genetic and environmental factors must ultimately undergird research on human aggression, the weight of the evidence accumulated thus far suggests that psychosocial variables are more promising prospects for intensive investigation.

In regard to the third question, the data on gender differences cannot be dismissed. Clinical evidence alone substantiates the thesis that gender differences are clearly manifested in overt aggressive activity. However, the discrepancies between investigators' reports on whether these gender differences are well established must be resolved. The fact that hard data underlie some of these conclusions suggests that the question warrants more visionary research to disentangle this issue. Similarly, the etiology of gender differences should be taken out of the current controversial arena.

In regard to the fourth question, the historical concern with hyperactivity as a syndrome of developmental psychopathology reflects a persistent effort to identify and better define the behaviors that enter into the clinical picture. As a result, accumulated evidence clearly suggests that hyperactivity and aggression in childhood appear to function as narrow-band syndromes. Research in this area has been profitable and may provide evidence for meaningful intervention.

Finally, to answer the last question posed in this chapter, the relationship of the more severe forms of antisocial activity to acts of childhood violence is still poorly understood. And even though the facts indicate that this index of developmental psychopathology is relatively low, the gravity of the offenses involved warrants continuing study.

REFERENCES

Achenbach, T. M. (1978). The child behavior profile: I. Boys aged 6–11. *Journal of Consulting and Clinical Psychology, 46,* 478–488.

Achenbach, T. M. (1980). DSM-III in light of empirical research on the classification of child psychology. *Journal of the American Academy of Child Psychiatry, 19,* 395–412.

Achenbach, T., & Edelbrock, C. (1978). The classification of child psychopathology: A review and analysis of empirical efforts. *Psychological Bulletin, 85,* 1275–1301.

Achenbach, T. M., & Edelbrock, C. S. (1983). Taxonomic issues in child psychology. In T. H. Ollendick & M. Hersen (Eds.), *Handbook of child psychopathology* (pp. 65–94). New York: Plenum Press.

American Psychiatric Association. (1968). *Diagnostic and statistical manual of mental disorders* (DSM-II) Washington, D. C.

American Psychiatric Association. (1980). *Diagnostic and statistical manual of mental disorders* (DSM-III) (3rd ed.). Washington, D. C.

Anastasi, A. (1958). Heredity, environment and the question "How?" *Psychological Review, 65,* 197–208.

Baker, D., Teifer, M. A., Richardson, C. E., & Clark, G. R. (1970). Chromosome errors in men with antisocial behavior. *Journal of the American Medical Association, 214,* 869–878.

Bempass, E. R., Fagelman, F. D., & Brix, R. J. (1983). Intervention with children who set fires. *American Journal of Psychotherapy, 37,* 328–345.

Block, J. H. (1976). Issues, problems, and pitfalls in assessing sex differences: A critical review of the psychology of sex differences. *Merrill-Palmer Quarterly, 22,* 283–308.

Borganonkar, D. S., & Shah, S. A. (1974). The XYY chromosome male—or syndrome? In A. G. Steinberg & A. G. Bearn (Eds.), *Progress in medical genetics* (Vol. 10). New York: Grune & Stratton.

Burg, C., Hart, D., Quinn, P. O., & Rapoport, J. L. (1978). Newborn minor physical anomalies and prediction of infant behavior. *Journal of Autism and Childhood Schizophrenia, 8,* 427–439.

Campbell, S. B. (1983). Developmental perspectives in child psychopathology. In T. O. Ollendick & M. Hersen (Eds.), *Handbook of child psychopathology* (pp. 113–140). New York: Plenum Press.

Campbell, S. B., Endman, M. W., & Bernfield, G. (1977). A three-year follow-up of hyperactive preschoolers into elementary school. *Journal of Child Psychology and Psychiatry, 18,* 239–249.

Campbell, S. B., Schleifer, M., Weiss, G., & Perlman, T. (1977). A two-year follow-up study of hyperactive preschoolers. *American Journal of Orthopsychiatry, 47.*

Chess, S. (1960). Diagnosis and treatment of the hyperactive child. *New York State Journal of Medicine, 60,* 2379–2385.

Christiansen, K. O. (1977a). A review of studies of criminality among twins. In S. A. Mednick & K. O. Christiansen (Eds.), *Biosocial bases of criminal behavior* (pp. 45–88). New York: Gardner Press.

Christiansen, K. O. (1977b). A preliminary study of criminality among twins. In S. A. Mednick & K. O. Christiansen (Eds.), *Biosocial bases of criminal behavior* (pp. 89–108). New York: Gardner Press.

Conners, C. K. (1969). A teacher rating scale for use in drug studies with children. *American Journal of Psychiatry, 126,* 884–888.

Conners, C. K. (1970). Symptom patterns in hyperkinetic, neurotic and normal children. *Child Development, 41,* 667–682.

Conners, C. K. (1973). Rating scales for use in drug studies with children. *Psychopharmacology Bulletin,* Special Issue, *Pharmacotherapy of Children,* 24–84.

Craig, M. M., & Glick, S. J. (1963). Ten years' experience with the Glueck social prediction table. *Crime and Delinquency, 9,* 249–261.

Crowe, R. R. (1972). The adopted offspring of women offenders: A study of their arrest records. *Archives of General Psychiatry, 27,* 600–603.

DeFries, J. C., & Plomin, R. (1978). Behavior genetics. In M. R. Rosenzweig & L. W. Porter (Eds.), *Annual review of psychology, 29,* 473–515.

Dela Cruz, F. F., Fox, R. H., & Roberts, R. H. (Eds.) (1973). Minimal brain dysfunction. *Annals of the New York Academy of Science,* Vol. 205.

Dixon, L. K., & Johnson, R. C. (1980). *The roots of individuality: A survey of human behavior genetics.* Monterey, CA: Brooks/Cole.

Doll, E. A., Phelps, W. M., & Melcher, R. T. (1932). *Mental deficiency due to birth injuries.* New York: MacMillan.

Erhardt, A. A., & Baker, S. W. (1974). Fetal androgens, human central nervous system differentiation, and behavior sex differences. In R. C. Freidman, R. M. Richart, & R. Vande Weile (Eds.), *Sex differences in behavior* (pp. 53–76). New York: Wiley.

Erhardt, A. A., & Money, J. (1967). Progestin-induced hermaphroditism: IQ and psychosexual identity in a study of ten girls. *Journal of Sex Research, 3,* 83–100.

Eme, R. (1979). Sex differences in childhood psychopathology: A review. *Psychological Bulletin, 86,* 574–595.

Farrington, D. P. (1983). Offending from 10 to 25 years of age. In K. T. Van Dusen & S. A. Mednick (Eds.), *Prospective studies of crime and delinquency* (pp. 17–38). Boston: Kluwer-Nijhoff.

Farrington, D. P., & West, D. J. (1981). The Cambridge study in delinquent development. In S. A. Mednick & A. E. Baert (Eds.), *Prospective longitudinal research.* Oxford: Oxford University Press.

Feshbach, S. (1970). Aggression. In P. Mussen (Ed.), *Carmichael's manual of child psychology* (Vol. 2, pp. 159–260). New York: Wiley.

Firestone, P., Lewy, F., & Douglas, V. I. (1976). Hyperactivity and physical anomalies. *Canadian Psychiatric Association Journal, 21,* 23–26.

Gersten, J. C., Langner, T. S., Eisenberg, J. G., Simcha-Fagan, O., & McCarthy, E. D. (1976). Stability and change in types of behavioral disturbance of children and adolescents. *Journal of Abnormal Child Psychology, 4,* 111–128.

Group for the Advancement of Psychiatry (1966). *Psychopathological disorders in childhood. Theoretical considerations and a proposed classification.* New York: Author.

Gruber, A. R., Heck, E. T., & Mintzer, E. (1981). Children who set fires: Some background and behavioral characteristics. *American Journal of Orthopsychiatry, 5,* 484–488.

Halverson, C. F., & Victor, J. B. (1976). Minor physical anomalies and problem behavior in elementary school children. *Child Development, 47,* 281–285.

Hamparian, D. M., Schuster, R., Dinitz, S., & Conrad, J. P. (1978). *The violent few.* Lexington, MA: Heath.

Havighurst, R. J., Bowman, P. H., Liddle, G. P., Matthews, C. V., & Pierce, J. V. (1962). *Growing up in River City.* New York: Wiley.

Hines, M. (1982). Prenatal gonadal hormones and sex differences in human behavior. *Psychological Bulletin, 92,* 56–80.

Hook, E. W. (1973). Behavioral implications of the human XYY genotype. *Science, 179,* 139–150.

Hook, E. B., Marden, P. M., Reiss, N. P., & Smith, D. W. (1976). Some aspects of the epidemiology of human minor birth defects and morphological variants in a completely ascertained newborn population (Madison Study). *Teratology, 13,* 47–56.

Hyde, J. S. (1984). How large are gender differences in aggression? A developmental meta-analysis. *Developmental Psychology, 20,* 722–736.

Jacobs, P. A., Brunton, M., Melville, M. M., Brittain, R. P., & McClement, W. F. (1965). Aggressive behavior, mental subnormality and the XYY male. *Nature, 208,* 1351–1352.

Knight, R., Prentky, R., Schneider, B., & Rosenberg, R. (1983). Linear causal modeling of adaptation and criminal history in sexual offenses. In K. T. Van Dusen & S. A. Mednick (Eds.), *Prospective studies of crime and delinquency* (pp. 181–208). Boston: Kluwer-Nijhoff.

Langhorne, J. E., Jr., Loney, J., Paternite, C. E., & Bechtoldt, H. P. (1976). Childhood hyperkinesis: A return to the source. *Journal of Abnormal Psychology, 85,* 201–209.

Leonard, M. F., Landy, G., Ruddle, F. H., & Lubs, H. A. (1974). Early development of children with abnormalities of the sex chromosomes: A prospective study. *Pediatrics, 54,* 208–212.

Loeber, R. (1982). The stability of antisocial and delinquent child behavior: A review. *Child Development, 53,* 1431–1446.

Loeber, R., & Dishion, T. J. (1983). Early predictors of male delinquency: A review. *Psychological Bulletin, 94,* 68–99.

Loeber, R., Dishion, T. J., & Patterson, G. R. (1984). Multiple gating: A multistage assessment procedure for identifying youths at risk for delinquency. *Journal of Research in Crime and Delinquency, 21,* 7–32.

Loney, J. (1974). The intellectual functioning of hyperactive elementary school boys: A cross-sectional investigation. *American Journal of Orthopsychiatry, 44,* 754–762.

Loney, J., Langhorne, J. E., & Paternite, C. E. (1978). An empirical basis for subgrouping the hyperkinetic/minimal brain dysfunction syndrome. *Journal of Abnormal Psychology, 87,* 431–441.

Loney, J., Kramer, J., & Milich, R. (1981). The hyperkinetic child grows up: Predictors of symptoms, delinquency, and achievement at follow-up. In K. Gadow & J. Loney (Eds.), *Psychosocial aspects of drug treatment for hyperactivity* (pp. 381–416). Boulder: Westview Press.

Loney, J., Whaley-Klahn, M. A., Kosier, T., & Konboy, J. (1983). Hyperactive boys and their brothers at 21: Predictors of aggressive and antisocial outcomes. In K. T. Van Dusen & S. A. Mednick (Eds.) *Prospective studies of crime and delinquency,* (pp. 181–208). Boston: Kluwer-Nijhoff.

Lush, J. L. (1937). *Animal breeding plans.* Ames, IA: Collegiate Press.

Maccoby, E. E., & Jacklin, C. N. (1974). *The psychology of sex differences.* Stanford, CA: Stanford University Press.

Maccoby, E. E., & Jacklin, C. N. (1980). Sex differences in aggression: A rejoinder and reprise. *Child Development, 51,* 964–980.

MacFarlane, J. W., Allen, L., & Honzik, M. P. (1954). *A developmental study of the behavior problems of normal children between twenty-one months and fourteen years.* Berkeley: University of California Press.

Marden, P. M., Smith, D. W., & McDonald, M. J. (1964). Congenital anomalies in the newborn infant, including minor variations. *Journal of Pediatrics, 64,* 357–371.

Marwit, S. J., & Stenner, A. J. (1972). Hyperkinesis: Delineation of two patterns. *Exceptional Children, 38,* 401–406.

Mednick, S. A., Gabrielli, W. F., Jr., & Hutchings, B. (1983). Genetic influences in criminal behavior: Evidence from an adoption cohort. In K. T. Van Dusen & S. A. Mednick (Eds.), *Prospective studies of crime and delinquency* (pp. 39–56). Boston: Kluwer-Nijhoff.

Mendelson, W., Johnson, N., & Stewart, M. A. (1971). Hyperactive children as teenagers: A follow-up study. *Journal of Nervous and Mental Disease, 153,* 273–279.

Meyer-Bahlburg, H., & Erhardt, A. (1982). Prenatal sex hormones and human aggression: A review, and new data on progestogen effects. *Aggressive Behavior, 8,* 39–62.

Milich, R., & Loney, J. (1979). The role of hyperactive and aggressive symptomatology in predicting adolescent outcome among children. *Journal of Pediatric Psychology, 4,* 93–112.

Milich, R., Loney, J., & Landau, S. (1982). Independent dimensions of hyperactivity and aggression: A validation with playroom observation data. *Journal of Abnormal Psychology, 91,* 183–198.

Mitchell, S., & Rosa, P. (1981). Boyhood behavior problems as precursors of criminality: A fifteen-year follow-up study. *Journal of Child Psychology and Psychiatry, 22,* 19–33.

Money, J., & Erhardt, A. (1972). *Man and woman, boy and girl.* Baltimore: Johns Hopkins University Press.

Money, J., & Schwartz, M. (1976). Fetal androgens in the early treated adrenogenital syndrome of 46XX hermaphroditism: Influence on assertive and aggressive types of behavior. *Aggressive Behavior, 2,* 19–30.

Moore, D. R., Chamberlain, P., & Mukai, L. (1979). A follow-up comparison of stealing and aggression. *Journal of Abnormal Child Psychology, 7,* 345–355.

Morrison, J. R. (1980). Childhood hyperactivity in an adult psychiatric population: Social factors. *Journal of Clinical Psychology, 41,* 40–43.

Ney, P. G. (1974). Four types of hyperkinesis. *Canadian Psychiatric Association Journal, 19,* 543–550.

Nielsen, J. (1970). Criminality among patients with Kleinfelter's syndrome and XYY syndrome. *British Journal of Psychiatry, 117,* 365–369.

Nielsen, J., & Christensen, A. L. (1974). Thirty-five males with double Y chromosome. *Psychological Medicine, 4,* 28–37.

Noel, B., Dupont, J. P., Revil, D., Dussuyer, I., & Quack, B. (1974). The XYY syndrome: Reality or myth? *Clinical Genetics, 5,* 387–394.

Oettinger, L., Majorski, L. V., Limbeck, G. A., & Gauch, R. (1974). Bone age in children with minimal brain dysfunction. *Perceptual and Motor Skills, 39,* 1127–1131.

Olweus, D. (1979). Stability of aggressive reaction patterns in males: A review. *Psychological Bulletin, 86,* 852–875.

Osborn, S. G., & West, D. J. (1978). The effectiveness of various predictors of criminal careers. *Journal of Adolescence, 1,* 101–117.

Owen, D. R. (1972). The 47, XYY male: A review. *Psychological Bulletin, 78,* 209–233.

Pfeffer, C. R., Plutchik, R., & Mizruchi, M. S. (1983a). Predictors of assaultiveness in latency age children. *American Journal of Psychiatry, 140,* 31–35.

Pfeffer, C. R., Plutchik, R., & Mizruchi, M. S. (1983b). Suicidal and assaultive behavior in children: Classification, measurement, and interrelations. *American Journal of Psychiatry, 140,* 154–157.

Prinz, R., Connor, P., & Wilson, C. (1981). Hyperactive and aggressive behaviors in childhood: Intertwined dimensions. *Journal of Abnormal Child Psychology, 9,* 191–202.

Quay, H. C. (1979). Classification. In H. C. Quay & J. S. Werry (Eds.), *Psychopathological disorders of childhood.* New York: Wiley.

Quinn, P. O., & Rapoport, J. L. (1974). Minor physical anomalies and neurological status in hyperactive boys. *Pediatrics, 53,* 742–747.

Quinn, P. O., Renfield, M., Burg, C., & Rapoport, J. L. (1977). Minor physical anomalies: A newborn screening and 1-year follow-up. *Journal of American Academy of Child Psychiatry, 16,* 662–669.

Rapoport, J. L., Quinn, P. O., & Lamprecht, F. (1974). Minor physical anomalies and plasma dopamine-beta-hydroxylase activity in hyperactive boys. *American Journal of Psychiatry, 131,* 386–390.

Reinisch, J. M. (1974). Fetal hormones, the brain and human sex differences: A heuristic integrative review of the recent literature. *Archives of Sexual Behavior, 3,* 51–90.

Reinisch, J. (1981). Prenatal exposure to prenatal progestens increases potential for aggression in humans. *Science, 211,* 1171–1173.

Robins, L. N. (1966). *Deviant children grown up: A sociological and psychiatric study of sociopathic personality.* Baltimore: Williams & Wilkins.

Robins, L. N. (1978). Sturdy childhood predictors of adult antisocial behaviour: Replications from longitudinal studies. *Psychological Medicine, 8,* 611–622.

Robins, L. N., & Ratcliff, K. S. (1979). Risk factors in the continuation of childhood antisocial behavior into adulthood. *International Journal of Mental Health, 7,* 96–116.

Ross, D. M., & Ross, S. A. (1976). *Hyperactivity: Research, theory, and action.* New York: Wiley.

Rutter, M. L. (1967). A children's behaviour questionnaire for completion by teachers: Preliminary findings. *Journal of Child Psychology and Psychiatry and Allied Disciplines, 8,* 1–11.

Rutter, M., Lebovici, S., Eisenberg, L., Sneznevskij, A. V., Sadoun, R., Brooke, E., & Lin, T. Y. (1969). A triaxial classification of mental disorder in childhood. *Journal of Child Psychology and Psychiatry, 10,* 41–61.

Rutter, M. L., Tizard, J., & Whitmore, K. (Eds.). (1970). *Education, health and behaviour: Psychological and medical study of childhood development.* New York: Wiley.

Rutter, M., Shaffer, D., & Shepherd, M. (1975). *A multi-axial classification of child psychiatric disorders.* Geneva: World Health Organization.

Sandberg, S. T., Rutter, M., & Taylor (1978). Hyperkinetic disorder in child offenders. *Developmental Medicine and Child Neurology, 20,* 279–299.

Sandberg, S. T., Wieselberg, M., & Shaffer, D. (1980). Hyperkinetic and conduct problem children: Some epidemiological considerations. *Journal of Child Psychology and Psychiatry, 21,* 293–312.

Scarpitti, F. R. (1964). Can teachers predict delinquency? *Elementary School Journal, 65,* 130–136.

Schacher, R., Rutter, M., & Smith, A. (1981). The characteristics of situationally and pervasively hyperactive children: Implications for syndrome definition. *Journal of Child Psychology and Psychiatry, 22,* 375–392.

Schleifer, M., Weiss, G., Cohen, N. J., Elman, M., Cvejic, H., & Kruger, E. (1975). Hyperactivity in preschoolers and the effect of methylphenidate. *American Journal of Orthopsychiatry, 45,* 38–50.

Sears, R., Maccoby, E., & Levin, H. (1957). *Patterns of child rearing.* Evanston, IL: Row, Peterson.

Smith, D. W. (1976). *Recognizable patterns of human malformation* (2nd ed.). Philadelphia, PA: W. B. Saunders.

Sroufe, L. A., & Rutter, M. (1984). The domain of development psychopathology. *Child Development, 55,* 17–29.

Steg, J., & Rapoport, J. L. (1975). Minor physical anomalies in normal, neurotic learning disabled and severely disturbed children. *Journal of Autism and Childhood Schizophrenia, 5*, 299–307.

Stewart, M. A., & Culver, K. W. (1982). Children who set fires: The clinical picture and a follow-up. *British Journal of Psychiatry, 140*, 357–363.

Stewart, M. A., Pitts, F. N., Craig, A. G., & Dieruf, W. (1966). The hyperactive child syndrome. *American Journal of Orthopsychiatry, 36*, 861–867.

Stewart, M. A., Cummings, C., Singer, S., & DeBlois, C. (1981). The overlap between hyperactive and unsocialized aggressive children. *Journal of Child Psychology and Psychiatry, 22*, 35–45.

Tieger, T. (1980). On the biological basis of sex differences in aggression. *Child Development, 51*, 943–963.

Uniform Crime Report for the United States (1983). Federal Bureau of Investigation, United States Department of Justice. Washington, D. C.: United States Government Printing Office.

Waldrop, M. F., & Goering, J. D. (1971). Hyperactivity and minor physical anomalies in elementary school children. *American Journal of Orthopsychiatry, 41*, 602–607.

Waldrop, M. F., & Halverson, C. F. (1971). Minor physical anomalies and hyperactive behavior in young children. In J. Hellmuth (Ed.), *The exceptional infant* (Vol. 2). New York: Brunner/Mazel.

Waldrop, M. F., & Halverson, C. F. (1972). Minor physical anomalies: Their incidence and relationship to behavior in a normal and a deviant sample. In R. C. Smart & M. S. Smart (Eds.), *Readings in child development and relationships* (pp. 146–155). New York: Macmillan.

Waldrop, M. F., Pederson, F. A., & Bell, R. Q. (1968). Minor physical anomalies and behavior in pre-school children. *Child Development, 39*, 391–400.

Waldrop, M. F., Bell, R. Q., McLaughlin, B., & Halverson, C. F. (1978). Newborn minor physical anomalies predict short attention span, peer aggression, and impulsivity at age 3. *Science, 199*, 563–565.

Wender, P. H. (1971). *Minimal brain dysfunction in children.* New York: Wiley.

Werry, J. S., & Quay, H. C. (1971). The prevalence of behavior symptoms of younger elementary school children. *American Journal of Orthopsychiatry, 41*, 136–143.

West, D. J., & Farrington, D. P. (1973). *Who becomes delinquent?* London: Heinemann.

Witkin, H. A., Mednick, S. A., Schulsinger, F., Bakkestrom, E., Christiansen, K. O., Goodenough, D. R., Hirschorn, K., Ludsteen, C., Owen, D. R., Philip, J., Rubin, D. B., & Stocking, M. (1977). Criminality, aggression, and intelligence among XXY and XYY men. In S. A. Mednick & K. O. Christiansen (Eds.), *Biosocial bases of criminal behavior* (pp. 165–188). New York: Gardner Press.

Wolfgang, M. E. (1983). Delinquency in two birth cohorts. In K. T. Van Dusen & S. A. Mednick (Eds.), *Prospective studies of crime and delinquency,* (pp. 7–16). Boston: Kluwer-Nijhoff.

Wolfgang, M., Figlio, R. M., & Sellin, T. (1972). *Delinquency in a birth cohort.* Chicago: University of Chicago Press.

Yalom, I. D., Green, R., & Fisk, N. (1973). Prenatal exposure to female hormones. *Archives of General Psychiatry, 28*, 554–561.

CHAPTER 3

A Neurological View of Violence

JONATHAN H. PINCUS

The problem of defining aggression—and thus differentiating it from violence—has already been discussed in Chapter 2 by David Crowell and continues to be an issue throughout this book. The position taken in this chapter is that it is clinically useful to consider extreme aggression or violence as a separate category of behavior. This is based on the observation that acts of repeated or extreme personal violence that are committed with little or no provocation are truly rare, as pointed out by Evans and Scheuer in Chapter 4. Considering the opportunities for this form of self-expression, physical acts of violence against persons are unusual in adulthood and even in adolescence.

Furthermore, though a violent career is usually thought of as being a consequence of a disadvantaged upbringing, this formulation does not appear to correspond to the facts. With respect to extreme violence, middle-class or upper-class individuals have been frequently implicated (Elliott, 1982); clearly, the vast majority of disadvantaged individuals are not criminals and most criminals are not violent.

Thus, whatever factors determine aggressive behavior in general, it seems possible that specific causes may be found for explaining the fact that relatively small numbers of children are repeatedly violent. My thesis in this chapter is that brain impairments are evident in such children and account for the violent behavior.

Recent textbooks of child neuropsychology do not discuss violence, and discussion of aggression is generally limited to aggressive traits that are supposedly part of attention deficit disorder with hyperactivity and thus appear to have a possible correlation with neurological "soft signs" (e.g., Rutter, 1983; Spreen, Tupper, Risser, Tuokko, & Edgell, 1984). There is, however, a great

JONATHAN H. PINCUS • Department of Neurology, Yale University School of Medicine, New Haven, Connecticut 06520.

deal of suggestive circumstantial evidence relating abnormalities of cerebral functioning to extreme violence in children. This chapter is not intended to be a review of all this evidence. The focus is on specific data that appear to indicate the importance of considering the presence of organic brain dysfunction in extremely violent children and the utility of identifying such children rather than focusing widely on many aspects of aggressiveness.

To begin the discussion, I will briefly review what we know about the neurological system that is seen as primarily involved in the regulation of aggressive behavior—that is, the limbic system.

THE LIMBIC SYSTEM AND VIOLENCE

The limbic system is a meeting place for the disciplines of psychology, psychiatry, and neurology. More of a philosophical concept than a discrete anatomical or physiological system, it is the ring of gray matter and tracts bordering (hence the name *limbic*) the hemispheres in the medial portions of the brain that play a role in emotions. Phylogenetically, many of the areas designated as the limbic system are among the oldest portions of the cortex; in lower creatures these structures largely subserve smell and have traditionally been called the rhinencephalon. Although other regions of the brain also play a role in emotional functioning, the concept of the limbic "system" seems justified. Stimulation and ablation studies demonstrate consistent interrelationships of its various components and the importance of these components to emotional functioning.

It was Papez (1937) who first pointed out that the limbic system was possibly related to emotional behavior and visceral reactivity. He regarded the hippocampus as a regulator of hypothalamic centers concerned with emotional response. On the basis of his observations of patients with rabies (which affects the hippocampus and causes emotional and behavioral changes such as anxiety and paroxysms of rage and terror), Papez predicted that following stimulation of the hippocampus there could be prolonged active discharges in its own structures with very little spread to neocortical areas because of the interconnections between the limbic system components. He predicted that these "reverberating circuits" of discharge within the limbic system would produce marked alterations in the subjective emotional life of an individual.

The idea of a phylogenetically ancient, deep, central portion of the nervous system that influences behavior and thought not under conscious neocortical control is consistent with Freudian concepts of instinctual drive. The sense of smell in lower animals would seem to be closely associated with memory, instinct, and emotion, for it is often smell that alerts an animal to danger and provokes fear, flight, or fighting, as well as sexual arousal and mating. Although the sense of smell is less important in human life, it is postulated that these rhinencephalic structures and the limbic system in man are still involved with emotions, memory, and visceral responses and that disturbances of the limbic system disrupt these responses.

The gray matter components encompassed by the term *limbic system* include numerous structures in the anterior and medial portions of the temporal lobe and outside the temporal lobe. The richness of interconnections among regions of the limbic system is too elaborate to be described here, and, in fact, not all of the interconnections are known.

Efforts to establish the function of the system's various components have included stimulation and ablation studies in animals and to some extent in man. These have yielded evidence that these components influence learning. memory, emotional states, visceral and endocrine responses, and overt behavior, particularly aggressive, oral, and sexual activity. It is not possible to define the function of each component because none of them appears to act as a center for a particular function. As Papez predicted, there is a tendency after stimulation of limbic components for prolonged afterdischarges, which spread throughout the system. (e.g., MacLean, 1952, 1954).

The behavioral and cognitive changes produced by animal studies of ablation and stimulation of the limbic system are of considerable theoretical interest since they closely resemble aspects of human behavior commonly seen as clinical disorders. Of special relevance for this present discussion is the fact that stimulation of portions of the amygdala produces rage and fear reactions in animals. Similar reactions have been seen after stimulation of the midbrain gray matter or the placement of destructive lesions in the septum. Sensations of fear have also been described in conscious human beings while this region was stimulated during surgery. Chewing, gagging, retching, bladder contractions, increases in respiration, pulse, and blood pressure, and increased ACTH secretion have all been produced by stimulation of the amygdala and other sites in the limbic system. Such phenomena are clinically similar to the manifestations of complex partial (psychomotor) epilepsy, which, together with the characteristic anterior temporal spikes seen in the EEG of patients with complex partial epilepsy, has led some clinicians to apply the term "limbic system" to such seizures (Fulton, 1953).

Behavioral alterations (e.g., docility, loss of natural fear, compulsive oral activity, and heightened indiscriminate sexual activity) were noted by Kluver and Bucy (1939) after bilateral removal of the amygdaloid nuclei and overlying hippocampal cortex in animal studies. Similar changes have been noted in man after bilateral temporal lobectomies, which, if performed somewhat caudal to the amygdala, also produce profound loss of memory for recent events. Malamud (1967) reported on 18 patients with intracranial neoplasms of the limbic system, all of whom had originally been diagnosed as having psychiatric disorders.

Subacute and chronic forms of viral encephalitis also tend to affect the medial portions of the temporal lobes which are associated with the limbic system (Glaser & Pincus, 1969) and characteristically give rise to behavioral symptoms resembling various psychiatric disorders. In patients being examined for epilepsy, electrical stimulation of the amygdala and the hippocampus has produced brief alterations mimicking complex partial seizures that persist only during the passage of current; after such stimulation, however, mood and thought disturbances persist for hours (Stevens, Mark, Erwin, Pacheco, & Suematsu, 1969).

NEUROLOGICAL STUDIES OF VIOLENT CHILDREN

As noted at the beginning of this chapter, repeated violence is committed by very few (Wolfgang, 1975) and is not encountered only in the lower socioeconomic classes (Elliott, 1982). If such acts were committed predominantly by those with evidence of abnormalities of cerebral functioning as reflected in the neurological examination, psychological testing, or EEG, it would shift the focus of some investigations into the causes of such violence from the social environment to the individual brain. Is there something neurologically different about some violent individuals that might explain why they are violent?

To address this question, Lewis, Shanok, Pincus, and Glaser (1979) studied a group of juvenile offenders incarcerated in a "reform school" in Connecticut. The study sample consisted of 97 boys, all of whom were evaluated by a neurologist and psychiatrist; psychological tests and an EEG recording were included in the evaluations. After all the data had been collected, each child was placed in a category ranging from 1 (least violent) to 4 (most violent), on the basis of total past history and records rather than only the current charge.

To determine whether the degree of violence might be significantly (statistically) related to neuropsychiatric differences, Lewis and her colleagues redivided the 97 subjects into two groups: those children rated 1 or 2, constituting the less violent group, and those rated 3 or 4, constituting the more violent group. In the more violent group ($N = 78$), 31% had both minor and major neurological signs; 44% had major neurological signs; 71% had minor neurological signs; and 81% had either minor or major signs. In the less violent group ($N = 19$), none had both minor and major signs; 12% had major neurological signs; 35% had minor neurological signs; and 41% had minor or major signs. Each of these differences between the groups was statistically significant.

For the purposes of this analysis, major neurological signs were considered to include a history of generalized seizures, an abnormal EEG, abnormal head circumference, and/or Babinski signs. Minor neurological signs included choreiform movements and the inability of the subject to skip.

Symptoms suggesting complex partial seizures were quite common among the 97 delinquent boys. A loss of fully conscious contact with reality was observed in 31%, dizziness or blackouts in 30%, impaired memory for acts committed in 23%, lapses of auditory comprehension in 20%, *déjà vu* more than once per week in 20%, and an abnormal EEG and/or history of generalized seizures in 24%. There was a significant positive correlation between the numbers of such symptoms and the degree of violence ($p < .001$). Among the individual symptoms, the correlation with violence was higher for memory impairment for violent and nonviolent acts ($p < .001$), EEG abnormality ($p < .05$) and automatisms (repetitious meaningless motor acts) ($p < .05$).

Two clinicians agreed that 18 of the boys (19%) most likely had suffered complex partial seizures, on the basis of the boys' having had experienced well-documented episodes, observed by others, of lapses of fully conscious contact with their environment which were followed by confusion, fatigue, or sleep during which the subject's memory was impaired or absent. Fourteen of these 18 boys who were considered to have experienced complex partial seizures at some time had abnormal EEGs, and 7 of the 14 had a history of generalized seizures, while one boy with a normal EEG also had a history of generalized seizures. All 18 were in the more violent group.

On the basis of historical data, it seemed highly probable that five of the subjects had committed violent acts during a seizure, though in no case was EEG/video monitoring performed on the subjects. However, all five of the youngsters who were considered to have performed violent acts during seizures had also been violent at times when seizures were not occurring clearly.

Intelligence as measured on the WISC-R indicated a tendency for the less violent children to function somewhat better intellectually than the more violent, but overall differences between the two groups were not striking. The more violent group did somewhat less well on the verbal section of the WISC-R, but both groups scored relatively well on the picture completion and picture arrangement subtests; both groups received their poorest scores on vocabulary subtests; and both were several years behind their expected reading grade. The two groups differed significantly only in reading grade, arithmetic, and the ability to remember four numbers backward, the more violent group being at a significant disadvantage in each case.

The most striking differences psychiatrically between the two groups were that a significantly greater proportion of very violent children demonstrated or gave clear histories of paranoid symptomatology and were significantly more likely than their less aggressive peers to be loose, rambling, and illogical in their thought processes during interviewing. Depressive symptoms were common in both groups. There were histories of mental illness in the families of the more violent boys and reports of alcoholism in the fathers, although information about fathers was often unreliable.

In this particular study (Lewis *et al.*, 1979), virtually all the subjects came from the lowest echelons of society, and most were from broken homes with multiple social problems including criminality, alcoholism, and mental illness in parents. Most of the subjects had histories of disruptive behavior beginning before puberty and often during the first decade. A social factor that strongly distinguished the more violent from the less violent children was a history of extreme physical abuse by parents or parent substitutes. The two samples in the study also differed significantly in their exposure to violence, in that the more violent children had witnessed extreme violence directed at others, mostly in their homes, more frequently than the less violent children. Specifically, 75% of the more violent group had been abused and 33% of the less violent group (p < .003). Seventy-nine percent of the more violent group had witnessed extreme violence as compared with 20% of the less violent group (p < .001).

Lewis and her colleagues concluded that there were three factors distinguishing the more violent from the less violent delinquents: (a) neurological deficits (including seizures), (b) psychiatric abnormalities (paranoia, looseness), and (c) the experience of abuse. There is independent evidence that each of these factors may increase the likelihood of producing an extremely violent individual.

Although we have been arguing the case for brain impairment, violence experienced at home in early childhood is also probably an important etiological factor in the development of a propensity for violence; and, of course, brain impairment may well result from violence as well as vice versa. Among 2,143 families in a national survey, Straus and Gelles (1981) reported a 3.4% annual incidence of at least a single episode of very severe violence by parents toward a child. A study by Knudsen (1981) of approximately 4,000 undergraduate students who took an introductory psychology course at the University of Iowa revealed that 7% had been seriously physically abused at home. This prevalence figure was obtained from students who were virtually all white, middle-class subjects, a third from rural, a third from urban, and a third from suburban areas. The figure rose to 9% when witnessing the abuse of a sibling was included. Knudsen defined abuse as beating severe enough that medical services were necessary. Though these incidence and prevalence figures are shockingly high, it must be noted that the figures in studies of violent individuals are 10 times higher. (Lewis *et al.,* 1979; Loberg, 1983)

The well-known prevalence of the experience of childhood abuse among parents who are themselves child abusers also supports the hypothesis that the experience of abuse is an important etiological factor in subsequent violent behavior; however, there have been no prospective studies to date on the victims of child abuse with respect to their adult behavior. It is, in fact, reasonable to hypothesize that exposure to abuse early in life sets up a "template" of behavior which is often followed in later life.

Although there appear to be neurological factors in violence, it is clear that they are interactive with environmental factors, and perhaps particularly with abuse.

Table 1
Arrest Rate for Serious Offense

Socioeconomic class	ADD[a] $n = 110$ (%)	Control $n = 88$ (%)	
Lower	58	11	$p < .01$
Middle	36	9	$p < .05$
Upper	52	2	$p < .001$

[a]ADD = attention deficit disorder.
Note. From ''A prospective study of delinquency in 110 adolescent boys with attention deficit disorder and 88 normal adolescent boys'' by J. H. Satterfield, C. M. Hoppe, & A. M. Schell, 1982, *American Journal of Psychiatry, 139.* Copyright 1982 by the American Psychiatric Association. Reprinted by permission.

Brain Damage and Violence

There is some evidence that minimal brain damage, which may involve damage to the limbic system, predisposes to criminal behavior, including violence.

In one study, for example, Satterfield, Hoppe, and Schell (1982) obtained serious offense records on a group of 198 boys 14 to 20 years of age, of whom 110 had been diagnosed between the ages 6 and 12 as suffering from attentional deficit disorder (ADD) (formerly called minimal brain damage) and 88 of whom had no such history. Rates of single and multiple offenses and institutionalization for delinquency were significantly higher in the ADD subjects. About half of the ADD subjects had been arrested at least once for a serious offense after the diagnosis of ADD was made. Serious offense was defined as robbery, assault with a deadly weapon, automobile grand theft, theft, and burglary. Only one

Table 2
Multiple Arrest Rate for Serious Offense

Socioeconomic class	ADD[a] (%)	Control (%)	
Lower	45	6	$p < .001$
Middle	25	0	$p < .001$
Upper	28	0	$p < .001$

[a]ADD = attention deficit disorder.
Note. From ''A prospective study of delinquency in 110 adolescent boys with attention deficit disorder and 88 normal adolescent boys'' by J. H. Satterfield, C. M. Hoppe, & A. M. Schell, 1982, *American Journal of Psychiatry, 139.* Copyright 1982 by American Psychiatric Association. Reprinted by permission.

ADD subject had been arrested before being given that diagnosis. Offender rates did not vary significantly as a function of socioeconomic class (Tables 1 and 2). Again, however, there may be an interaction with environmental factors (see Evans & Scheuer, Chapter 4 of this volume).

Epilepsy and Violence

Most of the studies investigating the relationship of epilepsy and violence have used adult subjects. Although this book is concerned with childhood violence, these studies are nevertheless worth considering for their implications for childhood violence, which often continues into adulthood.

Abnormalities appearing in the EEG are prevalent among violent prisoners. In a study of 1,250 individuals in jail for crimes of aggression, Williams *et al.* (1969) found abnormal EEGs in 57% of the habitual aggressors and in only 12% of those who had committed a solitary aggressive crime, after prisoners who were mentally retarded or epileptic or who had sustained serious head injury were separated from the group. Among habitual aggressors with EEG abnormalities, more than 80% had temporal lobe involvement.

In a study of more than 400 violent prisoners in a large penitentiary, Mark and Ervin (1970) discovered that half had symptoms suggestive of epileptic phenomena and one-third had abnormal EEGs, although fewer than 10% had frank temporal lobe epilepsy. It was also apparent that these people had a characteristic social history, which included multiple physical assaults, aggressive sexual behavior including attempted rape, many traffic violations, serious automobile accidents, and pathological intoxication.

A good deal of attention has been given to the question of whether patients with generalized and complex partial (psychomotor) seizures have a propensity toward violence before, during, after, or between seizures. From the review of experimental data earlier in this chapter, one might predict that such an association exists; however, it has not been found.

There are several ways in which seizures and violence could be theoretically related:

1. An episode of directed violence could be the automatism of a complex partial seizure.

The directed aggression reported during epileptic attacks by Saint-Hilaire, Gilbert, and Bouner (1980), Ashford, Schulz, and Walsh (1980), and Mark and Ervin (1970) have been ascribed to "fear, defensive kicking and flailing" by Delgado-Escueta, Mattson, King, *et al.* (1981), who also, however, reported seven patients who demonstrated aggression toward inanimate objects or another person during seizures recorded with scalp electrodes. Of these seven, "one had aggressive acts that could have resulted in serious harm to another person";

nevertheless, Delgado-Escueta *et al.* concluded that the commission of murder or manslaughter during psychomotor automatisms was a "near impossibility." However, as their study did not select patients from a population with known aggressive behavior, violence, and psychosis, did not study any patients who were on trial for violent crimes during epileptic attacks, and did not for the most part use depth electrodes, it left open the possibility that more harmful acts of aggression could characterize the automatisms of criminals with epilepsy or violence-prone patients with psychosis and epilepsy.

In a study by Smith (1980) of three excessively violent male patients, one of whom had experienced grand mal seizures, depth electrodes were implanted in and around the amygdala with continual recordings for three to seven weeks. The recordings demonstrated that the episodic rage attacks of all three men were associated with spiking discharges in the amygdala; and the study further showed that this behavior could be reproduced by stimulation. In only one of the patients was there a clear indication of an ictal basis for violent behavior from the surface EEG recordings.

2. Directed violence could be an outgrowth of the encephalopathy associated with a seizure or the postictal state.

There have been many reports of *status epilepticus* presenting as prolonged confusional states (Somerville & Bruni, 1983), and there has been at least one report of a man who frequently entered a confused paranoid state immediately after a generalized seizure and who killed his wife while in this state (Gunn, 1982). The latter report is the more impressive because its author had previously reported that there is very little evidence relating violent crimes to epileptic phenomena.

3. Anxiety, fear, or anger could precipitate a seizure, possibly by inducing hyperventilation.

In this way aggressive actions could cause a seizure. The confusional state associated with such a seizure or its postictal period might allow continued aggression to occur unhindered by the inhibitions that intact cortical function might bring to bear on the situation. Even if such a seizure were brief, lasting less than half a minute (Delgado-Escuete *et al.*, 1981), the postictal period could be much longer.

4. Brain damage that predisposes an individual to violence might also cause seizures.

This perspective, proposed forcefully by Stevens and Hermann (1981), regards epilepsy as an epiphenomenon in relation to violence or any other behavioral deviation but identifies limbic brain damage as a critical etiological feature in the pathogenesis of psychopathology in epileptics. The preponderance of evidence points toward the conclusion that some patients with partial epilepsy and a focus of abnormality in the temporal lobe have a vulnerability to personality change (Bear & Fedio 1977; Trimble 1983), but the role of epilepsy *per se* in this vulnerability is moot. Possibly epileptic discharges in sensitive regions of the brain that do not result in clinical seizures can give rise to nonictal behavioral disorders, that is, the "interictal" or "subictal" state.

5. Violence and epilepsy may be only coincidental.

There have been many reports of an impressive association between complex partial seizures and violence. For example, Falconer, Hill, Meyer, and Wilson (1958) reported the 38% of patients with temporal lobe epilepsy showed pathological aggressiveness. Among 666 cases of temporal lobe epilepsy studied by Currie (1971), 7% were found to be aggressive. Glaser (1967) reported aggressive behavior in 67 of 120 children with limbic epilepsy. Serafetinides (1965) also found aggressiveness to be a characteristic of temporal lobe epilepsy.

The prevalence of symptoms suggesting psychomotor seizures in violent individuals was evident in the previously cited study by Lewis *et al.* (1979), who evaluated the psychiatric-psychological status of 285 children referred from the juvenile court and reviewed the psychiatric, medical, and electroencephalographic records of those who manifested psychomotor seizures symptoms. Among the 285 children in this study, 18 had experienced loss of conscious contact with reality. Four of the children had histories of automatisms often associated with psychomotor seizures and four had experienced *déjà vu*. Of the 18, 8 had been arrested for crimes of violence, including 2 who committed murder, and 6 who were referred for milder violations had attacked other individuals. In all, 14 of the 18 had engaged in acts of violence. It should be noted that violent attacks against persons constitute 8% of the offenses for which children are referred to the juvenile courts and 9% of the juvenile offenders referred for psychiatric evaluation. The incidence of arrest for violence was significantly higher in the group with psychomotor symptoms ($\chi^2 = 11.4$, $p<0.001$). In the group with psychomotor symptoms, 11 of 14 EEGs were abnormal, with three demonstrating temporal foci.

It is also interesting that more than 75% of the prisoners studied by Mark and Ervin (1970) had histories of significant periods of unconsciousness from head injury or disease, and that 15 of the cases studied by Lewis *et al.* (1979) had a similar history of events known to be associated with brain injury, such as perinatal problems including infection or prematurity, serious accidents with head trauma, or other disease. These studies strongly support the concept that violence has neurological determinants.

On the other hand, there have also been reports in which no association between psychomotor seizures and violence was demonstrated. In a study of 100 children with a variety of neurological problems including seizures, outbursts of rage were described in 36 (Ounsted, 1969). But the patients who had only psychomotor epilepsy were said to be uniformly intelligent and conforming children who had not had outbursts at any time. Perhaps the most important of the reports in which no association between complex partial epilepsy and violence was demonstrated was that of Rodin (1973), who studied 57 patients with psychomotor epilepsy and photographed them during their seizures. There were no instances of ictal or postictal aggression. A review of 700 case histories of patients in an epilepsy clinic revealed only 34 patients who had committed aggressive acts, and the presence or absence of psychomotor epilepsy in these patients was not a relevant variable.

Possible explanations for the contradictions in these two groups of studies relate to varying definitions of aggression, violence, and complex partial seizures, and to the selection of patients as well. In some parts of the country, for instance, a propensity toward violence in patients may affect their referral. Violence may be dealt with by schools or the police, with or without consultation with physicians, some of whom may not be aware of the possibility that the suspect's behavior is influenced by seizures. Also, the referral of violent epileptics to a neurology or an epilepsy clinic may be more or less likely, depending on the local authorities.

In addition, some seizures units with video/EEG monitoring equipment discourage the admission of episodically violent individuals, as the personnel in the units are unprepared to handle violent patients and fear that their equipment may be damaged. This kind of selectivity has severely limited the number of prolonged EEG studies of violent individuals and probably has lowered the reported prevalence of violence among epileptics so monitored (Delgado-Escueta *et al.*, 1981).

Physicians who have cared for large numbers of seizure patients would agree that violence and aggressive acts do occur in patients with complex partial seizures, but they would disagree as to whether the incidence of violence in the form of epilepsy is more or less frequent than in the general population.

The problem of the definition of violence and aggression is also important, as suggested at the beginning of this chapter. Fighting among children, particularly boys, is certainly not unusual (Detre & Jarecki, 1971). But it may well be that some authors, not wishing to "give epileptics a bad name," have discounted acts of personal violence as being within the normal range and missed a possible association between violence and complex partial seizures. Certainly, the tremendous variation in reports about such an association or its absence, as well as the general lack of clarity in defining violence and aggression, suggest that methodological problems have yet to be overcome and that various studies on the association of violence and epilepsy are not comparable.

Drugs and Violence

Alcohol: Pathological Intoxication. The state of pathological intoxication is not synonymous with ordinary drunkenness. It is a state in which the individual engages in a violent act after drinking, an act about which he will later have little or no recollection. Such behavior may sometimes be elicited by small amounts of alcohol, much less than would be required for ordinary intoxication. Blood alcohol levels below 30 mg/100ml have been recorded in these cases. Pathological intoxication is not associated with slurred speech and incoordination and may last for only a few minutes. It occurs most often when alcohol is imbibed in circumstances conducive to violence, such as at a bar or a party; and it has been difficult to reproduce this state of intoxication by administering alcohol in any quantity in a laboratory setting or by intravenous injection. Those who become pathological intoxicated, it is said, may not be chronic alcoholics, and the condition is said not to be limited to individuals with a criminal disposition. It is relatively rare, however, even among brain-damaged individuals. Yet 90% of pathological intoxication cases are associated with brain damage, epilepsy, retardation, or psychosis (Bowman & Jellinck, 1941). EEG changes may also be associated with episodes of pathological intoxication (Thompson, 1963). There may, of course, be an interplay among environmental and organic factors in the induction of pathological intoxication, which, were it understood, might shed light on the complex relation between brain dysfunction and violence. Interestingly, at the Epilepsy Center at Yale it has never been possible to induce aggressive behavior or epileptiform EEG changes by administering alcohol in a clinical setting to a patient whose history suggests pathological intoxication. Nine such patients have been studied with EEG and clinical observation during the administration of alcohol toward the levels of legal intoxication (100g/ 100 ml, R. H. Mattson, personal communication).

Some have questioned the existence of "pathological intoxication" or refer to it simply as "intoxication." It is possible that alcohol nonspecifically worsens an organic brain syndrome and thus precipitates violence.

Although many serious crimes are committed by individuals who are drinking or taking drugs, many who drink and also abuse drugs do not commit serious crimes and especially not homicide. A number of different variables may affect the relationship between alcohol or any drug and violence. These include the premorbid personality, the immediate environment, the type of drug, multiple drug interactions, and the dosage and expectation of the effect of the drug in the individual taking it.

Alcohol has been the most completely studied of all drugs in relation to violence. It has been shown that 50%—83% of murderers were drinking at the time of the murder (Roslund & Larson, 1979; Shupe, 1954). Loberg (1983) compared severely belligerent and nonbelligerent alcoholics. The severely belligerent subjects had started drinking 11 years earlier than the nonbelligerent group. There was significantly more prealcoholic impulsivity and conduct disorder in the belligerent alcoholics, who also exhibited a deviant MMPI personality profile of paranoid type with extreme irritability, hostility, tension and restlessness, and very unhappy home backgrounds, often marked by physical aggression by their fathers. This study strongly suggests that some individuals bring to the effects of alcohol vulnerabilities consisting of neurological defects, personality defects, and life history qualities, especially the experience of abuse, that increase the risk of violent behavior under the influence of alcohol. The similarities of Loberg's severely belligerent álcoholics to the nonalcoholic violent delinquent group in the Lewis, Pincus, Shanok, and Glaser (1982) study are striking. In another study, Holcomb and Anderson (1983) investigated the effects of alcohol and multiple drug abuse on violent behavior in a sample of 110 men charged with capital murder. The group who had not been using alcohol or other drugs at the time of the crime had the smallest percentage of offenders who "overkilled" the victim (8%). This group also included the largest percentage who had a reason for killing the victim (80%); only 6% claimed not to be able to remember the crime, and 39% were paranoid. The drugs-only group was the most likely to overkill and to have no apparent motive for murder; 44% could not remember the actual event; and 72% were paranoid. The alcohol-using groups were intermediate. Wolfgang (1958) also argued that alcohol at the scene of homicide enhanced the likelihood and viciousness of the killing. These results support the conclusion that there is an association between alcohol abuse and violence and also between multiple drug abuse and violence. However, the prevalence of paranoia in the Holcomb and Anderson (1983) study and the fact that 45% of the accused murderers had received psychiatric treatment prior to committing homicide seem to suggest that alcohol and drug abuse cause violence primarily in the predisposed.

It is also possible that the immediate environment influences the prevalence of violence in another way: at least two studies indicate that there is a strong assocation between alcohol use and increased chances of becoming a homicide *victim* (Budd, 1982; Rouzioux, Parisot, Picard, Vermont & Isnard, 1985).

Heroin. A thorough study of criminal behavior and heroin use was performed by Taylor and Albright (1981). The sample consisted of 1,328 randomly sampled patients and former patients in drug treatment. There was a strong positive association between the number of predrug arrests and the total number of arrests, suggesting that predrug criminality probably has an effect on the future criminal activities of the heroin user. This evidence supports the Robins and Murphy (1967) conclusion that criminals are more likely to become heroin users and that nondrug criminality predates heroin use.

The types of crimes that have been associated with the use of heroin have been crimes that generate income. Of these, armed robbery and assault are also crimes of violence, and significant associations have been found with heroin use.

There is also considerable evidence that treatment of heroin addiction reduces criminality among heroin users. In a longitudinal study of intermittently addicted heroin users, Nurco, Shaffer, and Ball (1984) found that there was a general tendency for criminal activity to increase over successive periods of narcotics addiction as well as a general tendency for criminality to diminish over successive periods of nonaddiction. In this study, violent crime was committed by a minority and was exclusively associated with periods of narcotics addiction. It is unlikely that heroin itself induced violent behavior, however, because of its calming effect; violence among heroin addicts seems to be mainly for income generation (Tinkenberg, 1973).

The effect of treatment in eliminating criminality has been questioned by Taylor and Albright (1981), who studied the situation of former narcotics addicts after they left treatment. They found that there was a strong association between the number of arrests after leaving treatment and the number before drug use, and there was also an association between the number of arrests after leaving treatment and the total number of arrests before treatment. Thus, the longer the heroin user has been involved with crime, the less likely it is that treatment of his heroin addiction will reduce nondrug criminal behavior.

Phencyclidine HCL (PCP). Twelve of 16 chronic PCP users in a residential drug community reported acts of violence associated with PCP use. In two, violence was directed solely toward themselves, but 10 others reported 20 separate incidents of PCP-related violence toward others. One of these had had no previous history of violence or psychosis though he had used PCP for six years (Fauman, 1979). These findings and others (Wright, 1980) suggest that violence might be directly caused by PCP without predisposing factors. However, the data are too fragmentary to separate the variables that might influence causality.

It might be mentioned here that the short half-life of cocaine (one hour) has limited studies of its contribution to violence.

GENETIC STUDIES RELATING TO VIOLENT BEHAVIOR

Some studies have suggested that habitual violent acts may be genetically determined, as an XYY chromosome abnormality appears to be associated with tall stature and aggressiveness (Hook & Kim, 1970; Jacobs, Prince, Richmond, and Ratecliff, 1971). However, more recent data seem to indicate that as much as 90% of the XYY population may remain outside mental hospitals and prisons (Gerald, 1976), and therefore the significance of this genetic factor is in doubt. Concordance rates for delinquency in twin studies are higher in monozygotic than in dizygotic twins, but the evidence is not conclusive (Slater & Cowie, 1971).

TREATMENT OF VIOLENCE

Anticonvulsant and antipsychotic drugs are not a panacea for controlling violence in nonepileptic, nonpsychotic offenders (Goldstein, 1974), although this is not to say that these medications may not help individual patients (Lion, 1975; Monroe, 1975; Tupin, Smith, & Clanon, 1973). Also, according to anecdotal statements, sedating medications such as barbiturates and minor tranquilizers usually worsen violent behavior. As mentioned above, this is also the case with alcohol. However, when violence is a concomitant of bipolar depression, lithium may be effective; it has been shown to reduce aggressive behavior in a double-blind controlled study in a penal institution (Marini & Sheard, 1977; Sheard, Marini, & Bridges, 1976).

The beta-blocker propanolol has been used to treat rage attacks in brain-damaged individuals. The starting dose was 20 mgs. t.i.d. and this was doubled every two days, rarely to more than 480 mgs. Propanolol apparently does not work in the presence of haloperidol or phenothiazines and takes approximately two weeks to control violent outburts effectively (Elliot, 1981). Other accounts of the successful use of propanolol to prevent violence in brain-damaged individuals have appeared (Elliott, 1977; Schreier, 1979; Williams, Mehl, and Yudofsky, 1984; Yudofsky, Williams, & Gorman, 1981).

Despite these optimistic reports, it seems unlikely that anticonvulsant, antipsychotic, or beta-blocking medications would work in individuals whose violent behavior is semiadaptive, predatory, or motivated by loyalty to a cause, even if brain damage were a factor in such individuals. One might predict a greater effectiveness of pharmacotherapy in brain-damaged individuals who demonstrate episodic violence that seems remarkably atypical or alien to their baseline personality. Controlled studies have yet to be done, and they face nearly insuperable ethical problems. Such research must be conducted in prison populations to control compliance and to validate behavioral data, but incarcerated individuals commonly are not regarded as being free to give informed consent to participate. Studies of incarcerated minors would be even more difficult from the ethical point of view. Psychosurgery involving stimulation or ablation of limbic areas, as described by Mark and Ervin (1970), is ethically even more controversial and in any case appears to be of limited clinical use.

A further problem in such research is that violent individuals are often presented to neurologists and psychiatrists not as patients but as prisoners, and physicians are not then asked what treatment would prevent future violence but rather to what extent the individual is responsible for his past violent behavior. Psychotherapy also seems to be of limited use. In a study of juvenile delinquents, one-third of whom were violent, at a well-organized residential center in which they received psychotherapy, 75% were found to have had two reconvictions or more after release from the center (Hartelius, 1965). Roughly the same rate of recidivism has been noted in populations of untreated violent criminals (Gibbens, Pond, & Stafford-Clark, 1959).

VIOLENCE AND RESPONSIBILITY

A question frequently brought up in the courts and the media regarding violence and its etiologies is that of the responsibility of the perpetrator of violent acts. Our legal system generally operates under the presumption of free will. This is basically a philosophical and religious concept, not a scientific or medical one, from which it follows that people are responsible for their actions. The law recognizes, however, that the operation of free will in certain circumstances is constrained by diseases of the brain. Accordingly, the M'Naughten, irresistible impulse, mental incapacity, and diminshed responsibility rules have been developed, and the plea of innocence by reason of one of these rules has become conventional for defendants charged with serious crimes. Attorneys for defendants charged with homicide, arson, and assault commonly seek to prove that their clients' responsibility for their actions was significantly diminished when the crimes were committed. To buttress this opinion, attorneys turn to psychiatrists and neurologists for medical testimony.

Unfortunately, free will has no measurable parameters. The social scientist often assumes that genetic endowment and life experience form our personalities and greatly influence or fully determine our responses. Where does free will enter this equation? The mingling of legal and religious concepts with science has produced a murky swamp of belief and facts that is very difficult to negotiate. For neurologists, the legal question often centers around the issue of whether or not the so-called episodic dyscontrol syndrome has a physiological basis.

There are many types of behavioral disorders that society is prepared to tolerate, but the line is usually drawn at those that may harm others. The decision whether, when, and how long to incarcerate an individual who has acted dangerously in the past is not an easy one to make. Most authorities agree that it would be necessary to detain two or three times as many patients or prisoners unnecessarily in order to ensure that those who are a danger to society do not leave a hospital or prison prematurely (Lancet, 1982). Those who are detained in a hospital may be unjustifiably deprived of their civil rights. Several such patients in the United States have been judged unconstitutionally detained, and this has led to the release of many mentally ill people against the advice of their clinicians. However, follow-up of these patients has shown a much lower incidence of violence than was predicted (Cocozza & Steadman, 1974; Steadman &

Keveles, 1972; Thornberry & Jacoby, 1979). Unfortunately, there is no way of predicting when repeat offenses are likely to occur, and a long period of follow-up is necessary because repetition of arson, rape, and homicide may take place many years after release (Soothill & Pope, 1973; Soothill, Jack, & Gibbens, 1976).

Until 1970, attorneys rarely used the insanity defense and then only in cases of homicide because, if successful, it resulted in prolonged and indefinite incarceration of the criminal in a facility for the "criminally insane." A change in the interpretation of the law which forbade the incarceration in such facilities of individuals who have become "sane" has led to the increased popularity of the "temporary insanity" defense (or the equivalent thereof), as an individual judged not guilty by reason of insanity who has been committed must now be released as soon as he is no longer considered mentally ill.

There were 53 successful uses of the insanity defense in New York State (mostly for homicide) between 1965 and 1971 and 225 successful uses of it between 1971 and 1976. The average length of stay in mental health facilities was 369 days (Kolb, Carnahan, Steadman, & Wright, 1978).

The current situation is undesirable. Individuals convicted of first degree murder now serve an average of nine years in prison, whereas those found innocent of murder by reason of diminished mental capacity or insanity serve one to three years in an institution (Singer, 1978). Yet about 20% of the prisoners in New York State jails are receiving psychiatric therapy. By what logic are they in prison while others are free on the basis of mental incapacity or diminished responsibility? (Carnahan, 1981).

The use of physicians' testimony has often been embarrassing to the medical profession. Such testimony is often biased and uninformed and is never subjected to peer review. Perhaps a better procedure would be to allow a jury to ascertain guilt and then submit the facts concerning the perpetrator's mental state to a panel of informed, objective medical professionals who would determine whether there were mitigating factors that should influence sentencing. The insanity defense may well have to be discarded and the concept of diminished capacity used only for mitigating sentences, not exculpation (e.g., manslaughter instead of murder).

In my opinion, the preponderance of evidence does indicate that extreme violence as a behavioral syndrome is organically determined. Moreover, since the best predictor of aggressive or violent behavior is a history of aggressive or violent behavior, and since the tendency to recidivism persists at least until the fourth decade of life (Robins, 1966), it would appear reasonable to me to separate very violent individuals from society in some manner until their thirties or until some truly effective therapeutic measure is developed, at least in individual cases.

CONCLUSION

Extreme and repeated aggression or violence with little or no provocation occurs in a very small percentage of the population and appears to have neurological and possibly genetic components. Aggression and violence may originate in the limbic system of the brain, which is an important anatomical and physiological substrate for emotion and visceral reactivity. There also appears to be a positive correlation between extreme and repeated aggression or violence and neurological abnormalities, including brain damage and epilepsy, although the neurological abnormality does not necessarily imply the presence of violent behavior. Symptoms such as paranoia and loose associations also strongly correlate with violence, and the use of alcohol and other drugs exacerbates violence in the predisposed. The most important environmental factors that correlate positively with aggression and violence are abuse and observed abuse, but socioeconomic level *per se* does not appear to be an important factor.

Violence is very difficult to treat: neither drug therapy nor psychotherapy appears to prevent recidivism in all cases, but each may be helpful in selected cases.

In regard to the insanity plea for repeatedly violent offenders, it is recommended for the protection of the public that the law be changed.

REFERENCES

Ashford, J. W., Schulz, S. C., & Walsh, F. O. (1980). Violent automatism in a partial complex seizure. *Archives of Neurology, 37,* 120.

Bear, D. M., & Fedio, P. (1977). Quantitative analysis of interictal behavior in temporal lobe epilepsy. *Archives of Neurology, 34,* 454.

Bowman, K. M., & Jellinck, E. M. (1941). Alcoholic mental disorders. *Quarterly Journal of Studies on Alcohol, 2,* 312.

Budd, R. D. (1982). The incidence of alcohol use in Los Angeles County homicides. *American Journal of Alcohol Abuse, 9,* 105–111.

Carnahan, W. (1981). Violence and the legal system. Paper originally presented at a meeting of the *International Society for Research on Aggression,* Wheaton College, Norton, MA.

Cocozza, J. J., & Steadman, H. J. (1974). Some refinements in the measurement and prediction of dangerous behavior. *American Journal of Psychiatry, 131,* 1012.

Currie, S. (1971). Clinical course and prognosis of temporal lobe epilepsy. *Brain, 94,* 173.

Delgado-Escueta, A. V., Mattson, R. H., King, L., *et al.* (1981). The nature of aggression during epileptic seizures. *New England Journal of Medicine, 305,* 711.

Detre, T. P., & Jarecki, H. G. (1971). *Modern psychiatric treatment.* Philadelphia: J. B. Lippincott.

Elliott, F. A. (1977). Propanolol for the control of belligerent behavior following acute brain damage. *Annuals of Neurology, 1,* 489–491.

Elliott, F. A. (1981, August). Personal communication. Paper originally presented at a meeting of the *International Society for Research on Aggression,* Wheaton College, Norton. MA.

Elliott, F. A. (1982). Neurological findings in adult minimal brain dysfunction and the dyscontrol syndrome. *Journal of Neurological and Mental Diseases, 170,* 680–687.

Falconer, M. A., Hill, D., Meyer, A., & Wilson, J. (1958). Clinical, radiological and EEG correlations with pathological changes in temporal lobe epilepsy and their significance in surgical treatment. In M. Baldwin & P. Bailey (Eds.), *Temporal lobe epilepsy*. Springfield, IL: C. C. Thomas.

Fauman, M. A. (1979). Violence associated with phencyclidine abuse. *American Journal of Psychiatry, 136*, 1584–1586.

Fulton, H. H. (1953). Discussion. *Epilepsia 2*, 77.

Gerald, P. S. (1976). Current concepts in genetics: Sex chromosome disorders. *New England Journal of Medicine, 294*, 706.

Gibbens, T. C. N., Pond, D. A., & Stafford-Clark, D. (1959). Followup study of criminal psychopaths. *Journal of Mental Sciences, 105*, 108.

Glaser, G. H. (1967). Limbic epilepsy in childhood. *Journal of Nervous and Mental Diseases, 144*, 391.

Glaser, G. H., & Pincus, J. H. (1969). Limbic encephalitis. *Journal of Nervous and Mental Diseases, 149*, 59.

Goldstein, M. (1974). Brain research and violent behavior: A summary and evaluation of the status of biomedical research on brain and aggressive violent behavior. *Archives of Neurology, 30*, 1.

Gunn, J. C. (1982). Violence and epilepsy. *New England Journal of Medicine, 306*, 299.

Hartelius, H. (1965). Study of male juvenile delinquency. *Acta Psychiatry Scandanavia, 40*, 7.

Holcomb, W. R., & Anderson, W. P. (1983). Alcohol and multiple drug use in accused murderers. *Psychological Report, 52*, 159–164.

Hook, E. B., & Kim, D. S. (1970). Prevalence of XYY and XXY karyotypes in 337 non-retarded young offenders. *New England Journal of Medicine, 283*, 410.

Jacobs, P. A., Prince, W. H., Richmond, S., & Ratecliff, R. A. W. (1971). Chromosome surveys in penal institutions and approved schools. *Journal of Medical Genetics, 8*, 49.

Kluver, H., & Bucy, P. C. (1939). Preliminary analysis of functions of the temporal lobes in monkeys. *Archives of Neurology and Psychiatry, 42*, 979.

Knutsen, J. F. (1981, August). Personal communication. Paper originally presented at a meeting of the International Society for Research on Aggression, Wheaton College, Norton, MA.

Kolb, L., Carnahan, W. W., Steadman, H., & Wright, J. (1978). *The insanity defense in New York*. New York: State Department of Mental Hygiene.

Lancet (1982). Editorial, Dangerousness, *2*, 1341.

Lewis, D. O., Pincus, J. H., Shanok, S. S., & Glaser, G. H. (1982). Psychomotor epilepsy and violence in a group of incarcerated adolescent boys. *American Journal of Psychiatry, 139*, 882.

Lewis, D. O., Shanok, S. S., Pincus, J. H., *et al.* (1979). Violent juvenile delinquents: Psychiatric, neurological, psychological and abuse factors. *Journal of the American Academy of Child Psychiatry, 18*, 307–319.

Lewis, D. O., Shanok, S. S., & Pincus, J. H. (1982). A comparison of the neuropsychiatric status of female and male incarcerated delinquents: Some evidences of sex and race bias. *Journal of the American Academy of Child Psychiatry, 21*, 190.

Lion, J. R. (1975). Conceptual issues in the use of drugs for the treatment of aggression in man. *Journal of Nervous and Mental Diseases, 160*, 76.

Loberg, T. (1983). Belligerence in alcohol dependence. *Scandanavian Journal of Psychology, 24*, 285–292.

MacLean, P. D. (1952). Some psychiatric implications of physiological studies on frontotemporal portion of limbic system (visceral brain). *Electroencephalography and Clinical Neurophysiology, 4*, 407.

MacLean, P. D. (1954). The limbic system and its hippocampal formation: Studies in animals and their possible relation to man. *Journal of Neurosurgery, 11*, 29.

Malamud, N. (1967). Psychiatric disorder with intracranial tumors of the limbic system. *Archives of Neurology, 17,* 113.

Mark, V. H., & Ervin, F. R. (1970). *Violence and the brain.* New York: Harper & Row.

Marini, J. L., & Sheard, M. H. (1977). Antiaggressive effect of lithium in man. *Acta Psychiatry Scandanavia, 55,* 269.

Monroe, R. R. (1975). Anticonvulsants in the treatment of aggression. *Journal of Nervous Mental Diseases, 160,* 119.

Nurco, D. N., Shaffer, J. W., & Ball, J. C. (1984). Trends in the commission of crime among narcotics addicts over successive periods of addiction and nonaddiction. *American Journal of Drug and Alcohol Abuse, 10,* 481–489.

Ounsted, C. (1969). Aggression and epilepsy: Rage in children with temporal lobe epilepsy. *Journal Psychosomatic Research, 13,* 237.

Papez, J. W. (1937). A proposed mechanism of emotion. *Archives of Neurology and Psychiatry, 38,* 725.

Robins, L. N. (1966). *Deviant children grown up: Sociological and Psychiatric study of sociopathic personality.* Baltimore: Williams & Wilkins.

Robins, S. L. N., & Murphy, G. E. (1967). Drug use in a normal population of young negro men. *American Journal of Public Health, 57,* 1580–1596.

Rodin, E. A. (1973). Psychomotor epilepsy and aggressive behavior. *Archives of General Psychiatry, 28,* 210.

Roslund, B., & Larson, C. A. (1979). Crimes of violence and alcohol abuse in Sweden. *International Journal of Addiction, 14,* 1103–1115.

Rouzioux, J. M., Parisot, P., Picard, J., Vermont, J., & Isnard, E. (1985). Role of acute alcoholism in violent deaths. Statistics of the Lyon Medical Legal Institute. *Presse-Med 14,* 1017–1023.

Rutter, M. (1983).

Saint-Hilaire, J. M., Gilbert, M., & Bouner, G. (1980). Aggression as an epileptic manifestation: Two cases with depth electrode study. *Epilepsia 21,* 184.

Satterfield, J. H., Hoppe, C. M., & Schell, A. M. (1982). A prospective study of delinquency in 110 adolescent boys with attention deficit disorder and 88 normal adolescent boys. *American Journal of Psychiatry, 139,* 795.

Schreier, H. A. (1979). Use of propanolol in the treatment of postencephalitis psychosis. *American Journal of Psychiatry, 136,* 840.

Serafetinides, E. A. (1965). Aggression in temporal lobe epileptics and its relation to cerebral dysfunction and environmental factors. *Epilepsia 6,* 33.

Sheard, M. H., Marini, J. L., & Bridges, C. I. (1976). The effect of lithium on impulsive, aggressive behavior in man. *American Journal of Psychiatry, 133,* 1409.

Shupe, I. M. (1954). Alcohol and crime: A study of the urine alcohol concentration found in 882 persons arrested during or immediately after the commission of a felony. *Journal of Crime, Law and Criminology, 44,* 661–664.

Singer, A. C. (1978). Insanity acquittal in the 1970's: Observation on empirical analysis of one jurisdiction. *Mental Disability Law Reporter 406,* 417.

Slater, E., & Cowie, V. (1971). *The genetics of mental disorders.* London: Oxford University Press.

Smith, J. S. (1980). Episodic rage in limbic epilepsy and the dyscontrol syndrome. In M. Girais & L. G. Kilah (Eds.), Elsevier, North Holland: Biomedical Press.

Somerville, E. R., & Bruni, J. (1983). Tonic status epilepticus presenting as confusional state. *American Neurology, 13,* 549.

Soothill, K. L., Jack, A., & Gibbens, T. C. N. (1976). Rape: A twenty-two year cohort study. *Medical Science and Law, 16,* 62–69.

Soothill, K. L., & Pope, P. J. (1973). Arson: A twenty-year cohort study. *Medical Science and Law, 13,* 127–158.

Spreen, Tupper, Risser, Tuokko, & Edgell, (1984).

Steadman, H. J., & Keveles, G. (1972). The community adjustment and criminal activity of the Backstrom patients, 1966–1970. *American Journal of Psychiatry, 129,* 304–310.

Stevens, J. R., & Hermann, B. P. (1981). Temporal lobe epilepsy, psychopathology and violence: The state of the evidence. *Neurology 31,* 1127.

Stevens, J. R., Mark, V. H., Erwin, F., Pacheco, P., & Suematsu, K. (1969). Deep temporal stimulation in man: Long latency, long lasting psychological changes. *Archives of Neurology, 21,* 157.

Straus, M., & Gelles, R. J. (1981). *Behind closed doors: Violence in the American family.* New York: Doubleday.

Taylor, P. L., & Albright, W. J. (1981). Non-drug criminal behavior and heroin use. *International Journal of Addiction, 16,* 683–696.

Thompson, G. N. (1963). Electroencephalogram in acute pathological alcoholic intoxication. *Bulletin of the Los Angeles Neurological Society, 28,* 217.

Thornberry, T. P., & Jacoby, J. E. (1979). *The criminally insane in a community follow up of mentally ill offenders.* Chicago: University of Chicago Press.

Tinkenberg, J. (1973). *Drugs and crime in drug use in America. Vol. 1. Patterns and Consequence of Drug Use.* Washington, D.C.: U.S. Government Printing Office.

Trimble, M. R. (1983). Personality disturbances in epilepsy. *Neurology, 33,* 1332.

Tupin, J. P., Smith, D. B., Clanon, T. L., *et al.* (1973). The long term use of lithium in aggressive prisoners. *Comparative Psychiatry, 14,* 311.

Williams, D. T. (1969). Neural factors related to habitual aggression.

Williams, D. T., Mehl, R., & Yudofsky, S. (1984). The effect of propanolol on uncontrolled rage outbursts in children and adolescents with organic brain dysfunction. *Journal of the American Academy of Child Psychiatry,*

Wolfgang, M. (1975). Delinquency and violence from the viewpoint of criminality. In U. S. Fields & W. H. Sweet (Eds.), *Neural bases of violence and aggression.* St. Louis, MO:

Wolfgang, M. E. (1958). *Patterns in criminal homicide.* Philadelphia: University of Pennsylvania Press.

Wright, H. H. (1980). Violence and PCP abuse. *American Journal of Psychiatry, 137,* 752–753.

Yudofsky, S., Williams, D., & Gorman, J. (1981). Propanolol in the treatment of rage and violent behavior in patients with chronic brain syndrome. *American Journal of Psychiatry, 138,* 218.

CHAPTER 4

Analyzing Response Relationships in Childhood Aggression
The Clinical Perspective

IAN M. EVANS AND ALICE D. SCHEUER

The empirical study of aggression and violence in children occurs at many different levels of analysis, as is well illustrated by the other chapters of this volume. Each level is legitimate and equally necessary for providing a systematic conceptualization of the phenomenon. Although our understanding may be far from complete, the accumulation of surprisingly consistent findings that will be reported later in this book reveals the basic adequacy of a multilevel conceptualization for designing the broad requirements of therapeutic and preventative programs. At the same time, the clinician (who may be defined loosely as any formally designated agent of social change), even when oriented toward indirect community or family interventions, must ultimately deal with individual children revealing unique constellations of problems. Clinicians thus face the unenviable task of having to consider each of the many levels when assessing and treating individual cases of aggressive behavior. Effective clinical decision making in these circumstances represents a complex intellectual juggling act that is increasingly being recognized as a judgment task requiring unifying assumptions or an overall heuristic conceptual framework.

The purpose of this chapter, therefore, is not to try to review every aspect of

At the time the conference was planned, Ian M. Evans was with the Department of Psychology, University of Hawaii at Manoa.

IAN M. EVANS • Department of Psychology, University Center at Binghamton, State University of New York, Binghamton, New York 13901. ALICE D. SCHEUER • Department of Psychology, University of Hawaii at Manoa, Honolulu, Hawaii 96822.

the clinical treatment of aggression, but to concentrate on the elements of a framework that might be useful for analyzing aggressive behavior in individual children. Treatments aplenty can be deduced from the research to be presented by the other authors. One of the major themes—one that dominated the conference—is that aggression in children is multiply determined. For the clinician this means it must be multiply remediable as well. In order for research findings, whether basic or applied, to be usable in orchestrating effective individual interventions, a model of individual behavior is needed that provides a conceptual framework whereby general principles can be translated to serve the unbounded judgments required in the clinical setting. In this chapter we will consider two basic features of such a framework: (a) aggressive behavior as part of a behavioral system or repertoire of responses and (b) aggressive behavior as having a variety of dimensions, other than topography, that determine its clinical relevance.

A convenient theory within which our discussion can be cast is social behaviorism (Staats, 1975). Much of Staats's unifying theory as it pertains to childhood psychopathology is consistent with general behaviorally oriented clinical approaches. However, certain of Staats's concepts of response organization and development are particularly valuable for analyzing response dimensions and relationships. According to Staats, the individual child's personality can be thought of as a system of interrelated behaviors—basic behavioral repertoires—learned through prior experience but functioning in an interactive, causative manner so as to influence subsequent experience and learning. Three broad subsystems can be identified: the emotional-motivational personality system, the language-cognitive, and the sensory-motor. Relationships between affect and behavior (including covert behavior, or cognition) are mediated by stimuli acquiring, through principles of learning, three functions: an emotion-arousing or attitudinal function (A), a reinforcing function (R), and a directive or cue function (D). Of special importance to developmental processes is the assumption that behavioral elements within the basic repertoires facilitate (or are prerequisites for) the acquisition of additional elements. This Staats refers to as the principle of "cumulative-hierarchical learning." Abnormal behavior can be classified into two categories: aspects of the basic behavioral repertoire necessary for successful adjustment that are deficient and aspects that are present but are inappropriate and detrimental. These deficits and excesses both are shaped by and in turn shape the child's environment. For instance, a child's aggressive behavior might cause other peers to avoid social interactions, thus creating a deficit environment not conducive to the learning of more effective social skills.

Social behaviorism, like behaviorism in general, assumes that behaviors of specific clinical interest (and aggression in particular) are socially determined as well as socially defined. They are, therefore, inseparable from the interaction between an individual and his or her social milieu and are not analogous to the pathological symptoms of organic disease. Much of the empirical work on aggression, on the other hand, concerns children who have been identified as aggressive by society, following the disease model; and since clinicians typically see only such children who have been referred and designated as difficult by some social agency (including families), one might think that studies of these children would be more useful than studies of the acquisition and maintenance of aggressive behaviors *per se*. However, as the former draw into their rubric children whose common feature is social identification and not the variables controlling aggressive behavior, they may illuminate broad relationships but do not provide the detail needed for assessment and intervention. Thus, paradoxically, it is the underlying processes of learning prosocial and antisocial behavior that represent the most relevant data base for the clinician. To illustrate this point, it is worth considering the attributes of aggressive behavior that appear to be particularly important for the social identification of problem children, looking first at legal criteria and then at psychopathological definitions.

AGGRESSION AND JUVENILE CRIME

Much aggressive behavior in children comes to the attention of clinicians as a result of the involvement of the judicial system—acts and threats of personal injury or property destruction salient enough to warrant legal sanction. Thus it would seem at first that there should be some sort of continuum of severity from initial appearances of aggressive behavior in the young child, through repeated occurrences to the point at which aggression is a characteristic response mode, to escalation of conduct so unacceptable that it is considered a mental health "disorder," and finally to the perpetration of aggressive and violent crime. Natural histories of socially unacceptable behavior, however, indicate that this is not so. For instance, when specific problem behaviors in young children (e.g., temper tantrums or noncompliance) are studied longitudinally, there are striking discontinuities among children when they are 3, 4, and 8 years of age (Richman, Stevenson, & Graham, 1982). One reason for this, of course, is that the *form* of any behavior would be expected to show developmental changes, even if its *function* (say, coercive control over others) remained the same. Societal expectations, for instance, render a physical fight between two preschoolers less socially significant than a physical fight between two adolescents, which has a very different attitudinal value. One reason for this is that as children mature in physical strength and acquire more elaborate sensory-motor repertoires for inflicting harm (such as gaining access to, and skill in the use of, weapons) the lethality risks of hostile interpersonal confrontations increase. Consequently, while such violent episodes as murder, assault, and robbery are occasionally reported in children less than 10 years old, there is a sudden dramatic increase from 10 through 14 years of age, as opportunities, skills, and social demands change.

There are other reasons why crimes of aggression are not the end points of an escalating progression of socially undesirable behavior. To become identified as a juvenile offender certainly requires that some law has been violated. However, there is a decided capriciousness in the identification system (being arrested and charged), as criminologists have repeatedly emphasized (see Chesney-Lind, Chapter 8 of this volume). Thus, the transformation of aggressive behavior into the legal status of a juvenile offence is not simple. One youngster could on one occasion be involved in a fist fight that happened to come to police attention, whereas another child could habitually push, kick, and threaten other children without ever being called delinquent. One of us was recently asked to evaluate a 14-year-old youth who had been arrested for setting fire to a village trash-dumping site near his house, thereby risking damage to some surrounding homes. This was his first offence and was motivated, according to his account, by the discovery of toxic wastes at the landfill, on which he blamed his mother's recently detected terminal cancer. Appropriate anger in his emotional-motivational repertoire led to inappropriate sensory-motor actions that resulted in his arrest and, in fact, to his sentencing to a detention center.

Further complications that have greatly interested sociologists are the social class and ethnic and other cultural differences that mediate police arrest and court sentencing decisions, especially with respect to the initial use of police intervention as a management tactic for children's antisocial behavior. Another critical feature, then, in the discontinuity between adjudicated criminal acts and general adjustment problems is the nature of the victim. First, it is the presence of a victim that defines criminal behavior as aggressive: there are clear differences legally between index offences (acts against persons or property) and non-index offences (social rule violations with no obvious victim, such as gambling, vandalism, and drug abuse). Of special importance is the extent to which the victim of the aggressive crime is known to the perpetrator. Criminal behavior, unlike aggression in general, is characterized by the victim's being outside the perpetrator's immediate family and social circle. This is why, it might be argued, child, spouse, and parent abuse have been identified as criminal acts only recently, with changing societal definitions and demands. In any event, knowing or not knowing the victim represents an important element in the control of aggression. In situations wherein empathy for others can be reduced (e.g., involving strangers or people who can be labeled with negative value statements), or wherein fear of retaliation is minimal, the initiation of aggressive acts becomes much more probable.

Situational determinants are complex, however, since in a high proportion of rare but seriously aggressive crimes, such as murder, the victim is well known to the killer. In one frequently cited study (which, like so many others, is somewhat confounded by the fact that the data are based on crimes actually solved by the police), 33% of criminal homicides took place within family altercations, whereas only 7% were related to robbery (Wolfgang, 1958). Here the anticipation of consequences appear to have been overridden by the emotional-motivational antecedents. This is supported by the finding that before an aggravated assault involving youths there has typically been an angry verbal and/or social interaction (Pittman & Handy, 1964). Also, homicides and assaults by teenagers are frequently preceded by the victim's being the first to strike a blow or show a dangerous weapon in an argument. In view of the importance of these situational variables it is not surprising that repeated acts of the most serious forms of juvenile violence against persons are quite rare (see Crowell, Chapter 2 of this volume).

The clinician who is asked to predict the probability of future aggressive behavior faces a complex decision when the exact circumstances evoking aggressive behavior are not known and the future probabilities of such situations are not calculable. However, it is helpful to understand something of the interactions within the individual's social system. Aggressive acts may indeed be highly situational and yet occur against a backdrop of less serious deficits in the child's repertoire. An example of this analysis was presented to the first author when he was the consultant for an evaluation of a 16-year-old boy who had been in a secure facility since committing murder three years before. He had killed a man who had befriended him and was forcing him to engage in homosexual activities. Part of the assessment involved determining the exact features of this eliciting situation: clearly, homosexual assault might be a low probability future event, but if the aggression could be elicited in any situation in which the boy was being taken advantage of, his dangerousness was much greater.

In conclusion, the clinician working with a child who has committed murder or physical assault is not necessarily faced with a client who is on the extreme of some aggressiveness dimension, although the action itself represents a violent extreme. The appropriate assessment and treatment plan cannot take place without a consideration of the dimensions of more typically occurring behaviors and their roles in the child's social repertoire for handling conflict situations, regulating anger, exerting self-control, and so on. It is thus useful to make the distinction, common in the animal aggression literature, between defensive attack (occurring only in circumstances of high levels of fear) and angry aggression (for example, see Blanchard, O'Donnell, & Blanchard, 1979). The former appears to be rare in human situations and receives some social sanction. (One might note that the recent debate surrounding the New York subway vigilante was essentially concerned with whether his aggressive behavior was motivated by fear or by anger.)

The assumption that overt physical acts of aggression are dynamically regulated by emotional responses is essentially similar to the standard behavior therapy model in which avoidance behavior is motivated by anxiety. In Staats's (1975) A-R-D theory, situations eliciting anger (the attitudinal component) can also elicit attack behaviors (the directive component) when such behaviors have been acquired by reinforcement in the past. The interesting twist is that, as predicted by the two-factor theory of avoidance, situations that arouse fear as well as anger will "inhibit" the overt expression of aggression by eliciting avoidance behavior. The significance of this for teaching prosocial, noncriminal behavior will be seen in a later section.

PSYCHOPATHOLOGY AND CHILDHOOD AGGRESSION

We have briefly considered some dimensions of individual aggressive behavior that relate to children who might be referred to clinicians because they have come to the attention of the judicial system. The second major avenue of clinical referral is through the child mental health system, in which case it may be presumed that the children's violation of social rules has impacted only the immediate social context of family, peers, and perhaps school. In reality, of course, the social factors already mentioned determine whether a child is treated as emotionally disturbed or delinquent, and Staats's social behaviorism theory helps clarify those dimensions of the individual repertoire that also determine the judgment. Categorical and labeling models, however, tend to confuse matters. For example, one category in DSM-III is essentially isomorphic with judicial definitions of delinquent behavior. To be diagnosed as conduct disorder, aggressive type (whether socialized or undersocialized), the child must be chronically involved in such activities as vandalism, rape, assault, mugging, or theft involving a specific victim, such as purse-snatching or armed robbery. On the other hand, the criteria for nonaggressive types of conduct disorder specify activities that might or might not be criminal (status) offences, such as lying at home and breaking rules at school. These psychiatric diagnostic categories do not, therefore, parallel each other and are certainly not based on the empirical work carried out by developmental psychopathologists (see also Chapter 2 for a survey of these studies).

The major research tactic of developmental psychopathology does not, in our view, provide an entirely adequate description of response relationships. The approach is to rely on parent or teacher ratings of the presence or absence of very loosely described behavioral tendencies, to subject these ratings to multivariate statistical analyses, and to look for dimensions of response covariance (e.g., Achenbach & Edelbrock, 1978; Quay, 1979). This strategy has been extensively critiqued in behavioral assessment on a number of grounds (Evans & Nelson, 1986). Chief among these are (a) the incomplete range of behaviors entered into the original checklist of behavior problems, (b) the ambiguity of the items and the lack of a common set of scaling criteria, and (c) the statistical definition of a cluster failing to indicate the actual pattern of co-occurrence of the different behaviors (Evans, 1986). Because of poor item definition and other problems inherent in rating scales, the agreement between raters on the most commonly used instruments is quite low (Gould, Wunch-Hitzig, & Dohrenwend, 1981). Offord, Rae-Grant, Szatmari, and Boyle (1983), for instance, found correlations of only .35 between parent and teacher ratings on Achenbach and Edelbrock's (1981) Child Behavior Checklist. Part of the low agreement can be attributed to the well-documented finding that children's social repertoires vary considerably across settings, so that parents and teachers actually have different samples of behavior to aggregate and rate. Another major reason for poor agreement is that the raters use idiosyncratic judgment criteria. Thanks to the excellent work of Forehand and his colleagues (e.g., Griest, Wells, & Forehand, 1979) we are gaining some clinical insights into how depression and stress influence parents' ratings of their children. As is predicted by A-R-D theory, a parent's emotional-motivational repertoire influences the emotional valence of the child's inappropriate behavior and hence the labels used to describe it.

Despite these numerous limitations, the analysis of rating scales has the one advantage of being able to consider large samples of normal children, rather than only those who have been referred for clinical services. The resultant identification of very general clusters of problem behaviors does have some clinical utility. For instance, it is possible to track certain dimensions of behavior across developmental transitions in which the form of the behavior varies as a function of age or opportunity. A specific example is that clusters labeled "hostile aggression" and "anger/defiance" show up in preschool children when teacher ratings are analyzed, although the specific behaviors of these children (spitting, tearing, throwing) would not be seen in older children. On the other hand, traditional behavioral assessments, focusing on the exact measurement of topographically defined aggression, have resulted in certain anomalies when identifying response classes that are not derived from common motivational elements of the basic repertoire. To mention just one example of this problem, Murphy, Hutchison, and Bailey (1983) admitted that their observational system could not differentiate between "repeatedly striking a person in anger vs. a playful slap" (p. 33). Raters, however, by observing many different instances of behavior in their contexts, can assign individual events to more meaningful response classes. Also, very broad classes have emerged from the work of Achenbach and Edelbrock (1984). These authors have argued that the behavior problems of children, whether young or old, tend to fit into two "broad-band" clusters: undercontrolled behavior (incorporating the narrower clusters of hyperactivity, aggression, and delinquent behavior), and overcontrolled behavior (anxiety, depression, and somatic complaints).

These clusters could be thought of as representing deficits in basic behavioral repertoires. If, it might be argued, both hyperactive and aggressive behavior can be conceptualized as undercontrolled, then it follows that interventions in both cases could be targeted toward self-control deficits. As the relationship between designated syndromes of hyperactivity and aggression is discussed in some detail in Chapter 2, we will use these two behavioral categories just to illustrate some of the possible response interrelationships of significance to the clinician.

The most obvious relationship emerges in light of Staats's principle of cumulative hierarchical learning. If the preschool or early elementary school child has not learned the behavior of being able to sit still in the classroom at the appropriate times, whatever other behaviors are engaged in at those times will have a disruptive effect on the teacher and the other students. These behaviors are then apt to be called deliberately disruptive or aggressive. Also, clumsy, poorly coordinated children (those with a sensory-motor repertoire deficit), as Staats (1975) observed, are more likely to bump into other children and damage their possessions. At this point a cycle of real aggression may be easily initiated: the child is sharply reprimanded by the teacher, derided by the other children, and possibly punished by parents for misbehaving at school and being annoying at home. Not surprisingly, the child may respond with anger and overt aggression, perhaps damaging property and fighting with other children.

The point must be made, however, that not every instance of the co-occurence of aggression and hyperactive behavior would fit such a developmental model. It is also possible that some basic deficit mediates the two patterns separately—for instance, the inability to exert self-control over impulsive responses of any kind (the "undercontrolled" factor of the research findings). The clinician must formulate hypotheses regarding various possibilities and use various assessment strategies to answer individual questions. The second author recently assessed a 10-year-old boy who had a five-year history of referrals for hyperactive behavior and aggressive acts and who thus presented a problem as to where intervention should be directed. Her assessment revealed that in certain circumstances he could sit and concentrate for comparatively long periods of time, when the tasks were highly favored activities such as putting together jigsaw puzzles. The deficit was therefore not merely in attending behavior *per se,* but in the range of settings that controlled attending. She therefore devised versions of his academic work in which puzzles were used as a metaphor: words and images fitting together to make imaginary pictures, numbers and letters to make equations, and so on. Puzzles were also used as part of a home-based reward program for improved behavior. Although this strategy addresses only one area in which the child has been experiencing problems, and other treatment is necessary, including family therapy, its initial effect was to reverse the child's labelling of himself as incapable of performing or relating well because of his "illness." Over time, with continued effort, this may be expected to raise the level of his academic and prosocial behavior and to help reverse teacher, peer, and parental designations.

AGGRESSION IN CHILDREN WITH HANDICAPS

In the previous section we used hyperactivity to illustrate how a behavioral systems model conceptualizes two behavior patterns, aggression and overactivity, not as two disorders or syndromes but as interactive components of the child's basic repertoires. These components might arise quite independently from a basic skill deficit (e.g., impulse control), may interact causally by reciprocal effects on the environment (e.g., hyperactive behavior results in rejection and hostility from others), or may represent a superficial social labelling effect (e.g., aggressive behavior is called hyperactive by professionals).

It might now be instructive to consider a related area, one in which aggressive responding is obviously secondary to other clinical problems and in which aggression research itself is rarely carried out. A significant number of children with severe intellectual handicaps (moderate to severe mental retardation) and other developmental disabilities, such as autism and severe learning disabilities, exhibit aggressive behavior that interferes with their educational programs and general social and community adjustment. Kicking, biting, scratching, hair-pulling, and so on are often seen in younger children with handicaps and can become more serious acts of aggression in older children and young adults. Societal response to this behavior is often out of all proportion to the actual harm the children can inflict, frequently resulting in recommendations of a more restrictive school placement or institutional care and thus in a still more deficient environment for the child (Leduc & Dumais, in press). In fact, the most important criterion identified by teachers and other professionals for judging a behavior to be in need of change is that it is dangerous to others (Voeltz, Evans, Freedland, & Donellon, 1982). It is also fairly well established that such excess behaviors are more likely to interfere with community and vocational adjustment than simply having few skills.

Aggression directed against others, however, is not the only category of excess behavior that might be revealed by children with severe handicaps: self-stimulation and self-injurious behavior are also reported with some frequency, especially in institutional settings (Borthwick, Meyers, & Eyman, 1981). In the early days of behavior modification the most commonly used strategy to remediate this range of problem behaviors involved some kind of negative consequence or punishment procedure, in which an unpleasant or painful event was administered contingent upon the aggressive behavior. These techniques represented a significant clinical advance over treatments involving sedative drugs or physical restraints. Within recent years, however, the scientific, practical, and ethical value of punishment has been seriously questioned (Evans & Meyer, 1985; LaVigna & Donnellan, in press). Ethically, the use of punishment with any child is seen as dehumanizing and demeaning and a violation of civil rights including freedom from harm. Practically, the methods are unsuitable for normalized environments such as public schools, small group homes, and the other community settings in which children with handicaps are now being served. Further, there are also negative effects on the persons delivering the punishment, as would be obvious from considerations of the context of this book. Scientifically and theoretically, however, the major limitations of negative consequences and punishment procedures are that they are far less effective than was once believed. Along with other decelerative techniques, they serve to reduce still further the limited skill repertoires of children with handicaps. There is also growing evidence that punishment contingencies may reduce the specific target behavior but have negative collateral effects, or side effects (Voeltz & Evans, 1982). In addition, the punishment techniques rarely continue to be effective in new environments or once the specific contingencies are withdrawn. Finally, as Staats (1975), among others, has pointed out, the emotional responses elicited by the punishment may duplicate the emotional responses controlling the overt aggressive behavior in the first place. All these arguments suggest that some of the current work being carried out to remediate excess behaviors in children with handicaps provides a useful natural test of response relationship concepts of aggression.

    In regard to why reducing aggressive behavior through punishment produces side effects and limited generalization and maintenance of treatment gains, a widely accepted explanation is that the aggressive behavior, however negatively it may be judged by society, does serve specific functions for the child with a handicapping condition. Doubtless these functions are similar to those served by aggression in nonhandicapped children; however, they are somewhat easier to discern in individuals with limited alternative competencies. Probably the most obvious function is that the aggression represents an active form of coercion, whereby the child forces others to do something they might otherwise not want to do. This is most commonly seen in peer interactions at school, although when this kind of domination is perpetrated by nonhandicapped children it seems less likely to be brought to clinical attention. A second important function is passive coercion, in which the child uses aggressive behavior to avoid a situation or to prevent something from happening to him or her, or to escape from an ongoing aversive situation. Escape is quite frequently seen in students who are being required to complete some task that is too difficult or boring. Throwing materials, pushing over the table, and grabbing at the psychologist's clothes are all examples of aggressive intrusions that we have seen successfully terminate teaching or testing attempts. Avoidance is seen typically when the student with a severe handicap is asked to do some chore and reacts so violently that the caregiver backs off and discontinues the request.

In addition to these manipulative functions, there are also communicative functions. The aggression occurs in response to events provoking distress or anger. Instead of being able to explain verbally that the situation is upsetting, the student may react with a violent outburst. This suggests that there are skill deficiencies in both social interaction and communication and that the design of effective curriculum-based interventions requires a rather detailed assessment of the social communicative function. To do so, an instrument such as the Assessment of Social Competence developed by Meyer and her colleagues (Meyer *et al.*, 1985) might prove useful. Two social competency functions in this instrument are especially relevant. One of these, *provides negative feedback,* suggests how aggressive behavior can fulfill such a function. Level 3 of the function is defined as "increases negative affect directed to a particular person in response to a disliked situation or event," and an example is "ignores an interruption by a peer, but if interruption continues might push or hit peer." Level 4 of the same function has as an example "walks across the room to avoid contact with a typically troublesome peer," clearly a more desirable form of the function. Level 8 indicates what a really sophisticated version of a social behavior achieving the same effect as hitting might look like: "expresses negative opinions and dislikes in an appropriately assertive way, clearly specifying the source of the concern— for example, rejecting help from someone by politely saying that he or she can do the task alone." Another relevant function is *coping with negatives.* Level 2 of this function involves persisting in behavior that is bothersome to others, for example, "continues to tug on person's clothes for attention even though that person has asked him or her to stop." Level 6 involves responding to negative feedback by switching to another behavior; and Level 8, the highest level, requires anticipating negative feedback and switching strategies before it occurs—for instance, "notices a friend seems uninterested in his or her suggested activity and proposes an alternative."

By analyzing the function of aggressive behavior in such detail it is possible to see that the behavior does represent, however inappropriately, a level of social competence. As all levels described in the instrument fulfill the same general function, the therapeutic implications are that the child should be taught alternative and desirable forms of the behavior at approximately the same level. There is an expanding set of evidence supporting the efficacy of these strategies (Carr & Durand, 1985; Meyer & Evans, 1986). Generally the available studies show the value of teaching specific alternative skills to replace the aggressive behavior—for instance, teaching signs to severely handicapped students that convey such meaning as "Please leave me alone," "I want to stop," "This is making me angry." However, there are also broad–based remedial curricula that can be developed to reduce aggression at a number of levels. Examples of such efforts are general compliance training, curriculum changes that emphasize respect for others, or vocational training to enhance the student's access to environments with a richer density of reinforcement and hence improved feelings of self-worth. As these strategies are very similar to social skills training approaches, we will discuss them in a little more depth in the next section.

One final point must be made concerning aggressive behavior in developmentally disabled children. Insofar as some syndromes of mental retardation, autism, learning disability, and the like are related directly to neurological dysfunction, it would seem likely that for some students with handicaps there will be a certain percentage of aggressive episodes that can be traced back more directly to neurological causes, as discussed by Jonathan Pincus in Chapter 3 of this volume. One of us has recently described two clinical examples of such a pattern (Evans, 1982). Both of the children were girls, one 5 years old and one 7 years old. They were not severely handicapped but had language problems of sufficient severity that they were receiving special education services. They were referred, quite coincidentally, at about the same time by their respective families, for severe outbursts of aggressive behavior. The younger of the two would become violent over minor provocations, such as not being able to find her shoe, being gently reprimanded, or being asked to wait, and would attack whoever happened to be nearby, punching, kicking, and scratching. The older girl's outbursts, which occurred only at home, were sometimes directed at others and sometimes at herself—for instance, she once badly injured her toes by kicking at the sliding glass doors to the porch. She would also regularly awake up at night screaming but would scratch and claw at her parents if they came in to try to comfort her. Needless to say, both children had been seen by a variety of mental health professionals before coming to a specialized diagnostic facility for children run by the State of Hawaii's Department of Health. Careful assessment immediately revealed that these behaviors, though certainly not random as they were triggered by annoyances in one girl and never occurred at school in the other, were not manipulative in intent, nor did they have precursors that could be considered anger-related. Additionally, their form and contexts were not like the conduct disorder behaviors described earlier: the younger child's outbursts were preceded by a few moments of motor tic-like behavior, and the older child slept, or acted as though nothing had happened, once the episode was over. Referral to a pediatric neurologist confirmed, as expected, that the children both showed temporal lobe seizure patterns in their EEGs. Their aggressive behavior, however, could not be interpreted simplistically as being only seizure-related. For one thing, anti-convulsant medication improved only certain aspects of the behavior such as the nighttime waking episodes. Also, the older girl seemed to have acquired some self-control ability, and both girls were being treated very circumspectly by their families, although the parents originally had expressed a great deal of negative feeling over the constant disruption of normal family life. These cases illustrate that the control of aggression through learning alternative skills may be valuable even when significant neurological dysfunction is causally implicated.

AGGRESSION AND SOCIAL SKILLS

We have argued that the analysis of aggressive behavior in children with handicaps reveals the degree to which such behaviors may be seen as the reciprocal of prosocial behaviors, particularly in communicating with and exerting some control over others. In a social behaviorism analysis this would be conceptualized as the child's having inappropriate behaviors as a direct consequence of specific deficits in his or her skills repertoire. There are two other important aspects of response organization, however. One is based on the principle of cumulative hierarchical learning, whereby responses are seen not as static but as escalating social interactions and affecting attitudes and other aspects of the child's social and emotional repertoire. The other is that deficits *per se* may not really exist but that fundamental elements of the basic behavioral repertoires are regulating a wide variety of other day-to-day interactions. An example of this might be a response in the language-cognitive repertoire whereby the actions and intentions of others are misinterpreted, which limits the availability of cues for prosocial interactions (specific data supporting this will be described presently). In other words, the analysis of social skills as they relate to aggression goes beyond the specific reciprocal functions mentioned, into broader interactions within the individual's response system. These will be briefly identified in this next section.

One of the most important organizational concepts relevant to the present discussion is that acts easily identifiable as physically aggressive are only part of the cluster or complex of activities that characterize aggressive children. Hops and Greenwood (1981) used very broad observational categories to try to define the features that most clearly differentiated children considered highly aggressive by their teachers. These were teasing and provoking fights; striking back to teasing by others; always arguing in verbal interchanges; using threatening, coercive tactics to force peer submission; speaking to others in cross, impatient tones; and typically saying unkind things to other children.

From these increasingly rich descriptions of the social interactions of aggressive children we can understand why some social skills programs have focused very broadly on a variety of strategies for dealing with peers. A good example is the program developed by McGinnis, Goldstein, Sprafkin, and Gershaw (1984). The elements they specifically designed to provide alternatives to aggression are: (a) using self-control, such as asking authority figures for permission; (b) responding to (ignoring) teasing; (c) avoiding trouble; (d) staying out of fights; (e) problem solving; (f) accepting consequences; (g) dealing with an accusation; (h) negotiating with peers and teachers. Although very general, these categories are defined in terms of specific behavioral objectives, so that the program is quite structured. It will be noted that a strong emphasis is on avoiding the early stages in the chain of aggressive confrontations. The influence of Spivack and Shure's (1974) original problem-solving skills program is also very strong in most of these packages.

A more incisive approach is to try to identify the exact features of social skill deficiency that is the "prerequisite" deficit in the repertoires of aggressive children. A nice example of this approach is provided by the work of Dodge (1980). His central thesis is that aggressive children have biased social cognitions ("labels," in Staats's theory). They tend to overattribute hostile intention to peers, even in situations in which any hostile attribution is unwarranted. When exposed to an ambiguous provocation by another child, very aggressive boys do not judge the event to be accidental, as do less aggressive boys. Aggressive children are not likely to exhibit this attribution bias when they observe interactions between two other peers—an important finding as it substantiates that their misconstructions vis-à-vis themselves are not due to more global errors of judgment.

Aggressive children seem to believe that others are hostile towards them, and when they make that determination they are more likely to respond aggressively; thus it cannot simply be concluded that their peers are, indeed, typically approaching them in a very hostile fashion. However, Dodge and Frame (1982) did show that aggressive children are often the targets of aggression by others.

It still must be explained, of course, why such attributional biases arise in the first instance; one possibility is that there is a tendency to make hostile attributions when judgments are made hastily (Dodge & Newman, 1981). This suggests additional intriguing relationships between impulsive behavior, hyperactivity, and aggression. It is also necessary to explain why the attribution of hostile intention to peers does not invariably result in aggressive behavior. As already suggested, the presumption of counteraggression or retaliation causes many children to withdraw in such situations.

It remains to be seen whether clinical interventions focused on specific social-cognitive deficits will be more or less effective than when focused on a wider variety of social skills. Certainly the broader the treatment package, the less need the clinician has to try to identify the exact deficits of individual clients. Goldstein's (1981) programs are really like curriculum packages that can be used widely with many children. One thing does appear to be clear: merely talking about these skill deficits and problem-solving strategies, without providing rich opportunities for rehearsal and practice in natural settings, is unlikely to be effective. Children have innumerable direct opportunities to learn behavior in real-life, highly reinforcing, and salient circumstances. Clinicians have to match those learning experiences to effect meaningful change.

OTHER RESPONSE RELATIONSHIPS

Throughout this chapter, but especially in the preceding section, we have tried to emphasize the importance of considering aggression as a complex component of the child's total repertoire of behaviors, which seems to us more productive than using traditional personality descriptions or labeling specific children as aggressive. This systemic view of individual behavior has had considerable impact on the development of indirect behavioral manipulations. The types of response relationships possible are determined by the level of analysis at which the behaviors are described (Voeltz & Evans, 1982). For example, complex actions or "routines" fill available time and are thus substitutable, one for the other, according to economic principles. Thus broadly disruptive behaviors in schoolchildren (hitting, kicking others, property destruction) were effectively eliminated in one study by providing the students with clear opportunities to engage in constructive activities such as organized games (Murphy, Hutchison, & Bailey, 1983). Conceptually, this type of intervention represents the provision of alternative behaviors that are specific. It is also possible (and almost always necessary, clinically) to reinforce unspecified instances of nonaggression. The arrangement of such contingencies has long been considered central to the control of violence (Berkowitz, 1962).

Another structural approach to analyzing childhood aggression is to consider the precursors to more violent incidents. As we have already mentioned, acts of criminal violence are often preceded by hostile interchanges, and it may be these events, early in the chain, that can best be prevented by social skills training. In general, even though nonaggressive behavior may predominate in individual repertoires, it is obvious that aggression becomes more probable in anyone in certain provoking circumstances. This, of course, is why the clinical assessment of aggressive children requires consideration of the developmental concepts of angry and/or hostile aggression and instrumental aggression as separable categories. Aggressive behaviors, like others, may have more than one function, and understanding these functions through systematic observation is important. The consequences of aggressive acts are not inevitably the attainment of positive objectives. For example, Bjerke (1981) showed that aggressive acts (usually conflicts over objects such as toys) resulted in positive consequences for very young children only 20% of the time, and in negative consequences 62% of the time (negative consequences being counterattacks by the victim, or adult intrusion). As mentioned earlier in this chapter, another example has repeatedly been confirmed in the literature on children with handicaps: a major function of their inappropriate behavior is to escape an aversive situation. In other words, much childhood aggression is negatively reinforced. It follows that punishment of overt aggression, in the absence of reduction of anger or external negative conditions, would result simply in the child's being more selective of the conditions under which aggressive acts are committed, such as picking on smaller or more fearful children who are less likely to retaliate. It should also be mentioned that negative social consequences are not always aversive; if mother's, teacher's, or peer's attention is more desirable than their annoyance is negative, signs of someone else's anger will become a positive affective stimulus, maintaining the behavior that produces it (Staats, 1975).

The assumption that within individual response systems overt acts of aggression are "dynamically" regulated, as mentioned earlier, is an important guide for clinical assessment. Decisions must be made as to whether the anger elicited in social situations is unreasonably intense, or the child lacks social skills once anger has been aroused, or the fear of the consequences to the aggressive episode is not sufficiently intense. All three dynamics have been considered in the treatment literature. In regard to fear of consequences, we may reinterpret it as the acquisition of internalized social prohibitions, and there is an extensive developmental psychology literature on just this topic (e.g., Aronfreed, 1968). The internalizing by the child of externally imposed rules of conduct is most probably mediated by anticipatory fear of retaliation, or consequent aversive (guilt) feelings, although verbal representation of these rules and feelings is also important, as Eliot Turiel explains in Chapter 11. Reasoning with children, or explaining the consequences of their actions, still represents the manipulation of affect through the denotative and conotative meanings of words (Staats, in press). One reason that induction has so repeatedly been found to be a more effective parental discipline strategy than externally imposed punishments seems to be that through internalized principles the language repertoire can direct the "fear" most precisely to where it belongs—that is, to the prosocial position of fearing to hurt or humiliate the victim. Punishment, on the other hand, by a third party, simply creates fear of exhibiting the transgression in the presence of that person.

In addressing a lack of self-control skills in the aggressive child, it is important to see that self-control is a response repertoire that is overlaid on the basic processes just described. For instance, one could enhance self-control by encouraging the child to think ahead to the consequences for the victim of aggression (empathy), or the consequences for the perpetrator if the victim should retaliate. This technique, called covert punishment in adult behavior therapy, is one we have used successfully with aggressive teenagers. Most self-control programs, however, have focused on inhibiting the response to anger or on the anticipation and avoidance of social confrontations (e.g., Novaco's, 1975, anger management program).

More of this type of work has been done with adolescents and college students than with younger children, presumably reflecting clinical assumptions about when sources of control begin to shift from parents and other caregivers to individuals themselves. Nevertheless there is a promising literature developing on self-control training for impulsive children. Camp, Blom, Herbert, and van Doorninck (1977) developed a "think aloud" program focused mostly on interpersonal problem situations rather than just self-restraint. Coats (1979) found an effect of self-instructional training on verbal but not on physical aggression (showing, again, how forms of aggression can be differentiated and the more acceptable ones selectively permitted). Urbain and Kendall (1981) focused on self-restraint (stop and think), problem solving, and empathy training, but, as Kendall and Braswell (1985) commented in a review of these and other studies, the results have been less encouraging than with nonaggressive impulsive children. Whether the interventions have been too weak, or too artificial, or the self-control techniques not implemented later by the children, or the wrong target component identified, is not yet known.

CONCLUSION

In the latter two sections of this chapter the individual response repertoires of children who are judged as highly aggressive were considered in terms of skill deficiencies, either those running counter to aggression itself, or as components of more appropriate responding to provoking situations. Empirical treatment studies have often focused on modifying one feature of these patterns, such as teaching a self-control skill or an assertion skill. An approach to clinical intervention based on social behaviorism principles, particularly those discussed in this chapter, would result in the design of multifaceted interventions, with many of the elements being woven into a general fabric of planned treatment. For instance, parents could be encouraged to increase their level of social reinforcement for instances of nonaggression and to give the child greater responsibility, even though the primary focus of therapy might be on teaching better self-control skills and altering hostile attributions. Clearly, the planning of these systems interventions (Evans, 1985) requires rapid assessment of potential for change. Thus, modifications in parental reinforcement patterns would not be expected of, or asked from, parents who are already exhibiting problems in handling socioeconomic stress (Wahler & Graves, 1983) or depression (Forehand, Wells, McMahon, Griest, & Rogers, 1982), or who have a strong cultural belief in the value of aggressive solutions to child discipline problems (Dubanoski, Evans, & Higuchi, 1978). Eventually, of course, some way of changing these familial and social conditions must be found in order to optimize the development of prosocial behavior. This is why community models of intervention, which Clifford O'Donnell emphasizes in Chapter 12, are rightly in vogue.

In other words, there is nothing in our perspective, based on behavioral organization concepts, to deny that ultimately effective interventions require rearrangement of very specific family interaction problems, as described so well by Teru Morton in Chapter 6 of this volume. Understanding child abuse or the influences of the media and other social agencies is critical to the long-term reduction and prevention of aggression in children; however, these notions are so excellently dealt with in later chapters that we have not extended the social behaviorism model to them. Similarly, it is no contradiction, and might in fact assist in the design of community interventions, to relate the aims, objectives, and patterns of influence of these more general systems to the unique systems of responses that make up the repertoires of individual children. In fact, it is our contention that the social behaviorism model allows for a logical, and thus better unified, extension to the systems of influence from peers, parents, families, and social institutions. It also suggests possibilities for integration of the many and varied intervention strategies at the clinical level that have been promoted for assisting very aggressive children to make a happier and more adaptive adjustment to the adult world.

REFERENCES

Achenbach, T. M., & Edelbrock, C. S. (1978). The classification of child psychopathology: A review and analysis of empirical efforts. *Psychological Bulletin, 85,* 1275–1301.

Achenbach, T. M., & Edelbrock, C. S. (1981). Behavioral problems and competencies reported by parents of normal and disturbed children age 4 through 16. *Monographs of the Society for Research in Child Development, 46* (whole number 188).

Achenbach, T. M., & Edelbrock, C. S. (1984). Psychopathology of childhood. *Annual Review of Psychology, 35,* 227–256.

Aronfreed, J. (1968). *Conduct and conscience: The socialization of internalized control over behavior.* New York: Academic Press.

Berkowitz, L. (1962). *Aggression: A social psychological analysis.* New York: McGraw-Hill.

Bjerke, T. (1981). Aggression in young organisms: Why does it occur despite aversive stimulation? In K. Immelmann, G. W. Barlow, L. Petrinovich, & M. Main (Eds.), *Behavioral development.* Cambridge: Cambridge University Press.

Blanchard, R. J., O'Donnell, V., & Blanchard, D. C. (1979). Attack and defensive behaviors in the albino mouse. *Aggressive Behavior, 5,* 341–352.

Borthwick, S. A., Meyers, C. E., & Eyman, R. K. (1981). Comparative adaptive and maladaptive behavior of mentally retarded clients of five residential settings in Western states. In R. H. Bruininks, C. E. Meyers, B. B. Sigford, & K. C. Lakin (Eds.), *Deinstitutionalization and community adjustment of mentally retarded people.* Washington, D.C.: American Association on Mental Deficiency.

Camp, B. W., Blom, G., Herbert, F., & van Doorninck, W. (1977). "Think aloud": A program for developing self-control in young aggressive boys. *Journal of Abnormal Child Psychology, 5,* 157–168.

Carr, E. G., & Durand, V. M. (1985). The social-communicative basis of severe behavior problems in children. In S. Reiss & R. Bootzin (Eds.), *Theoretical issues in behavior therapy.* New York: Academic Press.

Coats, K. I. (1979). Cognitive self-instructional training approach for reducing disruptive behavior in young children. *Psychological Reports, 44*, 127–134.

Dodge, K. A. (1980). Social cognition and children's aggressive behavior. *Child Development, 51*, 162–170.

Dodge, K. A., & Frame, C. L. (1982). Social cognitive biases and deficits in aggressive boys. *Child Development, 53*, 620–635.

Dodge, K. A., & Newman, J. P. (1981). Biased decision making processes in aggressive boys. *Journal of Abnormal Psychology, 90*, 375–379.

Dubanoski, R. A., Evans, I. M., & Higuchi, A. A. (1978). Analysis and treatment of child abuse: A set of behavioral propositions. *Child Abuse and Neglect, 2*, 153–172.

Evans, I. M. (1982). *Assessment of aggression and temporal lobe seizure disorder: Two case reports*. Unpublished manuscript. State University of New York at Binghamton.

Evans, I. M. (1985). Building systems models as a strategy for target behavior selection in clinical assessment. *Behavioral Assessment, 7*, 21–32.

Evans, I. M. (1986). Response relationships and the triple-response-mode concept. In R. O. Nelson & S. C. Hayes (Eds.), *The conceptual foundations of behavioral assessment*. New York: Guilford.

Evans, I. M., & Meyer, L. H. (1985). *An educative approach to behavior problems: A practical decision model for interventions with severely handicapped learners*. Baltimore: Paul H. Brookes.

Evans, I. M., & Nelson, R. O. (1977). Assessment of child behavior problems. In A. R. Ciminero, K. S. Calhoun, & H. E. Adams (Eds.), *Handbook of behavioral assessment*. New York: Wiley.

Evans, I. M., & Nelson, R. O. (1986). The behavioral assessment of children. In A. R. Ciminero, K. S. Calhoun, & H. E. Adams (Eds.), *Handbook of behavioral assessment* (2nd ed.). New York: Wiley.

Forehand, R., Wells, K. C., McMahon, R. J., Griest, D. L., & Rogers, T. (1982). Maternal perceptions of maladjustment in clinic-referred children: An extension of earlier research. *Journal of Behavioral Assessment, 4*, 145–151.

Goldstein, A. P. (1981). Social skill training. In A. P. Goldstein, E. G. Carr, W. S. Davidson, & P. Wehr (Eds.), *In response to aggression: Methods of control and prosocial alternatives*. New York: Pergamon Press.

Gould, M. S., Wunch-Hitzig, R., & Dohrenwend, B. S. (1981). Estimating the pervalence of childhood psychopathology: A critical review. *Journal of the American Academy of Child Psychiatry, 20*(3), 462–476.

Griest, D. L., Wells, K. C., & Forehand, R. (1979). An examination of predictors of maternal preceptions of maladjustment in clinic-referred children. *Journal of Abnormal Psychology, 88*, 277–281.

Hops, H., & Greenwood, C. R. (1981). Social skills deficits. In E. J. Mash & L. G. Terdal (Eds.), *Behavioral assessment of childhood disorders*. New York: Guilford.

Kendall, P. C., & Braswell, L. (1985). *Cognitive-behavioral therapy for impulsive children*. New York: Guilford.

LaVigna, G. W., & Donnellan, A. M. (In press). *Alternatives to punishment: Non-aversive strategies for solving behavior problems*. New York: Irvington Press.

Leduc, A., & Dumais, A. (In press). Applications of social behaviorism in psychiatric institutional settings: A case study of organizational change. In I. M. Evans (Ed.), *Unifying behavior therapy: Contributions of paradigmatic behaviorism*. New York: Springer.

McGinnis, E., Goldstein, A. P., Sprafkin, R. P., & Gershaw, N. J. (1984). *Skill-streaming the elementary school child: A guide for teaching prosocial skills*. Champaign, IL: Research Press.

Meyer, L. H., & Evans, I. M. (1986). Modification of excess behavior: An adaptive and functional approach for educational and community contexts. In R. H. Horner, L. H. Meyer, & H. D. B. Fredericks (Eds.), *Education of learners with severe handicaps: Exemplary service strategies*. Baltimore: Paul H. Brookes.

Meyer, L. H., Reichle, J., McQuarter, R., Cole, D., Vandercook, T., Evans, I. M., Neel, R., & Kishi, G. (1985). *Assessment of Social Competence (ASC): A scale of social competence functions.* Minneapolis: University of Minnesota, Consortium Institute for the Education of Severely Handicapped Learners.

Murphy, H. A., Hutchison, J. M., & Bailey, J. S. (1983). Behavioral school psychology goes outdoors: The effect of organized games on playground aggression. *Journal of Applied Behavior Analysis, 16,* 29–35.

Novaco, R. W. (1975). *Anger control: The development and evaluation of an experimental treatment.* Lexington, MA: Lexington Books.

Offord, D. R., Rae-Grant, N. I., Szatmari, P., & Boyle, M. H. (1983, October). *The Ontario child health study: Methodology and some results.* Paper presented at the meeting of the American Academy of Child Psychiatry, San Francisco.

Pittman, D. J., & Handy, W. (1964). Patterns in criminal aggravated assault. *Journal of Criminal Law, Criminology, and Police Science, 55,* 462–473.

Quay, H. C. (1979). Classification. In H. C. Quay & J. S. Werry (Eds.), *Psychopathological disorders of childhood.* New York: Wiley.

Richman, N., Stevenson, J., & Graham, P. J. (1982). *Pre-school to school: A behavioral study.* London: Academic Press.

Spivack, G., & Shure, M. (1974). *Social adjustment of young children.* San Francisco: Jossey-Bass.

Staats, A. W. (1975). *Social behaviorism.* Homewood, IL: Dorsey Press.

Staats, A. W. (In press). Unifying behavior therapy: Contributions of paradigmatic behaviorism. In I. M. Evans (Ed.), *Paradigmatic behavior therapy: Critical perspectives on applied social behaviorism.* New York: Springer.

Urbain, E. S., & Kendall, P. C. (1981). *Interpersonal problem-solving, social perspective-taking and behavioral contingencies: A comparison of group approaches with impulsive-aggressive children.* Unpublished manuscript, University of Minnesota.

Voeltz, L. M., & Evans, I. M. (1982). The assessment of behavioral interrelationships in child behavior therapy. *Behavioral Assessment, 4,* 131–165.

Voeltz, L. M., Evans, I. M., Freedland, K., & Donellon, S. (1982). Teacher decision making in the selection of educational priorities for severely handicapped children. *Journal of Special Education, 16,* 179–198.

Wahler, R. G., & Graves, M. G. (1983). Setting events in social networks: Ally or enemy in child behavior therapy? *Behavior Therapy, 14,* 19–36.

Wolfgang, M. E. (1958). *Patterns of criminal homicide.* Philadelphia: University of Philadelphia Press.

CHAPTER 5

Potential Relations between the Development of Social Reasoning and Childhood Aggression

ELLIOT TURIEL

In this chapter the topic of childhood aggression and violence is considered from a different and more speculative perspective than that of the other contributions to this volume. Whereas all the other contributors have been engaged in research on the sources and nature of aggression or in efforts toward its prevention, my research has dealt primarily with children who are, for the most part, nonaggressive.

My research efforts have been directed at uncovering the structures and processes of the development of social judgments. This research has included investigations of children and adolescents, as well as their understandings of social organization, social rules and social conventions. Analyses of children's judgments about some forms of aggression have been included in the research: namely, judgments regarding persons inflicting harm upon one another. The research has also examined how children distinguish social rules pertaining to moral issues, such as the infliction of harm, from rules pertaining to nonmoral issues of a conventional nature.

The present chapter is devoted to a consideration of aggression from the perspective of children's moral and social judgments. Although the ideas discussed here stem from work with nonaggressive, nonviolent children, their inclusion here is based on the premise that information derived from research on children's developing social reasoning may have important implications for an

ELLIOT TURIEL • Division of Educational Psychology, Department of Education, University of California, Berkeley, California 94720.

understanding of the sources of influence on childhood aggression and possible ways of preventing it.

The first part of the chapter deals with explanations of children's moral judgments and concepts of social convention. The categories of morality and convention are defined and related to developmental hypotheses. Research is briefly described that deals with children's moral judgments (especially their judgments regarding individual rights and the harming of persons) and their conceptions of the conventions of social systems. The latter part of the chapter deals with implications of this research for the prevention and control of childhood aggression. Two issues are considered: (1) how best to facilitate the development of moral judgments and (2) how individuals' judgments about social organization influence their aggressive behavior.

First, however, I will describe two examples of the research by others which do bear directly on aggression and serve to form links with my research on the development of social judgments. The first example comes from research by George Gerbner and his colleagues (Gerbner & Gross, 1981; Gerbner, Gross, Morgan & Signorielli, 1980) of the Annenberg School of Communication at the University of Pennsylvania, on the influences of television viewing on children's thinking and behavior. Since 1967 Gerbner and his colleagues have conducted large-scale investigations of children and their viewing of television, and Gerbner has recently concluded that heavy exposure to violence on television influences only a small percentage of children to engage in violent behavior. Although Gerbner considers even this small effect to be medically and socially important, he has stated that the findings indicate that the overwhelming majority of children do not become more violent through exposure to television.

In his review of aggression in the *Manual of Child Psychology,* Feschbach (1970) also maintained that insofar as the mass media have an influence on aggressive behavior, the influence is small and limited. Nevertheless, the extent to which television viewing produces aggressiveness in children is a controversial issue, as is attested to by discussions in other chapters of this volume. The Gerbner and Feschbach interpretation of research findings suggests that at least the effects of exposure to television violence are neither obvious nor massive; however, there may be more involved in the process than simple direct modeling of observed actions on the part of children. Gerbner's analyses also indicate that children make inferences and construct judgments about the events they observe on television; and his research has shown that one of the consequences of heavy television viewing for many children is that they become more concerned about the effects of violence on victims and more worried about themselves as possible victims of violence.

Moreover, the impact of television goes beyond the effects of isolated incidents to which children are exposed. Television provides a symbolic environment conveying messages about the maintenance of the social order. Approaching televised content as constituting a general system of communicated messages (rather than as exposure to isolated elements), Gerbner and Gross (1981) proposed that much of the content, including the depiction of acts of violence, serves to communicate messages about the rules, power distribution, and conventional norms of the social order. The patterns of violence portrayed on television (e.g., types and status of people who are victims and victimizers) depict a social structure of power, dominance, and hierarchy that supports, rather than subverts or questions, the established social system.

The first research example, then, illustrates that judgments about the social world are relevant to how children observe and interpret aggressive actions in a symbolic medium. In Gerbner's analysis, television does not depict only aggressive acts, which children may or may not imitate; it also depicts the reactions of victims of aggression, which may lead children to a concern with the effects of violence on themselves and others. Television on the whole also portrays a constituted social system, with its rules, conventions, and hierarchical order, which includes aggressive acts.

We may now consider a second research example that also bears directly on aggressive behavior. This example comes from Milgram's (1963, 1974) well-known experiments on obedience to authority. In those experiments, adult subjects were instructed to administer electric shocks to another person. This was done in the guise of an experiment on the effects of physical punishment on human learning. The subject's task was to administer shocks of increasing voltage each time a person in the role of the learner made an error in the learning task. Although the learner was not actually receiving the shocks, virtually all the subjects were convinced that the learner was being shocked and experiencing great pain. Insofar as the subject hesitated or protested at inflicting the shocks, the experimenter acted out the role of the authority and insisted on the continuation of the experiment. In one experimental condition it was found that 65% of the subjects followed the experimenter's instructions and continued shocking the other person to the very end of the scale.

The Milgram experiment, therefore, provides findings that are in contrast with those of the Gerbner studies. Whereas the majority was influenced to inflict harm in one of the Milgram experimental conditions, the large majority was not influenced to do so in the case of Gerbner's research. However, there are also similarities in the two investigations. In both cases social organization plays a central role. As we have seen, television programming communicates the social order in the Gerbner studies, and social order in the form of authority and scientific legitimacy is an important component of the influences upon individual behavior in the Milgram experiment.

The Gerbner and Milgram studies have been mentioned to illustrate how both morality and social organization can be involved in social actions. Aggression is directly related to morality in that it involves inflicting harm and violating rights. Aggression is also related to the conventional social organization in which it takes place. For now, however, I put these examples aside in order to consider the development of moral judgments and concepts of convention.

CHILDREN'S MORAL JUDGMENTS

It is evident that aggression has been a topic of great interest to social scientists for many years. The issue of aggression and its resultant harm to persons, especially in childhood, is often singled out because of its importance in society and the agreed-upon need for preventing aggression. Many researchers have attempted to deal with the problem by studying the psychology of aggression and especially its antecedents. Many others have searched for solutions to the problem by looking into ways of preventing and controlling it. This very volume and the conference from which it stems, devoted to the study of the sources of influence and the prevention and control of childhood aggression, is reflective of the prominence and concern given to the topic. Aggression is a practical moral issue.

Much of the research has been based on the presumption that aggressive acts constitute the unit of analysis. In that case, aggressive behaviors are generally associated with dispositional types and/or environmental contingencies. Our research on the development of social reasoning can contribute to an understanding of aggression by providing ways of placing the topic into more general categories of social judgments formed by individuals and thereby placing aggressive actions (and their consequences) into the context of how individuals perceive and conceive the social world and social relationships. The most obvious category of social judgment on aggressive acts is morality.

The consensus that exists about the undesirability of aggression, as well as the imperative to prevent it, are consistent with the defining features of morality. Harm, welfare, rights, and justice have been identified as the basic elements of the moral realm (Dworkin, 1978; Gewirth, 1978; Rawls, 1971). Morality has also been characterized (e.g., Gewirth, 1978) as pertaining to obligatory requirements in interpersonal relations. Moral prescriptions entail judgments about issues such as justice, fairness, human rights, and welfare of persons. In addition to being obligatory, moral prescriptions are generalizable and impersonal and are not defined by existing features of social organization. They are generalizable in the sense that they are judged to apply across situations and to everyone in similar circumstances; they are impersonal in that they are not based on individual preferences or personal inclinations. In that moral prescriptions are based on generalizable judgments of justice, rights, and welfare, they would not be defined by existing features of social organization.

This is not to say that morality does not apply to institutional or social organizational practices; but although moral prescriptions are applied to social organizational practices, those practices do not constitute the grounds for moral prescriptions. Accordingly, morality is not determined by general agreement nor is its validity alterable by consensus. Correspondingly, moral prescriptions are not subject solely to existing social rules or the dictates of authority. Moral prescriptions differ from those norms of behavior determined by convention (or general agreement) which are specific to a group or social system.

Our research with children was, in part, designed to ascertain at which ages they make moral judgments and to determine the characteristics of such judgments. One question posed in a series of studies was whether children apply the criteria of obligatoriness, generalizability, and impersonality in their moral judgments. Some of these studies (Nucci & Turiel, 1978; Smetana, 1981; Weston & Turiel, 1980) included very young children (3 to 5 years of age) and others have included older children and adolescents (Davidson, Turiel, & Black, 1983; Nucci, 1981; Nucci & Nucci, 1982; Smetana, 1982; Turiel, 1983).

These studies have been reviewed elsewhere in some detail (Smetana, 1983; Turiel, 1983). For the present purpose, it is important to point out that young children do make distinctive moral judgments in which they apply some of the criteria defining the moral domain. One of our procedures in this research has been to present young children with descriptions of morally relevant social actions (e.g., hitting, stealing, lying) and pose questions tapping their judgments about those actions. In order to determine whether children regard moral issues as obligatory, nonalterable, and generalizable beyond specific social contexts, we posed the following types of questions: Would hitting be all right if there were no rule prohibiting it? Would it be all right if an authority permitted it? Would it be legitimate for a school to have a rule permitting children to hit each other?

Results from various studies show that young children's moral judgments are not contingent upon rules or authority. With regard to both verbally presented situations (Smetana, 1981) and observed actual events (Nucci & Turiel, 1978), young children judged moral acts to be wrong even if no rule existed prohibiting the acts. Correspondingly, children gave negative evaluations to social institutions permitting people to act in ways that are physically harmful to others. They stated it would be wrong for a school not to have policies regulating such actions. The children also judged such actions as wrong even if they were acceptable to persons in authority. Through these types of findings it has been possible to ascertain that young children begin to form moral understandings in which they evaluate actions harmful to persons as wrong in and of themselves. Young children's moral evaluations are based on assessments of the consequences of actions independent of social order or institutional practices. It is not social rules or authority dictates that form the ground for young children's judgments of right and wrong.

More extensive analyses have been made of older children's moral reasoning. One study (Davidson *et al.*, 1983) serves to illustrate the types of findings obtained. In this study two interrelated aspects of social judgments were assessed, using the same criteria applied to moral issues in the studies with younger children. Among the criteria measured were judgments as to whether the act is right or wrong if there is no rule, if an authority permits it, if it does not lead to punishment, and if the act is accepted by group consensus. In addition to assessing criteria, children's reasons or justifications for evaluations of courses of action were examined. To assess criteria and justifications, children (ages 6 to 10 years) were presented with brief hypothetical stories depicting social transgressions. The stories presented a variety of actions deliberately designed to be more or less familiar to children (for instance, the theft of a toy from a school generally is a more familiar event to children than an employee's embezzling money from his employer).

Direct assessments were made of children's familiarity with the events. The purpose of this procedure was to determine whether children's reasoning about familiar events would differ from their reasoning about unfamiliar events. It is perhaps not surprising, but nevertheless of interest, that the event assessed to be familiar to the greatest number of children dealt with a child (a bully) aggressing upon other children. The issue of physical harm was more familiar to children than issues such as theft, scapegoating, embezzlement, and dereliction of duty.

As in the case of younger children, it was found that the familiar events, especially those dealing with aggression and harm, were judged by the criteria of obligatoriness and generalizability. That is, the children's negative evaluations of acts of aggression were not based on the existence of rules or sanctions, nor were they determined by the dictates of authorities or by group consensus. The assessments of justifications for these evaluations revealed that the avoidance of harm to persons and concern for others' welfare were the most significant justifications for children. Furthermore, an age difference in children's justifications was observed. The younger children (the 6- to 8-year-olds) made judgments about the avoidance of harm in a unidirectional, absolutistic, and inflexible way. They focused solely on the avoidance of harm. The older children, in contrast, also focused on the need for concern with reciprocity and mutuality. The older children, however, justified moral prescriptions and rules on the basis of harm as well as on the basis of reciprocal rights and mutual obligations.

Similar and more extensive findings have been obtained in additional studies of the moral criteria and justifications of children and adolescents. The research has also shown that the characteristics of children's moral reasoning differ from their reasoning about conventionality. Whereas aggression is directly related to moral judgments, it is indirectly related to concepts of convention. Before considering those relations, the characteristics of children's conventional concepts will be outlined.

CHILDREN'S UNDERSTANDING OF SOCIAL COORDINATION AND CONVENTION

Earlier it was stated that morality is not defined by consensus. Although there may often be consensus over moral prescriptions, that does not constitute the grounds for their conceived validity. In contrast, convention is determined by consensus or generally accepted societal practices. Conventions are determined by systems of social organization. Conventions (e.g., uniformities in forms of address or modes of dress) are arbitrary acts that have a role in the makeup of the social system in that they serve to coordinate social interactions. Consequently, alternative courses of action can serve the same functions in different social systems; conventions are characterized by relativity or specificity rather than generalizability.

The emergence of distinctively moral judgments in young children suggests that the criteria they apply to moral issues might differ from those applied to issues of social convention. The research has indicated this to be the case. As an illustrative example of how children distinguish morality from convention, consider the following excerpt from an interview with a 5-year-old boy (Weston & Turiel, 1980).

> *This is a story about Park School. In Park School the children are allowed to hit and push others if they want. It's okay to hit and push others. Do you think it is all right for Park School to say children can hit and push others if they want to?*
> No. it is not okay.
> *Why not?*
> Because that is like making other people unhappy. You can hurt them that way. It hurts other people, hurting is not good.
> *Mark goes to Park School. Today in school he wants to swing but he finds that all the swings are being used by other children. So he decides to hit one of the children and take the swing. Is it okay for Mark to do that?*
> No. Because he is hurting someone else.

The 5-year-old boy was also told about a boy who took his clothes off in school because he was warm from running around; he was then asked if that was all right.

> No, because it's a school and other people don't like to see you without your clothes on. It looks silly.
> *I know about another school in a different city. It's called Grove School. . . . At Grove School the children are allowed to take their clothes off if they want to. Is it okay or not okay for Grove School to say children can take their clothes off if they want to?*
> Yes. Because that is the rule.
> *Why can they have that rule?*
> If that's what the boss wants to do, he can do that.
> *How come?*
> Because he's the boss, he is in charge of the school.

Bob goes to Grove School. This is a warm day at Grove School. He has been running in the play area outside and he is hot so he decides to take off his clothes. Is it okay for Bob to do that?
Yes, if he wants to he can because it is the rule.

This 5-year-old boy, like most of the other children in the study, accepted the legitimacy of the institutional policy regarding the conventional issue of dress. His responses suggest that he is a budding or intuitive sociologist, concerned with the role of authority and the status of rules within social groups. His evaluation of a policy permitting nakedness is based on the existing rule and the jurisdiction of the authority. Note, however, that he does not apply those considerations to the infliction of harm. Although the same social organizational features—rules and authority jurisdiction—were present, they were not the basis for his evaluation of the validity of the institutional practice.

It may be said in general that children make both sociological judgments about the social-organizational functions of conventions and moral judgments about the functions of justice, rights, and welfare. In the various studies mentioned in the previous section about moral judgments, assessments were also made of the criteria children and adolescents apply to conventional issues and transgressions. Conventional issues were judged to be contingent on the existence of rules, the dictates of authority, or institutional practices. That is, conventional acts were considered to be acceptable in the absence of a rule pertaining to the act, or alterable by an authority and institutional practice.

Moreover, children and adolescents do not regard conventions as generalizable. They take a relativistic orientation and evaluate conventions by their social context. For example, conventions are judged to be legitimately variable in different cultural or societal contexts. Overall, the criteria applied to conventional issues reflect conceptualizations of the meaning and functions of uniformities in coordinating systems of social organization.

FACILITATING MORAL DEVELOPMENT

The research studies considered thus far offer examples of the types of results that reflect children's moral and conventional judgments. The pattern of findings has been consistent in a number of studies (see also Dodsworth-Rugani, 1982; Nucci & Herman, 1982; Pool, Shweder, & Much, 1983; Smetana, 1982; Smetana, Kelly, & Twentyman, 1984). In all these studies it has been found that children apply differing sets of criteria to moral and conventional issues. It has also been found that children's justifications for courses of action in the moral domain differ from those in the conventional domain. The research, therefore, suggests that morality and convention represent basic and separate categories of social judgments stemming from children's interactions with the social environment.

We have seen that an important component of children's developing morality is the judgments they make regarding aggression and harm. Very young children make judgments about harm, using the criteria of obligatoriness, impersonality, and generalizability. Furthermore, those judgments are not reducible to the learning of social rules, authority expectations, societal norms, or conventions. It should be stressed, however, that I am not suggesting that all children develop the kinds of moral judgments that lead them away from aggressiveness or violence. Nor do I claim that children always or consistently manifest in their behavior preconceived judgments about harm. Rather, I am simply suggesting that the information obtained in research on mainly nonaggressive children's moral reasoning and social-rule learning should be taken into account in attempts to understand aggressive behavior. This information may also be useful in efforts at preventing children from harming others.

Another proviso is in order. The implications drawn from the research, which are meant to be suggestive for further work, apply primarily to common and not extreme forms of aggression that occur among children and adolescents or even between adults and children. Much of the aggression studied by those examining the influences of television falls in this category. The types of aggressive acts examined in experimental settings, as in studies of imitation or modeling, also belong in this category. It is not at all clear how our research on social judgments relates to the very serious examples of aggression of a criminal nature or those that have been associated with psychopathology.

There are two general issues stemming from our work that have a bearing on the topic of aggression. One is the question of how the development of children's moral judgments occurs and what that suggests for facilitating such development. The second is the issue of how children's moral judgments are related to their actions. Obviously, one way of preventing aggression is to promote moral development. However, the research showing that children generally form prescriptive judgments at a very early age suggests that it is also important to consider how such judgments are translated into action. In dealing with each of these issues, it is necessary to account for not only children's thinking about harm, but also their thinking about the rules, authority, and conventions of the social system.

In considering these issues I will make use of the two examples mentioned earlier, the studies by Gerbner and those by Milgram, which directly pertain to aggressive behavior. The Gerbner analyses bear mainly on the question of how to facilitate moral development, the Milgram findings on the relationship between judgments and action.

It will be recalled that Gerbner and his colleagues found that, on the one hand, only a small number of children become more aggressive as a consequence of exposure to violence on television, and that, on the other hand, many children become more concerned with the effects of violence on victims and develop an increased concern about being victims of violence themselves. These patterns of children's reactions to events portrayed on television are consistent with one of the hypotheses that has emerged from our own research, namely, that children actively make judgments about the events experienced in their social environments. Insofar as children make conceptual discriminations between social domains, the implication is that they do not simply accommodate to the social environment. Rather, they structure their experiences and make inferences about social interactions. Children attempt to make sense of the social world, constructing ideas about how people ought to relate to each other and about the rules and conventions in systems of social organization.

Gerbner's findings from the research on children's reactions to a symbolic medium are in accord with the interpretation of social development as entailing inferences and the construction of judgments. Gerbner's analyses indicate that children attend to more than one facet of the scenarios they observe; they also attend to the multidimensional facets of depicted actions of violence. In addition to processing the actions of the perpetrators of violence, children attend to the reactions of victims and the consequences of violent acts (the hurt experienced by victims). It is the relations among persons, including the perpetrators of violent acts and the victims, that constitute one of the experiential bases for children's inferences and constructed prescriptions about how people ought to behave toward one another (Turiel, 1983).

In this way, Gerbner and Gross (1981) have provided a broadened conception of the ways in which actions depicted in a symbolic medium can influence the observer. Whereas the tendency of researchers is to focus solely on the ways in which the action of the aggressor impacts on observers, Gerbner and Gross have observed that aggression involves at least two participants who engage in very different acts and experience different reactions. Aggressive acts, therefore, can be broken down into three simple but significant components: the act of the perpetrator, the reactions of the victim, and the relationship between them. This analysis shows that there is more to take into account than whether or to what extent the perpetrator serves as a model for the observer.

The depiction of aggressive as well as other types of acts on television was further discussed by Gerbner and Gross. They proposed also that television constitutes a symbolic environment whose influences are not limited to specific actions, messages, or even isolated programs, and that analyses of the influences of television should account for the total or "system-wide" context:

> The world of television drama consists of a complex and integrated system of characters, events, actions, and relationships. It is a total symbol system composed largely of stories whose effects cannot be measured with regard to any single element or program seen in isolation. (Gerbner & Gross, 1981, p. 156)

This is both a methodological and substantive consideration. On the methodological side, it is being proposed that the events of analysis include more than specific acts or isolated instances of what television portrays. On the substantive side, the implication is that viewers process the relationships among the parts and structure symbolic systems from the medium as a whole.

Considered from this viewpoint, television does not merely shape or model specific attitudes and behaviors of young viewers; rather, it influences how individuals interpret and structure the totality of this symbolic system. Nevertheless, the impact of television on children's development is likely to be limited since it is a symbolic and passive mode of relating to observed events. It does not entail reciprocal interactions. Accordingly, the structuring activities of children are not most strongly influenced by their television viewing.

By the same token, television viewing would not be the ideal way of fostering children's creative, interpretive activities. However, this does not at all imply that efforts at reducing violence on television should be curtailed. From a moral point of view, the messages conveyed through the depiction of violence on television are not the most beneficial. Insofar as the medium communicates ideas and information, it can be put to better use than the presentation of violence for its entertainment value.

We must look, therefore, to additional sources for evidence that children's social development is associated with their interpretive activities. Such evidence comes from a body of research that has examined children's natural and active relationships through study of the influences of different types of child-rearing methods on moral development. In several studies (see Aronfreed, 1968, and Hoffman, 1970, for reviews) a variety of measures of children's moral development (including measures of judgment and other indices such as behavioral and guilt responses) have been correlated with assessments of the ways in which parents discipline and raise their children. A typology including three main methods of discipline was identified. Those methods are power assertion, love withdrawal, and what has been called induction. Power assertion includes physical punishment and deprivation of material goods. Love withdrawal refers to discipline involving disapproval, blame, or withdrawal of attention. Induction refers to methods in which parents communicate a rationale for their requirements that the child act in certain ways. In this case, the parents provide explanations or reasons for their prescriptions, such as pointing out to the child possible harmful consequences to others.

A major finding obtained by several researchers is that the induction method is most closely correlated with measures of children's moral development. Explicit communication with children regarding the reasons for courses of action is the most effective way of promoting positive, nonaggressive behavior. Parents who use punishment or love withdrawal as the means of dealing with their children are not as effective as those who reason with them. In fact, there is a fair amount of evidence indicating that physical punishment by parents increases the likelihood of aggressive behavior in their children (Feschbach, 1970). Therefore, it is just those types of experiences that might be expected to shape or mold children's behavior—punishment, reward, praise, and disapproval—that turn out to be the least effective and even counterproductive. It is interactions of a reciprocal nature entailing the communication of ideas about social relations and serving to engage the child's thought that most adequately stimulate the development of nonaggressive behavior.

This research on childrearing in conjunction with our research on social reasoning and Gerbner's work on the influences of television viewing all point to the significance of children's social reasoning for an understanding of aggression and its prevention. An important if obvious implication of these convergent findings is that one avenue toward the prevention of childhood aggression is the promotion of the development of moral judgments. This capitalizes on young children's inclinations toward the avoidance of harm (as seen in the research on moral reasoning), their budding empathy for the welfare of others (as seen in the research on the influences of televised aggressive acts), and their receptivity to explanations of reasons for avoiding aggression (as seen in the research on child-rearing methods).

Although it is obvious that promoting development may be one means of preventing aggression, if the relevance of social judgments is accepted, what is not so obvious is how to go about doing so. Our knowledge regarding the most effective ways of facilitating the development of moral judgments is still quite limited. The findings from the child-rearing research strongly point to the relative value of communicating explanations and reasons over physical and psychological punishment. However, the child-rearing research does not provide a basis for specifying the methods and content of communications that most productively stimulate development.

Developmental and educational psychologists have long stressed the importance of providing an optimal match between the level of communication and the level of the child's thinking (Hunt, 1971; Kohlberg, 1971; Turiel, 1969). Optimal matching is considered to occur when the level of the communication is sufficiently close to the child's competence so as to be comprehended and sufficiently distant so as to challenge the child's thinking and thereby stimulate change.

However, there is another and perhaps prerequisite type of matching suggested by the research on morality and convention that has not been given sufficient attention until recently (Nucci, 1982). The research showing that children's moral judgments are distinct from their understandings of the rules, authority, and conventions of social systems indicates that in order to promote children's judgments about aggression and the infliction of harm it is necessary to provide communications relevant to that domain.

If morality and convention form two separate categories of social reasoning, each with its distinctive features, then instruction or communication aimed at facilitating the development of a given domain ought to pertain to that domain. Nucci (1982) has referred to this kind of matching as domain-appropriate instruction. Instruction that fails to coordinate the substance of the communication with the domain of the event is then domain-inappropriate. As an example, domain-inappropriate communication would occur when a teacher attempts to teach a child that harming others is wrong by simply asserting that a rule prohibits the act, or that it is socially unacceptable, or that it contradicts the authority's commands. While communications about customs, rules, and authority is domain-appropriate in efforts to teach children about the conventional social order, it fails to coordinate the nature of the communication with the ways children (and adults) conceptualize morally relevant actions.

This is not to say that the conventional domain is unimportant or that the development of children's concepts of social organization should be ignored. Rather, it is to say that focusing on the social context or institutional requirements in reacting to moral transgressions (to take an example from Nucci, as when a teacher admonishes a child for hitting another with statements such as "We do not hit at school," or "You are not respecting our rules") is not likely to be a forceful argument for children who structure moral events in terms of fairness or justice. With regard to morally relevant acts, especially those relating to harm, effective communications would focus on the nature of the action, its consequences to persons, the emotional reactions of victims, and, especially with older children, on issues of reciprocity and mutual rights and expectations.

The proposition that children's reactions to adult communications and injunctions are influenced by the coordination of the substance of those communications with the domain of the event has further been supported by very recent research (Nucci, 1984). In Nucci's study children drawn from the third, fifth, seventh, and ninth grades were presented with depictions of children's transgressions along with examples of teachers' verbal responses to the transgressions. The depicted transgressions included some in the moral domain (e.g., hitting, stealing) and some in the conventional domain (e.g., swearing, violation of dress codes). Some of the teachers' responses to these transgressions reflected an orientation to consequences of actions and the perspective of the victims and others focused on rule adherence and social order. The children were presented with different combinations of transgressions and teacher responses. In some cases the transgressions were coupled with domain-appropriate teacher responses: teachers responded to moral transgressions with references to consequences and victims' reactions, and teachers responded to conventional transgressions with reference to rules and social order. In other cases the combinations were reversed, so that the transgressions were coupled with domain-inappropriate teacher responses.

Children's evaluations were obtained through ratings of the content of the responses to each transgression and of teachers who were depicted as consistently responding in either domain-appropriate or domain-inappropriate ways. On both measures it was found that children at all ages gave higher ratings to teachers' responses that were coordinated with the domain of the transgression than to responses that were domain-inappropriate. Thus, the findings showed that children are aware of discrepancies between the nature of the transgressions and the types of messages communicated to them by adults. Furthermore, the results indicate that children react more positively to messages that are coordinated with the domain of the transgression. Stated more concretely, the findings show that children respond more positively to moral injunctions when teachers provide reasons dealing with the fairness or justice of the act than when they invoke rules, order, or authority. In turn, children respond more positively to reasons dealing with the necessity of rules, order, and authority when they are associated with conventional transgressions than when they are associated with moral transgressions.

Other research also indicates that in normal circumstances a foundation does exist for domain-appropriate, coordinated communications. A series of observational studies with preschoolers (Much & Shweder, 1978; Nucci & Turiel, 1978: Nucci, Turiel, & Gawrych, 1983) and grade-school children (Nucci & Nucci, 1982) have shown that social interactions are generally differentiated by domain. These studies have documented that, for the most part, the social interactions and communications occurring among children and between adults and children in the context of moral transgressions differ from those in the context of conventional transgressions. These observational studies have supported the propositions that children's social judgments are constructed through their active, reciprocal social interactions and that the types of interactions stimulating the development of moral judgments differ in kind from interactions producing the development of nonmoral social judgments (Turiel, 1983).

Nucci's (1982, 1984) concepts of domain-appropriate and domain-inappropriate communications may have utility in comprehending the potential influence on young viewers of forms of aggression depicted on television. It may be that the portrayal of violence on television fuses messages about aggression and messages about the power and status structure of social organization. As noted by Gerbner and Gross (1981), the pattern of television violence is one in which society's dominant groups are consistently portrayed as prevailing over those of lower status and lesser power. That is, the patterns of violence convey the roles and hierarchies in social organization. Therefore, aspects of the constituted social order are couched in the morally relevant interactions of people inflicting harm on others. This is an example of the crossing of domains in that the conventionally constituted social organization is communicated through interactions (infliction of harm) with moral requirements that are not determined by conventional practices. In this example the conventional order is used to structure aggressive acts. Such a fusion of morality and convention may indeed pose difficulties for children's judgments in situations that include components of the two domains (Turiel & Smetana, 1984). The coordination of domains is relevant to the issue of how children's moral judgments are related to their actions—an issue stemming from research on the development of social reasoning as having a direct bearing on the topic of aggression. However, the promoting of children's moral judgments is no simple matter; it is an issue still requiring a good deal of research.

RELATIONSHIP BETWEEN SOCIAL JUDGMENTS AND ACTION

We have seen that at a relatively early age children form the foundations for the types of moral judgments that have a bearing on aggression. On that basis it was suggested that one productive avenue to consider in preventing aggression is the promotion of moral judgments in children. However, it is not sufficient to deal solely with the development of moral reasoning since children, and adults for that matter, do not always apply their judgments about harm in consistent ways. The second example of research including aggressive behavior outlined at the outset of this chapter—Milgram's experiments on obedience to authority—is informative in this regard. The finding from one of Milgram's experimental conditions was mentioned earlier: the majority of subjects (65%) went along with the experimenter's commands and administered the electric shocks to another person to the very end of the scale.

These findings show that people do not always act in accordance with their judgment about avoiding harm to others. It can be assumed, with some confidence, that most of the adult subjects had formed the judgment that inflicting harm on others is wrong; and in all likelihood those subjects did not normally inflict harm on others. Moreover, during the experiment almost all subjects expressed a good deal of concern about the harm inflicted on the person being shocked and continued administering the shocks to the other person with much conflict and vacillation (Milgram, 1974). Although they went along with the authority, the subjects were also concerned with the other person's welfare.

Subjects experienced conflict because the experimental situation pitted moral and conventional-social organization components against each other. They were faced with a conflict between moral and social organizational considerations. This experimental situation is multifaceted. It includes the conventional-social organization component of an experimenter in a position of authority regarding scientific procedures and goals and also a moral component relating to physical harm to persons. To maintain the experiment, subjects would have had to continue harming another person, whereas to avoid inflicting harm they would have had to disrupt the scientific aims of the experiment.

It is proposed that in their behavioral choices subjects were attempting to coordinate moral and conventional-social organizational judgments (Turiel & Smetana, 1984). This proposition is supported by the findings of a series of other less well known experimental conditions in Milgram's study. In six other experimental conditions it was found that the majority of subjects (in some cases 100%) acted in accordance with their moral judgments and refused to continue administering the electric shocks to the other person. Those experimental conditions had the same general structure as the original experiment, with the exception that there were systematic variations in the salience of either the moral or the social organizational component. In some experimental conditions, the salience of the harm component was increased, for instance, by making the victim visible to the subject. In other conditions, the salience in the force of the experimenter's authority was decreased, by making the experimenter's presence less apparent to the subject by the delegation or diffusion of authority or by other means. (For descriptions of the details of the different experimental conditions see Milgram, 1974 and Turiel, 1983.)

A greater incidence in the number of subjects refusing to administer shocks to the victim under these experimental conditions indicates that they were indeed coordinating moral and conventional judgments. Taken as a whole, Milgram's experiments actually show that in certain circumstances people go along with an authority and inflict harm to another, but in other circumstances they actively refuse to do so. In all the experimental conditions the subjects displayed concern with both the moral and organizational components. The application of those concerns varied by the structure of the social situation, so that harm was sometimes inflicted in spite of the concern with avoiding it when there was a strong concern with maintaining the organization of the social system.

As far as behavior in the Milgram situation is concerned, it appears that adults are not unidimensional in their orientation to aggressive acts. It is likely that individual children and adolescents also display systematic variability in their aggressiveness. The Milgram findings point to one of the sources of such variability. Judgments about the legitimacy of conventionality and social organization may sometimes override moral judgments and lead to acts of aggression and resultant harm to others.

An understanding of how moral and conventional judgments are coordinated is particularly relevant to the behavior of adolescents. To a much greater extent than younger children, adolescents become involved in more or less well organized social groups. It is generally acknowledged that the demands of the social groups with which adolescents become identified can take on moral significance for them. Our own research has confirmed this expectation (Geiger & Turiel, 1983; Turiel, 1978, 1983). Cross-sectional and longitudinal studies were conducted to determine whether there are age-related changes in thinking within the conventional domain. Those studies showed that children and adolescents conceptualize conventions as shared knowledge related to the organization of social systems and as serving the function of coordinating social interactions. Developmental changes do occur in the ways in which social organization is conceptualized and in the understanding of the connections between conventions and social organization. Stated generally, from late childhood to early adolescence there is a shift from a conception of social organization based on a system of concrete rules and authoritative dictates to one based on a hierarchical organization with a system of roles, rules, and norms.

In forming conceptions of hierarchically organized social systems, adolescents also manifest attitudes of increased commitment to the maintenance of social groups. Analogously with what occurred in the Milgram experimental situation for adults, adolescents may very well be faced with strong conflicts between group or social-organizational demands and moral imperatives. Like the behavioral outcomes observed in the Milgram experiments, such situations of conflict could lead to aggressive acts. Therefore another source of aggression may be the conflicts engendered by developing social-organizational concepts that produce strong group commitments on the part of adolescents.

Once again, therefore, it appears that aggressive actions are related to more than one aspect of individuals' developing social judgments. Aggression is related to both the moral and conventional domains. For adolescents, especially, acts of aggression would at times be due to their inadequate coordinations of moral judgments with those concepts of conventionality that produce strong group commitments. More than likely, group commitments are less of a factor prior to adolescence. Children lack experience in organized groups and have still undeveloped concepts of hierarchically organized social systems. Nevertheless, aggressiveness in children is also related to more than one aspect of their developing social judgments. There is research evidence suggesting that children's psychological attributions contribute to the ways in which they relate to others in situations entailing aggressive responses.

One example of this comes from research by Dodge (1980) with groups of children judged to be more or less aggressive by their teachers. In a devised experimental situation the children were confronted with a frustrating experience caused by an unknown child. The subjects were led to believe that a puzzle they had assembled in order to win a prize was disassembled by another child who was not seen but could be heard in an adjoining room. The child who had disassembled the puzzle was depicted as acting with hostile intent (with the intention to disrupt the activity), benign intent (the act was accidental), or ambiguous intent (the intent was not specified). The aggressive and nonaggressive children reacted to the frustrating experience in similar fashion when the other child's intentions were depicted as hostile or benign. Both groups reacted with greater aggression to the hostile intention than to the benign intention. Interestingly, the aggressive children were even more likely than the nonaggressive children to offer help to the child with benign intent. It was only when the other child's intentions were ambiguous that the reactions of the two groups differed in the hostility expressed. In that case, the aggressive group reacted more aggressively than the nonaggressive group, and in about the same way as it had reacted to the hostile intent.

In looking at the total degree of aggressiveness in reaction to all three types of intent, we see that the children classified as aggressive by teacher ratings did display more aggression than the children classified as nonaggressive. However, a hostile intent on the part of a child evoked the same degree of aggressiveness from all the children. It was only the reactions to unclear intentions that discriminated between the aggressive and nonaggressive children. Thus, children's psychological attributes also have a bearing on aggressive behavior. As other findings by Dodge (1980) have shown, the aggressive children were more likely to attribute hostile intentions to others when the actual intentions were unknown to them. For reasons that are not yet apparent, when the actor's intentions are unclear certain children impute hostile intentions whereas other children do not.

Other research (Jancaterino, 1983) suggests that, in general, children expect other children to be highly influenced to commit aggressive acts by situational forces. Children have implicit psychological theories that lead them to attribute a fair amount of aggressiveness to other children in certain social circumstances. Jancaterino obtained evaluations from children (ages 6 to 10 years) of physically harmful acts and their predictions as to whether or not other children would engage in such acts in specified social-environmental contexts, such as attending a school that permits hitting or having parents who permit it. Whereas most of the children evaluated physically harmful acts as wrong, most children predicted that other children would engage in aggressive acts in each of the social contexts permitting it.

CONCLUSION

As seen throughout this chapter, aggression in children as well as adolescents is related to more than one aspect of their social judgments. Along with moral judgments and concepts of convention, psychological attributions are implicated in aggressive behavior. Children's views that others have a propensity for aggressiveness may be another source of conflict that would increase the likelihood of aggression on their part.

In addition to fostering the development of moral judgments from an early age, it may be useful to educate children and adolescents in their abilities to coordinate their moral judgments with their psychological attributions and their understanding of conventional social systems.

REFERENCES

Aronfreed, J. (1968). *Conduct and conscience: The socialization of internalized control over behavior*. New York: Academic Press.

Davidson, P., Turiel, E., & Black, A. (1983). The effect of stimulus familiarity on the use of criteria and justifications in children's social reasoning. *British Journal of Developmental Psychology, 1*, 49–65.

Dodge, K. A. (1980). Social cognition and children's aggressive behavior. *Child Development, 51*, 162–170.

Dodsworth-Rugani, K. J. (1982). *The development of concepts of social structure and their relationship to school rules and authority*. Unpublished doctoral dissertation, University of California, Berkeley.

Dworkin, R. (1978). *Taking rights seriously*. Cambridge, MA: Harvard University Press.

Feschbach, S. (1970). Aggression. In P. H. Mussen (Ed.), *Carmichael's manual of child psychology* (Vol. 2). New York: Wiley.

Geiger, K., & Turiel, E. (1983). Disruptive school behavior and social convention in early adolescence. *Journal of Educational Psychology, 75*, 677–685.

Gerbner, G., & Gross, L. (1981). The violent face of television and its lessons. In E. L. Palmer (Ed.), *Children and the faces of television: Teaching, violence, selling*. New York: Academic Press.

Gerbner, G., Gross, L., Morgan, M., & Signorielli, N. (1980). The "mainstreaming" of America: Violence profile No. 11. *Journal of Communication*, 10–29.

Gewirth, A. (1978). *Reason and morality*. Chicago: University of Chicago Press.

Hoffman, M. L. (1970). Moral development. In P. H. Mussen (Ed.), *Carmichael's manual of child psychology* (Vol. 2). New York: Wiley.

Hunt, D. (1971). Matching models and moral training. In C. M. Beck, B. S. Crittenden, & E. V. Sullivan (Eds.), *Moral education: Interdisciplinary approaches*. Toronto: University of Toronto Press.

Jancaterino, W. (1983). *The relationship between children's understanding of social influences and their moral evaluations of harm*. Unpublished doctoral dissertation, University of California, Santa Cruz.

Kohlberg, L. (1971). Stages of development as a basis for moral education. In C. M. Beck, B. S. Crittenden, & E. V. Sullivan (Eds.), *Moral education: Interdisciplinary approaches*. Toronto, University of Toronto Press.

Milgram, S. (1963). Behavioral study of obedience. *Journal of Abnormal and Social Psychology, 67*, 371–378.

Milgram, S. (1974). *Obedience to authority*. New York: Harper & Row.

Much, N., & Shweder, R. A. (1978). Speaking of rules: The analysis of culture in breach. In W. Damon (Ed.), *New directions for child development, Vol. 2: Moral development*. San Francisco: Jossey-Bass.

Nucci, L. (1981). The development of personal concepts: A domain distinct from moral or societal concepts. *Chid Development, 52*, 114–121.

Nucci, L. (1982). Conceptual development in the moral and conventional domains: Implications for values education. *Review of Educational Research, 49*, 93–122.

Nucci, L. (1984). Evaluating teachers as social agents: Students' ratings of domain appropriate and domain inappropriate teacher responses to transgressions. *American Educational Research Journal, 21*, 367–378.

Nucci, L., & Herman, S. (1982). Educational implications of behavioral disordered children's classifications of moral, conventional and personal issues. *Journal of Abnormal Child Psychology, 10*, 411–426.

Nucci, L., & Nucci, M. (1982). Children's social interactions in the context of moral and conventional transgressions. *Child Development, 53,* 1339–1342.

Nucci, L., & Turiel, E. (1978). Social interactions and the development of social concepts in preschool children. *Child Development, 49,* 400–407.

Nucci, L., Turiel, E., & Gawrych-Encarcion, G. (1983). Children's interactions and social concepts: Analyses of morality and convention in the Virgin Islands. *Journal of Cross-Cultural Psychology, 14,* 469–487.

Pool, D. L., Shweder, R. A., & Much, N. C. (1983). Culture as a cognitive system: Differentiated rule understandings in children and other savages. In E. T. Higgins, D. N. Ruble, & W. E. Hartup (Eds.), *Social cognition and social development: A sociocultural perspective.* Cambridge, England: Cambridge University Press.

Rawls, J. (1971). *A theory of justice.* Cambridge, MA: Harvard University Press.

Smetana, J. (1981). Preschool children's conceptions of moral and social rules. *Child Development, 52,* 1333–1336.

Smetana, J. (1982). *Concepts of self and morality: Women's reasoning about abortion.* New York: Praeger.

Smetana, J. (1983). Social cognitive development: Domain distinctions and coordinations. *Developmental Review, 3,* 131–147.

Smetana, J., Kelly, M., & Twentyman, C. T. (1984). Abused, neglected, and nonmaltreated children's conceptions of moral and social-conventional transgressions. *Child Development, 55,* 277–287.

Turiel, E. (1969). Developmental processes in the child's moral thinking. In P. H. Mussen, J. Langer, & M. Covington (Eds.), *Trends and issues in developmental psychology.* New York: Holt.

Turiel, E. (1978). The development of concepts of social structure: Social convention. In J. Glick & A. Clarke-Stewart (Eds.), *The development of social understanding.* New York: Gardener Press.

Turiel, E. (1983). *The development of social knowledge: Morality and convention.* Cambridge: Cambridge University Press.

Turiel, E., & Smetana, J. (1984). Social knowledge and action: The coordination of domains. In W. M. Kurtines & J. L. Gewirtz (Eds.), *Morality, moral behavior, and moral development: Basic issues in theory and research.* New York: Wiley.

Weston, D., & Turiel, E. (1980). Act–rule relations: Children's concepts of social rules. *Developmental Psychology, 16,* 417–424.

PART III

FAMILIAL AND SOCIETAL ISSUES

CHAPTER 6

Childhood Aggression in the Context of Family Interaction

TERU MORTON

This chapter unfolds on the premise that the family system is the initial, if not primary, context in which childhood aggression can best be understood. Three basic features of family living will be reflected here. First, the family is an arena in which the young infant is inducted into social life and is taught, intentionally or accidentally, a range of social influence strategies, ways in which to influence the enveloping environment—that is, the family. Aggression is one of these modes of social influence. Second, the family is also an arena of conflict, or competing needs and desires, as well as finite resources. Construed in this sense, family members exist in a give-and-take economy wherein they must strike a bargain, each with every other member, about what they are exchanging, what the fair rate of exchange is to be, and how interdependent their existence shall be. This bargaining process thus inherently entails conflict and sometimes also aggression. Third, the family operates as a system; the aggregate of individuals must stay together and yet permit change in individual members and their interdependent relationships.

The attempt will be made to highlight the importance of considering the entire family constellation in determining the meaning and function of childhood aggression. The validity of physiological and genetic contributions to aggression is acknowledged in the ensuing discussion of individuals' aggressive behavior. However, the focus here is on the social framing of aggression and on the reciprocal influence of child aggression and family interaction dynamics.

This chapter is divided into two sections. In the first, the argument for considering childhood aggression as both a cause and a symptom of family

TERU MORTON • Department of Psychology, University of Hawaii at Manoa, Honolulu, Hawaii 96822.

dysfunction will be developed. In making this case, description will proceed from individual to interpersonal and then to systemic levels of analysis. Aggression is now widely acknowledged to be multiply determined, and consequently a diverse assortment of theories assist in explicating the ways in which child and family functioning are related. The case for understanding childhood aggression in the family context having been developed, the second section will then discuss treatment directed at the dysfunctional family.

UNDERSTANDING CHILDHOOD AGGRESSION IN THE FAMILY CONTEXT: COERCIVE FAMILY INTERACTION

Let us begin by considering the socially aggressive child, that young or preadolescent child who represents the bulk of referrals to child guidance clinics for aggressive conduct disorder problems. Such children rely inordinately on the use of aversive means of getting what they want to maximize their immediate payoff, with such behaviors as having tantrums, hitting, fighting. and shouting. These problem children are usually described by their harried parents or teachers as difficult to control, disobedient, irritable, bossy, or coercive (Patterson, 1982; Reid & Hendricks, 1973).

Such coercive behavior occurs to some extent in all young children, and indeed it is the task of parents and other socializing agents to teach children effective alternatives to the inflicting of pain in influencing others and firmly to discourage aggressive, noxious strategies in favor of more prosocial techniques for social influence and control.

When such socialization for alternatives to aggression is not adequate, the use of coercion will continue to characterize a developing child, although the topography of the aggressive behavior will change. The extremely coercive four-year-old or five-year-old has already established a mode of relating to others that, if left untreated, will probably continue (Olweus, 1976, 1979). Coerciveness appears to operate, traitlike, across situations, so that the coercive child at home is found to behave similarly on the school playground (Harris & Reid, 1981). Indeed, child conduct problems, unlike child neuroses, tend to maintain or become worse with age (Olweus, 1979). The finding reported by Eron et al. in Chapter 10 of this volume, that childhood aggression predicts aggression levels across generations, indicates the persistence of the use of pain infliction as an instrument for social control. Thus the preschool child whose whining, yelling, and hitting are not brought under control may graduate to teasing, verbal attacks, and argumentativeness. The use of coercion is extremely effective in the short run, and, once developed, a coercive strategy for getting what one wants can effectively become a lasting style.

Parent–Child Interaction

All very young children manipulate their social environments by using aversive methods. Fretting and other compelling if noxious vocalizations by infants prompt parental appeasement attempts, and the contingent response of the infants then serves to maintain this parental engagement (Bell, 1971; Lewis & Lee-Painter, 1974; Moss & Robson, 1968). Although infants and toddlers may lack the intentionality of older children and caregiving adults, their behavior may nonetheless be just as powerful in terms of social control (Bell & Harper, 1977). The high rates of aversive behavior by young preschool children have been documented by several researchers. Such noxious coercive attempts to influence as demanding, hitting, and shouting occur every few minutes in normal pre-schoolers with their mothers, but this aversive mother-directed behavior drops by more than 50% by age 4 (Fawl, 1963).

Control-oriented instrusions upon the child also occur at high rates from caregivers during these early childhood years. Young toddlers and preschoolers are normally monitored rigorously by their mothers, who issue commands and disapprovals (aversive disciplinary messages) every few minutes, and even school-age children receive such maternal "hawking" messages approximately every four minutes (Patterson, 1976). Tantrum rates drop by more than half between the ages of one and four and are replaced by other behavior patterns at a rate influenced by the parental training method (Goodenough, 1931). Although all of these noxious child behaviors may function as crude instruments of social control, the quality of the aggression changes. Angry outbursts, instrumental in eliciting immediate parental attention and relief from discomfort, are increasingly replaced by aggression, which is less simply instrumental and more hostile, person-directed, and retaliatory (Dawe, 1934; Hartup, 1974).

Socialization research has most typically presumed a unidirectional causality, with parental child-management techniques viewed as shapers of the developing child's social behaviors. Rollins and Thomas (1979), reviewed 235 such studies published between 1960 and 1974. They concluded that (a) aggressiveness correlated with other behavior problems as well as academic and later delinquency problems and (b) this "social incompetence" was generally associated with lack of parental supportiveness and inordinate use of coercive rather than inductive control attempts by the parent. If a young child, striving to master new developmental tasks, is warmly and positively encouraged and supported, he or she will gain in self-efficacy and personal competency in mastering the social and physical world. Without such support, that child will be less attracted to the nonsupportive parent and hence less likely to respond imitatively to him or her, and the development of prosocial alternatives may therefore be retarded. If a parent uses a great amount of punishment, unqualified power assertions, and other such coercive control attempts, and relatively fewer inductive efforts (e.g., reasoning, explanations of consequences for behavior, and discussion of feeling–behavior relationships), the child will not so readily acquire noncoercive social behavior.

Induction, relying on language, provides the child with considerable information about the parents' wishes and values. By helping the child internalize what parents value as socially competent, then, reasoning and explanation facilitate the development of a common understanding between parent and child over the meaning and effectiveness of various problem-solving or conflict-resolution strategies. The importance of parental supportiveness and induction, and of the sparing use of punishment, in socially aggressive children has been underscored by others (e.g., Steinmetz, 1979). Still others have pointed to a probable curvilinear relationship between punishment and child aggression, such that overly lax permissiveness and a high degree of punishment are both associated with child aggression, while a moderate amount of firm enforcement (power assertion) in conjunction with ample reward for more socially competent behavior decreases aggressiveness in children and thus reduces the need for future punishment (Eron, Walder, & Lefkowitz, 1971). Olweus, in his research on determinants of the bully or "whipping boy" phenomenon (1978, 1980), found an additive contribution of parents' use of power-assertion methods and a difficult child temperament; and even more strongly determinant were maternal negativism and permissiveness concerning the child's aggression.

Other researchers have examined the different responses to aggressive outbursts by contrasting short-term and long-term methods of termination. Many techniques effective in the short-term are counterproductive for long-term elimination of aggression. Thus, soothing, coaxing, or granting a child's desire are effective in stopping a tantrum immediately, but serve to reinforce future aggressiveness. Reasoning, scolding, and spanking may be relatively ineffective in controlling an immediate aggressive episode, but are effective in long-term aggression training, presumably because they promote inhibitory mechanisms (Goodenough, 1931). Punishment inhibits aggression only in a narrow sphere of activity and may in fact prompt displacement (Miller, 1948) to other contexts in which, in all likelihood, the caretaker is not present. Further, punishment appears to retard both a child's social development (Hoffman, 1970) and cognitive development (S. Feschbach, 1974). Alternatives to a high degree of punishment include eliminating frustrating and aversive stimuli impinging upon the child such as exposure to the irritable aggressiveness of others, and also substituting competing responses such as cooperation and socially supportive behavior. Indeed, it appears that there is an inverse relationship between empathy and aggression, with the empathic response having an inhibitory effort upon aggressive behavior (S. Feschbach, 1974).

To summarize to this point, research on childrearing variables contributing to the rearing of an nonaggressive child underscores the importance of parental warmth and affection, positive reinforcement and the use of induction, and a parental orientation to the long-term elimination of aggression through facilitation of prosocial alternatives to aggression. The highly aggressive child, in contrast, is exposed to less parental support and reasoning and to more negative, punitive, coercive, and short-term techniques of control. Highly aggressive children, reared in such a fashion, are likely to be low in empathy and cognitive-emotional development, and relatively inattentive and nondiscriminating in regard to social stimulation (S. Feschbach, 1974; Rollins & Thomas, 1979).

The earlier work on the relationship between parental values and socialization techniques and subsequent child behavior tended to presume that the child was influenced by the parent, and not that the parent was also being influenced by the child's behavior. Further, such studies typically relied on self-report and even retrospective accounts of the parents or on global ratings of child aggression or competence. The last decade has witnessed the rapid expansion of detailed observational accounts of parent–child interaction, largely rooted in an increasingly broadening social learning tradition. Such studies have examined rates of various parent and child behaviors, often analyzed in terms of temporal sequence or conditional probability. The purpose of such interactional studies has been to describe the systems of *mutual* reinforcement contingencies that shape and maintain child behavior, both desired and undesired. These studies tend to support previously established relationships between parental disciplinary behavior and child behavior and have offered richly detailed description of the minutiae of day-to-day exchanges between the caregiver and the child.

The next section describes the mutually frustrating parent–child interaction that has been implicated in the fostering of childhood aggression.

The Shaping of a Coercive Child

Since the late 1960s, Gerald Patterson and his associates at the Oregon Social Learning Center have been researching the reinforcement systems surrounding young aggressive children and the most effective ways of correcting such systems. This programatic investigation of childhood aggression has been presented in an integrated manner in Patterson's *Coercive Family Process* (1982), although numerous reports of this line of inquiry have appeared since 1967 (e.g., Patterson, 1976, 1980; Patterson, Littman & Bricker, 1967; Patterson & Reid, 1967; Patterson, Reid, Jones, & Conger, 1975). These researchers have been most influential in drawing attention to the nature of a coercive interaction and have described the fostering of an aggressive child in terms of a dynamic process rather than a static condition.

Patterson, using the reinforcement language of Skinnerians, has coined the concept of the "coercion trap" of spoiled or oppositional children. According to this, a child's aversive "mand" or directive, is responded to by the targeted adult's positive reinforcement of that mand. The parent has now been negatively reinforced by elimination of aversiveness, and the child has been positively reinforced for behaving aversively. Thus, for example, if a child whines for candy at the supermarket and the mother "gives in" to avoid a worse scene, the child becomes more likely to use some similar aversive method of social influence and the mother will be more likely to give in. Alternatively, if the mother requests that the child "put that glass back," and the child explodes and strikes out at her, whereupon the mother shrugs and stops nagging, the child's aggressive outburst has been negatively reinforced (it has turned off the mother's aversiveness), while the mother, too, has been negatively reinforced by halting the tantrum before it escalates.

Two other features of such coercive sequences are necessary to fully understand the coercion trap. One is the reciprocity of aversiveness, or attack and counterattack, which has been observed in both laboratory (O'Leary & Dengerink, 1973) and naturalistic settings (Patterson, Littman, & Bricker, 1967; Rausch, 1965). That is, when one perceives that another is using a coercive strategy on oneself, one is likely to respond with a counterattack. The other aspect of coercion sequences that contributes to their entrapping qualities is that coercive interchanges escalate in intensity. Thus, the spiraling sequence of attack and counterattack becomes more coercive, more painful, and more violent. Eventually, one person will give in and adopt the role of "victim" to terminate the overly painful exchange. Again, however, the "winner" is negatively reinforced for the intensity of the aversiveness and for the escalation. In the future, this winner will initiate new exchanges with a higher level of intensity and will employ rapid escalation as an increasingly sure-fire, albeit primitive, mechanism of conflict resolution. Comparative studies have shown that parents of normal children are effective about 75% of the time when they punish their child's behavior, whereas parents of aggressive children are faced with escalation of the child's aversiveness when they attempt to punish coerciveness (Kopfstein, 1972; Patterson, 1976; Snyder, 1977).

In sequential analyses of the coercion process, Patterson (1982) examined four types of stimulus function for a coercive behavior: antecedents of a coercive behavior associated with either increases or decreases in conditional probability (facilitating and inhibiting stimuli, respectively), and consequences of a coercive behavior that either increased or decreased the probability of occurrence (accelerating or decelerating stimuli, respectively). Such analyses were applied to coercive behaviors of members of various families to illustrate the disorder of a coercion trap. In one particularly deteriorated family condition observed in minute detail for a 48-hour period, sequential analysis of the contingencies of interaction between a mother and her child demonstrated the entrapment of an inept mother. Given that the child behaved hostilely, the mother could either respond or ignore the behavior; the probability of the child's continuing to be hostile was .45 with the first tactic, and .56 with the second (Patterson, 1982). This victimized mother was in a lose–lose situation wherein the child would continue to be coercive irrespective of the mother's disciplinary technique.

Once a child's coercive style has been permitted to become highly developed, it becomes ever more convenient to give in for short-term reprieve from pain and ever more costly (in the short run) to employ a long-term effective technique. In mother–child relationships characterized by this kind of coercion, the child is receiving very effective training in being aversive and coercive, and the mother is becoming ever more trapped in terms of her long-range goals of extinguishing, or at least rechanneling, such aggression.

The parents of socially aggressive children do in fact employ ineffective child management techniques. They positively reinforce aggression and fail to reward and often even punish nonaggressive, prosocial behavior (Johnson, Wahl, Martin, & Johansson, 1973; Snyder, 1977). Not only, then, are the child's coercive strategies successful and noncompliance accepted, but the socially aggressive child is also likely to be the recipient of an inordinate amount of aversive intrusions from other family members, particularly the mother. The mothers of aggressive children are very punishing, although their punishment is ineffective. Since the child is likely to receive punishment, or at least aversive, coercive messages from the mother no matter what he or she does, and since little reward is likely to make compliance worthwhile, the child might just as well be coercive. And as fully one-third of the child's coercive responses are merely counterattacks to the aversive intrusions of others, the child's continued use of coercion pays off substantially: about 40% of the time it serves as an effective counterattack to quell the aversive intrusion of another (Patterson, 1982). While coercion sequences occur early and briefly in homes without especially aggressive children, these sequences in problem-ridden mother–child dyads are four to five times more common and are of much longer duration.

This, then, is the frustrative environment enveloping the difficult aggression-prone youngster. This child, in attempting to master developmental tasks, is learning that the use of pain as an influence strategy is effective, or at least as effective as any other attempt to influence. Social learning research has described well the reciprocal use of aversiveness by caregiver and child as each attempts to influence and control the other. We continue next with a description of the contagion of this coercive process characteristic of parent–child interaction in families with aggressive children.

Contagion of the Coercive Process

When the competitive use of pain as an attempt to influence is sufficiently high, a kind of contagion occurs among the intensely interdependent members of a family. Several aspects of this contagion process are described here—the augmenting potential of other children in the family, the victimization of the mother, and the increasing negativity within all interrelated family dyads.

When there are other children in the family, there are also more victims on whom the coercive child may practice. One study of coercive interchange among children in a nursery school setting demonstrated that the victim of an intrusive attack by another child could effectively terminate that attack about two-thirds of the time. This success against coercion, however, led to an increased likelihood that the victim would then initiate his or her own attacks later (Patterson, Littman, & Bricker, 1967). Coercion as a powerful influence strategy can thus be learned by a passive child, by being first the victim, then the counterattacker, and finally the initiator. In short, nonaggressive siblings of a conduct-disordered child learn the effectiveness of coercion by observing the success of the target child, or by counterattacking effectively. If siblings are also highly aggressive, the target child will have many more opportunities to witness their successful coercions and more opportunities to practice retaliation. Recent work suggests that sibling aggression plays a much larger part in training socially aggressive children than was originally thought (Gully, Dengerink, Pepping, & Bergstrom, 1981; Patterson, 1979).

The mothers in families with aggressive children are key figures. A large number of studies now confirm that these mothers are especially likely to be entrapped in coercion sequences. They initiate many more coercive episodes and are more likely to be the receiver of coercive attacks than any other member of the family (Patterson, 1980). In families with problem children, the child's rapidly escalating coercion is disproportionally directed at the mother—50%, with the remainder of the child's attacks and counterattacks directed at the siblings but not the father.

Patterson's pilot scalogram analyses suggest that there may be a progression in the disruption of mothering skills that is tantamount to the victimization of the mother (Patterson, 1979, 1980). This progression, although not conclusively demonstrated at this point, appears consistent with the interaction data collected to date at the Oregon Social Learning Center. The progression begins with high rates of aversive stimuli from a child in conjunction with ineffective child management techniques—that is, failing to pair parental commands and scolding with effective punishment. This results in mother–child coercion sequences in which the mother escalates her aggression level at a slower rate than does the child. The problem child "challenges" the inept mother with rapid escalation of coercive responses until the mother and the rest of the family are engaged in mutually aversive exchanges, and negativism and coerciveness characterize much of the family interaction. This deteriorated state of affairs reflects the incipient breakdown of the family system.

While all members of the family are now behaving coercively toward one another, the next phase involves one person, the target child, emerging as a primary victimizer. This child delivers an inequitably greater number of aversive consequences to others than he or she receives. Finally, the mother clearly falls victim to the "monster child," so that the child punishes the mother more often than the mother punishes the child. The child now "runs the family," having toppled the mother, and maintains a disrupted family through high rates of coercion. This contagion of coercion, originally centered in the parent–child relationship but eventually suffusing the entire family system, thus involves what Patterson refers to as the "victimization of the mother." Indeed, Patterson's interpretation of the descriptive interaction data and the sequential patterns found within it has been instrumental in drawing attention to the hellishly entrapped mother of an aggressive child. This "unacknowledged victim" (Patterson, 1980) of an increasingly out-of-control child is thought to be a key figure in the eventual disruption of the entire family system.

Mothers have been more directly implicated in the fostering of aggressive children than have fathers. In most families, mothers have most responsibility for child care and more parent–child interaction than do fathers (Fagot, 1974). It is also true that most parent–child interaction research has involved only the female caretaker; much more is known, therefore, about her parenting than about that of her mate, if she has one. Still, the existing comparative studies attest to her much greater influence. The father's interaction with his child may be said to be less directly influential in the child's development than the mother's in normal families, and paternal influence decreases even more in disturbed families (Goodstein & Rowley, 1961; Liverant, 1959; Olweus, 1981; Patterson, 1976, 1980).

In families without especially aggressive children, the father may play with children more than the mother (Clark-Stewart, 1978; Lamb, 1976), while the mother is responsible for the majority of monitoring and moment-to-moment discipline. In homes with an aggressive child, this appears to be even more often the case, with fathers, when present, simply failing to attend as much to the child but still finding more occasion to play or interact nonaversively with the children (Patterson, 1982). In such disturbed families, the father–child interaction will be coercive as is mother–child interaction, but not to the same degree and not with the same frequency.

While fathers of aggressive children do not seem as directly implicated in their child's growing coerciveness, the mothers appear strikingly irritable and overwhelmed. They are more likely to engage in coercive episodes with their child, to initiate frustrating interchanges, to retaliate, and to continue an irritable exchange regardless of what the child does (Patterson, 1982). This irritability of the mother has been related not only to the child's antisocial behavior, but also to ineffective family problem-solving and the perception of these mothers that they experience an undue number of daily hassles (Forgatch & Wieder, 1981; Johnson & Lobitz, 1974). Additionally, mothers of aggressive children categorize the behavior of the children differently than do mothers of normal children. They classify more of the children's acts as deviant and are therefore more likely to punish those children (Johnson & Lobitz, 1974; Wahler & Afton, 1980). These attentional and attributional processes, wherein these mothers perceive intentional control attempts from others when none exist and do not selectively discriminate but rather view too many actions as aversive or irritating, may be at least in part a result of their psychological distress, particularly their depression, anger, and low self-esteem.

While mood states do not differentiate fathers of normal children from those with an aggressive child, the mothers of aggressive children describe themselves as much more seriously distressed than mothers of nonaggressive children (Rutter, 1966). Comparative studies have shown such mothers to be more acutely distressed than mothers without aggressive children on MMPI indices of disturbance (Anderson, 1969; Goodstein & Rowley, 1961; Patterson, 1976, 1980; Wohlking, Dunteman, & Bailey, 1969). As well as being depressed and angry, with low self-esteem, these victimized mothers may also report feeling confused, isolated, anxious, and incompetent at mastering the instrumental tasks before them.

The poor self-concept and level of depression in these mothers is incompatible with effective parenting (McClean, 1976) but could be viewed as either the cause or the consequence of having an out-of-control child. Patterson (1982) has theorized that while becoming caught in coercion traps is a simple function of inadequate parenting and high rates of child aversiveness, sustained immersion in the coercive process results in feelings of depression and helplessness. As the mother's depression increases, she makes increasingly negative attributions about both herself and others, her irritability and the overall coerciveness within the family increase, and the balance of pleasant to unpleasant events within the home shifts in the negative direction, thus furthering the mother's depression and sense of helplessness and hopelessness. Heatherington, Cox, and Cox (1980) have produced cross-lag correlations to suggest that earlier child aggression results in later maternal depression in divorcing families. It also seems reasonable that a coercive, out-of-control child is the consequence of a depressed, distracted, nonperceptive parent and that reciprocal influence processes are in operation—as they usually are in a long-term intimate family relationship.

The increasingly out-of-control child, the emotional distress of the mother, and the contagion of coercion processes occur concomitantly with a growing negativism. The aversive and defensive characteristics of exchange between the mother and the identified aggressive child appear to be found increasingly in the relationships between each of these family members and others in the family. Patterson (1980) has described the contagion of coerciveness from its intense concentration within the mother–child dyad until negativism suffuses the whole family system. Wahler (Wahler, 1980; Wahler & Afton, 1980; Wahler, Leske, & Rogers, 1979) has also viewed this negativism as a byproduct of coercion traps and has referred to it as "social insularity," or a narrowing of the family interaction style. The mutual hostility processes, the escalating retaliatory sequences, and the dominance of a coercive mode of engagement are held to erode the positive reinforcement value of each member for every other member. As family members grow more irritable and punishing toward one another, their ability to attract one another—to implement reward as an influence strategy—diminishes, and the family interaction becomes increasingly more hostile and negative. The more the coercive mode of conflict management spreads, the more the escalating hostility and irritability lead to a mounting negativism—a negative "set" or attitude toward other family members. Increasingly, family members come to expect attack, respond defensively or in a retaliatory fashion, and feel entrapped in a system of irritable and irritating individuals. This quality of negativism, defensiveness, and restricted communication range is a telling symptom of a dysfunctional family system, a theme to which we will return later.

In summary, the recent research on *in vivo* interaction between a parent and an aggressive child has highlighted the coercion trap, in which both parent and child participate in mutually frustrating each other. Rather than establishing an effectively cooperative relationship in which the child may profitably develop prosocial, nonaggressive means of social influence under the parent's guidance, these parent–child dyads become entrapped in a coercion process that reduces their attractiveness to one another. Coercion is a primitive but effective influence strategy in the short run, but in the long run it results in predictably and mutually held negative attitudes. As contagion of the coercive process gains momentum, effective socialization of young children becomes increasingly less probable and aggression becomes increasingly more rewarding, while nonaggression and compliance become increasingly less fruitful. Research on this process has pointed to the key role of the primary caretaker, the mother, and the behavioral, affective, and cognitive deterioration she experiences. That is, her ineffective parenting becomes even less effective in her orientation toward escape from coercive entrapment, so that she is more likely to reward undesirable behavior and less likely to behave in a way that fosters nonaggressive alternatives. She becomes more depressed and irritable, feeling trapped and out of control. She also shows poor ability to discriminate the desirability of her child's behaviors and those of others who impinge upon her, and her attitude and perceptual bias become increasingly more negative. In an extreme stage of progression, then, a coercive child may be seen as coming from a dysfunctioning family system.

The discussion will turn next to the marital relationship and the ways in which it may play a role as both cause and effect in the case of childhood aggression.

THE MARITAL RELATIONSHIP

An important element in the family with an aggressive child is the unsatisfactory and conflicted marital relationship. Numerous studies now exist suggesting that when a family has an especially aggressive child, both spouses (in two-parent households) tend to report more dissatisfaction with their marriage. The many studies establishing the robust relationship between marital problems and child problems are reviewed elsewhere (Margolin, 1981). Couples with an aggressive child can be seen to engage in unusually high levels of coercive exchange themselves (Steinmetz, 1979), to report feeling depressed, angry, and low in self-esteem (Patterson, 1980; Weiss & Birchler, 1978), and to be "blaming the other" considerably. The more dissatisfied the couple is with the marriage, or with one another, the more aggressive and aversive they report the child to be (Oltmanns, Broderick, & O'Leary, 1977). Although childhood disorders and marital disruptions are commonly understood to coexist within families, the explanations for this vary widely. Furthermore, all of the theoretical propositions to date are grossly underresearched and in need of more empirical validation. Social learning theory proposes that parental modeling of coercion and poor problem solving encourages a child to act similarly. Sociologically rooted concepts of roles and role strain suggest that the pivotal position of the mother-wife is an unduly vulnerable one, so that distress in either the spousal or parent–child relationship may easily spread through mother-wife role strain to the other relationship. Family systems theories provide the constructs of scapegoating, triangulation, and enmeshment to explain the way in which the aggressive symptoms of the child serve to maintain the troubled marriage. Each of these propositions will now be discussed in turn.

Modeling

It is within the family that children receive their most salient instructions for interpersonal relating and problem solving. If a child observes mother and father engaging in hostile, defensive, or coercive interactions, social learning theory would suggest that the child will be likely to learn to engage in those forms of interaction as well.

Research on interaction characteristics distinguishing satisfactory and unsatisfactory marital relationships has repeatedly underscored the defensiveness, rigidity, and negativeness of dysfunctional relationships in contrast to the greater supportiveness, spontaneity, and positiveness of exchange in good relationships (Alexander, 1973; Birchler & Webb, 1977; Winter & Ferreira, 1969). Distressed couples are distinguished by their affect, which is negative and lacking in warmth, by their attribution of malevolence and their presumption of exploitive and competitive intent on the part of the other, and by behavior that is much more frequently defensive, aversive, and coercive than supportive and rewarding (Alexander, 1973; Birchler, 1972; Rausch, 1965). Further, there is some evidence that such couples reciprocate aggression more than they reciprocate affection or support.

Sequential analyses of marital interactions in naturalistic and game situations suggest that, as might be expected, couples high in marital satisfaction are much better problem solvers than those reporting low marital satisfaction. Gottman et al. (Gottman, 1979; Gottman, Markman, & Notarius, 1977), in their comparative interaction studies, found that effective problem-solving couples begin with validations of the other, avoid negative exchanges, and are likely to end the discussion in a noncoercive contracting sequence. Epstein and Santa-Barbara (1975) reported that in a mixed-motive game situation, effective couples began with mutual exploitation as prompted by the nature of the game but moved quickly through discussion to a cooperative framework for the maximizing of joint profits, expressed much appeasement regarding the consensually perceived cooperative context, and then finally resolved the problem through maximization of joint profit. Children exposed to such effective parental conflict resolution procedures as modeled by these experimental couples are presumably witnessing the use of supportive, inductive, and cooperative techniques of conjoint problem solving.

Distressed couples, in contrast, were likely to move quickly to a mutually destructive, competitive stance and express high levels of exploitive and defensive intentions. Each member emphasized defensive self-enhancement or self-validation more than supportive listening and presumed negative and exploitive intentions on the part of the other (Epstein & Santa-Barbara, 1975). In naturalistic exchanges, the dysfunctional married pair began not with mutual validation but with cross-complaining loops, moving next to negative exchange loops. They were then unlikely to enter into a contract loop at the end of the discussion (Gottman et al., 1977). Such spousal exchanges are likely to model for observing children the competitive, mutually debilitating coercion process with its key features of escalating hostility and defensive retaliation.

Researchers on family violence provide further evidence for the view that conflict-resolution attempts such as coercion, aggression, and violence may "run in families," presumably because of modeling. Thus, those who use violence in managing conflict with their child or spouse are likely to report having been abused as children or having observed the use of violence between their parents (Gelles, 1972; Gelles & Straus, 1974). Steinmetz (1977) has reported a correlation of physical aggression in spousal versus parent–child pairs of about .50. Straus (1978) reported that in families in which spouses are known to use violence in their problem solving with one another, there are higher rates of violence directed at their children—29% higher than in families in which there is no spouse–spouse violence employed. Thus, the use of physical aggression in parenting becomes much more likely when physical aggression is used as a conflict-management technique within the marriage.

It appears that family conflict management may be conceptualized as a continuum, with highly aggressive and ineffective conflict-management families on one end and nonviolent, effective problem-solving families on the other.

Recent family interaction studies provide support for this heuristic proposal. Reid, Taplin, and Lorber (1981), for example, compared interactive behaviors in family triads in which there was child abuse, an aggressive child but not known child abuse, or a nonaggressive child. They found mother–child aggressiveness and spouse–spouse aggressiveness to be arrayed along this continuum. Mothers, rather than fathers, were again found to be especially involved in parent–child coerciveness, with child abuse dyads at one end and normal child discipline dyads at the other end of the continuum. Similarly, Reid *et al.* reported that the spouses in families with an aggressive child directed more aggression at one another than did spouses in families with a normal child, with spouses in the child-abusing families even more aggressive and coercive with one another. They speculated from their findings that when parent–child and spouse–spouse conflict operate together at high rates in a family, child abuse becomes highly probable. Burgess and Conger (1978) compared interaction in families in which there was child abuse, child neglect, and a normal child. These families fell along a continuum with the abnormal families more silent, more negative, and less active than the normal-child families, whereas the child-neglect families were even more extreme than the child-abuse families. Also, Steinmetz (1977, 1979), in studying family use of violent and nonviolent conflict management, reported that methods used to solve marital conflicts appeared to be similar to methods used within the family for child discipline, as well as to methods used by that child for resolving conflict with siblings or extrafamilial peers.

The research available on family violence supports earlier interaction research findings that methods of influence and conflict resolution run in families. When physical aggression or escalating coercion is used within the spousal dyad, it is likely to be found in the parent–child dyad as well. Although there is no direct evidence to date that poor problem solving between husband and wife provides a model for the observing child to imitate, the descriptive data are not inconsistent with a modeling interpretation. When coercion and escalating hostility characterize exchanges between parents, they may be implicitly sanctioned as a family conflict-resolution mode. A young coercive child may in fact learn through observation the topographic changes in coerciveness required in maturity, rather than that effective conflict resolution is characterized by nonviolent cooperation and mutual appeasement.

Role Strain of the Mother-Wife

According to sociological role theory, when an individual has trouble meeting role expectations, or when more than one role is held by that individual and the demands of these roles are in conflict, that individual will experience stress, or role strain. The woman who wears the hats of both mother and wife and who feels inadequate in either of the relationships with child or husband will therefore experience role strain. The inadequate parenting skills and poor self-evaluations of mothers with aggressive children have already been described. These victimized mothers are exemplars of a role-strained person. If, in addition, such a woman perceives herself as being an inadequate wife, or if she is torn by competing demands from her offspring and her husband, then the stress would be even greater, putting her at yet greater risk for emotional distress, behavioral disorganization, and generally declining levels of performance. The mothers of aggressive children report difficulties with their marriages as well as with their children, and the attendant psychological stress has previously been noted. The difficulties posed by an aggressive child are born more by the wife, and she more than her husband appears to be the main link between a problem-laden marital relationship and a problem child. Indeed, the role of the female caretaker may be the single most important role in establishing the level of overall functioning in the family, certainly in families in which the children are young and demanding of much maternal time, energy, and attention.

Given a demanding and difficult child and the attendant strain on the mother, the husband may serve as an important support system for her. He may actively share the burden of monitoring, training, and disciplining the child, as in the symmetrical or equal parenting advocated by some (Baumrind, 1979; Chodorow, 1978). He may provide sympathetic validation and encouragement to his wife as she attempts to control and direct the child. He may back up her efforts at discipline and control, aligning collaboratively with her to present a united front on major parent–child confrontations or serving as a crisis manager. Or he may provide positive and restorative experiences for her quite apart from child-care considerations. If, however, a husband does not provide adequate support for a strained wife, or if he provides aversive experiences that further stress her, her role strain and attendant dysfunction may result in increasingly inadequate relationships within the family as she becomes increasingly irritable, depressed, and negative in attitude.

Too much unrelieved stress for the mother has been viewed as one of the major causes of the noncompliant, aggressive, and out-of-control behavior of children affected by marital separation or divorce (Heatherington, 1972; Heatherington, Cox, & Cox, 1978, 1979, 1980; Wallerstein & Kelly, 1980). The greater risk of elevated childhood aggression in broken homes appears to be due not to the father's absence *per se,* but rather to the psychological distress of the single parent and the poor quality of the parent–child relationship (Barry, 1979; Rickard, Forehand, Atkeson, & Lopez, 1982). Single mothers with an adequate level of well-being, in comparison to unhappily married mothers, have been found to provide more positive attention to their children (Rickard *et al.,* 1982) and to have a lower probability of aggressiveness in their children (Horne, 1980). If a psychologically overwhelmed mother attempts to reduce her role strain by exiting from her stressful marriage, her depression and negativism are likely to result in even more disrupted and ineffective parenting, so that her resultant lack of a support system and vulnerable condition may prevent her from regaining control of her child's aggression.

Wahler and his colleagues (Wahler, 1980; Wahler & Afton, 1980; Wahler & Fox, 1980; Wahler, Leske & Rogers, 1979) has described a subset of mothers referred to child guidance clinics for an overly aggressive child. These "insular mothers" are likely to be found in multi-problem, crisis-ridden, low-education, and poverty-stressed families. The distinguishing feature of this kind of mother, however, is that she has little community contact, and whatever contact she does have she describes as coercive. On days when she interacts with relatives and community agency helpers, this mother has been found to be more coercive and coercion-bound with her aggressive child. On days when she interacts with friends, she is less coercive and coerced by her child. Her few friends are people with whom she interacts but perceives no apparent attempts at control in their exchanges. The contacts with her relatives and agency personnel, on the other hand, are unsolicited, and she perceives the community as "manding," threatening, unfriendly, and instrusive. Wahler has analyzed these aversive contacts as mands from the viewpoint of the mother. The mother complies with them, which is reinforcing to both parties, but once the agency people stop calling on her, she is unlikely to continue taking their suggestions or advice. These insular mothers are disturbed in behavior, affect, and perceptual or attributional systems—similar to the victimized mothers described by Patterson's group at the Oregon Social Learning Center, only more so. In turn, these mothers have much in common with the battered woman described by Walker (1981) in her feminist perspective on domestic violence. This woman has low self-esteem, believes all myths about battering relationships, believes no one will be able to help her resolve her predicament except herself, is a traditionalist in the home, strongly believes in family unity and the prescribed sex role stereotype, and accept responsibility for the batterer's actions. There is not enough carefully collected data on the degree to which the distressed mother of an aggressive child is in turn the recipient of spouse abuse, but it does appear to be the case that these mothers are experiencing debilitating stress to varying degrees, and this stress might be termed role strain.

For role strain without adequate external supports, two other major remedies exist. One is that expectations of a stressful role can be made more modest so that they are easier to meet. If a mother feels she is not fulfilling her child-management role, she can readjust her expectations by concluding that her child is not trainable, but merely a hopelessly coercive bully whom she must defend herself against; this self-justifying attribution is not without its costs, however. Similarly, the mother can point to other difficulties such as uncontrollable peer influences and (often very real) external crises such as poverty impinging upon the family. An alternative to reducing the mother's role expectations is withdrawal from one of two competing roles—that is, giving up either the mother role or the wife role. Neither of these choices is easy, however, and such proactive strategy is likely to be blocked by feelings of resentment, guilt, anger, entrapment, and helplessness.

Role-strain theory acknowledges the bidirectionality of influence between marital and child problems because of the queenpin role of the wife and mother. Marital conflict and disagreement can distress her and drain her of the energy and motivation necessary to effectively monitor and discipline a difficult child. Conversely, the exhaustion, depression, and anger associated with having an aggressive child may distress the mother sufficiently that she is blaming, aversive, and irritable with her husband, behavior which eventually contributes to marriage problems.

Processes of Scapegoating, Triangulation, and Enmeshment

Theories of family systems have focused primarily on the family as a whole but have also emphasized the way in which a difficult child and a disturbed marriage may be mutually sustaining. The mechanisms of scapegoating, triangulation, and enmeshment are usually construed to argue more for the way in which a symptomatic child "acts out" the pathology of the parents' spousal relationship, although they too are amenable to bidirectional causality.

A couple facing unresolved marital conflict or a growing rift in the relationship may divert their attentions and anxieties from this threatening problem by scapegoating one of their children. Parents may thus unite to protect a fragile child, focusing such undue attention upon that fragility that the weakness is reinforced and the development of strengths discouraged or denied. Similarly, they may present a united front to an initially irritable or irritating child, blaming and attacking this child until he or she has developed full-blown aggressive symptoms. The most direct illustration of scapegoating has been found in families with psychosomatic children. Minuchin's experiments (Minuchin, Rosman, & Baker, 1978) demonstrated that the child's involvement in the marital conflict alleviated the parents' stress although it was symptom-maintaining for the child. Direct evidence that aggressive children might also be scapegoats for marital distress was not provided by Minuchin et al. (1978), but indirect support is provided by a number of researchers. Patterson (1982), for example, has observed that although all the children in clinic-referred families are inordinately aversive and coercive, parents seem to single out one child for special treatment which is not given to the other children. Indeed, in a number of his studies it has been shown that the target child is sometimes *less* aversive and coercive than his or her siblings. Additional, albeit indirect, evidence of scapegoating lies in the repeated finding that parents' description of a child's aggression level correlates less well with overt child behaviors than with the parents' psychological or mood states (Griest, Forehand, Wells, & McMahon, 1980; Griest, Wells, & Forehand, 1979). Family systems theory would posit that this child's aversiveness was detouring parental anxieties about their own conflictual relationship and thus permitting them to maintain a position of coorientation.

Processes of triangulation and enmeshment are also invoked to explain the "unholy triangle" pattern of dysfunctional families (Haley, 1978). Triangulation occurs when one spouse withdraws and the other spouse forms a tight and enmeshed relationship with one of the children, often an opposite-sex child, as in "Daddy's girl" or a mutually dependent relationship between a permissive mother and her increasingly demanding young son. The enmeshment of a mother and an aggression-prone child in coercive involvement has been described in an earlier section. The coexistence of a socially aggressive child and a conflicted marriage may be more likely when the child is a boy (Rutter, 1966, 1971). According to the propositions of triangulation and enmeshment, the overinvolvement of the mother with the attacking and attacked child is necessary to maintain the fragile balance in the marriage; but this parent–child enmeshment may in turn, through escalating coercion, develop into greater problems. Although little direct evidence exists for this explanation for the development of socially aggressive children, it is congruent with the picture of the overinvolved mother, the relatively uninvolved father, and the common concurrence of an aggressive child with marital disturbance. Systems theory maintains that this *family structure,* although bound for increased turbulence as coercion and aggression escalate, serves to maintain the marriage.

In summary, disturbance in the spousal relationship and aggressiveness in a child commonly occur together. A conduct-disordered child comes from a coercion-riddled family, and the marriage, too, in this family is often a negative and conflicted one. Explanations for the relationship between marriage dynamics and the emergence of childhood aggression vary. The inadequate problem-solving efforts of the spouses may model inadequate problem-solving for the child, teaching the child in effect that this is a normative, or at least most effective, method for resolving conflict. Alternatively, the role strain of the mother, who is "spread too thin" and functions as the familial "storm center," may make her ineffective in maintaining both the parental and spousal roles adequately. This in turn may result in her increased disturbance and deterioration, so that stresses from either relationship are in effect transmitted through her inept management to the other relationship. At the same time, her declining performance and stresses from outside the family may disable her further, thereby precipitating further family breakdown. Or, from yet another perspective, the child's aggressiveness may serve systems-maintaining functions, operating to hold a marriage together. In this case, the child's aggression "excuses" the mother and father from marital engagement, which is too threatening, while still imposing an obstacle to terminating the marriage, which is also too threatening. When this is the case, the child may well become a scapegoat with aggressive responses rewarded and prosocial responses disregarded, and the attendant self-fulfilling prophecy that the aggressive symptomatology is increasing is permitted to develop further.

Modeling explanations typically assume that parental behaviors "cause" child behaviors; systems explanations typically assume that marital problems cause child problems; and role-strain theory suggests that reciprocal causality is most probable. Yet all explanations might begin by granting that family life operates as a system of reciprocal influences, with change in one unit or subsystem affecting all other units and subsystems in the family. Thus, parents may adopt a primitive coerciveness with one another which is first evidenced in parent–child interchanges with the target child, or a troublesome child may not only maintain marital discord but cause it.

We have progressed in this discussion from an initial examination of how aggression is manifested in young children and how parenting variables are thought to determine socialization for aggression. We then proceeded to a description of the ongoing mutually maintained coercion trap characteristic of parent–child interactions and how coercive processes may spread to characterize the entire family. We have further examined the differential roles of the two parents and the ways in which a problematic relationship between spouses may be reciprocally related to the shaping of aggressive children. Because it is a presumption here that aggressive children come from dysfunctional families, we turn now to an examination of the family as a whole, with the understanding that aggression as a social behavior must be understood in its full social context.

FAMILY ORGANIZATION

Childhood aggression, if extreme or prolonged, is argued to be a correlate of a dysfunctional family system. In normal development, the youngster poses a considerable strain upon the family, particularly upon the caregivers, until increasing social competence and concomitantly diminishing dependence permit more freedom, flexibility, and differentiation within the family. When acquisition of social competence is slow, prolonged strain upon family members results. If contagion of coercion processes is allowed to occur, stress, conflict, and poor family problem solving prevent adequate family functioning.

Interactional research comparing dysfunctional and functional family systems reveals the poor quality of communication in families in which one or more members are deviant. Dysfunctional families in interaction are more silent, talk less frequently and with less equality, have fewer positive interruptions and more negative and defensive exchanges, and are generally less active than normal families (Alexander, Barton, Schiavo, & Parson, 1976; Mischler & Waxler, 1968; Winter & Ferreira, 1969). The insularity, or narrowed communication range employed by family members with one another, has been repeatedly observed.

In the previous section, the common concurrence of child aggressiveness and marital problems was discussed. Methodologically sound research on interactions between spouses and between both parents and children in the same situation are relatively rare. Snyder (1977), however, conducted a reinforcement-contingencies analysis of families with both a behavior problem child and parents low on marital satisfaction in contrast to families without such problems. This study found that problem families were deviant across all members and all subunits. Problem-family members behaved more negatively to all other family members and provided each other with no systematic contingencies for good behavior. In normal families, each person's pleasing behaviors were generally rewarded and displeasing behaviors punished by the recipient. In problem families the probability of receiving a positive, negative, or neutral consequence was virtually independent of the preceding behavior. Further, punishment accelerated displeasing behavior in all problem-family dyads, whereas it suppressed displeasing behavior in normal family dyads. Snyder concluded that the lack of contingencies resulted, over time, in problem families' having reduced responsiveness to social reinforcers. Lack of systematic and meaningful consequation, general negativism of interactive behavior, and defensive reciprocity or retaliation are thus characteristics of the entire family and not merely of selected dyads in problem families. All family members are contributing to the development and maintenance of one another's deviant behavior.

In this section, discussion will therefore focus on the family system as a whole, on the premise that childhood aggression can be most meaningfully understood and treated within this framework. The family system is commonly held to be a living system with morphostatic qualities that permit it to maintain its integrity as a long-term group and yet to change to more adaptive levels of functioning as necessitated by stresses from both within and outside the system. To carry out its functions, the family must stay together, maintaining sufficient order and structure to sustain relatively consistent group culture, yet permitting individuals within it to develop. The family, viewed over the family life span, must be a dynamic system which changes as individuals grow older and members join or leave the group, and which adapts to circumstances impinging upon the system from without. The following discussion will examine the dysfunctional families in which aggressive children are thought to be imbedded. Consistent with this level of analysis, dysfunction will be discussed along two primary dimensions of family functioning, cohesion and adaptability (Olson, Sprenkle, & Russell, 1979a).

Family Cohesion

Family cohesion refers to the emotional bonding that family members have with one another and the degree of individual autonomy they experience (Olson, Sprenkle, & Russell, 1979a). The regulation of independence–connectedness is an important characteristic of family life. Families vary within and across cultures in how interdependent their members are, but families also vary in this dimension across the family life span. In the family with infants or young children, the family cohesion is high by necessity; the offspring are highly dependent on the caretaker(s), and the tasks of socializing them and of spousal concordance in this process require a high level of interdependence. As children mature, however, they are typically granted more autonomy, freedom, and status equality as they demonstrate requisite levels of social competence. If either extreme of the cohesion dimension—enmeshment or disengagement—becomes a characteristic mode of family functioning, the family system is likely to be dysfunctional. Crises from developmental changes within the family are likely to result in a "flip-flop" between extreme engagement and disengagement as an ineffective means of restoring a viable equilibrium.

Currently there are no adequate longitudinal studies of family systems in which an aggression-prone child is imbedded. The data that do exist suggest, however, that families with antisocial children and adolescents may indeed evidence difficulties with the regulation of cohesion. Too much permissiveness— that is, granting of too much independence and autonomy to a child who is still socially incompetent—may be followed by parental "crackdowns" as socializers attempt to control increasingly deviant and resistant behaviors (Burgess & Conger, 1978). Patterson (1982) has reported on a certain kind of nonaggressive but antisocial child who steals and commits other kinds of crimes against property. The parents of these "pure stealers" are distant and disengaged, refusing to acknowledge the antisocial actions of their wandering and unsupervised children. Patterson has not yet been able to collect adequately long-term follow-up data on these disengaged families with the young stealers, but he has speculated that they are at high risk for later adolescent and adult delinquency.

The social aggressors are the coercive, aggressive children on whom this chapter is centered. The reciprocal influence between their disordered conduct and the disorganization of the family has been characterized in terms of enmeshed coercive processes. This is still only speculation until long-term developmental research is forthcoming on these families, but it is conceivable that these extreme and prolonged aversive and enmeshed exchanges will become sufficiently painful to participants that they will flee from one another when they can, finding time apart preferable to mutual involvement and engagement (Birchler, Weiss, & Vincent, 1975; Gottman *et al.,* 1977; Rosenblatt, Titus, & Cunningham, 1979). The uncorrected young social aggressor will spend increasing amounts of time away from home, and spouses will withdraw from one another or from the children (Burgess & Conger, 1978). Family violence research documents oscillation between nonengagement and violent overengagement (e.g., Burgess & Conger, 1978). When mutual engagement is coercive and unrewarding and problem solving is ineffective, escape from the situation is desirable. Out of sight is out of mind—but only until engagement is once again necessitated. Prolonged disengagement is not an effective way of solving problems either, so when problem solving is again attempted, difficulty in achieving an equilibrium of separation and connection occurs.

Several studies of families with delinquent children illustrate the problems of regulating cohesion typical of families with antisocial children. Minuchin's studies of families of delinquents (Minuchin, 1974; Minuchin, Montalvo, Guerney, Rosman, & Schumer, 1967) described the disengagement of the father and the enmeshment of the mother and the conduct-disordered child as a modal pattern, along with either extremely enmeshed or disengaged patterns, and sometimes with reversal from unrelatedness to entrapped coercive sequences. When engaged, members of dysfunctional families are unable to come to closure—that is, to complete effective problem-solving sequences. When disengaged, they were described as having no feeling of belonging, not knowing how to request help when it was needed, operating in isolated orbits, and often being under the influence of deviant peer pressures.

Reiss (1971), comparing these families with others having either a schizophrenic or a normal adolescent, characterized the families with one or more delinquent children as interpersonal-distance sensitive. Each member had his or her own environment in the extrafamilial world, rather than a shared support group of similar families to support and validate family-wide values and beliefs. Each of the family members was indifferent to how the others in the family viewed him or her and all were characterized by high levels of defensiveness, regarding the acceptance of opinion or advice from others as a sign of weakness and fiercely defending their own ideas. Delinquent families have also been described by other researchers as fiercely defending their own individual autonomy and having very limited identification with the family group (Glueck & Glueck, 1950). With such extreme and erratic disengagement, there is not much base for cooperative family problem-solving.

Another aspect of the cohesion dimension of family functioning is boundary regulation, both around individuals, between family subsystems, and around the family. These boundaries, ideally, are semipermeable, permitting help and supportive information into the system or subsystem but keeping deviant and unwanted intrusive elements out. The insular mother described earlier, the multiproblem crisis-prone families often reported in the family violence literature, and the dysfunctioning families referred to helping agencies but quickly dropping out of treatment are all illustrative of ineffective boundary regulation. Dysfunction in this area often results in the intrusion of agency personnel into the home, followed by the brief uniting of family members to close out the intruder. This collusion of family members is often understood as a collaborative family effort to prevent change in family functioning which threatens wholly to debilitate the tenuous system equilibrium.

Family Adaptability

The other dimension of family functioning is the adaptability of the system, the ability of the group to change its power structure, role relationships, and relationship rules in order to function optimally in response to situational and developmental stresses. Issues of control and discipline, rules about rights and responsibilities, and modes of social influence are subsumed under this dimension (Olson *et al.*, 1979a).

Earlier, in exploring structural aspects of relationships, I have argued that a viable relationship between two persons requires mutuality of relationship definition, or agreement between both parties on (1) the nature of resources exchanged, (2) the form of justice being employed in distributing these resources fairly, and (3) the nature and degree of interdependence between the two parties (Morton & Douglas, 1982). If there is disagreement about any of these aspects of the relationship, there is relationship crisis (Morton & Douglas, 1982; Morton, Alexander, & Altman, 1976), and conflict will ensue until a new agreement can be arrived at or the relationship terminated. In family power terms, a power struggle may occur if there is dispute over bases of power, distribution of power, or the interdependence of family members—that is, the stake each member has in sacrificing individual profit for maximizing shared profits. Adaptability of a family system thus rests on the ability of family members to reach agreement on their mutual regulation, both the structure and the process of mutual interpersonal influence and control.

Conflicts of interest, however, are inherent in the intensely related social group called the family. Because members have different desires and the family has only a finite number of resources, a competitive base for family living must be assumed. According to conflict theory, conflict most productively leads to confrontation, which, when concluded, leads to change. It appears that some relationships and some families as a whole, however, become stuck in conflict, never proceeding to effective confrontation and change. Such families accomplish merely *regulation* of conflict, as in simmering disputes and power struggles, rather than conflict *resolution,* which requires processes such as discussion, bargaining, negotiation, compromise, and sometimes sacrifice.

Klein and Hill (1979) have synthesized the theory and research on determinants of family problem-solving effectiveness, or the degree to which family problems are solved to the mutual satisfaction of family members. In their analysis, family interaction processes are of central importance. When family members are withdrawn, unsupportive, restricted in their communication range, and unwilling or unable to employ elaborate language codes, they will be relatively ineffective in resolving their disputes and coorienting to a common task. When family members do not agree on the legitimacy of parental power and authority, there will be higher levels of retaliatory defensiveness rather than mutual support. And when the family cannot employ an orderly, rational approach to discussion of problems, as in the random-type families reported by Kantor and Lehr (1975), family problem-solving effectiveness is hindered. The acute dysfunctioning of a deteriorated aggression-employing family is associated with all of these deficits.

Whereas sociologists have examined problem solving at the family group level, psychologists have approached it at an individual skill level. At this level, good problem solving is seen as a set of steps: (1) definition of the problem; (2) formulation—that is, clearly operationalizing all relevant aspects of the problematic situation; (3) brainstorming, or the generation of the various alternatives available; (4) estimation of rewards and costs for each alternative's outcome; (5) implementation of the selected solution; and (6) verification—that is, a cost–reward reappraisal of the solution's effectiveness compared to other, more promising solutions (D'Zurilla & Goldfried, 1971). Problem-solving effectiveness is positively associated with social competence and psychological adjustment in a wide range of populations. Further, problem-solving skills can be taught, resulting in improved social competence and psychological adjustment (D'Zurilla & Goldfried, 1971; Heppner, 1978). Shure and Spivak (1978) have shown that interpersonal cognitive problem-solving skills can be taught to children from preschool age to adolscence, again resulting in improved social adjustment. Aggressive children are retarded in their problem-solving skills, and families who interact coercively are mutually entrapping in their inabilities to use more effective problem-solving strategies.

In highly coercion-bound families, indeed, there may be such cognitive distortion by individual members and such accusing, defense-producing communication styles that the first step of agreeing on the definition of the problem cannot be accomplished. Problem perception is a critical initial step in the problem-solving process. But formulating a problematic interpersonal situation in the most solvable way requires that one person refrain from stereotyping the other and instead attempt to interpret the thoughts, feelings, and motivation of the other in that specific situation (Kieren & Tallman, 1972; Klein & Hill, 1979). In distressed couples and families, members tend to make global and nonspecific attributions about each other. They tend to see each other as intentionally injurious or self-aggrandizing and to ignore the specifics of the problematic situation from the other's point of view. Their cognitions, in short, are egocentric. Their behavior, powerful in eliciting retaliatory actions, is paradoxically motivated by feelings of powerlessness (Tedeschi, Gaes & Rivera, 1977; Tedeschi, Smith, & Brown, 1974).

Coercion-ridden families with aggressive children are likely to be low in problem-solving effectiveness. They have failed to make effective adaptation to a difficult child, to an overly stressed and inadequate caretaker, or to a disturbed marital relationship. In turn, such families are at high risk for further family deterioration if they are unable to change the rules for governing power, legitimacy, justice, and interdependence. Faced with a problem, such families will avoid it. If it is unavoidable, the family's ineffective problem-solving attempts will end in escalating coercive processes, quite possibly resulting in an explosion of intense family violence. The cycle of interactions in coercion-ridden families is thus from predictably negative narrow-range interactive patterns to episodes of runaway escalation, chaotic control attempts, and destructive power struggles.

In the language of social exchange theory, the account of accumulated rewards and costs is going bankrupt. Instead of operating on a long-term reciprocity basis, permitting a cool-headed, objective assessment of the entrapment, family members are increasingly under response-control contingencies (Melges & Harris, 1970; Tedeschi et al., 1977). That is, they are operating with a primitive tit-for-tat reciprocity model, as evidenced by their hostile exchanges. Each member is caught up in the immediate moment, retaliating to specific environmental contingencies, forgetting, or never comprehending, the long-term payoff of peaceful settlement through arriving at a common goal. Family members caught up in a coercive process are not able to see the relationship between the immediate present and the future. They are not able to see their individual roles in the overall process. Indeed, given the need to defend and justify themselves, each member punctuates the sequence of coercive exchange in a way to validate himself or herself and invalidate the others. Each member feels unfairly attacked by other family members and retaliates as defensively as possible. Such a family can manage conflict but cannot resolve it.

The molar analysis of the entire family system suggests that families with aggressive children may be at high risk for further problems because they have difficulty in regulating cohesion and responding adaptively to crises. These family system constructs, in combination with the developmental trajectory of progressive family dysfunction, provide a useful means of understanding the interface of childhood aggression and family disturbance.

The goal of this section has been to promote the view that childhood aggression can be profitably understood in the context of family interaction dynamics. By focusing on the family as a system with its own developmental course, the variable "meanings" of childhood aggression have been highlighted. The case of an aggressive child may reflect only a lack of parenting skills in combination with a particularly difficult child. Or it can signify a problem-prone parent, spousal relationship, or entire family system. Problems may exist concurrently in behavioral, cognitive, and affective domains, and, again, may involve not just the child, but other relationships as well. A view of family conflict, power, and problem solution based on exchange theory furthers understanding of how bargains may be struck but may also need renegotiation, as individual and relational developmental processes create stresses leading to new confrontations and new bargains. Families are not merely systems and exchange economies; they are also groups of thinking, feeling people. This discussion, however, has largely neglected personality-based descriptions of aggressive children and their family members, attempting instead to describe how interpersonal influence modes, attributional styles, and affective mood states interact with family interaction dynamics.

Reciprocal influences and equilibrium-maintaining dynamics have been presumed throughout the foregoing discussion. Given the multilevel interdependence of family members with one another, absolute statements of linear causality concerning childhood aggression and family dynamics seem premature at this point. Future work examining the theoretically presumed causes, consequences, and correlates of childhood aggression will, one hopes, consider the entire family constellation and provide descriptive data permitting examination of circular causal processes and patterns. In addition, developmental analyses are necessary for furthering our understanding of the different meanings and functions of childhood aggression across the life-span of the family. Family interaction dynamics are different when the aggressive child is the first-born of a young couple than when he or she is the last in a line of already delinquent offspring. The mounting evidence that violence runs in families suggests the importance of long-term longitudinal studies examining intergenerational patterns of transfer— again, not just at the level of individual aggression but in terms of the family processes that emerge and attenuate over time. Finally, attention to problem-solving processes, including patterns of coercion and effective communication modes, appears promising. The painful conclusion concerning family deterioration is this: the less effectively a family solves problems, the more incapacitating and numerous the problems it will have to face. Greater knowledge of the most critical ingredients of problem solving at the family level, coupled with an improved technology for improving the problem solving of its members, is necessary.

We turn next to a discussion of treatment for the entire family.

TREATING CHILDHOOD AGGRESSION THROUGH FAMILY THERAPY: REPROGRAMMING THE FAMILY SYSTEM

Given the embeddedness of aggressive children in family systems, it is not surprising that treatment within the family is widely held to be the treatment of choice. Aggressive children and juvenile delinquents are often successfully treated in individual therapy, group therapy, and institutional settings, but once they have returned to their family homes, the original dynamics fostering their coercive antisocial patterns are likely to reinstate the original level of deviant conduct (Gurman & Kniskern, 1978). Without change in the family system, individuals cannot be expected to maintain a new behavioral repertoire. Family therapy is now extensively used for childhood disorders (Masten, 1979). As Gurman and Kniskern (1978) point out in their review of family therapy outcome research, every study that has compared family therapy with other types of treatment finds family therapy equal to or superior to individual therapy.

The entire family system may be dysfunctional or at risk for future deterioration, as the earlier section suggests; therefore childhood aggression may best be addressed by a focus on the family as a whole. Professional clinicians from numerous disciplinary and theoretical perspectives engage in family treatments. All professionals working to treat aggressive behavior in the family context must assess the stage in the family life span to determine the nature and extent of family dysfunction and to consider how to use the referral person or problem to enter the system.

Many of these families will not voluntarily request professional assistance for their problems. If, indeed, the family members have given up on hopes of better family life, or if they have difficulty identifying or objectifying a problem, a problem may eventually be identified for them by the community. Police, school personnel, social service and child protection agencies, and the courts not uncommonly become the identifiers of the problem, whether it is child abuse, spouse abuse, schoolyard aggression, or teenage delinquency. These identified problems may be only a partially accurate assessment of the family problems.

Other families may voluntarily seek help for one of these difficulties, particularly for treatment of an aggressive child. Again, however, there may be other features that will make effective treatment and long-term maintainance of treatment gains difficult. Families also may not present the most important problem, but merely a superficial one, either because the central problem is seen as not treatable or because it is too threatening to acknowledge publicly, as in collusive spouse abuse situations. Dysfunctional families, we have noted, want help with only a little part of the system. By whatever referral trajectory the family comes to the attention of a helping professional, a better examination of the full family is the mode of choice.

The use of marriage and family therapy has increased rapidly in the last fifteen years, though there is considerable diversity in the goals and techniques of therapy, as well as differing assumptions about the nature of human functioning and pathology. The behavioral approaches have been oriented toward target symptom behaviors such as aggressiveness, and evaluation of the treatment effectiveness in changing the symptomatic behaviors has been assessed. The nonbehavioral approaches, however, have not usually been oriented to specific target behaviors. Family therapists commonly adopt such treatment goals as improvement of communication, clarification of roles, increased individuation of members, and other changes in the overall family; removal of individual target symptoms is typically a lower priority. Thus, the degree to which nonbehavioral approaches are effective in treating childhood aggression *per se* is not very well documented.

In this section, the behaviorally based child-management approach, especially as it applies to childhood aggression, will be discussed. Then attention will turn to marital therapy, and finally we will consider the need for family therapies impacting on family problem solving and address some of the problems of resistance, collusion, and coercion in family therapy.

Child-Management Training

A large number of efforts have now been mounted to teach parents how to manage their children more effectively. Gordon and Davidson (1981) have reviewed the work on behavioral parent training, which has been characterized by well-described treatment packages and a strong emphasis on empirical evaluation of outcome and of specific techniques. In this approach, the therapist serves as a consultant, teaching the parents to use behavior change principles. The aggressiveness of the referred child is seen as the result of inconsistent and coercive parenting efforts, and parents are assisted in changing their own parenting behavior to decrease aggressive or aversive behavior and increase positive, prosocial behavior.

After careful baseline assessment of parent and child behavior in the home through home observation, self-report, and interview, parents are taught to track carefully their child's behavior, pinpointing problems and their antecedents and consequences. They are assisted in making a functional analysis of the ways in which reinforcement contingencies are maintaining the child's noxious behavior and taught to use such learning principles as shaping, time out, and positive and negative reinforcement consistently to decrease aggressive behavior and to increase more desirable behavior. It is assumed, in this approach, that the parents are motivated but simply unskilled at changing their own behavior.

Patterson and his colleagues have produced a large body of work on the outcome of therapy to reduce childhood aggression through parent training. His most recent work (1982) chronicles well the evolution of the child-management approach. Originally parent training was offered in a highly structured educational approach. In later years, new modules were added to teach parents and children the principle of contract negotiation, problem solving, and communication. By 1975, Patterson was reporting:

> For about a third of the families, it is sufficient to adopt the simplest possible strategy, e.g., teach the parent the specific skills for changing child behaviors. Another third seem to require more than this, including the teaching of negotiation skill, resolution of marital conflict and depression being the most common—If these problems are not dealt with, we believe the long-term follow-up will show the treatment to have been ineffective. The remaining third fail despite our best efforts. (Patterson, 1975, p. 29)

New technology continued to be developed. The marital subsystem was given more attention, as was improving poor feelings of self-efficacy and depression in the mother. Reluctant fathers were paid to encourage their participation, and breakage fees were exacted if therapy was prematurely terminated. The treatment was made less structured and more interactive, and more supervisional support was provided to parents in their efforts to increase their parenting skills. All these measures appeared to contribute to the steady improvement in treatment effectiveness.

By 1982, the Oregon Social Learning Center studies were suggesting considerable effectiveness for those families receiving their treatment. By the end of treatment, substantial changes were evident in the child's overall rate of coercive behavior, and the parents' global rating of the child was substantially more positive. Furthermore, aversive behavior rates had declined to normal levels, not only for the identified child but also for the mother and other children in the family. Parents were properly consequating desirable and undesirable behaviors, and coercive episodes were brought to within normal range. Moreover, the mother's psychological adjustment, particularly her depression, was brought into a normal range as she experienced treatment success. By 1982, Patterson's group had 12- to 18-month follow-ups demonstrating maintenance of treatment gains.

Recent concern with establishing generalization has prompted studies to determine the degree to which parent training effectively improves overall family functioning. Evidence is accruing that training in these behavior modification procedures improves the mother's depression and low sense of self-efficacy (Johnson & Lobitz, 1974), increases the marital satisfaction of both parents (Oltmanns et al., 1977), reduces sibling aggression (Arnold, Levine, & Patterson, 1975), and increases family cohesion (Karoly & Rosenthal, 1977). A long-term follow-up study of 40 children treated at the Regional Intervention Program in Pittsburg reported impressive maintenance and generalization of treatment gains three to nine years after treatment (Strain, Steele, Ellis, & Timm, 1982). The parents and children were acting in positive ways within the home, parents were using consistent parenting techniques, and the children were behaving and being seen as no different from other, nonaggressive, schoolmates.

In this study, then, generalization from the home to the school and maintenance across a long time span were found. Generalization was, incidently, related to only one demographic variable: the younger the child when parents were trained, the more extensive the generalization.

Gordon and Davidson (1981) have offered a thorough review of the work in this area, concluding that it is indeed an effective intervention method for discrete, well-specified behavior problems. However, the effectiveness of this kind of parent training as the only form of intervention may be limited if the parents do not have sufficient control over their environment, if their marital problems prevent them from cooperative and collaborative parenting, or if one or both parents is too maladjusted psychologically—that is, depressed (Kniskern & Gurman, 1981; Gordon & Davidson, 1981).

The involvement of the father enhances training effectiveness, but rarely are fathers involved in these interventions (Gordon & Davidson, 1981). Furthermore, dropout rates are typically high, and those who drop out are the more disturbed families with more deviant children (Kent, 1976). When the child's deviance is more extreme and complex, and the family simultaneously more distressed, child management alone does not appear as effective. Patterson feels, however, that lengthier and open-ended therapy using more sophisticated and advanced clinical skills will successfully alter even these more troubled systems (Patterson, 1975).

Wahler and his colleagues (Wahler, 1980; Wahler & Afton, 1980; Wahler, Leske, & Rogers, 1979) have shown that the insular mothers of lower-class father-absent ghetto families with truant childhood stealers may not profit from such an approach because of these mothers' defensive attributions and selective attention. These mothers can be taught parenting technology with an attendant decrease in their children's coercion, but they continue to blame the children for coercing them and continue to view the children's behavior from a vague, abstract level of negativism. Treatment gains in the Wahler studies, once the therapist withdrew, were lost within a year.

Other researchers have criticized the common lack of inclusion of children in therapy sessions and the overemphasis on the use of parental coercive control, which gives parents a technical but not a conceptual shift in the way they relate to their children (Gurman & Kniskern, 1978, 1981).

Perhaps most salient for the present argument in favor of full family treatment is the "capricious quality of the deviancy labeling process" as noted by Gurman and Kniskern (1978). As discussed earlier, many of the target children brought in to child guidance clinics are not abnormally aggressive or more aggressive than their siblings. There is also evidence that the mother's depression predicts her labeling of the child as aggressive more than does the actual behavior of the child. Again, from the systems point of view, the child's aggressiveness may be functional for the family system, which will resist actual change of the perceived symptoms in an effort to maintain its tenuous equilibrium. DeWitt (1978) has argued that treatment of many childhood problems may have in fact been unnecessary, since the child was not actually deviant but was simply perceived to be deviant by the family.

It is probable that some caretakers will be so dysfunctional that they will be unable to profit from child-management training. They may be so emotionally distressed that they are unable to think or see clearly. Such poor problem solvers will have faulty modes of problem perception and ineffective methods of solution. These parents may well require individual psychotherapy if they are to continue in their parenting role.

Simply training parents to use effective parenting techniques can be quite effective, then, when inadequate parenting skill is the primary problem, as it appears to be in many cases referred to child guidance clinics. But when there are other problems, the intervention must be more extensive and must consider the whole family. Many child-management training programs have begun to include marital therapy in the treatment package. We turn to this focus next.

Marriage Therapy

Marital therapies increasingly show a blending of social learning and systems constructs. Concepts of wholeness, homeostasis, and circular causality are easy to acknowledge in the social exchange system of two people, with parallels in mutuality of interdependence and reciprocal causality. Both social learning and systems-oriented approaches tend to focus on the present ongoing interaction between spouses, on the implicit rules that govern the interaction, and on the larger meanings derived from that behavior.

Earlier social-learning-based approaches employed reinforcement constructs similar to those found in the child-management training approaches—for example, contracting for more pleasing and less displeasing behavior exchanges. This approach was effective in improving marital satisfaction (Weiss, Hops, & Patterson, 1973), but only in couples already functioning relatively well. More seriously distressed couples were unable to reach contracting because of their inept, abrasive, and "issue expanding" communication (Rausch, Barry, Hartel, & Swain, 1974). Until such couples learn to communicate nonaversively—to withhold disrespectful, insulting, and injurious behavior and coercive episodes—they are not able to complete the problem-solving sequence to the point of contracting (Rosenblatt et al., 1979). Thus, more recent social-learning approaches to marital therapy are focusing on improvement of communication as a prerequisite to problem solving. Indeed, in reviewing the outcome research to date, Jacobson (1978) concludes that restructuring or facilitating improved communication may be the *sine qua non* of marital therapy.

Communication enhancement involves increasing the appropriate expression of feelings, increasing positive verbal interactions, identifying nonproductive communication patterns that interfere with problem solving, and teaching problem-solving skills. In such therapy, each spouse is trained to be assertive rather than aggressive, and interaction is altered from destructive, mutually defensive exchanges to more positive, problem-oriented discussion (Jacobson & Margolin, 1979). The emphasis in this kind of training is to help the couple resolve conflict by nonaggressively confronting the conflictual issue and moving cooperatively toward a mutual compromise. Such effective problem solving is thought to be rewarding because both spouses participate noncoercively yet assertively. It thereby increases their mutual attraction as well as their ability and motivation to conjointly approach another difficulty together.

The work of Weiss (Weiss, 1978, 1980; Weiss & Birchler, 1978) places special stress on "objectification" and "support-understanding." To truly solve an interpersonal conflict, the parties must be able to objectify the problem and to use a common vocabulary which describes overt and objectively evident behaviors as well as subjective personal feelings. This training to conjointly distinguish subjective reactions from a consensual reality is a tacit nudging of the parties beyond the egocentric, self-justificatory and retributionary stances of people in extended unresolved conflict.

It has been suggested that one way to reduce childhood aggression would be to enhance the moral development of their socializing adults (N. Feschbach, 1974). The morality of cooperation, the most advanced stage of moral development in Piagetian theory (Piaget, 1932), requires that each person understand the give-and-take formulation of the relationship and that each recognize that short-term sacrifice can lead to longer-term benefit. The spouses must be able to objectify the problem, provide support and understanding, learn to react nondefensively, and correct misunderstanding in a supportive, cooperative way. Problem solving requires not only defining the problem satisfactorily but then taking time to think it through and determine consensually how both will benefit.

Marital therapy, if there is a troubled marriage in the home with an aggressive child, is in fact an excellent way to enhance the adults' abilities to solve child-related problems cooperatively. Effective spousal problem solving has been shown to be positively related to effective parenting and effective problem solving by offspring within the family. Certainly when a couple has difficulty resolving conflict in the home, enhancing their problem-solving effectiveness will improve the level of functioning family-wide.

Marital therapies are generally effective about two-thirds of the time (Kniskern & Gurman, 1981), and there is a markedly better chance of positive outcome when both spouses are involved in the therapy sessions. Indeed, while treatments involving both spouses produce a 65% rate of positive change in assorted measures of behavioral interaction, attitude and affect, and global ratings of marital satisfaction, this positive outcome shrinks to 48% when individual therapy for marital problems is employed. This striking finding has prompted Gurman and Kniskern to suggest that treating an individual for a relationship problem is not only ineffective but actually destructive.

We turn next to a consideration of family therapy, which is increasingly considered the mode of choice for complex family-based problems, including those involving childhood aggression.

Family Systems Therapy

In effect, family therapy occurs whenever assessment and treatment planning address the meaning or function of the symptomatic behavior, such as childhood aggression, within the family context as well as the nature of the family dysfunctioning. All family therapies would concur that a symptom cannot be understood apart from the context in which it occurs and the function it serves. All family therapy approaches likewise may be characterized as attempts to enhance the effectiveness of family problem solving so that the family can operate as a cohesive and flexible group on its own. Thus, such therapies focus on helping families orient to accepting problems in a way that will ensure effective solution. Many therapy techniques are directed to helping a family conceptualize the problem in a viable manner, a difficult feat in a fractured, defensive, and blaming group. Unlike the traditional educational approach of early behavior modification treatments, which assumed willingness and rational cooperation from clients ostensibly seeking help, family systems therapies are all based on the presumption that the family as a unit will be resistive and collusive in attempting to keep a fragile equilibrium. Thus, although the goals are similar to the child-management and marriage therapy approaches described earlier— cooperative mutual control, supportive family relationships, enhanced communication, and improved problem solving—techniques are often quite different.

The two dominant traditions are the behaviorally based and the family-systems therapeutic approaches. The social-learning approaches, which stress skills training, have been described earlier. The family-systems therapists more typically view family disturbance in terms of boundary diffusion or rigidity and focus on changing role-governed behavior to rule-governed interaction by altering interaction patterns. The family systems therapeutic approach is the only treatment approach to the family that emerged from work with marriage and family groups rather than from individualistic treatment modes, as have the social-learning treatments. It thus offers provocative treatment strategies for breaking resistance to change in family systems.

The behavioral and systems approaches appear to be converging in many respects, as previously noted. Proponents of both approaches have pointed to the "systems-behavioral" intervention model of Alexander and his colleagues at the University of Utah as one useful direction in which to proceed (Alexander & Barton, 1976, 1980; Alexander et al., 1976; Barton & Alexander, 1981). This group has shown the most impressive results to date for families of court-referred adolescent delinquents. Later relabeled "functional family therapy" (Barton &

Alexander, 1981), this approach assumes that family interaction is patterned and that patterns are linked functionally. That is, the concern is with the outcome a regular pattern produces in regulating interpersonal distance and intimacy, and the purpose of that behavioral process can be understood only after the fact. The therapist, observing *in vivo* interaction of all family members, notes how they consensually punctuate the stream of interaction to derive meaning and then intervenes to help members achieve the same functions in less costly ways.

In treating families of teenage delinquents, Alexander *et al.* used a "therapy first, education second" approach. The first part of treatment in this model was focused on breaking through family system resistance and providing the right cooperative mental set. This "therapy" focused on relabeling motivational states, helping family members see the interdependence of behaviors and feelings, neutralizing blame attributions, and moving the entire family into a cooperative set so that they could see that change would benefit everyone. The focus was, like that of strategic systems therapy, to change attributions of malevolence with reframing and the use of paradox. By simply changing the context in which they found themselves, members of the family began to talk cooperatively, developing enthusiasm or motivation for maintaining a new communication pattern. The most effective family therapy approach to the delinquent population documented so far, this treatment was effective in making all members' interactions more supportive rather than defensive, in introducing more effective problem-solving interventions. and in reducing recidivism to the family court by more than half, as compared to waiting list and alternative family treatments. Further, the recidivism of siblings was also reduced, 250% more than under alternative treatment conditions. Similar approaches with female juvenile delinquents and their families have suggested that such treatment improves family functioning on family-wide measures of cohesion and adaptability.

In reducing family resistance and collusion, family therapy techniques often involve relabeling of behavior and definition of the problem in a way that all will accept. Cognitive reframing or relabeling is used to change attributions about intent or malevolence. Thus the persistent squabbling of two siblings is no longer "trying to get under Mom's skin" but "trying to sort things out;" and a adolescent's insolence is relabeled as an age-appropriate bid to be seen as more grown-up. Also employed are paradoxical directives, which "appear absurd because they exhibit an apparently contradictory nature, such as requiring clients to do what in fact they have been doing, rather than requiring that they change, which is what everyone else is demanding" (Hare-Mustin, 1976, p. 128). The successful use of paradoxical interventions is being increasingly reported in therapy for children and adults with various problems. It appears even more valuable in reducing group resistance and is currently being adopted in behavioral treatments for marriage (Weiss, 1978).

The "therapy first, education second" edict of the Alexander group is helpful in addressing the dysfunctional families who present an aggressive child as the referral problem. That the family will cooperate in supporting the child's change is not a certainty; therefore it is essential to assess the family interaction system to determine whether the problem is indeed solely the child's aggressiveness or a more disturbed family pattern.

Once an understanding of the overall family interaction context is obtained, the meaning of the childhood aggression becomes more apparent. If the therapist perceives the central problem to be maternal depression, marital rift, coercive aggressive conflict-management styles throughout the family, or sufficient dysfunction that the family is poorly equipped to solve problems effectively, then the therapist has the difficult task of helping the family to define the problem differently, in a way that all can accept and that can then be solved. The family systems therapist in such a circumstance will typically not accept the family's interpretation of the problem directly. He or she will support it in words but undermine this interpretation over time in other ways to further redefinition of the problem. To do this, of course, requires achieving acceptance by the family by establishing rapport and a cooperative, supportive environment in which family members find themselves behaving cooperatively and with mutual supportiveness. The family that finds itself effectively solving therapist-maneuvered problems will thus find itself interacting successfully. Dysfunctional families interact differently from normal families only in situations which they perceive to be competitive ones; in cooperative contexts their communication patterns are as effective as those of normal families (Barton & Alexander, 1979). Members of dysfunctional families are problem-laden and perceive too many of their interactions as competitive. If the therapist can effectively stage a cooperative context for the rehearsal of family problem-solving efforts, therapy is likely to be effective.

Considering the entire family constellation is therefore necessary in the family-treatment modality. This does not negate the utility of individual- or dyadic-focus subtreatments. Thus, individual treatments for anger control, assertion training, communication or problem-solving skills, and affective problems of self-esteem, depression, and the like may be part of the overall reprogramming of the family system. The child-management or parent-training programs that extend beyond this focus to deal with personal or marital issues of the parents are an example of multiple subtreatments or treatment goals within the family framework context. Given what is known about the family dynamics of homes with aggressive children, then, parenting training will sometimes be the treatment mode of choice, with or without adjunct treatment for other areas of family problem solving.

In this section, the argument has been made that childhood aggression should be viewed as a potential symptom of a dysfunctional family in designing effective psychotherapy. Focusing on the family system as a whole allows assessment of the nature and degree of family pathology and permits design of a treatment to reprogram the family system that will be accepted. Families maintain their boundaries as living systems, and dysfunctional families are even more resistive to change agents, since such families have less problem-solving capacity. Thus, the professional attempting to restore effective problem-solving capabilities to the distressed family must be prepared to encounter family dynamics that resist easy change.

The comparatively high level of effectiveness for child-management training has been noted. For treating a discrete problem of childhood aggression, this is clearly a powerful method and the method of choice. Because the marital relationship is the major source of authority and problem-solving expertise, however, marital therapy may also be usefully incorporated into treatments directed at treating dysfunctional family systems for which the presenting problem is an aggressive child. That individual treatments for cognitive, affective, and behavioral problems may well be appropriate for individual members in dysfunctional families is also quite probable. It has been argued, however, that attention to the larger family framework and the effective problem solving of its members is essential to both effective treatment and long-term maintenance of treatment gain.

Family therapy is still to some degree in its infancy, and more research on therapy process and outcome is essential. In particular, the field will be aided by approaches that assess all family members and family-wide interaction as well as specific symptoms. The social-learning therapies have been target-oriented but have often failed to examine the degree to which change in one member or one relationship within the family system effects change in other members and other relationships. It is unfortunate, for example, that the detailed behavioral analyses of relationships in families with aggressive children have, by and large, failed to assess the marital relationship in these families as well. By the same token, the family-systems therapy research has all too often considered communication, roles, and power constructs while failing to measure adequately specific presenting symptoms such as childhood aggression.

Earlier it was argued that there may be a trajectory of family deterioration, in which coercive processes and ineffective problem solving breed more of the same. Greater attention to mapping the progress of such deterioration and an increasingly improved technology for treating relationship dysfunction may permit eventual illumination of what treatment or treatment combinations are most effective at what stages of the family lifespan and at what stages of deterioration. At present, it appears that childhood aggression, if caught early enough, can be effectively brought under control if there are no other problems in the family. Because such additional problems may well exist, professionals working with aggressive children should be prepared to reprogram the family if it is required.

REFERENCES

Alexander, J. F. (1973). Defensive and supportive communication in normal and deviant families. *Journal of Consulting and Clinical Psychology, 40,* 223–231.

Alexander, J. F., & Barton, C. (1976). Behavioral systems therapy for families. In D. H. Olson (Ed.), *Treating relationships.* Lake Mills, IA: Graphic.

Alexander, J. F., & Barton, C. (1980). Intervention with delinquents and their families: Clinical, methodological, and conceptual issues. In J. P. Vincent (Ed.), *Advances in family intervention assessment and therapy.* Greenwich, CT: JAI Press.

Alexander, J. F., Barton, C., Schiavo, R. S., & Parson, B. V. (1976). Systems-behavioral intervention with families of delinquents: Therapist characteristics, family behavior, and outcome. *Journal of Consulting and Clinical Psychology, 44,* 656–664.

Anderson, L. M. (1969). Personality characteristics of parents of neurotic, aggressive, and normal preadolescent boys. *Journal of Consulting and Clinical Psychology, 33*(5), 575–581.

Arnold, J., Levine, A., & Patterson, G. R. (1975). Changes in sibling behavior following family intervention. *Journal of Consulting and Clinical Psychology, 43,* 683–688.

Barry, M. (1979). A research project in successful single-parent families. *American Journal of Family Therapy, 7,* 65–73.

Barton, C., & Alexander, J. F. (1979). *Delinquent and normal family interaction in competitive and cooperative conditions.* Paper presented at the annual meeting of the American Psychological Association, New York.

Barton, C., & Alexander, J. F. (1981). Functional family therapy. In A. S. Gurman & D. P. Kniskern (Eds.), *Handbook of family therapy.* New York: Brunner/Mazel.

Baumrind, D. (1979). *New direction in socialization research.* Paper presented at the Society of Research in Child Development, San Francisco, California.

Bell, R. Q. (1971). Stimulus control of parent or caretaker behavior by offspring. *Developmental Psychology, 4,* 63–72.

Bell, R. Q., & Harper, L. V. (1977). *Child effects on adults.* Hillsdale, NJ: Erlbaum.

Birchler, G. R. (1972). *Differential patterns of instrumental and affiliative behavior as a function of degree of marital distress and level of intimacy.* Unpublished doctoral thesis, University of Oregon.

Birchler, G. R., & Webb, L. F. (1977). Discriminating interaction patterns in happy and unhappy marriages. *Journal of Consulting and Clinical Psychology, 45* (3), 494–495.

Birchler, G. R., Weiss, R. L., & Vincent, J. P. (1975). Multi-method analysis of social reinforcement exchange between maritally distressed and nondistressed spouse and stranger dyads. *Journal of Personality and Social Psychology, 31* (2), 349–360.

Burgess, R. L., & Conger, R. D. (1978). Family interaction in abusive, neglectful, and normal families. *Child Development, 47,* 1163–1173.

Chodorow, N. (1978). *The reproduction of mothering, psychoanalysis, and the sociology of gender.* Berkeley, CA: University of California Press.

Clark-Stewart, K. A. (1978). And daddy makes three: The father's impact on mother and young child. *Child Development, 49,* 466–478.

Dawe, H. C. (1934). An analysis of two hundred quarrels of preschool children. *Child Development, 5.* 139–157.

DeWitt, K. N. (1978). The effectiveness of family therapy: A review of outcome research. *Archives of General Psychiatry, 35,* 549–561.

D'Zurilla, T. J., & Goldfried, M. R. (1971). Problem solving and behavior modification. *Journal of Abnormal Psychology, 78,* 107–126.

Epstein, N. B., & Santa-Barbara, J. (1975). Conflict behavior in clinical couples: Interpersonal perception and stable outcomes. *Family Process,* March, 51–65.

Eron, L. D., Walder, L. O., & Lefkowitz, M. M. (1971). *Learning of aggression in children.* Boston: Little Brown.

Fagot, B. (1974). Sex differences in toddlers' behavior and parental reaction. *Developmental Psychology, 10* (4), 554–558.

Fawl, C. L. (1963). Disturbances experienced by children in their natural habitats. In R. Barker (Ed.), *The stream of behavior.* New York: Appleton-Century-Crofts.

Feschbach, N. N. (1974). The relationship of child-rearing factors to children's aggression, empathy, and related positive and negative social behaviors. In J. DeWit & W. W. Hartup (Eds.), *Determinants and origins of aggressive behavior.* The Hague: Mouton & Co.

Feschbach, S. (1974). The development and regulation of aggression: Some research gaps and a proposed cognitive approach. In J. DeWitt & W. W. Hartup, (Eds.), *Determinants and origins of aggressive behavior.* The Hague: Mouton & Co.

Forgatch, M., & Wieder, G. (1981). *The parent–adolescent naturalistic interaction code (PANIC).* Unpublished manuscript. Eugene, OR: Oregon Social Learning Center.

Gelles, R. J. (1972). *The violent home.* Beverly Hills, CA: Sage.

Gelles, R. J., & Straus, M. A. (1979). Violence in the American family. *Journal of Family Issues, 35* (2), 15–39.

Glueck, S., & Glueck, E. (1950). *Unraveling juvenile delinquency.* Cambridge, MA: Harvard University Press.

Goodenough, F. L. (1931). *Anger in young children.* Minneapolis: University of Minnesota Press.

Goodstein, L. D., & Rowley, V. N. (1961). A further study of MMPI differences between parents of disturbed and nondisturbed children. *Journal of Consulting Psychology, 25* (5), 460–464.

Gordon, S., & Davidson, N. (1981). Behavioral parent training. In A. S. Gurman & D. P. Kniskern (Eds.), *Handbook of family therapy.* New York: Brunner/Mazel.

Gottman, J. M. (1979). *Marital interaction: Experimental investigation.* New York: Academic Press.

Gottman, J. M., Markman, H., & Notarius, C. (1977). The topography of marital conflict: A sequential analysis of verbal and nonverbal behavior. *Journal of Marriage and the Family, 39,* 461–477.

Griest, D. L., Forehand, R., Wells, K. C., & McMahon, R. J. (1980). An examination of differences between nonclinic and behavior problem clinic-referred children and their mothers. *Journal of Abnormal Psychology, 89,* 497–500.

Griest, D. L., Wells, K. C., & Forehand, R. (1979). An examination of maternal perceptions of maladjustment in clinic-referred children. *Journal of Abnormal Psychology,* 1979, *88*(3), 277–281.

Gully, K. J., Dengerink, H. A., Pepping, M., & Bergstrom, D. (1981). Research note: Sibling contributions to violent behavior. *Journal of Marriage and the Family,* 333–337.

Gurman, A. S., & Kniskern, D. P. (1978). Research in marital and family therapy: Empirical, clinical, and conceptual issues. In S. L. Garfield & A. E. Bergin (Eds.), *Handbook of psychotherapy and behavior change (rev. ed.).* New York: Wiley.

Gurman, A. S., & Kniskern, D. P. (1981). Family therapy outcome research: Knowns and unknowns. In A. S. Gurman & D. P. Kniskern (Eds.), *Handbook of family therapy.* New York: Brunner/Mazel.

Haley. J. (1978). *Problem solving therapy.* San Francisco: Jossey-Bass.

Hare-Mustin, R. (1976). Paradoxical tasks in family therapy: Who can resist? *Psychotherapy: Theory, Research and Practice, 13,* 128–130.

Harris, A., & Reid, J. B. (1981). The consistency of a class of coercive child behaviors across school settings for individual subjects. *Journal of Personality and Social Psychology, 9,* 219–227.

Hartup, W. W. (1974). Aggression in childhood: Developmental perspectives. *American Psychologist, 29,* 336–339.

Heatherington, E. M. (1972). Effects of father absence on personality development in adolescent daughters. *Developmental Psychology, 7*(3), 313–326.

Heatherington, E. M., Cox, M., & Cox, R. (1978). The aftermath of divorce. In I. J. Stevens & M. Mathews (Eds.), *Mother/child, father/child interaction.* Washington, D.C.: Association for the Education of Young Children.

Heatherington, E. M., Cox, M., & Cox, R. (1979). Family interaction and the social, emotional and cognitive development of children following divorce. In V. Vaughan & T. Brazelton (Eds.), *The family: Setting priorities.* New York: Science and Medicine.

Heatherington, E. M., Cox, M., & Cox, R. (1980). *Stress and coping in divorce.* Unpublished manuscript.

Heppner, P. P. (1978). A review of the problem-solving literature and its relationship to the counseling process. *Journal of Counseling Psychology, 25,* 366–375.

Hoffman, M. L. (1970). Moral development. In P. Mussen (Ed.), *Handbook of child psychology.* New York: Wiley.

Horne, A. (1980). *Aggressive behavior in referred and nonreferred one and two parent families.* Paper presented at the annual meeting of the American Psychological Association.

Jacobson, N. S. (1978). A review of the research on the effectiveness of marital therapy. In T. J. Paolino & B. S. McCrady (Eds.), *Marriage and marital therapy: Psychoanalytic, behavioral and systems theory perspective* (pp. 395–441). New York: Brunner/Mazel.

Jacobson, N. S., & Margolin, G. (1979). *Marital therapy.* New York: Brunner/Mazel.

Johnson, S. M., & Lobitz, G. K. (1974). The personal and marital adjustment of parents as related to observed child deviance and parenting behaviors. *Journal of Abnormal Child Psychology, 2,* 193–207.

Johnson, S. M., Wahl, G., Martin, S., & Johansson, S. (1973). How deviant is the normal child: A behavioral analysis of the preschool child and his family. In R. D. Rubin, J. P. Brady, & J. D. Henderson (Eds.), *Advances in behavior therapy* (Vol. 4). New York: Academic Press.

Kantor, D., & Lehr, W. (1975). *Inside the family.* San Francisco: Jossey-Bass.

Karoly, P., & Rosenthal, M. (1977). Training parents in behavior modification: Effects on perceptions of family interaction and deviant behavior. *Behavior Therapy, 8,* 406–410.

Kent, R. (1976). A methodological critique of "Interventions for boys with conduct problems." *Journal of Consulting and Clinical Psychology, 44,* 297–302.

Kieren, D., & Tallman, I. (1972). Spousal adaptability: An assessment of marriage competence. *Journal of Marriage and the Family, 34,* 247–256.

Klein, D. M., & Hill, R. (1979). Determinants of family problem-solving effectiveness. In W. R. Burr, R. Hill, F. I. Nye, & I. L. Reiss (Eds.), *Contemporary theories about the family* (Vol. 1). New York: Free Press.

Kniskern, D. P., & Gurman, A. S. (1981). Advances and prospects for family therapy research. In J. P. Vincent (Ed.), *Advances in family intervention, assessment and theory* (Vol. 2). Greenwich, CT: JAI Press.

Kopfstein, D. (1972). The effects of accelerating and decelerating consequences on the social behavior of trainable retarded children. *Child Development, 43,* 800–809.

Lamb, M. E. (1976). The role of the father: An overview. In M. E. Lamb (Ed.), *The role of the father in child development.* New York: Wiley.

Lewis, M., & Lee-Painter, S. (1974). An interactional approach to the mother–child dyad. In M. Lewis & L. A. Rosenblum (Eds.), *The effects of the infant on its caretaker.* New York: Wiley.

Liverant, S. (1959). MMPI differences between parents of disturbed and nondisturbed children. *Journal of Clinical Psychology, 23,* 256–260.

Margolin, G. (1981). The reciprocal relationship between marital and child problems. In J. P.

Vincent (Ed.), *Advances in family intervention, assessment, and theory* (Vol. 2). Greenwich, CT: JAI Press.

Masten, A. S. (1979). Family therapy as a treatment for children: A critical review of outcome research. *Family Process, 18,* 232–336.

McLean, P. D. (1976). Parental depression: Incompatible with effective parenting. In E. J. Mash, L. C. Handy, & L. A. Hamerlynck (Eds.), *Behavior modification approaches to parenting.* New York: Brunner/Mazer.

Melges, F. T., & Harris, R. F. (1970). Anger and attack: A cybernetic model of violence. In D. N. Daniels, H. F. Galula, & F. M. Ochberg (Eds.), *Violence and the struggle for existence.* Boston: Little, Brown.

Miller, N. E. (1948). Theory and experiment relating psychoanalytic displacement to stimulus response generalization. *Journal of Abnormal and Social Psychology, 43,* 188–178.

Minuchin, S. (1974). *Families and family therapy.* Cambridge: Harvard University Press.

Minuchin, F., Montalvo, B., Guerney, B., Roseman, B., & Shumer, F. (1967). *Families of the slums.* New York: Basic Books.

Minuchin, S., Rosman, B. L., & Baker, L. (1978). *Psychosomatic families.* Cambridge, MA: Harvard University Press.

Mischler, E., & Waxler, N. (1968). *Interaction in families.* New York: Wiley.

Morton, T. L., & Douglas, M. A. (1982). Growth of relationships. In S. Duck & R. Gilmour (Eds.), *Personal relationships. Vol. 2: Developing personal relationships.* London: Academic Press.

Morton, T. L., Alexander, J. F., & Altman, I. (1976). Communication and relationship definition. In G. L. Miller (Ed.), *Explorations in interpersonal communication.* Beverly Hills, CA: Sage.

Moss, H. A., & Robson, K. S. (1968). Maternal influence in early social visual behavior. *Child Development, 39,* 401–408.

O'Leary, M. R., & Dengerink, H. A. (1973). Aggression as a function of the intensity and pattern of attack. *Journal of Research in Personality, 7,* 61–70.

Olson, D. H., Russell, C. S., & Sprenkle, D. H. (1979a). Circumplex model of marital and family systems. II: Empirical studies and clinical intervention. In J. P. Vincent (Ed.), *Advances in family intervention, assessment, and theory* (Vol. 1). Greenwich, CT: JAI Press.

Olson, D. H., Sprenkle, D., & Russell, C. (1979b). Circumplex model of marital and family systems. I: Cohesion and adaptability dimensions, family types and clinical applications. *Family Process, 14,* 1–35.

Oltmanns, T., Broderick, J., & O'Leary, K. (1977). Marital adjustment and the efficacy of behavior therapy with children. *Journal of Consulting and Clinical Psychology, 45*(5).

Olweus, D. (1976). *Longitudinal studies of aggressive reaction patterns: A review.* Paper presented at the Twenty-first International Congress of Psychology, Paris.

Olweus, D. (1978). *Aggression in the schools: Bullies and whipping boys.* New York: Wiley.

Olweus, D. (1979). Stability of aggressive reaction patterns in males: A review. *Psychological Bulletin, 86* (4), 852–875.

Olweus, D. (1980). Familial and temperamental determinants of aggressive behavior in adolescent boys: A causal analysis. *Developmental Psychology, 16,* 644–660.

Patterson, G. R. (1975). *Families.* Champaign, IL: Research Press.

Patterson, G. R. (1976). The aggressive child: Victim and architect of a coercive system. In L. A. Hamerlynck, L. C. Handy, & E. J. Mash (Eds.), *Behavior modification and families: Theory and research* (Vol. 1). New York: Brunner/Mazel.

Patterson, G. R. (1979). Siblings: Fellow travelers in coercive family processes. In R. J. Blanchard (Ed.). *Advances in the study of aggression.* New York: Academic Press.

Patterson, G. R. (1980). Mothers: The unacknowledged victims. *Monographs of the Society for Research in Child Development, 1980, 45,* No. 113.

Patterson, G. R. (1982). *Coercive family process.* Eugene, OR: Castalia.

Patterson, G. R., & Reid, J. B. (1967). Reciprocity and coercion: Two facets of social systems. In C. Neuringer & J. Michael (Eds.), *Behavior Modification in Clinical Psychology*. New York: Appleton-Century-Crofts.

Patterson, G. R., Littman, R. A., & Bricker, W. (1967). Assertive behavior in children: A step toward a theory of aggression. *Monographs of the Society for Research in Child Development, 32* (5), 1–43.

Patterson, G. R., Reid, J. B., Jones, R. R., & Conger, R. E. (1975). *A social learning approach to family intervention. Vol. 1: Families with aggressive children*. Eugene, OR: Castalia.

Piaget, J. (1932). *The moral judgement of the child*. New York: Harcourt-Brace.

Rausch, H. L. (1965). Interaction sequences. *Journal of Personality and Social Psychology, 2* (4). 487–499.

Rausch, H. L., Barry, W. A., Hartel, R. K., & Swain, M. A. (1974). *Communication, conflict, and marriage*. San Francisco: Jossey-Bass.

Reid, J. B., & Hendricks, A. F. (1973). A preliminary analysis of the effectiveness of direct home intervention for treatment of pre-delinquent boys who steal. In L. A. Hamerlynck, L. C. Handy, & E. J. Mash (Eds.), *Behavior therapy: Methodology, concepts, and practice*. Champaign, Ill.: Research Press.

Reid, J. B., Taplin, P. S., & Lorber, R. (1981). A social interactional approach to the treatment of abusive families. In R. Stuart (Ed.), *Violent behavior: Social learning approaches to prediction, management, and treatment*. New York: Brunner/Mazel.

Reiss, D. (1971). Varieties of consensual experience. III: Contrasts between families of normals, delinquents and schizophrenics. *Journal of Nervous and Mental Disease, 152*, 73–95.

Rickard, K. M., Forehand, R., Atkeson, B. M., & Lopez, C. (1982). Examination of the relationship of marital satisfaction and divorce with parent–child interactions. *Journal of Clinical Child Psychology, 11*, 61–65.

Rollins, B. C., & Thomas, D. L. (1979). Parental support, power, and control techniques in the socialization of children. In W. R. Burr, R. Hill, F. I. Nye, & I. L. Reiss (Eds.), *Contemporary theories about the family* (Vol. 1). New York: Free Press.

Rosenblatt, P. C., Titus, S. L., & Cunningham, M. R. (1979). Disrespect, tension, and togetherness–apartness in marriage. *Journal of Marital and Family Therapy, 5* (1), 47–54.

Rutter, M. (1966). *Children of sick parents: An environmental and psychiatric study*. London: Oxford University Press.

Rutter, M. (1971). Parent–child separation: Psychological effects on the children. *Journal of Child Psychology and Psychiatry, 12*, 233–260.

Shure, M. B., & Spivack, G. (1978). *Problem-solving techniques in child rearing*. San Francisco: Jossey-Bass.

Snyder, J. J. (1977). A reinforcement analysis of interaction in problem and nonproblem families. *Journal of Abnormal Psychology, 86* (5), 528–535.

Steinmetz, S. K. (1977). *The cycle of violence: Assertive, aggressive, and abusive family interaction*. New York: Praeger.

Steinmetz, S. K. (1979). Disciplinary techniques and their relationship to aggressiveness, dependency, and conscience. In W. R. Burr, R. Hill, F. I. Nye, & I. L. Reiss (Eds.), *Contemporary theories about the family* (Vol. 1). New York: Free Press.

Strain, P. S., Steele, P., Ellis, T., & Timm, M. A. (1982). Long-term effects of oppositional child treatment with mothers as therapists and therapist trainers. *Journal of Applied Behavior Analysis, 15*, 163–169.

Straus, M. A. (1978). Wifebeating: How common and why? *Victimology: An International Journal, 2*(3–4), 443–458.

Straus, M. A., Gelles, R. J., & Steinmetz, S. K. (1979). *Violence in the American family*. New York: Doubleday/Anchor.

Tedeschi, J. T., Smith, R. B., III, & Brown, R. C., Jr. (1974). A reinterpretation of research on aggression. *Psychological Bulletin, 81*, 540–563.

Tedeschi, J. T., Gaes, G. G., & Rivera, A. N. (1977). Aggression and the use of coercive power. *Journal of Social Issues, 33* (1), 101–125.

Wahler, R. G. (1980). The insular mother: Her problems in parent–child treatment. *Journal of Applied Behavior Analysis, 13*, 207–219.

Wahler, R. G., & Afton, A. D. (1980). Attentional processes in insular and noninsular mothers: Some differences in their summary reports about child problem behaviors. *Child Behavior Therapy, 2*, 25–41.

Wahler, R. G., & Fox, J. J. (1980). Solitary toy play and time out: A family treatment package for children with aggressive and oppositional behavior. *Journal of Applied Behavior Analysis, 13*, 23–39.

Wahler, R. G., Leske, G., & Rogers, E. S. (1979). The insular family: A deviance support system for oppositional children. In L. A. Hamerlynck (Ed.), *Behavioral systems for the developmentally disabled. Vol. 1: School and family environments.* New York: Brunner/Mazel.

Walker, L. E. (1981). A feminist perspective on domestic violence. In R. B. Stuart (Ed.), *Violent behavior: Social learning approaches to prediction, management, and treatment.* New York: Brunner Mazel.

Wallerstein, J. S., & Kelly, J. B. (1980). *Surviving the breakup: How children and parents cope with divorce.* New York: Basic Books.

Weiss, R. L. (1978). The conceptualization of marriage from a behavioral perspective. In T. J. Paolino, Jr., & B. S. McCrady (Eds.), *Marriage and marital therapy: Psychoanalytic, behavioral and systems theory perspectives.* New York: Brunner/Mazel.

Weiss, R. L. (1980). Strategic behavioral marital therapy; Toward a model for assessment and intervention. In J. P. Vincent (Ed.) *Advances in family intervention assessment theory, Vol. 1.* Greenwich, CT: J.A.I. Press.

Weiss, R. L., & Birchler, G. R. (1978). Adults with marital dysfunction. In M. Hersen & A. S. Bellack (Eds.), *Behavior therapy in the psychiatric setting.* Baltimore: Williams and Wilkins.

Weiss, R. L., Hops, H., & Patterson, G. R. (1973). A framework for conceptualizing marital conflict, a technology for altering it, and some data for evaluating it. In L. A. Hamerlynck, L. C. Handy, & E. J. Mash (Eds.), *Behavior change: Methodology, concepts, and practice.* Champaign, IL: Research Press.

Winter, W., & Ferreira, A. (1969). Talking time as an index of intrafamilial similarity in normal and abnormal families. *Journal of Abnormal Psychology, 74*, 574–575.

Wohlking, W. D., Dunteman, G. H., & Bailey, J. P. (1967). Multivariate analyses of parents' MMPI's based on psychiatric diagnosis of their children. *Journal of Consulting Psychology, 31*, 521–524.

CHAPTER 7

Child Maltreatment

Prevalence, Consequences, Causes, and Interventions

JAY BELSKY AND JOAN VONDRA

Although serious aggressive behavior in children arises from many sources, few contemporary behavioral scientists would deny the clear link between childhood aggression and patterns of abusive, neglectful, and violent behavior within the home. Teru Morton, in the previous chapter. has provided a broad overview of patterns of family interaction. In this chapter we will be considering a specific pattern of family abuse and neglect of children.

In recent years the abuse and neglect of children in the United States has become a social problem attracting a great deal of attention from scientists, policymakers, and concerned citizens alike. Although exact definitions of child maltreatment are hard to come by and engender a great deal of debate, it is useful to think of child abuse and neglect as cases in which a child ''receives nonaccidental physical injury (or injuries) as a result of acts (or omissions) on the part of his parents or guardians that violate the community standards concerning the treatment of children'' (Parke & Collmer, 1975, p. 3).

Several aspects of this definition are noteworthy. First, acts of omission, as when a certain minimum standard of care is absent, are included, as well as acts

JAY BELSKY • College of Human Development, Department of Individual and Family Studies, Pennsylvania State University, University Park, Pennsylvania 16802. JOAN VONDRA • Mt. Hope Family Center, Department of Psychology, University of Rochester, Rochester, New York 14627. Work on this chapter was supported by grants from the National Science Foundation (No. SES-8108886), the National Institute of Child Health and Human Development (No. RO1HD15496-O1A1), the Division of Maternal and Child Health of the Public Health Service (No. MC-R-424067-02-0), and by the March of Dimes Birth Defects Foundation (Social and Behavioral Sciences Branch, No. 12-64), Jay Belsky, principal investigator.

of commission. as when a child is hit. Most child neglect can be subsumed under the notion of acts of omission. Consider, for example, the neglect of a parent who fails to attend to the physical needs of a sick child. (Note: The term *parent* throughout this paper shall be taken to mean either natural parent or one who serves in the absence of parents as primary caregiver.) A secondary noteworthy feature of this definition is the absence of the requirement that abusive or neglectful care be perpetrated with intent. Thus, as defined here, parents or guardians can be considered to mistreat their child whether or not they intend to do so. Finally, this definition recognizes that child maltreatment is a community-defined phenomenon: it must be viewed in terms of community norms and standards regarding the appropriate conduct of adults in caring for children.

This contextual nature of child abuse becomes most apparent when we recognize that although child abuse, as currently defined, has gone on through the ages, it is only recently that hostile and punitive child care has come to be considered abusive. Consider, for example, the fact that Roman law permitted fathers to sell, abandon, kill. or offer their children in sacrifice; or consider the Greek philosopher Aristotle's contention that "the justice of a mother or a father is a different thing from that of a citizen, for a son or a slave is property, and there can be no injustice to one's own property" (Radbill, 1974). Even the Bible can be read as permitting, if not encouraging, maltreatment: "Foolishness is bound in the heart of the child; but the rod of correction shall drive it far from him" (Proverbs 22:15); "Withhold not correction from the child, for if thou beatest him with the rod, he shall not die" (Proverbs 13:13). And, of course, the history of child labor in this country, as well as around the world, clearly documents the maltreatment of children as not being a modern phenomenon (Radbill, 1974).

Child abuse was recently "discovered" as a result of changing attitudes regarding the rights of children and the responsibilities of parents. Medical technology has also contributed to this discovery, as x-rays now enable physicians to identify multiple injuries to children in various stages of healing, indicating that an injury which brings a child to the attention of a physician may not be the result of an isolated event (Caffey, 1946). But it was not until Kempe (Kempe, Silverman, Steele, Droegemueller, & Silver, 1962) coined the phrase "the battered child syndrome" that attention was given to the seriousness of maltreatment and child abuse was formally declared to exist. Since that time, four basic issues have occupied the attention of individuals concerned with child abuse: its prevalence, its causes, the developmental consequences for the child and strategies for preventing and remediating this disturbing social problem.

In this chapter each of these concerns will be addressed. Our goal is to demonstrate that child abuse should be conceptualized as an extreme point on a continuum of parental function–dysfunction and that insight into its etiology and therefore its treatment can be gained from work not directly focused upon child maltreatment *per se*.

PREVALENCE

Despite the considerable attention that has been devoted to child abuse and neglect, valid and reliable data regarding the incidence and prevalence of the use of violence and aggression against children is flawed in a variety of ways. Most significantly, in spite of recent laws requiring teachers, physicians, and other community personnel to report suspected cases of child maltreatment, a great deal of abuse and neglect probably goes unreported by not being brought to the formal attention of authorities. Information based upon official statistics must be qualified by the fact that it represents only "caught" cases of abuse. A second problem plaguing current estimates of child abuse is that those states and localities keeping records do not employ uniform definitions of child abuse. In fact, the definition of abuse may frequently vary in order to mitigate concern about this social problem. Although some scientists and policymakers use the term to cover a wide spectrum of phenomena that hinder proper development of a child's potential, others use the term to focus attention more specifically on cases of severely injured children.

In an effort to improve knowledge of the incidence of abuse, a 1965 survey was conducted on 1,520 individuals. Three percent of this nationally representative sample reported knowledge of 48 different incidents of child abuse. Extrapolations from this sample to the national population resulted in the estimate that between 2.5 and 4.1 million adults knew of families involved in child abuse incidents (Gil, 1971). When coercive adjustments were applied to these data, it was estimated that 500,000 children in this country had been abused in the survey year (Light, 1973).

Despite this apparently scientific evaluation and analysis, it might be emphasized that opinions on the actual frequency of child abuse in the United States are quite varied. A report to the United States Senate in 1973 estimated that there were only between 30,000 and 40,000 instances of "truly battered children" each year, whereas Fontana (1971) proposed a figure of 1.5 million. Perhaps the most accurate summary of our knowledge regarding the prevalence of abuse was provided by Cohen and Sussman (1975), who argued that "the only conclusion which can be made fairly is that information indicating the incidence of child abuse in the United States simply does not exist."

In fact, it has been the case until very recently that most projections of incidence have actually been little more than educated guesses. In an effort to correct this sorry state of affairs, a national survey was undertaken in 1975 to estimate the amount of violence directed against children in their own homes. For purposes of the study, violence was defined as "an act carried out with the intention, or perceived intention, of physically injuring another person," and injury could range from slight pain, as in a slap, to murder. A broad definition of violence, which would include spanking as a form of violent behavior, was employed to estimate the frequency with which children are hit in their families.

A national probability sample yielded 2,143 completed interviews with 460 men and 1,183 women, focusing upon the tactics employed in dealing with family disputes (Gelles, 1978; Straus, 1979; Straus, Gelles, & Steinmetz, 1980). Among the respondents who had children between the ages of 3 and 17 living at home, 63% cited at least one violent episode during the survey year (1975), and 73% of the survey sample reported at least one violent occurrence during the entire course of raising children. As expected, milder forms of violence were reported more frequently. Slaps or spankings were mentioned by 58% of the respondents as having occurred in the previous year, and by 71% of the parents as having ever taken place. During the survey year, 41% of the parents admitted pushing or shoving a child, while 13% admitted to hitting the child. Throwing an object was less common, but still occurred in 5% of the families surveyed.

Even though the smallest percentage of parents reported exposing a child to the more dangerous types of violence, 3% still admitted to kicking, biting, or hitting a child with a fist in 1975. Slightly more than 1% of the respondents reported "beating up" a child in the survey year. Finally, .10%, or one in a thousand parents, claimed to have threatened their child with a gun or a knife in 1975, and about the same number actually admitted using a gun or a knife.

When these rates of violence are extrapolated to the total population of children 3 to 17 years of age living with both parents, an astoundingly large number of children appear to have been kicked, bitten, punched, beaten up, threatened with a gun or a knife, or actually attacked with a gun or knife. Of the nearly 46 million children between 3 and 17 years old who lived with their parents in 1975, we may estimate that between 3.1 and 4.0 million had been kicked, bitten, or punched by parents at some time in their lives; between 1.0 and 1.9 million were kicked, bitten, or punched in 1975; between 1.4 and 2.3 million had been "beaten up" while growing up; and between 900,000 and 1.8 million had had their parents use a gun or knife on them at some time. The implications for the perpetuation of aggressive behavior are dramatic.

When these data were summarized in the form of a child abuse index, measuring whether a parent had ever kicked, bitten, punched, hit with an object, beaten up, or used a knife or gun on their child, it was estimated that 14 out of every 100 American parents of children 3 through 17 years old had treated their children violently enough to be considered abusive. This means that of the 46 million children in these age groups in the United States who live with both parents, approximately 6.5 million are abused each year. Even when the abuse index is recalculated to consider only incidents as severe as, or more severe than, hitting the child with an object, abuse rates drop to three or four out of every hundred parents—1.7 million children per year. Clearly, child maltreatment, however defined, is not as isolated a phenomenon as most of us believe or would like to believe.

DEVELOPMENTAL CONSEQUENCES

Until recently, virtually all attention paid to child abuse has been devoted to understanding its causes. This, in and of itself, should not be surprising. Concern for etiology stems from concern for treatment. Given the general assumption that child abuse is bad for children, that in fact many die, are brain-damaged or otherwise permanently physically injured, and that the psychological as well as physical effects of abuse and neglect need to be remedied insofar as possible, it stands to reason that more attention has been paid to cause than to consequence. Nevertheless, what is the current state of our knowledge regarding the psychological consequences of maltreatment for the developing child, particularly with respect to the development of aggression?

Until the middle 1970s most of what was known about the development of maltreated children was based upon the clinical impressions and evaluations of practitioners dealing with abused neglected children. What was lacking, as a result, were firm grounds for drawing strong conclusions. Without sampling adequate groups of nonmaltreated children to compare with abused and neglected children, it was difficult to determine whether dysfunctional behavior displayed by maltreated children was a cause or consequence of the hostile or indifferent care they received at the hands of their parents. Consider, for example, the reports of child-care workers who characterized a group of abused children as "whiny, fussy, listless, chronically crying, demanding, stubborn, resistive, negativistic, pallid, sickly, emaciated, fearful, panicky, unsmily" and difficult to manage (Johnson & Morse, 1968). Given the recognition—emphasized in Chapter 6—that parent–child relations are a two-way street, there are certainly grounds for contending that such characteristics of children are as likely to contribute to as result from child abuse and neglect.

On the basis of more recent inquiry, especially studies using control groups of nonmaltreated children, it is possible to draw a tentative picture of the developmental consequences of child maltreatment. During the infancy years, abused children tend to display, not surprisingly, disturbances in affective expression, emotional maladjustment, and insecurity in their attachment relations to their mothers. In one recent investigation, abused and neglected infants between the ages of 12 and 26 months were observed in a laboratory setting to determine how they reacted to their parents and to strangers in a variety of social situations. Some of these situations involved the gradual and friendly approach of an unfamiliar adult which culminated in picking the baby up, a free play session involving mother and baby, the administration of standardized infant assessments, and a brief separation followed by reunion with mother and stranger. As predicted, the emotional responses of abused babied were characteristically different from those of normal infants. In general, the abused infants appeared sad, fearful, distressed, and often angry. Moreover, their play behavior tended to be aimless, disorganized, and inhibited (Gaensbauer, Mrajek, & Harmon, 1981).

In a follow-up investigation aimed at refining the clinical description of distorted affective communication as reflected in social interchange, abused children were observed in interaction with unfamiliar adults and while playing with inanimate objects (Gaensbauer & Sands, 1981). The primary interaction pattern observed in the maltreated children involved social and emotional withdrawal. Abused and neglected infants not only failed to initiate social contact but also failed to respond to pleasurable interactions; in fact, they tended to isolate themselves to prevent social interchange. In addition to such disturbed social patterns, affective communications were inconsistent and unpredictable in occurrence, and shallow or distorted in emotional content when they did emerge.

Complementing the findings of these investigations are the results of two studies focused upon abused toddlers in day-care settings and the quality of their infant—mother attachment. Abused one-year-olds, Egeland and Sroufe (1981) found, were significantly more likely to be classified as avoidantly attached to their mothers—a style of relating to caregiver that has been linked to subsequent developmental incompetence. In the second study, although abused and non-abused control toddlers were similar in the number of approaches they made to peers, children with a history of maltreatment approached caregivers only half as often as the control children. Moreover, in response to friendly advances by caregivers, abused toddlers were more likely to terminate social contact and to respond to such overtures by moving to the side of the caregivers or by backing up when approached by them. In fact, avoidance comprised 25% of the abused children's responses to encounters with peers and caregivers, but only 6% of the responses of controls to such encounters. Many of the abused children wriggled or pushed away from situations involving physical contact, as when a caregiver went to seat a child on her lap during story time (George & Main, 1979).

These findings, along with other clinical impressions suggesting that abused children tend to be inhibited and overly compliant, and rarely express pain or distress, most certainly convey a picture of psychological disturbance—a picture that, upon reflection, does not appear all that surprising. If the quality of care one receives is hostile and rejecting, the tendency to avoid others for fear of similar experiences appears to be both reasonable and potentially adaptive. After all, how does the child know for certain that the pain experienced at the hands of his abusive caregiver is not a routine cost of engaging in social interchange?

The other primary pattern of response to abuse chronicled by clinicians and scientists, particularly in older children, involves aggression. This is why the specific analysis of child abuse is critical for understanding the sources of social influence and control in childhood and violence. In many cases, severe temper tantrums and angry outbursts, including self-destructive behavior (e.g., head banging, self-biting), have been noted among maltreated children (Galdston,

1975; Green, 1978; Martin, 1976). In the observational study of abused and nonabused toddlers in a therapeutic day-care center described earlier (George & Main, 1979), it was found that acts of aggression against friendly caregivers occurred on the average of six times per two-hour observation; in contrast, nonabused control children engaged in similar aggressive acts only once per two-hour period. The incidence of aggression against agemates, it is interesting to note, was similar across groups in this study.

The findings just summarized have been extended through investigations of preschoolers and school age children. Observation of 3- to 5-year-olds engaged in free play with peers reveals greater aggression among children identified as maltreated as well as less tolerance for situations in which they could not have their own way (Herrenkohl & Herronkohl, 1981). Reidy (1977) also found that abused children, who averaged 6.4 years of age in the study, displayed more aggression than maltreated peers across a variety of situations, including fantasy, free play, and classroom situations. Violence, then, appears to be a consistent pattern displayed by abused children, many of whom are otherwise characterized by emotional unresponsiveness.

In terms of causation, a variety of underlying processes may account for the aggression that is repeatedly observed in abused children. One possibility that has been suggested to account for this aggression is that they simply are modeling the hostile interpersonal exchanges they have experienced. Complementing this notion is the observation that maltreated children are "hypervigilant" (Martin & Breezley, 1977); that is, they appear to be constantly on the alert for danger, scanning the environment for signs of impending attack. To the extent that this is indeed the case, such children may be quick to interpret any interruption or obstacle as such a danger sign and, as a result, respond aggressively because they perceive frustrating circumstances as a threat to them. Alternatively, because of the poor quality of care they have experienced, maltreated children may simply have failed to learn and develop the social skills required to engage others in harmonious interaction (see also Elliot Turiel's analysis of presocial development in Chapter 6 of this volume). In this regard, Straker and Jacobsen (1981) have recently reported that 5- to 10-year-olds with a history of abuse perform less well on tests of empathy than do nonabused agemates. Finally, aggression may simply be a response to the frustration caused when one cannot effectively communicate with, and thereby influence, another.

Whatever the exact process by which avoidant and aggressive behavior is promoted, it is clear that maltreated children run an increased risk of developing disturbed patterns of functioning. From the standpoint of several studies of parent–child relations. the effect of child abuse on child development is not surprising. Child abuse can be viewed as an extreme case of hostile, punitive rearing, which is well known to undermine, rather than support, the welfare of the developing human being.

THE ETIOLOGY OF CHILD ABUSE

By tradition, three general perspectives have been employed to account for the etiology of child maltreatment; these can be referred to as the psychiatric or psychological model, the sociological model, and the effect-of-child-on-caregiver model (Belsky, 1978a; Parke & Collmer, 1975).

The Psychiatric Model

The account of child maltreatment most widely subscribed to, by far, by the lay public falls within the psychiatric model, which focuses exclusive attention on the individual abusive parent. Essentially, the psychiatric model emphasizes the role that the parent plays since it is the parent who is the direct perpetrator of maltreatment. Probably the most compelling evidence that focuses attention on the psychiatric make-up of the individual abuser derives from reports linking parents' own child-rearing histories with subsequent parenting (e.g., Brown & Daniels, 1968; Spinetta & Rigler, 1972; Steele & Pollack, 1968). Repeatedly investigators have reported associations between maltreatment in one's own childhood and subsequent maltreatment of one's offspring. Although the data upon which such claims are based are fraught with methodological weaknesses (Belsky, 1978a; Jayaratne, 1977; Parke & Collmer, 1975), it would be unwise to disregard entirely insight into the etiology of child abuse that may be gained from other than hard scientific evidence. This should not imply, however, that such relations between prior rearing history and subsequent parenting are to be accepted at face value; clearly, not all parents who were maltreated while growing up maltreat their own offspring. Indeed, it is not even known whether one needs to have been maltreated in order to become a maltreating parent.

The Sociological Model

A radical sociological critique of the psychiatric model argues that the psychiatric perspective "blames the victim." That is, it fails to recognize that it is social conditions that create the stress which undermines family functioning, and cultural values and practices that encourage the societal violence and corporal punishment of children which are primarily responsible for child maltreatment (Gelles, 1973; 1975; Gil, 1971; Light, 1973). Parents are considered mere victims of such social forces. More specifically, sociological thinkers argue that in a society in which violence is rampant and frequently encouraged as a strategy for settling disputes in human relations, a society in which children are regarded as the property of their parents and in which beliefs like "spare the rod and spoil the child'' are promulgated, the fact that parent–child conflict eventuates in child abuse should not be surprising. In essence, the cultural soil is regarded as fertile for the maltreatment of children.

In addition to such critiques of contemporary American culture and society, empirical evidence has been amassed showing that child maltreatment is not evenly distributed throughout the population but tends to be more frequent in certain "sociological pockets." The fact that child abuse is more frequent in the lower socioeconomic strata of our society represents one such piece of evidence. And although it is likely that maltreatment is more easily identified in populations that use public hospitals and are subject to investigation from community agencies, this explanation alone does not account for the social class difference in suspected and reported cases of child maltreatment that have been documented repeatedly (Garbarino, 1976; Pelton, 1978).

Additional support for the sociological model of child abuse, especially the notion that social stress creates a climate in which child maltreatment can flourish, comes from data linking unemployment, labor market shrinkage, and social isolation with child abuse (Gelles, 1975; Giovannoni & Billingsley, 1970; Steinberg, Catalano, & Dooley, 1981). One national survey, for example, found unemployment to be the factor that most frequently differentiated child abusers from nonabusers (Gil, 1971; Light, 1973). With respect to social isolation, Garbarino (1977a) has pointed out that virtually every study that has considered the absence of social ties as a correlate of child abuse has discerned a positive relationship between such isolation and the occurrence of abuse or neglect.

When the possibility is considered that social isolation can be self-generating because of a dearth of interpersonal skills required for generating and maintaining reciprocal social relations, and that such interpersonal deficits may themselves result from a developmental history that fails to offer opportunities and occasions to develop these skills, it becomes apparent that the sociological and psychiatric explanations of child abuse may be more complementary than is often assumed (Belsky, 1980). Indeed, evidence to support the proposition that the tendency to isolate oneself may be a function of early developmental experience comes from a recent study, already reviewed, of the social behavior of abused toddlers (George & Main, 1979). Recall that careful observation of a sample of children in day care revealed that by the age of 18–24 months abused children had developed aberrant patterns for dealing with even friendly social encounters with day-care teachers, which itself served to decrease social interaction. Clearly if such interactive patterns remain in the behavior repertoire as one grows up, it is not difficult to understand how poor developmental experiences are later linked to stress occasioned by social isolation.

Such stress could be mitigated, no doubt, by a supportive marital relationship. But here clinical evidence tends to indicate that marital discord is often another correlate of child maltreatment (Elmer, 1967; Green, 1978; Young,

1964). When considered in light of the preceding analysis of social isolation, this should not be surprising, as it is likely that many of the social skills required for developing a supportive marital relationship are lacking in those who were maltreated as children. Thus, the maltreated child would appear to embark on a self-limiting and self-damaging course which may come, through a variety of ways, to approximate in later adulthood the same conditions provoking his or her own childhood mistreatment.

The Effect of Child on Caregiver Model

At about the same time Bell (1968) and others were working to redirect the study of socialization away from the "social mold" model (Hartup, 1978), which presumed unidirectional pathways of influence from parent to child, toward a model more consistent with reciprocal, bidirectional processes, child abuse researchers were reporting data consistent with the notion that children can influence the care they receive. Indeed, evidence to suggest that children might be partly responsible for the maltreatment they experience came from reports that a single child within a family was often the recipient of abuse (Brown & Daniels, 1968; Milowe & Lourie, 1964); that maltreated children exhibited deviations in social interaction and general functioning prior to their reported abuse (Gil, 1971; Birrell & Birrell, 1969; Johnson & Morse, 1968); and that prematurity and low birth weight characterized the perinatal histories of a disproportionate number of abused children (Elmer & Gregg, 1967; Fontana, 1971; Klein & Stern, 1971; Martin, Conway, Breezley, & Kempe, 1974).

Some of the most compelling evidence in support of this third model of the etiology of child maltreatment comes from experimental simulation studies designed to test propositions, derived from correlational data and clinical reports, implicating the child as a causal agent in the abuse process. One such study of premature infants, for example, demonstrated that individuals felt less sympathy for videotaped displays of crying premature infants than they did for crying full-term babies, most likely because the cries of the prematures were judged to be more aversive (Frodi et al., 1978). The fact that such babies tend to be less responsive and are frequently more difficult to care for (Goldberg, 1978) may help account for their increased risk of mistreatment.

With respect to older children, another simulation study nicely documents how adult–child conflict can escalate in intensity as a function of uncooperative child behavior (Parke & Sawin, 1977). Indeed, in this research, defiance by the child in the face of parental discipline served to escalate the severity of parental threats in such a way that it became very clear how the child could actively contribute to his own maltreatment by invoking, often in an apparently intentional manner, the hostility of his or her parent.

Ecological Integration

It has become apparent that a single model narrow in scope, whether emphasizing the personality and developmental history of abusive parents, or the social context in which they function, or the role children play in eliciting their own maltreatment, must inevitably fail in an attempt to account for the multifaceted processes at work in child abuse. In response to the widely recognized need to integrate these three distinct approaches to the etiology of child maltreatment, one of us (Belsky, 1980) offered an ecological synthesis of these approaches as being clearly complementary using a modified version of Bronfenbrenner's (1977) ecological framework.

Indeed, Belsky's review of past research highlighted the components of each of the three prior models. Specifically, the developmental history of persons who maltreat their offspring was underscored for the role it presumably plays in shaping their personalities and parenting behavior (ontogenic development). Also emphasized were the internal dynamics of family life (the microsystem), particularly stress-promoting child characteristics and behavior, such as fussiness, physical handicap, and disobedience. The support and assistance provided by the marital relationship, or the stress and conflict it generates, were also regarded as influential dimensions of family functioning. Similarly, an impoverished social network and concurrent social isolation, as well as unemployment, were singled out as salient neighborhood, community, and extrafamilial factors that undermine parenting (the exosystem). The broader cultural context (the macrosystem), which serves to permit or encourage violence in society, including the corporal punishment of children and the use of violent strategies in settling disputes, and which regards children as the property of parents, represented a final critical factor in the etiology of child maltreatment.

Determinants of Parental Competence

Available theory and research on the etiology of child abuse and neglect draw attention to three general sources of influence upon parental functioning: the parent's ontogenic origins and personal psychological resources, the child's characteristics as an individual, and contextual sources of stress and support. A basic assumption of this presentation is that these forces of influence are at work whether parental care is growth-promoting or abusive. In other words, we assume a continuum of care from high quality to low quality. In order to provide support for this claim, in the remainder of this section we will devote our attention to a consideration of research that does not directly address the etiology of child abuse but does nevertheless shed light on the determinants of parental competence and dysfunction. As we will soon discover, the research on nonabusive parenting is remarkably consistent with that bearing directly upon the etiology of child maltreatment. Furthermore, such research enables us to construct a developmental and contextual process model of the origins of individual differences in parenting which may serve as a guide for intervention efforts.

The Parent's Contribution. Research on child maltreatment indicates that parenting, like most dimensions of human functioning, may be influenced by enduring characteristics of the individual, characteristics that are, at least in part, a product of one's developmental history. To obtain a better sense of just how developmental history and personality influence parenting, it may be useful to consider briefly the kind of parenting that appears to promote optimal child functioning and to speculate on the type of personality most likely to provide such developmental care.

In the infancy period, detailed observational studies reveal that cognitive-motivational competence and healthy socioemotional development are promoted by attentive, warm, stimulating, responsive, and nonrestrictive caregiving (e.g., Clarke-Stewart, 1973; Stayton, Hogan, & Ainsworth, 1971; Yarrow, Rubenstein, & Pedersen, 1975). In regard to the preschool years, the work of Baumrind (1967, 1971) demonstrates that it is high levels of nurturance and control that foster the child's ability to engage peers and adults in a friendly and cooperative manner and to develop the capacity to be instrumentally resourceful and achievement-striving. And, as children grow older, parental use of induction or reasoning, consistent discipline, and expression of warmth have been found to relate positively to self-esteem, internalized controls, prosocial orientation, and intellectual achievement during the school-age years (e.g., Coopersmith, 1967; Hoffman, 1970; McCall, 1974).

Consideration of these findings and others suggests that, across childhood, parenting that is *sensitively* attuned to children's capabilities and to the developmental tasks they face promotes a variety of highly valued developmental outcomes, including emotional security, behavioral independence, social competence, and intellectual achievement (Belsky, Lerner, & Spanier, 1983). In infancy this sensitivity translates into being able to read babies' often subtle cues and to respond appropriately to their needs in reasonably brief periods of time (Ainsworth, Blehar, Waters, & Wall, 1978; Lamb & Easterbrooks, 1980). In childhood, sensitivity means continuing the warmth and affection provided in the early years but increasing the demands for age-appropriate behavior. Parents must be willing and able to direct children's behavior and activities without squelching their developing independence and industry. Ultimately, the sensitive and thus competent parent must be willing to wean the child from this overt control to permit the child's testing of personal limits through the exercise of internalized rules and regulations. Indeed, by the time the child reaches adolescence, the competent parent has set the stage so that the child has the psychological building blocks to encounter successfully the transition from childhood to adolescence.

What kind of person should be able to provide such developmentally flexible and growth-promoting care? The sensitive parent, one might argue, is able to put aside his or her own viewpoint and accurately appraise the perspective of others, is able to empathize with them, and, in addition, is able to adopt a nurturant orientation. It is difficult to imagine how a parent without the capacity to escape the egocentrism of his or her own psychological state and the ability to nurture others could recognize needs of children on a daily basis. Indeed, it is likely that only by possessing the skills outlined above would an individual, faced with the very real demands and challenges that parenting presents, not abdicate responsibility (as in neglectful or permissive rearing), or else rely on absolute power (as in child abuse or authoritarian rearing). Moreover, to function well as a parent an individual would likely need to experience a sense of control over his or her own life and destiny and feel that his or her own psychological needs were being met. Since the essence of parenting, especially in the childhood years, involves "giving," it seems reasonable that parents most able to do this in a sensitive, competence-inducing manner, will be mature, psychologically healthy adults. To what extent does the empirical literature support this contention, or its converse—that is, that dysfunctional parenting is likely to be provided by developmentally immature and psychologically unhealthy individuals?

Personality. The literature linking personality and parenting is not nearly as rich or extensive as one might expect. Nevertheless, the limited data that are available can be marshalled to provide some support for the notion that personal maturity and competent parenting covary. The first evidence in support of this contention comes from investigations linking maternal age to parental functioning, since age can be conceptualized as a marker or proxy of psychological maturity.

A recent study demonstrates that first-time mothers interact with their 4-month-old infants in a more positively affectionate, stimulating, and sensitive manner the older they are (Ragozin, Basham, Crnic, Greenberg, & Robinson, 1982). It is quite conceivable that early entry into parenting "forecloses" some of the individual development that, for example, the 30-year-old first-time parent has been able to experience by delaying motherhood. Thus, the differential timing of first birth and the personal development it either permits or limits may well explain why, for primiparous mothers, age and quality of parenting are positively related (Ragozin *et al.,* 1982).

The data on teenage mothers, who are presumably less psychologically mature than older mothers, are generally consistent with this line of reasoning.

Not only is there evidence that such young mothers express less desirable chil-drearing attitudes and have less realistic expectations for infant development than do older mothers (Epstein, 1979: Field, Widmayer, Stringer, & Ignatoff, 1980), but, from a more behavioral standpoint, it has been observed that they also tend to be less responsive to their newborns (Jones, Green, & Krauss, 1980) and to engage infants in less verbal interaction (Osofsky & Osofsky, 1970).

Data from a recent study of some 267 economically disadvantaged families from the Minneapolis–St. Paul area more directly implicate the role personality plays in shaping parenting. Those mothers who proved to be abusive or ne-glectful during their children's first few years displayed, prenatally and at three months postpartum, a configuration of personality attributes indicating that they were less psychologically complex and less well-integrated personally than mothers who did not maltreat their offspring (Brunnquell, Crichton, & Egeland, 1981). More specifically, these mothers received fewer optimal scores on sum-mary scales comprised of several specific personality and attitudinal assess-ments, including anxiety, locus of control, aggression, succorance, suspicion, and dependence. Indeed these inadeuate inadequate caregivers lacked under-standing of the complexity of a parent–child relationship, reacted negatively to pregnancy, were more aggressive and suspicious, and described themselves more negatively.

In addition to maintaining a reasonably positive sense of self and at the same time an ability to assume the perspective of others, the mature, healthy person-ality also is expected to appraise situations accurately in terms of his or her ability to exert control over the environment. Except in unusual circumstances (as when environmental events are beyond control), such an individual should operate from an internal locus of control, recognizing the influence that his or her own actions have upon the world. One would expect such internal locus of control to be associated with growth-promoting parenting, and in studies of infancy and preschool periods support for this prediction can be found. Mothers who score higher internally on locus of control measures demonstrate greater stimulation of and interaction with their infants (Schaeffer, Bauman, Siegel, Hosking & Sanders, 1980), and more warmth, acceptance, and helpfulness—versus disapproval—toward their preschoolers (Mondell & Tyler, 1981).

Evidence that is potentially more compelling in its demonstration of the influence of personal psychological attributes on parental functioning can be found in investigations of psychologically disturbed adults (Belsky, 1984). The disturbance in parental functioning receiving the most attention from investiga-tors interested in the personality–parenting link is depression. One of the most extensive and informative studies of this relationship and its developmental consequences for the child is provided by Weissman and her colleagues (Or-raschel, Weissman, & Kidd, 1980; Weissman & Paykel, 1974). Relying upon self-reports from semistructured interviews with 40 depressed and 40 nondisturbed, mostly middle- and low-income mothers, these investigators concluded that depressed parents provide a disruptive, hostile, rejecting home environment which, not surprisingly, undermines child functioning. This conclusion was based upon the fact that depressed mothers were only moderately involved in their children's lives, experienced difficulty communicating with them, and reported considerable friction in parent–child relations. Disorganization and chaos frequently resulted as mothers withdrew from all aspects of home management. The children themselves often responded to such noninvolvement with hyperactivity and excessive sibling rivalry (possibly for whatever limited attention the mother provided), while some even began to display acute symptoms of agitated depression themselves.

The research we have summarized to this point provides support for the general notion that an individual's personality can function to support or undermine his or her parenting ability. If our principal concern is the determinants of parenting, we must ask, in the face of such an observation, about the developmental origins of personality as they pertain to childrearing. Therefore, we now turn our attention to the developmental histories of parents under the assumption that earlier experiences shape personality which subsequently contributes to parenting. We reserve for a later section the role of immediate *contextual* stresses and supports with regard to parental mental health status.

Developmental History. Consistent with previously summarized research indicating that, in many cases, the abusive and neglectful behavior parents direct toward their children can be traced back to their own childhood experiences, there is also evidence that depression (another influential factor for parenting, as we have just seen) can itself be traced back to a parent's ontogenic history. As part of an investigation specifically concerned with the social origins of depressions, Brown and Harris (1978) conducted clinical interviews, psychological testing, and case-record reviews on some 114 randomly sampled clinic patients and 95 neighborhood controls. Separation from the mother prior to the age of 11 emerged as one important feature distinguishing female patients (4%) from controls (17%), though only those individuals who had lost a mother and also experienced a severely stressful life event or major difficulty actually became depressed.

The potential implications of such early experiences for parenting are suggested specifically by several studies revealing a direct association between early separation from parent(s) and subsequent parental dysfunction. For example, Frommer and O'Shea (1973a) found, in the course of clinical work at a day center for disturbed preschool children, that an unduly high proportion of the mothers whose children were disturbed, or who themselves reported difficulties in mothering, also reported a history of separation from one or both of their parents in childhood. In a second investigation replicating this general finding from the first study, Frommer and O'Shea (1973b) further observed that mothers reporting parenting difficulties who had experienced parental separation in their own childhood were also likely to be suffering from depression.

Having observed that early separation may be related to depression, as well as to mothering, one may find the results of still another English study especially intriguing. Hall, Pawlby, and Wolkind (1979) found, in their observational research on 68 primiparous working-class women, that not only was disruption in the family of origin by parental death, separation, or divorce associated with lower levels of mother–infant interaction but, possibly as a consequence of receiving less social stimulation, the children of such mothers displayed less linguistic competence when tested at age 27 months.

When these several studies concerned with the origins of depression and the consequences of separation are jointly considered, there certainly appears to be a basis for concluding that, at least in certain stressful conditions, developmental history influences psychological well-being, which in turn affects parental functioning and, as a result, child development. Indeed, a conclusion that can be drawn at this point is that, in general, supportive developmental experiences give rise to a mature, healthy person, who is then capable of providing the sensitive parental care that promotes optimal development.

Highly pertinent to this conclusion are the empirical and theoretical arguments summarized by McCandless (1967) regarding the intergenerational transmission of what Adorno termed the "authoritarian personality." Theory and data suggest that the authoritarian parent subscribes to a pattern of childrearing practices that promote intolerance of ambiguity, rigid, dichotomous ("black or white") attitudes and responses, conformity to parental or other "power models," extrinsic values and motivation, unrealistic social goals, self-devaluation and, ultimately, ethnocentrism. By practicing "all or none" reinforcement (i.e., treating a child alternatively as all good or all bad) which is contingent upon conformity to socially approved standards of behavior, by emphasizing status and power as gratification, by employing harsh disciplinary methods but also more extreme forms of rewards, and by setting themselves in the position of sole dispensers of rewards and punishments, these parents encourage formation of authoritarian personality attributes in their children. Of particular importance to this discussion, such parents, by so doing, also ensure that their own childrearing techniques will succeed them in raising still another generation of authoritarian individuals. Hence, the cycle of parenting–personality–parenting is perpetuated across generations. This is a particularly fitting case in point for illustrating the developmental sequence encompassed in our model. Needless to say, it represents but one of a multiplicity of paths linking individual and environmental factors with the parenting they engender. In the next section we take a counterperspective in order that we may consider the role played by the children themselves.

The Child's Contribution. Appreciation of children's contribution to the caregiving they receive is now so widely shared that it has affected our way of thinking about specific social policy-related concerns such as child abuse (Belsky, 1980; Friedrich & Boriskin, 1976; Parke & Collmer, 1975) and malnutrition (Pollitt, 1973; Rossetti-Ferreira, 1978; Zeskind & Ramey, 1978), as well as more general explanations of the developmental process itself (Sameroff, 1975). Although demonstrations of the effects of the child abound, there has been little effort expended on determining exactly which particular characteristics of individuality most strongly impact upon parenting (Belsky, 1981). In recent years, however, interest in individual differences in temperament has expanded considerably (see Hubert, Wachs, Peters-Martin, & Gandour, 1982, and Plomin, 1982, for reviews), especially in regard to identifying temperament styles that make parenting more or less difficult (Bates, 1980).

With regard to documentation of the specific effects of a child's difficult temperament on parenting, findings are mixed (Bates, 1980). Nevertheless, select evidence certainly does exist in support of the notion that difficult temperament, especially in infancy, can undermine parental functioning. Campbell (1979) reported, for example, that when mothers rated their infants as having difficult temperaments at 3 months, they interacted with them less and were less responsive to their cries at 3 and 8 months, in comparison to a set of matched controls. Similarly, Milliones (1978) discerned a significant negative association between mothers' perceptions of difficulty and outreach workers' ratings of maternal responsiveness to infants who averaged 11 months of age. And, as a final illustrative finding, Kelly (1976) reported that mothers of more difficult 4-month-olds tended to respond negatively to negative infant emotions. Interestingly, a follow-up analysis of these same mother–infant dyads at 12 months indicated that mothers of these difficult infants more often avoided social interaction with them than did other mothers with their own children (Sameroff, 1977).

Because the child's influence on parenting is so widely recognized by developmentalists, we have chosen not to treat this issue in detail. Nevertheless, the limited evidence just reviewed does illustrate the now well-accepted point that even in nonabusive samples, characteristics of children hypothesized to make them more or less difficult to care for do indeed appear to shape the quantity and quality of parental care they receive. A potentially important qualification, however, concerns the nonindependence of measures in these studies. Mothers who exhibit less desirable parenting behavior (e.g., unresponsiveness, social avoidance) may systematically differ in their perceptions and/or reports of their children's temperament and behavior. Perhaps the mother who finds little appeal in young infants is more likely both to focus on the difficult qualities of her own (or any) child and to minimize her interaction with the baby. Objective assessments of child characteristics are clearly necessary.

One further point worth noting is the fact that no study to date has examined the differential impact of such characteristics on fathers and mothers, either during infancy or subsequent developmental periods. Furthermore, although speculation abounds with respect to the need to consider child characteristics in the context of parent characteristics (e.g., personality, expectations), surprisingly little work illuminating such interactive processes is actually available. That which does exist may be marshalled to support the conclusion that neither temperament nor other child characteristics *per se* shape parenting, but rather that the "goodness of fit" between parent and child determines the development of parent–child relations (Lerner & Lerner, 1983).

Contextual Sources of Stress and Support. Although both parent and child contributions to differences in parenting have been addressed here, an ecological perspective on this topic requires consideration of the *context* of parent–child relations as well. For this purpose, one may turn to the abundance of evidence that highlights the generally beneficial impact on social support on both psychological and physical health. Some data indicate, for instance, that supports of all kinds, either formal or informal, enable individuals to cope with stress and thereby both lessen the risk of ill health and facilitate a more optimal recovery from illness (Caplan, 1974; Cassell, 1974; Cobb, 1976; Mitchell & Trickett, 1980; Powell, 1979).

Of particular significance to the topic of this discussion is research chronicling a relationship between support and general well-being in the case of parents (Colletta, 1983: Colletta & Gregg, 1981; Nuckolls, Cassell, & Kaplan, 1972). Not only does overall support positively influence psychological well-being in general and the mental health of parents in particular, but, possibly as a consequence, it is also related to parenting. Open-ended interviews by Colletta (1981) with three groups of mothers with preschoolers (low- and middle-income single parents and middle-income married mothers) revealed that total support (provided by friends, relatives, and spouse) was negatively associated with maternal restrictiveness and punitiveness. In fact, Colleta was led to conclude on the basis of her data that "mothers receiving the least amount of total support tended to have more household rules and to use more authoritarian punishment techniques" (p. 843). Consistent with these findings are results of a study indicating that the social support available to mothers of 3-year olds who had required intensive care as neonates predicted the extent to which the mothers were stimulating in their parenting (Pascoe, Loda, Jeffries, & Earp, 1981).

The fact that parenting appears to be positively associated with social support should not be surprising. As noted already, support and general well-being have been repeatedly linked. If one conceptualizes growth-promoting parenting as a dimension of mental health, then the link between parenting and support may be but one way in which the more general supportive–well-being relationship manifests itself. But even after highlighting such general associations, there remain two specific questions regarding the role of social support in an analysis of the determinants of parenting. How does support influence parenting, and from where does influential support derive? To address these questions, the following discussion is subdivided according to the function of support and its particular sources; and evidence pertinent to a more refined and more clearly differential understanding of how support affects parental functioning is reviewed.

Functions of Support. In line with the extensive literature on social support, it is likely that, in the case of parenting, social support functions in three general ways: (a) by providing emotional support, (b) by providing instrumental assistance, and (c) by providing social expectations (Caplan, 1974; Cassell, 1974; Cobb, 1976: Cochran & Brassard, 1979; Mitchell & Trickett, 1980; Powell, 1979). Emotional support can be identified as the love and interpersonal acceptance an individual receives from others, either through explicit statements to that effect or as a result of considerate and caring actions. Instrumental assistance can take a variety of forms, including the provision of information and advice as well as help with routine tasks such as child care, which Longfellow, Dill, Makosky, and Zur-Spiro (1981) found to predict levels of parenting stress. Finally, social expectations serve as guides about what is and is not appropriate behavior.

Expectations and advice, it is important to note, may not always serve as a truly helpful function or facilitate parenting. This would seem to be especially the case when expectations are inconsistent (Belsky, Robins, & Gamble, 1983; Lamb & Easterbrooks, 1980; Todd, 1980) or contrary to an individual's own inclinations (Minturn & Lambert, 1964; Powell, 1979; Stolz, 1967).

Each type of support cited above can function to influence parenting both directly and indirectly (Belsky, Robins, & Gamble, 1983). Direct effects are those which are targeted at parental behavior, whereas indirect effects are mediated by other factors. When a parent is praised, for example, by a neighbor or a teacher for her child's good behavior or for her skill in handling children, emotional support can be considered direct with respect to parenting; when a spouse lets his mate know she is loved and cherished in general, however, we may assume that such positive sentiments, though not directly targeted at parenting, nevertheless affect caregiving and may therefore be regarded as indirect forms of emotional support. Child abuse research highlights three distinct sources of stress and support that are likely to promote or undermine parental competence: the marital relationship, social networks, and employment.

The Marital Relationship. Belsky (1981) has argued that the marital relationship serves as the principal support system for parents. Although available evidence is not sufficient to document this claim, the effect of spousal relations on parenting has been suggested recently by studies of quite different developmental periods of the child (Belsky, Lerner, & Spanier, 1983).

During the infancy years the influence of fathers on child functioning may be primarily indirect, that is, mediated by the wife in her capacity as mother (Lewis & Weinraub, 1976; Parke, 1978; Pedersen, Yarrow, Anderson, & Cain, 1978). Several studies have begun to illuminate these types of indirect effects (Moss, 1974; Switzky, Vietze, & Switzky, 1979). Pedersen (1975, 1982; Pedersen, Anderson, and Cain, 1977), for instance, has found that tension and conflict between husband and wife (as reported by fathers) strongly and negatively correlated with independent observational evaluations of maternal feeding competence. The husband's esteem for his wife as a mother (i.e., direct emotional support), on the other hand, was positively related to feeding skill. On the basis of a comparable investigation of changes in mother–infant reciprocity across the first month of the baby's life, Price (1977) in fact concluded that the mother's "ability to enjoy her infant, and regard it with affection, may be in part a function of the quality of her relationship with her husband" (p. 7).

From a paternal perspective, Belsky (1978b) observed that in families marked by frequent communication between husband and wife about the baby fathers were highly involved with their 15-month olds, both when alone with them and while in their wives' presence. More recently, he and his colleagues found that at 1, 3, and 9 months of age, high levels of fathering and marital interaction positively covary with each other (Belsky, Gilstrap, & Rovine, 1983).

Investigations linking marital relations and parenting during the preschool years are generally consistent with the parent–infant studies just summarized. Bandura and Walters (1959) observed that mothers who seemed inclined to nag and scold their sons felt less warmth and affection toward their husbands. Complementing these findings are data from a study by Sears, Maccoby, and Levin (1957) indicating that mothers' professed esteem for their husbands was systematically related to the praise they directed at their preschool children.

During the school-age and adolescent years, high interspousal hostility has been linked to parental negativeness, the frequent use of punishment, and the infrequent use of induction or reasoning as a disciplinary strategy (Dielman, Barton, & Cattell, 1977; Johnson & Lobitz, 1974: Kemper & Reichler, 1976a; Morton, Chapter 6 of this volume). The reason for this is suggested by Olweus's (1980) recent work on the development of aggression. This researcher also found that the quality of the emotional relationship between spouses apparently influences mothers' negativism toward their adolescent sons, and this provokes aggressive, antisocial teenage behavior. The concluding link between provocative adolescent behavior and parental punitiveness is easily envisioned.

On a more positive note, and with respect to fathering, Heath (1976) observed that paternal competence is predicted by marital happiness and the ability

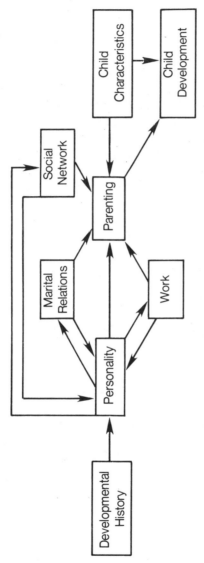

Figure 1. A process model of the determinants of parenting.

to communicate with one's spouse. The benefits of such marital harmony are evident in a current study of 6- to 11-year-old boys raised in reconstituted families comprising a stepfather and biological mother. These boys were found to be more socially competent than agemates reared in families comprising both biological parents (Santrock, Warshak, Lindbergh, & Meadows, 1982). This surprising result, further inquiry revealed, coincided with the more competent parenting displayed by the stepfathers. Most significant in terms of this discussion, however, is the observation that these more competent stepfathers, with more socially skilled stepsons, reported less marital conflict than did the biological fathers whose parenting and whose sons' functioning appeared less competent.

In sum, the data reviewed in this section strongly suggest that in order to understand parenting and its influence upon child development attention must be accorded to the marital relationship (Belsky, 1981). At the same time, it is essential to bear in mind the possibility that marital quality is itself a function of the developmental histories and the personalities of the individuals in the relationship. To the extent that this is true, a complete model of the determinants of parenting must necessarily consider the fact that developmental experience contributes to adult personality, which itself affects mate selection, marital functioning and, thereby, parenting behavior (see Figure 1).

Social Networks. If the marital relationship is the principal support system of parents, as we have suggested, it is likely that the interpersonal relations between parents and their friends, relatives, and neighbors—the significant others in their lives—function as the next most important system of support. And it is clear that the availability of significant others and the support received from them exert a beneficial impact upon parent–child relations (Aug & Bright, 1970; Hetherington, Cox, & Cox, 1977; Kessen, Fein, Clarke-Stewart, & Starr, 1975; McLanahan, Wedemeyer, & Adelberg, 1981; Toms-Olson, 1981). Powell (1979) discovered that the qualities of mothering during the infancy period which are predictive of child competence during the preschool years, namely verbal and emotional responsivity, are more characteristic of mothers who have weekly or more frequent contact with friends. Similarly, Crnic, Greenberg, Ragozin, Robinson, and Basham (1983) have found, in their study of the parents of preterm and term infants, that although assistance from friends did not relate to observed behavior *per se,* more positive maternal attitudes toward parenting were evident among mothers reporting more friends and/or greater support from those they did cite.

Turning to the preschool years, Abernethy (1973) found the presence of a tightly knit social network to be positively associated with mothers' sense of competence in the caregiving role. Beyond parental self-concept, supportive social network contact predicts maternal physical and temporal organization of her 3-year-old's environment, her avoidance of punishment and restriction (Pascoe *et al.*, 1981), and the degree to which teenage mothers are affectionate rather than hostile, indifferent, rejecting, and/or dissatisfied in their parental role (Colletta, 1981). Hess, Shipman, Brophy, and Bear (1968) reported not only that mothers who were well integrated in social networks were more likely to engage their preschoolers in goal-oriented tasks during structured interaction, but that the children of these presumably better-supported mothers performed more competently in both the structured task situations and in preschool as well.

Although social isolation, identified as a risk condition in the child abuse literature (Garbarino, 1977b), may be associated with less supportive parenting, it would be inappropriate to conclude on the basis of the above findings that more social network contact is always advantageous. Contact which would normally function supportively may become stressful if taken to an extreme (French, Rodgers, & Cobb, 1974). Indirect evidence of such a diminishing-returns effect can be found in Minturn and Lambert's (1964) cross-cultural study of parenting in six cultures. These investigators observed maternal warmth to be inversely related to the number of adult kin with young children that lived close to the mother, possibly as a result of social sanctions (stretched or violated in private) regarding public expressions of parent–child affection. When considered in conjunction with the results cited above, these data suggest the existence of some optimal but as yet unspecified degree of contact and support which, when surpassed or unrealized, serves to restrict or even undermine rather than enhance parenting. Indeed, what is probably most beneficial is what French *et al.* (1974) refer to as a "goodness of fit," representing the match between support desired and support received.

Work. The third and final contextual source of stress and support on parenting considered here is suggested by research that links unemployment and labor market shrinkage with child maltreatment (Light, 1973; Steinberg *et al.*, 1981). It is not only investigations of child abuse, however, that highlight the deleterious consequences of unemployment with respect to parent–child relations (Bronfenbrenner & Crouter, 1982). Over four decades ago, Komarovsky's (1940) detailed interview study of intact families with fathers on relief revealed that, especially in households with adolescent children, paternal authority declined with unemployment. Elder's (1974) investigation of children during the Great Depression documented similar consequences but in doing so was able to illustrate how families who were able to realign themselves in order to cope with a pattern of adversity could eventually derive benefits from the experience for adolescent offspring, especially sons.

Beyond the study of unemployment, one of the richest sources of information pertinent to the impact of work on parenting is found in the literature on maternal employment. Even though a sizable proportion of studies fail to document any such effects (e.g., Cohen, 1978; Hock, 1980; Schubert, Bradley-

Johnson, & Nuttal, 1980), several others do suggest that a mother's employment status influences both the quantity and quality of her own and her spouse's parenting behavior (see Bronfenbrenner & Crouter, 1982, for a review). The actual effect of maternal employment on child development appears to be mediated, however, by the mother's feelings about working—that is, by her psychological state vis-à-vis her role as worker. Not only is there evidence that mothers who are dissatisfied with their employment status have offspring whose development is less optimal than those whose mothers are satisfied with their work situation (Farel, 1980; Hock, 1979, 1980; Hoffman, 1961; Yarrow, Scott, De-Leeuw, & Heinig, 1962), but several studies, taking a more process-oriented perspective, suggest that parenting itself is compromised under such stressful conditions. In their previously mentioned investigation of 40 preschool family triads, Stuckey and her colleagues (1982) found that "parental negative affect was exhibited more frequently by parents with attitudes toward dual roles for women that did not match the employment status of the mother in their family" (p. 643). Similarly, Hoffman (1963) found that working mothers who liked their work displayed more affection and used less severe discipline with their children, while Yarrow *et al.* (1962) reported that mothers dissatisfied with their employment status reported more problems in childrearing. It appears to be the case, then, that it is not employment status *per se* that is principally influential, but how one feels about that status (i.e., about either staying home or going out to work). When one does what is not desired—often out of necessity—it stands to reason that psychological stress is experienced which then serves to undermine parental functioning.

Further insight into how employment influences parenting can be found in studies of men's work. In his longitudinal study of men in professional jobs, Heath (1976) found the characteristics Kanter (1978) referred to as "work absorption" related to paternal inadequacy. Specifically, the more time and energy fathers devoted to their occupations, the more irritable and impatient they were with their children, as indicated by both husbands' and wives' reports (Clark & Gecas, 1971; Moen, 1982; Pleck, Staines, & Lang, 1978). And in a somewhat different vein, Kemper and Reichler (1976b) and McKinley (1964) demonstrated that the father's job satisfaction is inversely related to the severity of punishment he dispenses and his reliance upon reasoning as a disciplinary strategy.

Relative Importance of Contextual Sources of Stress and Support. Throughout the preceding discussion of the roles that marriage, social networks, and work assume in supporting or undermining growth-promoting parental functioning, only the consequences of variation within any single sphere of influence have been considered. What remains to be addressed is the relative contribution made by each of these three contextual dimensions. We remain of the opinion that the marital relationship is the first-order support system, with inherent potential for exerting the most positive or negative effects on parental functioning. This appears reasonable if only because emotional investment is routinely greater in marriage, as is time spent in this relationship.

Two important studies have been reported recently that address this issue of the *relative* importance of marital support as opposed to certain other kinds of support. In Colletta's (1981) investigation of 50 adolescent mothers, the emotional assistance received from the family of origin (i.e., social network) was found to be most predictive of maternal attitudes and affectionate behavior; the support received from a boyfriend or spouse was next in order of importance, followed finally by the support of friends. In another investigation, comprised of 105 mothers and their full-term and pre-term 4-month-olds, "intimate support (from spouse) proved to have the most general positive effects, although community and friendship support appear[ed] valuable to maternal attitudes as well" (Crnic et al., 1983, p. 14). The fact that the availability of the spouse's support and the mother's satisfaction with the support given turned out to be the most significant predictors of the mother's positive attitude toward parenting and of the affect she displayed in face-to-face interaction led Crnic et al. to express strong agreement with our earlier conclusion. Consistent with our own thinking, the hypothesis was also advanced by Crnic et al. that over time, as children mature, the possibility of direct influences of social supports on children probably increases.

It is probably the case, however, that in certain conditions marriage plays a less influential role than that chronicled by Crnic et al. (1983). In circumstances such as single parenthood and teenage parenthood, social networks will presumably serve as the principal source of support, as Colletta's (1981) data indicate. The same may be true for traditional blue-collar marriages in which husband and wife roles typically serve more instrumental than intimate functions and in which neither friendship nor romance, and thus emotional support, are the principal reasons for the relationship. Young and Willmott's (1975) description of social network ties in East London, particularly those of mothers to their families of origin, clearly suggests this to be the case. With respect to occupation, it is unclear at present what its relative influence may be. The more important the work role is in one's hierarchy of identities, the more influence it is likely to exert.

It is unfortunately the case that both our assumption of the primacy of marital relations as a source of support and stress and our inclination to emphasize social networks as second in importance must remain speculative propositions. The reason for this is that no investigation to date has included each of the three contextual determinants of parenting discussed here in a comparative study design. A clear imperative for future research is indicated by this lacuna.

The Determinants of Parenting: A Process Model

This analysis of the determinants of parental functioning, which is most certainly consistent with research on the etiology of child abuse, indicates that parental functioning is multiply and reciprocally determined. We offer in Figure 1 a process model of the determinants of parenting that summarizes schematically the ideas discussed thus far in this chapter as well as several others which will now be advanced. As should be evident in Figure 1 and from our discussion up to this point, we presume that personality, social networks, work, marital relations, and child characteristics all directly influence parenting. Further, developmental history is presumed to shape personality and thereby parenting, through what is, consequently, an indirect effect.

Several of the arrows included in Figure 1 underscore two additional assumptions. The first of these is that the personality or psychological attributes of an individual affect the resources she or he will be able to draw on which will support or undermine parenting. Individuals vary in the quality of the marriages they participate in, the jobs they are able to find and hold, and the support and assistance they receive from friends, neighbors, and relatives. For this reason Figure 1 includes arrows linking personality to marriage, work, and social network and thereby underscores the fact that individuals can serve as producers of their own development (Lerner & Busch-Rossnagel, 1981).

Probably the most compelling evidence for such a process comes from a previously mentioned study of the developmental consequences of child abuse. Recall that George and Main (1979), in their observations of abused children in a day-care center, found that maltreated toddlers isolated themselves socially by failing to respond to friendly overtures and by avoiding many social exchanges. Quite conceivably such patterns are maintained as these and similar children grow up, one consequence of which is that social skills fail to develop; and this leads to the same absence of social network ties that has been repeatedly linked to abuse. In such circumstances it would be inappropriate to speak of social isolation as something done to the abuser, but rather as something the abuser-to-be generates himself (or herself).

The second basic assumption schematically represented in Figure 1 involves the process whereby contextual sources of stress and support function indirectly to enhance or undermine parental functioning. Up to this point we have spoken mainly in terms of the direct effect of these sources of influence on parenting. The possibility must be entertained, however, that the effect of marriage, social networks, and work on parenting may actually be mediated by their influence on general psychological well-being. For this reason, arrows are included in Figure 1 extending from these three contextual sources of influence to parent personality.

Brown and Harris's (1978) and Zur-Spiro and Longfellow's (1981) interview studies of urban women provide empirical support for this contention. These researchers have documented an association between the presence of a supportive husband or boyfriend and lower frequency of depression, which we have observed already to be related to parenting. With respect to the indirect influence of social networks on parenting, Cochran and Brassard (1979) hypothesized that the support which social networks provide can enhance self-esteem and as a consequence increase the patience and sensitivity that individuals exercise in the parenting role.

Finally, and with respect to the effect of work on general psychological well-being, Miller, Schooler, Kohn, and Miller's (1979) interviews with more than 500 women revealed that specific conditions of work, including closeness of supervision, routinization of job, and the substantive complexity of tasks performed "are related to effective intellectual functioning and an open, flexible orientation to others, while those that constrain opportunities for self-direction or subject the worker to pressures or uncertainties are related to ineffective functioning, unfavorable self-conceptions, and a rigid social orientation" (p. 91).

These latter personal characteristics could hardly be considered encouraging portents of sensitive, growth-promoting parenting practices. The potential implications for parental functioning of unfavorable effects of work on personality are even more apparent in Piotrkowski's (1979) small but intensive study of 13 working-class and middle-class families. Case analysis indicated that "work experience is brought into the family via the worker-parent's emotional state, which in turn determines in part the person's availability to family members, particularly children" (Bronfenbrenner & Crouter, 1982, p. 28). Note how consistent this perspective is with Heath's (1976) study linking energy invested in the job and irritability and impatience with children.

In summary, the process model detailed in Figure 1 assumes that parenting is determined by three principal sources of influence, the parent's psychological well-being, the child's unique characteristics, and the contextual sources of stress and support. Personality influences parenting directly as well as indirectly—for instance, by influencing the social support an individual has or does not have available, and is itself shaped by the parent's developmental history. Marriage, social networks, and work also influence parenting directly and indirectly, in this instance by influencing the parent's psychological well-being.

IMPLICATIONS FOR INTERVENTION

We have gone to considerable length to describe a model of parenting that is multiply, reciprocally, and even hierarchically determined, that draws upon a notion of life span development, and that incorporates causal elements originating in all levels of the developmental ecosystem. In this section it is our task to operationalize this model for the purpose of intervention. The value of a model, after all, is at least partly determined by its potential for practical application. Only after we recognize how the pieces fit together can we design effective strategies of intervention. A model, in effect, becomes the blueprint for change, as was argued in Chapter 6.

Before presenting our suggestions, we will very briefly summarize the approaches to intervention which have predominated in the past and which secure the greatest favor in the present. This is readily accomplished, as most parental interventions to date dealing with child abuse have been remedial in nature—that is, they have been designed to provide special services to parents already known to maltreat their offspring. Thus, with respect to child abuse and neglect, they are "after-the-fact" interventions.

Another principal characteristic of most interventions to date is that they have adopted single-focus strategies, usually with the parent as the target of intervention. Traditional psychotherapy represents such an approach, in that it deals principally with the perpetrating agent and not the context that fosters maltreatment or the child's contribution. Whereas such therapy deals with the emotional well-being of the client and thus seriously entertains and addresses the notion of personality contributions, behavioral approaches are concerned primarily with changing the behavior and cognition of the maltreating individual. It appears clear to us that successful intervention will depend upon elements contained in both the behavioral and the psychotherapeutic approaches. In the absence of personal incentives for change, parents are unlikely to adopt new techniques of child care. On the other hand, bringing new insight and emotional assistance to abusive parents without demonstrating alternative patterns of behavior or developing specific skills will probably prove equally fruitless. Surely, then, parents are best served by integrating the two philosophical stands in a program addressing both the interpersonal and the behavioral needs of maltreating parents.

Perhaps the best example of a multidimensional program is that offered by Parents Anonymous, the primary self-help group for abusive parents. Taking its cues from organizations like Alcoholics Anonymous, this group is guided by many of the same principles upon which the psychotherapeutic method is founded. It is expected, for example, that emotional support accompanied by the expression and exchange of feelings among individuals sharing a common problem will bolster parents' morale and facilitate personal motivation for change. In addition, self-help groups typically put members in touch with the services they require for optimal functioning—child care, drug or alcohol rehabilitation, professional psychological services, marital counseling, welfare assistance, and the like. Above and beyond either emotional support or instrumental assistance, a group like Parents Anonymous attempts to inculcate new parenting habits and skills as well as alternative means of responding to stressful events or circumstances, in part by sharing techniques that have been effective for other abusing parents. Suggestions for improvement in parenting are offered in an atmosphere of mutual concern and cooperation, making it that much more likely that parents will be responsive to them.

Not only do self-help groups typically connect parents to needed and available community services, but they also act to draw parents into new social networks composed of individuals sharing common concerns and interests. Given our previous discussion on the significance of such networks for adult psychological well-being and for parental performance, inclusion of this factor into the intervention program appears particularly advantageous. By incorporating such a feature, self-help groups foster competent parenting both directly and indirectly through the emotional support, instrumental assistance, and the nonthreatening social expectations they provide for parents as individuals as well as persons charged with the care of children.

Indirect evidence in support of these assumptions regarding effectiveness comes from an experimental study designed to reduce the stress associated with bearing a high-risk infant. Minde and his colleagues observed that parents of premature infants who participated in a self-help group appeared to cope more effectively with their babies (Minde *et al.,* 1980). Whether in the neonatal ward or at home three months after discharge, those mothers who had had the opportunity to share their feelings and experiences with other parents in the same stressful situation displayed more involvement, more interaction, and more concern about their infants' development than mothers who were randomly excluded from this supportive intervention. Moreover, at one year, the experimental mothers provided their infants more freedom and stimulation and judged their babies' competencies more accurately relative to their biological abilities. Possibly as a consequence, their infants displayed more social and exploratory behavior in playing, food sharing, and self-feeding.

Limits of Remediation

Remedial efforts are obviously subject to numerous limitations. Even programs which are relatively comprehensive in their focus suffer from factors such as the client's lack of motivation and fear of social stigma. Furthermore, by the time remediation is offered, the damage has already been done in terms of child costs, strained family relations, parental self-concept, and social labeling. Remediation is a post facto strategy, and after the fact is often too late for adequate reparation of the psychological and sometimes physical injuries inflicted. Moreover, remediation is beset by a host of problems concerning the efficacy and efficiency of its programs. There is frequently an excessive cost in time, energy, and money devoted to individual parents or families, particularly when traditional therapeutic or behavioral interventions are utilized. Not only are such programs unwieldy to implement, but the considerable expenditures of time and money severely restrict the number of families that can be served over any given period of time.

As if this were not enough, parental remediation efforts have notoriously poor success rates. Burgess and Richardson (1983) cite several evaluations of remedial interventions documenting the absence of any diminuation—and even occasional increases—in the incidence of inadequate or downright abusive parenting practices (Burgess, Anderson, Schellenbach, & Conger, 1981; Wolfe *et al.*, 1981; Cohn, 1949). Berkeley Planning Associates (1977) reported results confirming this poor prognosis for remedial intervention. Across the 11 different remedial projects conducted, 30% of the clients participating in the study exhibited "severe reincidence" of abuse or neglect *while still in treatment,* and only 42% of the participants were considered to exhibit a "reduced propensity" for maltreatment by the time treatment was terminated. Again, however, it should be noted that this success rate fluctuated considerably across projects, with the best outcomes characterizing programs utilizing lay and group services in addition to formal social services.

New Directions: Mini-interventions

The limitations of available remedial efforts, when coupled with the ideas that form the basis of the model of parenting presented here, suggest the importance of prevention efforts for improving parental functioning. These can be presented most clearly after several principles of intervention derived from, or related to, our model are articulated. In what follows, then, we detail a series of such principles and then illustrate their meaning by describing a set of interventions that could be implemented to improve parenting.

The basic characteristic of the model of determinants of parenting developed in this chapter is that parental functioning is multiply determined by forces of influence derived from the parent, the child, and the social context in which the parent–child relationship is embedded. Therefore our first principle of intervention states that efforts aimed at the multiple causes of parental incompetence, rather than at any single cause, are most likely to prove effective in improving parental functioning.

A second and related principle deriving from our model is that forces of influence that shape parenting do so both directly and indirectly. It stands to reason, then, that one should be able to enhance parental functioning by directly addressing both parental behavior (as in older behavior modification approaches) and the parent's psychological well-being (as in traditional psychotherapy), as well as by affecting those aspects of the ecology of parent–child relations that are linked to parenting. Thus, not only efforts to improve parental functioning directly but also efforts to make marriages more harmonious, social networks more supportive, and children more agreeable should—again, in theory—promote more competent caregiving.

The third principle of intervention is somewhat more complex and is based on ideas that permeate our entire approach. Fundamental to our analysis of the determinants of parenting is the contention that there is a continuum of influence, ranging from stress to support. This suggests that the very processes serving to undermine parental functioning and to generate child maltreatment in some cases also serve, when operating in a supportive as opposed to stressful mode, to generate parental competence. The basic principle we derive from this idea is that efforts need not focus exclusively on remedying already dysfunctional parenting or the childrearing of parents at risk for maltreating their offspring, since efforts geared toward enhancing the functioning of all parents may prove equally beneficial. Indeed, in certain respects such efforts may reduce the incidence of child abuse and neglect to an even greater extent than efforts targeted directly at this goal.

As we see it, a basic problem of remedial and preventive approaches in the past is that they identified a "problem population." Few of us like to admit to a problem; yet when a service designed to change things, especially parenting, is offered to a select few, the implications are by no means subtle: "You have a problem; you need to change." It is conceivable that this message does more to *undermine* intervention efforts than anything else, since it generates a certain degree of resistance in the recipient of services.

In view of these observations, we contend that successful interventions should be provided to the public at large and thus *not appear to be interventive services*. Instead they should be integrated into the natural ebb and flow of normal community life. How, exactly, might this be achieved? Furthermore, how would it be possible to provide services to many, rather than to a restricted few labeled "at risk," particularly in this day and age of budget restrictions? Services to many are likely to be more expensive, are they not?

In our minds, the key to the dilemma involves the attachment of "mini-interventions" to already existing social structures to which large numbers of families in the community already take access voluntarily. In certain respects, these services would be unnoticeable but would nevertheless have the potential for exerting influence. This notion of mini-interventions is based upon the idea that it would be the collective and cumulative impact of a variety of supportive experiences that would promote competent parenting. Further, such mini-interventions, especially when developed within and maintained by already operating community structures, should prove less costly and more viable than large-scale programs. Important in this regard is the fact that all intervention "eggs" would not be placed in the proverbial single basket. Thus, too much would not be expected of any single service, and failure of any one would not imperil the effectiveness of the entire effort.

We would be naive if we assumed that this abstract, conceptual discussion, in and of itself, could convey the message we are attempting to articulate. Therefore at this point we will provide some concrete illustrations of the kinds of mini-interventions that could be implemented to enhance parental competence and thereby prevent child maltreatment. Important to note here is the fact that in prevention or enrichment, unlike remediation, the time frame for interventions is not governed by the actions of the parent. Instead, systematic acquisition of parental knowledge and skills could be incorporated a priori into the developmental learning course of the individual. For this reason, we have organized the following presentation in terms of the life course, first considering efforts which could be initiated prior to parenting—prior even to adulthood—before moving on to the period of pregnancy and delivery and, finally, to parenting itself.

Parenthood. The finding that abusive parents tend to be somewhat younger on the average than the general population (Straus, Gelles, & Steinmetz, 1980) suggests that stress and/or skill deficits are greater among younger, less experienced parents. Research on teenage parents (Colletta, 1983; deLissovoy, 1975) and on parental psychological maturity (Brunnquell *et al.*, 1981; Ragozin *et al.*, 1982), chronicled earlier in the chapter, substantiate this. Consequently, if we are to ensure developmentally optimal parenting, efforts ought to be initiated prior to the age when young people begin the transition to parenthood.

Bronfenbrenner (1977) has suggested a basic strategy for addressing the age problem in parenting interventions that deserves serious consideration. Why not, he asks, begin formal training for parenthood at or even before adolescence? Our educational system represents the single *universal* experience for youth between the ages of 10 and 18, as well as a primary means for disseminating knowledge at this age. Not all young people attend church or summer camp or scouting; school attendance, on the other hand, is required by law. So widespread and pervasive a ''social service'' could certainly be utilized to everyone's advantage, with a minimum of disruption, when it comes to instruction in parenting skills. Regular, firsthand experience in school-based or school-coordinated day-care facilities, the plan Bronfenbrenner proposes, would essentially offer young people a practicum in parenthood.

Supervised caregiving, accompanied by formal lessons in child development and child management and by open discussions on general expectations and probable challenges, would serve three distinct and complementary functions. First, teenagers would acquire information with regard to both appropriate parenting practices and appropriate child expectations. Second, these young people would be provided an opportunity to develop accurate expectations about the pleasures and problems of parenting. Finally, they would be afforded a preview of their own responses to the role of caregiver. Perhaps this latter experience in itself would assist individuals in deciding whether or not they would prefer to take on that role; and this should help to contain the subsequent incidence of child abuse. Child maltreatment stemming from ignorance of child behavior and development (Blumberg, 1977; Galdston, 1965) should decline markedly as well. Furthermore, the early experience of responsibility derived from caring for children might enhance the self-esteem of those young people most in need of the ego support which their own homes fail to provide and which has been related to abuse (Green, Gaines, & Sandgrun, 1974; Melnick & Hurley, 1969). Even the mere opportunity to observe alternative models of childcare might aid in breaking the intergenerational transmission of abuse. In addition, one certainly cannot dispute the benefits to the community of providing supplementary and convenient day care.

The next logical step in the prevention sequence would be to ensure that any individual, and any teenager in particular, choosing *not* to become a parent, would not be trapped into assuming this role. In other words, we are making a strong plea for appropriate, accessible family planning services. This is a fundamental need in light of the fact that both research and rhetoric have repeatedly documented the costs of unwanted pregnancy. With all the skills in the world, the reluctant parent is unlikely to exhibit optimal caregiving. Both firsthand experience with children and the means to exercise personal reproductive choices are measures designed to minimize the number of teenagers and adults who become such reluctant parents.

Pregnancy and Birth. But what about those individuals who choose to assume a parenting role? What could be done to assist and instruct parents during the difficult months immediately prior to and following birth? There are innumerable opportunities that could be exploited at this time. Just consider the fact that parents-to-be, probably more than at any other time in their lives, seek the information, the encouragement, and the *assurance* of professionals. We could offer these concerned adults any number of mini-interventions implemented for no better reason than to ease or enhance the transition to parenthood.

Classes to prepare couples for childbirth are utilized on a large-scale basis across the nation and are supported by voluntary contributions from those who use them. They therefore represent an ideal community structure with which large numbers of families come into contact and which are not dependent upon tax revenue for support. At present, however, such classes focus almost exclusively upon the event of childbirth rather than the reality of parenthood that endures long past the birth experience. Yet there is much data to indicate that the transition to parenthood is often very stressful to families, frequently because the effects of parenthood on several domains of life are not recognized before the event. It would be useful, then, to amend childbirth education classes in ways that would enable couples to discover, during pregnancy, how having a baby is likely to influence work life, marital relations, relations with friends, neighbors, and relatives, as well as one's sense of self. This would be easy to do by having a small part of a weekly childbirth class devoted to an open discussion of expectations.

Such an opportunity to explore expectations would serve two important functions: (a) it would create a context in which people could get to know one another in a way that might lead to the development of friendships, and (b) it would provide couples with more realistic expectations regarding what the transition to parenthood occasions. That such consequences would promote optimal child development is suggested by the fact that friends and other social contacts represent important sources of instrumental assistance and emotional support, the absence of which is associated with child abuse and neglect. To the extent that the data we have summarized on the determinants of parenting highlight the influence of supportive social networks even in nonabusive samples, there exists even more reason to expect that the kind of intervention just proposed would enhance individual and family well-being.

The same arguments regarding the benefits of geographic propinquity suggested with respect to childbirth classes could be used to encourage hospitals to place together, in the same room, women from the same geographic areas who have recently given birth. In most hospitals, maternity patients are assigned rooms on a haphazard basis—whatever bed is available on the ward. But, if more than one bed is available, placing a woman in a room in which there is already a woman from her own neighborhood would indirectly encourage the establishment of social relationships that, conceivably, could endure and develop into a functional informal support system.

In addition to this slight modification of a context that most families engage in at some time, an additional procedure could be instituted to assist parents in "getting to know" their newborn infants. It is the policy in most hospitals to show mothers, before they are discharged from the maternity ward, how to bathe a newborn. Consider the potential advantages of expanding this into a demonstration for mothers *and* fathers of some of the behavioral competencies that newborns possess. By helping parents actively discover, early in the baby's life, that young infants can do more than eat, sleep, and cry (i.e., that they can see, hear, track an object, or respond to a soothing voice) hospitals would provide a foundation upon which sensitivity could develop.

In fact, all that would be required would be the training of maternity nurses to provide this relatively simple service on a routine basis. The provision of the service by nurses to all families bearing babies in the hospital would take advantage of the natural role of the nurse, as a trusted and familiar community agent working in a context that is routinely and voluntarily engaged by virtually all families. Again, the presumed impact upon families in their childrearing role would be indirect, as the service would never be presented as a means of enhancing parenting. To do so would risk the dangerous implication, described earlier, that there is something deficient in parents. Thus, the service would be introduced merely as part of a set of enjoyable activities intended to assist parents in getting to know their babies, on the assumption that such familiarity would enhance the quality of care that parents provide.

Much attention has been devoted recently to the notion of providing parents, both fathers and mothers, time alone with their newborn immediately after birth. It would be a most suitable extension of this prineiple to encourage both paternal and sibling involvement by routincly allowing each parent greater access to the newborn during the remainder of the hospital stay. What better context for starting families out in harmony than the supportive, growth-promoting hospital setting? Parents would be afforded a rare opportunity to interact with, care for, and enjoy their infants in an environment remarkably free from the burdens and strains of home and work life. Siblings could be familiarized with some of the basic needs, limitations, and competencies of the newborn in a relaxed, intimate, family-oriented setting. By establishing regular "family times," uncertainty, discovery, and wonderment could be shared among family members, and a brief period aimed at fostering maternal adjustment could be transferred into an initial step toward family adjustment as well.

From an intervention standpoint, we must exploit the fact that the entire period of childbirth represents a unique opportunity for bringing parents in contact with the information, the support, and the services designed to reinforce competent parenting. As we mentioned earlier, new parents and parents-to-be are particularly willing to establish just these sorts of contacts with those they view as knowledgeable in the field of obstetrics and child development. The vast majority of parents who utilize formal assistance during this period (childbirth classes, obstetricians, hospital services, etc.) could be subsequently assimilated into extended networks of support during parenthood. In the next section, we will see how supportive contact could be maintained and expanded as the child grows to maturity.

One of the greatest difficulties encountered by parents in meeting the needs of their children involves locating available services in a community. All too often there exists no easily approachable source that provides such information. The suggestion put forth here is that natural helpers who already function in a fairly circumscribed manner in the community be trained to be knowledgeable about available services. By broadening the information base of, for example, nurses and receptionists in physician's offices, and day-care personnel whom families see daily as they pick up their children after a day's work, families would be provided with easily accessible and approachable resource agents. If such persons who presently function in contexts that link families with the broader community were also trained to be careful listeners and empathic respondents, it is likely that parents would turn to them more readily for assistance that falls beyond the scope of their present circumscribed areas of expertise (e.g., pediatrics, child development).

In sum, it is suggested that if parents got the sense from receptionists at doctors' offices and from day-care personnel that these individuals were interested in them as people, not only as parents, and that these interested parties also had at their fingertips a wealth of useful information, then they would become frequently used support systems. Such support would no doubt affect parents' well-being and the care their children receive, thus indirectly serving the causes of both optimal parenting and optimal child development.

Any experience with families shows that time is a precious commodity for families these days, especially when both parents work. Since many parents spend the majority of their daytime hours in employment outside the home, the workplace is an intervention site, hitherto neglected, that is ripe for exploitation. Even a strategy as simple as a work-family bulletin board, with sign-up sheets for babysitting services, child transport carpools, or a children's clothing and furniture exchange, with service agency listings and/or birth announcements, might help in coordinating the needs of individual families by joining together previously unacquainted co-workers. At another level of sophistication, mini-interventions could consist of working with industries to develop modules on child care that could be used during lunch hours or coffee breaks, to alert parents to things they might like to know but do not have time to find out themselves. In an age in which dual-earner families are becoming the norm, information about family functioning and child care that was easily available at the worksite would surely be widely used. Imagine 15-minute coffee-break sessions devoted to topics such as (a) what to look for in selecting quality day care, (b) what to do if your child is sick and cannot go to day care, (c) nutritional needs of children at various ages, (d) behavioral problems of children, (e) the developing competencies of infants, toddlers, and preschoolers, and, as a final example, (f) effective strategies of discipline.

Essentially, coffee breaks could be used to provide information and expertise to parents who chose to use them to gather such knowledge. Such time would be planned not only to provide information but also to give parents a chance to talk. The goal here, of course, is to bring services *to* parents in a cost-efficient manner, rather than requiring parents to go and search out the services. It is assumed once again, in making such services widely available to all workers at a plant or factory, that this mini-intervention would not appear to be a special service, thus avoiding the negative consequences of stigmatization, but still indirectly supporting parental functioning. It is assumed, too, that such services would serve to reduce family stress and thereby enhance the mental health of parents and children alike.

The Child as a Determinant. We have repeatedly emphasized that parents do not raise their children independently of the context which supports or undermines their caregiving. We cannot, therefore, ignore the contribution that a colicky, irritable infant, a demanding toddler, a disruptive, disobedient schoolchild or teenager, or especially a mentally or physically handicapped child adds to the challenge of parenting. Certain children, we noted earlier, in and of themselves are at greater risk for maltreatment by their parents. Hence, prevention can and should address the child's contribution. We offer, in this section, two contrasting but complementary means of addressing this issue.

Parents can be prepared both psychologically and behaviorally for the unique characteristics their child possesses. Why not begin in the hospital, a logical starting place since abnormal and/or demanding characteristics of the child are often first identified there? On the neonatal ward, cases of prematurity or birth defects requiring special professional attention need also to be considered from the perspective of concerned parents, particularly if, as Belsky (1978a) suggests, extra caretaking demands translate into additional stress on parents. Allowing parents a more active involvement in their newborn's care, including them to a greater extent in discussions of treatment alternatives, and, especially, furnishing them with formal and informal supports during the early weeks and over the course of subsequent months might enable the parents of children with special problems to begin surmounting the odds stacked against them. Agencies specializing in services to handicapped children could place greater emphasis on the unique strengths and capabilities possessed by even the most incapacitated of children and on the needs of parents as psychological agents as well as caregivers. Training *parents* is equally important if not more important than training exceptional children, since the former not only engage in the day-to-day interaction with these children but also provide the context for their development. If parents to a large extent control—intentionally or not—developmental outcomes for children, and if children in turn play an important role in shaping parental behavior, then the many facilities and organizations identifying or caring for exceptional children must modify current policies and practices to ensure greater sensitivity to parental needs.

What of the child who only later develops or represents special behavioral or psychological problems? We need additional mechanisms to prevent or circumvent potentially explosive family situations by attending to child behavior problems when they first attract the notice of teachers, physicians, and/or other community service agents. When this is the case, the community service network should immediately assume a constructive role in mobilizing appropriate services for the child and supportive resources for the parents. Enlisting the help of a big brother–big sister program, a neighborhood job-training program, special resource services available through the school, or, if necessary, referring parents to

a child counselor or therapist might be the first step in preventing serious dysfunction, child or parental. Similarly, alerting parents to the range of services
available to the child, putting them in touch with relevant parent support groups,
or inviting them to attend organizational and social gatherings of relevant school,
church, or health groups might be the supplementary measure that would ensure
a responsive intervention's becoming a successful one.

There is all too frequently an inclination on the part of primary and other
caregivers to ignore or mutually disparage the aversive behaviors and/or characteristics of a child and to hustle him or her through the system with as little
commotion as possible. Such actions may occasion any combination of disas-
trous outcomes: overtaxed, rejecting, and eventually physically abusive parents,
alienated and/or delinquent youth, social crimes and misdemeanors committed
by such juveniles, and/or a drain on already overburdened corrective services
which are called upon too late for effective protection of any of the victims—
parents, child, or community. It is in everyone's best interests to expand an early
alert system comprising hospital, school, welfare bureau, and even church or
synagogue into a responsive and integrated service network. It is equally important to ensure that the response is a constructive one aimed at facilitating positive
outcomes rather than a reactive one seeking to allay aggravating symptoms by
the swiftest, most facile methods possible.

CONCLUSION

In this analysis we have strayed far from the specific issue of aggressive
children, but we have tried to emphasize the importance of a multilevel model to
consider social structures ranging from the family and social networks to the
policies of institutions and of government. By using parental aggression as a
social point and by identifying special points of contact with, or of vulnerability
within, the larger context in which parenting is embedded, social organizations
may be designed and utilized as keystones for optimal family functioning and
may thus reduce childhood aggression as an expression of family disruption.
Many, if not most, of the interventions described earlier do incorporate elements
of the social context for specific remedial or preventive purposes. Such efforts
may be supplemented by social programs aimed at one of two levels of change—
the first addressing problems within specific subsets of families, the second,
problems inherent in the very fabric of our society.

Ours is a heterogeneous and a changing population. The demographics of
the American family resemble less and less the prototypic ideals formulated in
the past and favored still by many traditionalists. If we are to foster the welfare of
the family, we cannot afford to ignore the structural and functional changes in
family life which have recently occurred and continue to occur. Our system of

social supports must reflect these changes by becoming increasingly sensitive to the special needs of alternative family forms. Research indicates that single parenthood, stepparenthood, dual-career marriages, and several other emerging trends in family structure require new or expanded social services corresponding to their unique needs. Support through childcare, information networks, work modules, and encouragement of social network extension—among the numerous mini-interventions that have been suggested—can all serve such a purpose. In keeping with the views outlined above, we see the role of social services as twofold: helping parents directly through information, skill-training, and instrumental assistance and teaching parents how to help themselves through social contacts and support groups. The specific forms that such assistance takes will, and in fact must, remain responsive to the changing needs of the family.

Several social scientists (e.g., Garbarino & Gilliam, 1980; Gil, 1971; Straus et al., 1980) have argued that the epidemic proportions of child abuse can be reduced only through a restructuring of sociocultural mores and manners. If positive exchanges between parent and child are encouraged by social support, negative exchanges may be permitted by social attitudes. For this reason, numerous investigators in the field of child abuse lament the current social and political tolerance for violence in our society. Violence begets violence in their minds, and violence is deemed by many to be a veritable American institution. Violence in the streets, violence on television (see chapter 9 in this volume), violence in the justice system, violence in the schools, and violence in the home are all coterminous. So long as corporal punishment, a common denominator of physical violence, is accepted and promoted as an appropriate disciplinary strategy, its misuse is assured. Similarly, to the degree that parents are reinforced in their perception of children as personal property, these children will be battered emotionally and perhaps physically as any piece of chattel might, depending on its owner. It is ultimately up to those who recognize the ills of society to rectify them, and this requires the active participation of established social agents and agencies that may be seen as comprising the very backbone of a society. Social expectations, then, are probably as vital to parenting outcomes as the provision of instrumental assistance and emotional support.

In describing our preferences with regard to the style, nature, and timing of intervention, we are acting on the basis of a larger underlying assumption about the role of society vis-à-vis the functioning of its individual members. When the topic is as universal as parenting, we suggest that the purpose of intervention should not be selective treatment for "needy" families, but routine assistance to all who could benefit from this aid. The idea is not to require parents experiencing difficulty to identify themselves through a special request for aid, but to ensure that services are not only available but actively promoted in every case of parenting. With all good intentions, it is too easy to imply condemnation of individual parents and so to foster the misperception that child abuse is a problem of individuals. On the contrary, the very essence of our model argues the opposite, that parenting is a cumulative result of social, economic, cultural, *and* individual psychological factors. If we are to gain the active support of the social systems we rely upon for any intervention effort, we must first convince the public at large that optimal parental functioning depends upon social conditions—public and private—that support the competence and well-being of the parent as caregiver and individual.

Parenting is a skill so fundamental in our lives that there is an inclination to take it for granted. Yet few would deny its profound impact on each and every individual, from the period of infancy up to the time of death. Indeed, this impact is of such consequence that *experiences* of parenting appear to be transmitted from one generation to the next. In view of this, the knowledge that a significant proportion of parents exhibit such serious deficiencies in their ability to care for children that society labels their parenting "abusive" is alarming, to say the least. When contrasted with the kind of parenting that produces competent, responsive, responsible individuals, the differences are more than striking; they are insupportable.

In this chapter we have explicated the route and the methods we consider most instrumental in eliciting change. What we have set forth is a model of the evolution of parenting, all parenting. By focusing on the relative value of each of three broad determinants of parenting—parental psychological resources, characteristics of the child, and contextual stresses or supports—we have proposed a model that can describe both extremes in parenting, competence and abuse. From this model we are able to formulate hypothetical relationships between specific variables of the family and the setting and the parental outcomes we expect to observe. The availability of such a model for identifying significant causal factors in the etiology of parenting styles and for associating them with positive or negative outcomes is the key to intervention. Once we recognize *what* should be changed and what form this change should take, and once we decide *how* best we can accomplish change, we have initiated the first vital steps toward an effective intervention effort. The course is laid, the tests drawn up; we have only to embark upon the path we have cleared through fact and conjecture in order to assess the adequacy of this model for guiding us to a successful conclusion.

REFERENCES

Abernethy, V. (1973). Social network and response to the maternal role. *International Journal of Sociology of the Family, 3,* 86–92.
Ainsworth, M. D. S., Blehar, M. C., Waters, E., & Wall, S. (1978). *Patterns of attachment.* Hillsdale, NJ: Erlbaum.

Aug, R. G., & Bright, T. P. (1970). A study of wed and unwed motherhood in adolescents and young adults. *Journal of the American Academy of Child Psychiatry, 9,* 577–592.

Bandura, A., & Walters, R. (1959). *Adolescent aggression.* New York: Ronald Press.

Bates, J. (1980). The concept of difficult temperament. *Merrill-Palmer Quarterly, 26,* 299–319.

Baumrind, D. (1971). Current patterns of parental authority. *Developmental Psychology Monographs, 4* (1).

Baumrind, D. (1967). Child care practices anteceding three patterns of preschool behavior. *Genetic Psychology Monographs, 75,* 43–88.

Bell, R. Q. (1968). A reinterpretation of the direction of effects in studies of socialization. *Psychological Review, 75,* 81–95.

Belsky, J. (1978a). A theoretical analysis of child abuse remediation strategies. *Journal of Clinical Child Psychology, 7,* 113–117.

Belsky, J. (1978b). Three theoretical models of child abuse: A critical review. *International Journal of Child Abuse and Neglect, 2,* 37–49.

Belsky, J. (1980). Child maltreatment: An ecological integration. *American Psychologist, 35,* 320–335.

Belsky, J. (1981). Early human experience: A family perspective. *Developmental Psychology, 17,* 3–23.

Belsky, J. (1984). The determinants of parenting: A process model. *Child Development, 55,* 83–96.

Belsky, J., Gilstrap, B., & Rovine, M. (1983). Stability and change in mother–infant and father–infant interaction in a family setting: 1-to-3-to-9 months. *Child Development, 55,* 692–705.

Belsky, J., Lerner, R., & Spanier, G. (1983). *The child in the family.* Reading, MA: Addison-Wesley.

Belsky, J., Robins, E., & Gamble, W. (1983). The determinants of parenting: Toward a contextual theory. In M. Lewis & L. Rosenblum (Eds.), *Social connections: Beyond the dyad.* New York: Plenum Press.

Berkeley Planning Associates. (1977). *Evaluation of child abuse and neglect demonstration projects, 1974–1977. Vol. 3: Adult client impact.* Hyattsville, MD: National Center for Health Services Research.

Birrell, R., & Birrell, J. (1969). The maltreatment syndrome in children: A hospital survey. *Medical Journal of Australia, 2,* 1023.

Blumberg, M. L. (1977). Treatment of the abused child and the child abuser. *American Journal of Psychotherapy, 31,* 204–215.

Bronfenbrenner, U. (1977). Toward an experimental ecology of human development. *American Psychologist, 52,* 513–531.

Bronfenbrenner, U., & Crouter, A. C. (1982). Work and family through time and space. In C. Hayes & S. Kamerman (Eds.), *Families that work: Children in a changing world.* Washington, D.C.: National Academy of Sciences.

Brown, G. W., & Harris, T. (1978). *Social origins of depression: A study of psychiatric disorder in women.* New York: Free Press.

Brown, J., & Daniels, R. (1968). Some observations on abusive parents. *Child Welfare, 47,* 89.

Brunnquell, D., Crichton, L., & Egeland, B. (1981). Maternal personality and attitude in disturbances of child-rearing. *American Journal of Orthopsychiatry, 51,* 680–691.

Burgess, R. L., & Richardson, R. A. (1983). Coercive interpersonal contingencies as a determinant of child abuse: Implications for treatment and intervention. In R. F. Dangel & R. A. Polster (Eds.), *Behavioral parent training: Issues in research and practice.* New York: Guilford.

Burgess, R. L., Anderson, E. S., Schellenbach, C. J., & Conger, R. D. (1981). A social interactional approach to the study of abusive families. In J. P. Vincent (Ed.), *Advances in family intervention, assessment and theory: An annual compilation of research* (Vol. 2). Greenwich, CT: JAI Press.

Caffey, J. (1946). Multiple fractures in the long bones of children suffering from chronic subdural hematoma. *American Journal of Roentgenology, Radium Therapy, and Nuclear Medicine, 56,* 163–173.

Campbell, S. (1979). Mother–infant interaction as a function of maternal ratings of temperament. *Child Psychiatry and Human Development, 10,* 67–76.

Caplan, G. (1974). *Support systems and community mental health.* New York: Behavioral Publications.

Cassell, J. (1974). Psychosocial processes and "stress": Theoretical formulation. *International Journal of Health Services, 4,* 471–482.

Clarke, R., & Gecas, V. (1971). *The employed father in America: A role comparison analysis.* Paper presented at the annual meeting of the Pacific Sociological Association.

Clarke-Stewart, K. A. (1973). Interactions between mothers and their young children: Characteristics and consequences. *Monographs of the Society for Research in Child Development, (6–7,* Serial No. 153).

Cobb, S. (1976). Social support as a moderator of life stress. *Psychosomatic Medicine, 38,* 300–314.

Cochran, M., & Brassard, J. (1979). Child development and personal social networks. *Child Development, 50,* 601–616.

Cohen, S. E. (1978). Maternal employment and mother–child interaction. *Merrill-Palmer Quarterly, 24,* 189–197.

Cohen, S., & Sussman, A. (1975). *The incidence of child abuse in the United States.* Unpublished manuscript, University of Delaware, Wilmington, Delaware.

Cohn, A. H. (1949). Essential elements of successful child abuse and neglect treatment. *Child Abuse and Neglect: The International Journal, 3,* 491–496.

Colletta, N. D. (1981, April). *The influence of support systems on the maternal behavior of young mothers.* Paper presented at the biennial meeting of the Society for Research in Child Development, Boston, MA.

Colletta, N. (1979). Support systems after divorce: Incidence and impact. *Journal of Marriage and the Family, 41,* 837–846.

Colletta, N. D., & Gregg, C. H. (1981). Adolescent mothers' vulnerability to stress. *Journal of Nervous and Mental Disease, 169,* 50–54.

Coopersmith, S. (1967). *The antecedents of self-esteem.* San Francisco: W.H. Freeman.

Crnic, K. A., Greenberg, M. T., Ragozin, A. S., Robinson, N. M., & Basham, R. (1983). Effects of stress and social support on mothers and premature and full-term infants. *Child Development, 54,* 1199–1210.

deLissovoy, V. (1975). Concerns of rural adolescent parents. *Child Welfare, 54,* 167–174.

Dielman, T., Barton, K., & Cattell, R. (1977). Relationships among family attitudes and child rearing practices. *Journal of Genetic Psychology, 130,* 105–112.

Egeland, B., & Sroufe, A. (1981). Attachment and early maltreatment. *Child Development, 52,* 44–52.

Elder, G. H., Jr. (1974). *Children of the Great Depression.* Chicago: University of Chicago Press.

Elmer, E. (1967). *Children in jeopardy: A case of abused minors and their families.* Pittsburgh: University of Pittsburgh Press.

Elmer, E., & Gregg, G. (1967). Developmental characteristics of abused children. *Pediatrics, 40,* 569–602.

Epstein, A. S. (1979, March). *Pregnant teenagers' knowledge of infant development.* Paper presented at the meeting of the Society for Research in Child Development, San Francisco, CA.

Farel, A. N. (1980). Effects of preferred roles, maternal employment, and sociographic status on school adjustment and competence. *Child Development, 50,* 1179–1186.

Field, T. M., Widmayer, S. M., Stringer, S., & Ignatoff, E. (1980). Teenage, lower-class, black mothers and their preterm infants: An intervention and developmental follow-up. *Child Development, 51*, 426–436.

Fontana, V. (1971). *The maltreated child*. Springfield, IL: Thomas.

French, J., Rodgers, W., & Cobb, S. (1974). Adjustment as person–environment fit. In G. Cochlo, D. Hamberg, & J. Adams (Eds.), *Coping and adaptation*. New York: Basic Books.

Friedrich, W., & Boriskin, J. (1976). The role of the child in abuse: A review of the literature. *American Journal of Orthopsychiatry, 40*, 580–590.

Frodi, A., Lamb, M., Leavitt, C., Donovan, W., Neff, C., & Sherry, D. (1978). Fathers' and mothers' responses to the faces and cries of normal and premature infants. *Developmental Psychology, 14*, 490–498.

Frommer, E., & O'Shea, G. (1973a). Antenatal identification of women liable to have problems in managing their infants. *British Journal of Psychiatry, 123*, 149–156.

Frommer, E., & O'Shea, G. (1973b). The importance of childhood experiences in relation to problems of marriage and family building. *British Journal of Psychiatry, 123*, 157–160.

Gaensbauer, T. J., & Sands, K. (1979). Distorted affective communication in abused/neglected infants and their potential impact on caretakers. *Journal of the American Academy of Child Psychiatry, 18*, 236–250.

Gaensbauer, T., Mrajek, D., & Harmon, R. (1981). Affective behavior patterns in abused and/or neglected infants. In N. Frodi (Ed.), *The understanding and prevention of child abuse: Psychological approaches*. London: Concord Press.

Galdston, R. (1965). Observations on children who have been physcially abused by their parents. *American Journal of Psychiatry, 122*, 440–443.

Galdston, R. (1975). Preventing the abuse of little children: The Parent's Center Project for the study and prevention of child abuse. *American Journal of Orthopsychiatry, 45*, 372–381.

Garbarino, J. (1976). A preliminary study of some ecological correlates of child abuse: The impact of socioeconomic stress on mothers. *Child Development, 47*, 178–185.

Garbarino, J. (1977a). The human ecology of child maltreatment: A conceptual model for research. *Journal of Marriage and the Family, 39*, 721–736.

Garbarino, J. (1977b). The price of privacy in the social dynamics of child abuse. *Child Welfare, 56*, 565–575.

Garbarino, J., & Gilliam, G. (1980). *Understanding abusive families*. Lexington, MA: D.C. Heath.

Gelles, R. (1973). Child abuse as psychopathology: A sociological critique and reformulation. *American Journal of Orthopsychiatry, 43*, 611–1973.

Gelles, R. (1975). The social construction of child abuse. *American Journal of Psychiatry, 132*, 363–371.

Gelles, R. (1978). Violence toward children in the United States. *American Journal of Orthopsychiatry, 48*, 580–592.

George, C., & Main, M. (1979). Social interactions of young abused children: Approach, avoidance and aggression. *Child Development, 50*, 306–318.

Gil, D. (1971). Violence against children. *Journal of Marriage and the Family, 33*, 639.

Giovannoni, J., & Billingsley, A. (1970). Child neglect among the poor: A study of parental adequacy in families of three ethnic groups. *Child Welfare, 49*, 196.

Goldberg, S. (1978). Prematurity: Effects on parent–infant interaction. *Journal of Pediatric Psychology, 3*, 137–144.

Green, A. H. (1978). Psychopathology of abused children. *Journal of the American Academy of Child Psychiatry, 17*, 92–103.

Green, A., Gaines, R., & Sandgrun, A. (1974). Child abuse: Pathological syndrome of family interaction. *American Journal of Child Psychiatry, 131*, 882–886.

Hall, F., Pawlby, S., & Wolkind, S. (1979). Early life experience and later mothering behavior: A study of mothers and their 20-week-old babies. In D. Schaffer & J. Dunn (Eds.), *The first year of life*. New York: Wiley.

Hartup, W. W. (1978). Perspectives on child and family interaction: Past, present, and future. In R. Lerner & G. Spanier (Eds.), *Child influences on marital and family interaction: A life-span perspective*. New York: Academic Press.

Heath, D. H. (1976). Competent fathers: Their personality and marriages. *Human Development, 19,* 26–39.

Herrenkohl, R. C., & Herrenkohl, E. C. (1981). Some antecedents and developmental consequences of child maltreatment. In R. Rizley & D. Cinchitti (Eds.), *New directions for child development*. San Francisco: Jossey-Bass.

Hess, R. D., Shipman, V. C., Brophy, J. E., & Bear, B. M. (1968). *The cognitive environments of urban preschool children*. University of Chicago: Graduate School of Education.

Hetherington, E., Cox, M., & Cox, R. (1977). The aftermath of divorce. In J. Stevens & M. Mathews (Eds.), *Mother–child, father–child relations*. Washington, D.C.: National Association for the Education of Young Children.

Hock, E. (1979). Working and nonworking mothers and their infants: A comparative study of maternal caregiving characteristics and infant social behavior. *Merrill-Palmer Quarterly, 26,* 79–101.

Hoffman, L. W. (1961). Mothers' enjoyment of work and its effects on the child. *Child Development, 32,* 187–197.

Hoffman, L. W. (1963). Mothers' enjoyment of work and its effects on the child. In F. I. Nye & L. W. Hoffman (Eds.), *The employed mother in America*. Chicago: Rand McNally.

Hoffman, M. L. (1970). Moral development. In P. H. Mussen (Ed.), *Carmichael's manual of child psychology* (Vol. 2). New York: Wiley.

Hubert, N., Wachs, T., Peters-Martin, P., & Gandour, J. (1982). The study of early temperament: Measurement and conceptual issues. *Child Development, 53,* 571–600.

Jayaratne, S. (1977). Child abusers as parents and children: A review. *Social Work, 22,* 5.

Johnson, S., & Lobitz, G. (1974). The personal and marital adjustment of parents as related to observed child deviance and parenting behaviors. *Journal of Abnormal Child Psychology, 2,* 193–207.

Johnson, B., & Morse, H. (1968). Injured children and their parents. *Children, 15,* 147.

Jones, F. A., Green, V., & Krauss, D. R. (1980). Maternal responsiveness of primiparous mothers during the postpartum period: Age differences. *Pediatrics, 65,* 579–583.

Kanter, B. (1978). Families, family processes, and economic life: Toward a systematic analysis of social historical research. In J. Demos & S. Boocock (Eds.), *Turning points: Historical and sociological essays on the family*. Chicago: University of Chicago Press.

Kelly, P. (1976). The relation of infant's temperament and mother's psychopathology to interactions in early infancy. In K. F. Riegel & J. A. Meacham (Eds.), *The developing individual in a changing world*. (Vol. 11). Chicago: Aldine.

Kempe, C., Silverman, E., Steele, B., Droegemueller, W., & Silver, H. (1962). The battered-child syndrome. *Journal of the American Medical Association, 181,* 17.

Kemper, T., & Reichler, M. (1976a). Fathers' work integration and frequencies of rewards and punishments administered by fathers and mothers to adolescent son and daughters. *Journal of Genetic Psychology, 129,* 207–219.

Kemper, T., & Reichler, M. (1976b). Marital satisfaction and conjugal power as determinants of intensity and frequency of rewards and punishments administered by parents. *Journal of Genetic Psychology, 129,* 221–234.

Kessen, W., Fein, G., Clarke-Stewart, A., & Starr, S. (1975, August). *Variations in home-based infant education* (Grant #OCD-CB-98). Washington, D.C.: Office of Child Development.

Klein, M., & Stern, L. (1971). Low birthweight and the battered child syndrome. *American Journal of Diseases of Childhood, 122,* 15–18.

Komarovsky, M. (1940). *The unemployed man and his family.* New York: Dryden Press.

Lamb, M., & Easterbrooks, M. (1980). Individual differences in parental sensitivity. In M. Lamb & L. Sherrod (Eds.), *Infant social cognition.* Hillsdale, NJ: Erlbaum.

Lerner, R., & Lerner, J. (1983). Temperament-intelligence reciprocities in early childhood: A contextual model. In M. Lewis (Ed.), *Origins of intelligence* (2nd ed.). New York: Plenum Press.

Lerner, R., & Busch-Rossnagel, N. (Eds.). (1981). *Individuals as producers of their own development.* New York: Academic Press.

Lewis, M., & Weinraub, M. (1976). The father's role in the infant's social network. In M. E. Lamb (Ed.), *The role of the father in child development.* New York: Wiley.

Light, R. (1973). Abused and neglected children in American: A study of alternative policies. *Harvard Educational Review, 43,* 556–598.

Longfellow, C., Dill, D., Makosky, V., & Zur-Spiro, S. (1981, September). *Stressful life conditions and the mental health of mothers.* Paper presented at the annual convention of the American Psychological Association, Los Angeles, CA.

Martin, H. P. (1976). Which children get abused: High risk factors in the child. In H. P. Martin (Ed.), *The abused child: A multidisciplinary approach to developmental issues and treatment.* Cambridge: Ballinger.

Martin, H., & Breezley, P. (1977). Behavioral observations of abused children. *Developmental Medical Child Neurology, 19,* 373–387.

Martin, H., Conway, E., Breezley, P., & Kempe, H. C. (1974). The development of abused children. Part I: A review of the literature. *Advances in Pediatrics, 21,* 43.

McCall, R. B. (1974). Exploratory manipulation and play in the human infant. *Monographs of the Society for Research in Child Development, 39,* (No. 155).

McKinley, D. (1964). *Social class and family life.* New York: Free Press.

McLanahan, S., Wedemeyer, N., & Adelberg, T. (1981). Network structure, social support, and psychological well-being in the single-parent family. *Journal of Marriage and the Family, 43,* 601–612.

Melnick, B., & Hurley, J. (1969). Distinctive personality attributes of child-abusing mothers. *Journal of Consulting and Clinical Psychology, 33,* 746–749.

Miller, J., Schooler, C., Kohn, M. L., & Miller, K. A. (1979). Women and work: The psychological effects of occupational conditions. *American Journal of Sociology, 85,* 66–94.

Milliones, J. (1978). Relationship between perceived child temperament and maternal behavior. *Child Development, 49,* 1255–1257.

Milowe, I., & Lourie, B. (1964). The child's role in the battered child syndrome. *Society for Pediatric Research, 65,* 1079.

Minde, K., Shosenberg, N. E., Marton, P., Thompson, J., Ripley, J., & Burns, S. (1980). Self-help groups in a premature nursery—A controlled evaluation. *Journal of Pediatrics, 96,* 933–940.

Minturn, L., & Lambert, W. W. (1964). *Mothers of six cultures: Antecedents of childrearing.* New York: Wiley.

Mitchell, R., & Trickett, E. (1980). Task force report: Social networks as mediators of social support. *Community Mental Health Journal, 16,* 27–44.

Moen, P. (1982). The two-provider family: Problems and potentials. In M. Lamb (Ed.), *Nontraditional families: Parenting and child development.* Hillsdale, NJ: Erlbaum.

Mondell, S., & Tyler, F. (1981). Parental competence and styles of problem-solving and play behavior with children. *Developmental Psychology, 17,* 73–78.

Moss, H. A. (1974). Communication in mother–infant interaction. In L. Krames, P. Pliner, & T. Alloway (Eds.), *Nonverbal communication.* New York: Plenum Press.

Nuckolls, C. G., Cassell, J., & Kaplan, B. H. (1972). Psychological assets, life crises and the prognosis of pregnancy. *American Journal of Epidemiology, 95,* 431–441.

Olweus, D. (1980). Familial and temperamental determinants of aggressive behavior in adolescent boys: A causal analysis. *Developmental Psychology, 16,* 644–660.

Orraschel, H., Weissman, M. M., & Kidd, K. K. (1980). Children and depression: The children of depressed parents; the childhood of depressed patients; depression in children. *Journal of Affective Disorders, 2,* 1–16.

Osofsky, J. J., & Osofsky, J. D. (1970). Adolescents as mothers. *American Journal of Orthopsychiatry, 40,* 825.

Parke, R. D. (1978). Parent–infant interaction: Progress, paradigms and problems. In G. P. Sackett (Ed.), *Observing behavior, Vol. 1: Theory and applications in mental retardation.* Baltimore: University Park Press.

Parke, R., & Collmer, C. (1975). Child abuse: An interdisciplinary review. In E. M. Hetherington (Ed.), *Review of child development research* (Vol. 5). Chicago: University of Chicago Press.

Parke, R., & Sawin, D. (1977, March). *The family in early infancy: Social interaction and attitudinal analyses.* Paper presented at the biennial meeting of the Society for Research in Child Development, New Orleans, LA.

Pascoe, J. M., Loda, F. A., Jeffries, V., & Earp, J. A. (1981). The association between mother's social support and provision of stimulation to their children. *Developmental and Behavioral Pediatrics, 2,* 15–19.

Pedersen, F. (1982). Mother, father and infant as an interactive system. In J. Belsky (Ed.), *In the beginning: Readings on infancy.* New York: Columbia University Press.

Pedersen, F. (1975, September). *Mother, father and infant as an interactive system.* Paper presented at the annual convention of the American Psychological Association, Chicago.

Pedersen, F., Anderson, B., & Cain, R. (1977, March). *An approach to understanding linkages between the parent–infant and spouse relationships.* Paper presented at the biennial meeting of the Society for Research in Child Development, New Orleans, LA.

Pedersen, F., Yarrow, L., Anderson, B., & Cain, R. (1978). Conceptualization of father influences in the infancy period. In M. Lewis & L. Rosenblum (Eds.), *The social network of the developing infant.* New York: Plenum Press.

Pelton, L. (1978). The myth of classlessness in child abuse cases. *American Journal of Orthopsychiatry, 48,* 569–579.

Piotrkowski, C. S. (1979). *Work and the family system: A naturalistic study of working-class and lower-middle-class families.* New York: Free Press.

Pleck, J. H., Staines, G. L., & Lang, L. (1978). *Work and family life.* (Final reports on work–family interference and worker's formal childcare arrangements, from the 1977 Quality of Employment survey). Unpublished manuscript, Wellesley College, Wellesley, MA.

Plomin, R. (1982). Childhood temperament. In B. Lahey & A. Kazdin (Eds.), *Advances in clinical child psychology* (Vol. 6). New York: Plenum Press.

Pollitt, E. (1973). Behavior of infant in causation of nutritional marasmus. *American Journal of Clinical Nutrition, 26,* 264–70.

Powell, D. (1979). Family–environment relations and early childrearing: The role of social networks and neighborhoods. *Journal of Research and Development in Education, 13,* 1–11.

Price, G. (1977, March). *Factors influencing reciprocity in early mother–infant interaction.* Paper presented at the biennial meeting of the Society for Research in Child Development, New Orleans, LA.

Radbill, S. (1974). A history of child abuse and infanticide. In R. Helfer & C. H. Kempe (Eds.), *The battered child.* Chicago: University of Chicago Press.

Ragozin, A. S., Basham, R. B., Crnic, K. A., Greenberg, M. T., & Robinson, N. M. (1982). Effects of maternal age on parenting role. *Developmental Psychology, 18,* 627–634.

Reidy, T. J. (1977). The aggressive characteristics of abused and neglected children. *Journal of Clinical Psychology, 33*, 1140–1145.

Rossetti-Ferreira, M. (1978). Malnutrition and mother–infant synchrony: Slow mental development. *International Journal of Behavioral Development, 1*, 207–219.

Sameroff, A. (1975). Transactional models of early social relations. *Human Development, 18*, 65–79.

Sameroff, A. (1977). Concepts of humanity in primary prevention. In G. Albee & J. Joffe (Eds.), *Primary prevention of psychopathology* (Vol. 1). Hanover, NH: University Press of New England.

Santrock, J. W., Warshak, R., Lindbergh, C., & Meadows, L. (1982). Children's and parent's observed social behavior in stepfather families. *Child Development, 53*, 472–480.

Schaefer, E., Bauman, K., Siegel, E., Hosking, J., & Sanders, M. (1980). *Mother–infant interaction: Factor analyses, stability and demographic and psychological correlates*. Unpublished manuscript, University of North Carolina, Chapel Hill, NC.

Schubert, J. B., Bradley-Johnson, S., & Nuttal, J. (1980). Mother–infant communication and maternal employment. *Child Development, 51*, 246–249.

Sears, R., Maccoby, E., & Levin, H. (1957). *Patterns of child rearing*. Evanston, IL: Row, Peterson.

Spinetta, J., & Rigler, D. (1972). The child-abusing parent: A psychological review. *Psychological Bulletin, 77*, 296–304.

Stayton, D., Hogan, R., & Ainsworth, M. (1971). Infant obedience and maternal behavior: The origins of socialization reconsidered. *Child Development, 12*, 1057–1069.

Steele, B., & Pollack, D. (1968). A psychiatric study of parents who abuse infants and small children. In R. Helfer & C. Kempe (Eds.), *The battered child*. Chicago: University of Chicago Press.

Steinberg, L., Catalano, R., & Dooley, D. (1981). Economic antecedents of child abuse and neglect. *Child Development, 52*, 975–985.

Stolz, L. M. (1967). *Influences on parent behavior*. Stanford, CA: Stanford University Press.

Straker, G., & Jacobson, R. (1981). Aggression, emotional maladjustment, and empathy in the abused child. *Developmental Psychology, 17*, 762–765.

Straus, M. A. (1979). Family patterns and child abuse in a nationally representative American sample. *Child Abuse and Neglect, 3*, 213–225.

Straus, M. A., Gelles, R. J., & Steinmetz, S. K. (1980). *Behind closed doors: Violence in the American family*. New York: Anchor Press.

Stuckey, M., McGhee, P., & Bell, N. (1982). Parent–child interaction: The influence of maternal employment. *Developmental Psychology, 18*, 635–644.

Switzky, L. T., Vietze, P., & Switzky, H. N. (1979). Attitudinal and demographic predictors of breast-feeding and bottle-feeding behavior by mothers of six-week-old infants. *Psychological Reports, 45*, 3–14.

Todd, D. M. (1980, September). *Social networks, psychological adaptation, and preventive/developmental interventions: The support development workshop*. Paper presented at the annual convention of the American Psychological Association, Montreal, Canada.

Toms-Olson, J. (1981). The impact of housework on childcare in the home. *Family Relations, 30*, 75–81.

Weissman, M. M., & Paykel, E. S. (1974). *The depressed woman: A study of social relations*. Chicago: University of Chicago Press.

Wolfe, D. A., St. Lawrence, J., Graves, K., Brehony, K., Bradlyn, D., & Kelly, J. A. (1981). *Intensive behavioral parent training for a child-abusive mother*. Unpublished manuscript, University of Western Ontario, London, Ontario.

Yarrow, L., Rubenstein, J., & Pedersen, F. (1975). *Infant and environment*. New York: Wiley.

Yarrow, M. R., Scott, P., DeLeeuw, L., & Heinig, C. (1962). Childrearing in families of working and nonworking mothers. *Sociometry, 25,* 122–140.

Young, L. (1964). *Wednesday's children: A study of child neglect and abuse.* New York: McGraw-Hill.

Young, M., & Willmott, P. (1957). *Family and kinship in East London.* London: Penquin.

Zeskind, P., & Ramey, C. (1978). Fetal malnutrition: An experimental study of its consequences on infant development in two caregiving environments. *Child Development, 49,* 1155–1162.

Zur-Spiro, S., & Longfellow, C. (1981, April). *Support from fathers: Implications for the well-being of mothers and their children.* Paper presented at the biennial meeting of the Society for Research in Child Development, Boston, MA.

CHAPTER 8

Girls and Violence
An Exploration of the Gender Gap in Serious Delinquent Behavior

MEDA CHESNEY-LIND

It is a timeworn assumption that males and females differ radically in their delinquency. Indeed, "real" delinquency was once thought to be an exclusively male preserve. Albert Cohen, in his widely cited work, *Delinquent Boys,* provides one of the clearest academic articulations of this position. Because "boys collect stamps and girls collect boys," Cohen felt it followed that the "problems of adjustment of men and women, of boys and girls, arise out of quite different circumstances and press for quite different solutions." The delinquent, he concluded, was essentially "a rogue male" (Cohen, 1955, p. 140).

Notions such as Cohen's, which relied heavily on simplistic conventional stereotypes about male and female misbehavior, were not refuted by careful research simply because there was extremely little interest in the female delinquent.

Criminologists' failure to address the issue of women and crime has seriously hampered efforts to understand not only why, when, and how women deviate or commit delinquent offenses, but the equally important questions of why, when, and how the society responds to their behavior. Moreover, this pattern of neglect has permitted and encouraged general theory-building research that is profoundly flawed by monosexism (Heindensohn, 1968). It is not too much to say that any theory or theories of deviance that fail to account for the behavior (either conforming or rule-violating), of over half of the population cannot, in the final analysis, be considered sound.

MEDA CHESNEY-LIND • Youth Development and Research Center, University of Hawaii at Manoa, Honolulu, Hawaii 96822.

In the last ten years, however, this pattern of scholarly neglect has appeared to be reversed, as the female criminal and, to some extent, her younger counterpart, were suddenly propelled into the limelight. Unfortunately, although this attention was long overdue, it was less a product of intellectual thoroughness than it was an attempt to discover a "dark side" of the women's liberation movement (Adler, 1975; Deming, 1977).

There was literally a rush to study women and crime as journalists, and some academics, began to focus on the popular idea that the women's movement was causing an increase in female delinquency and criminality. These writers were joined, somewhat later, by other academics who were more generally interested in women and crime. As a consequence, there has been a veritable explosion of writings on the female delinquent and her older counterpart, the female criminal. Regrettably, only portions of this work can be said to have brought about a greater understanding of either the dynamics of female delinquency or the treatment of these young women who come into the criminal justice system. Some of these writings have, if anything, muddied the intellectual waters and, in so doing, provided support for those who are seeking scientific legitimacy for patterns of personal and institutional sexism.

Nowhere has this journalistic and academic confusion been more pronounced than in discussions of girls' entry into nontraditional and often violent delinquency and crime. For example, Adler (1975), in her widely cited *Sisters in Crime,* says:

> Girls are involved in more drinking, stealing, gang activity, and fighting-behavior in keeping with their adoption of male roles. We also find increases in the total number of female deviancies. The departure from the safety of traditional female roles and the testing of uncertain alternative roles coincide with the turmoil of adolescent creating criminogenic risk factors which are bound to increase. (p. 95)

There also appeared to be some compelling evidence on this point for a period of time. Between 1960 and 1975 arrests of young girls increased by a startling 474% in comparison to only a 153% increase in the number of older women arrested. Along with these figures were even more dramatic increases in particular types of what might be called nontraditional offenses: murder up 452%, aggravated assault up 662%, and robbery up 777%.

Several comments must be made about these figures, however. The first and most obvious point is that such dramatic increases in female misbehavior, particularly in nontraditional areas, were calculated on extremely small base numbers. For example, the number of girls arrested for robbery increased from 346 to 3,033, but that latter figure represented less than 1% of the arrests of all young women during 1975 (FBI, 1974; Criminal Justice Research Center, 1978). Thus, percentage increases of this sort present a disturbing but incomplete picture of the total female delinquency problem.

Perhaps more importantly, however, these figures did not, as some sup-

Table 1

Rank Order of Adolescent Male and Female Arrests for Specific
Offenses, 1979, and Arrests of Youth for Violent Offenses

Male		Female	
Offense	Percentage of total male arrests	Offense	Percentage of total female arrests
Larceny theft	19.1	Larceny theft	27.5
Other offenses	13.6	Runaway	20.3
Burglary	12.5	Other offenses	13.2
Vandalism	7.0	Liquor laws	6.9
Liquor laws	6.4	Drugs	4.3
Disorderly conduct	6.2	Curfew	3.9
Arrest for serious violent offenses[a]	4.6	Arrest for serious violent crime	2.0
Arrest for all violent offenses[b]	8.5	Arrest for all violent offenses	7.1

[a]Serious violent arrest categories include murder, nonnegligent manslaughter, forcible rape, robbery, aggravated assault (all part one offenses)
[b]Includes arrests for other assaults (part two offenses)
Note. Compiled from data provided in the *Sourcebook of Criminal Justice Statistics* (1979, 1980), p. 350, by the Criminal Justice Research Center. Washington D.C.: U.S. Government Printing Office.

posed, augur a new trend in female criminality. Between 1975 and 1979, for example, the number of girls arrested for all offenses increased by a modest 11%, with the 1979 figures representing a slight (4.4%) decrease from the 1978 figures (Criminal Justice Research Center, 1978; Criminal Justice Research Center, 1982). In the nontraditional areas such modest gains, with even a loss, was the picture by 1979. Arrests of girls for murder were up 18%; assault arrests increased by 14.8%, forcible rape by 12.2%; and arrests of girls for robbery actually showed a decline of 10% (Criminal Justice Research Center, 1982).

The other fact, of course, is that the female contribution to the problem of serious delinquency (as measured by arrest data) is miniscule. Of those juveniles arrested for serious crimes of violence in 1979 (murder, forcible rape, robbery, and aggravated assault) only 10.2% were female. Indeed young women constituted only 20.5% of all arrests of youth during that period (Criminal Justice Research Center, 1982).

Essentially, when girls run afoul of the law, they are most frequently brought into the criminal justice system for minor crimes and status offenses (noncriminal actions such as running away from home, being truant, incorrigible, etc.). (See Table 1.) For example, in 1979 over a quarter of all young women who were arrested were taken into custody for larceny theft. Other studies (Steffensmeier & Steffensmeier, 1980; Hoffman-Bustamante, 1973) reveal that the vast majority of such arrests (perhaps as high as 80%) are for shoplifting.

Arrests of girls for runaway and other offenses account for about a third of all female arrests. These two categories are here grouped as status offenses since the category "other offenses" probably includes a large percentage of status offense arrests. For example, although national data on this point are unavailable, more detailed arrest data from Hawaii suggest that 74.5% of those girls arrested for other offenses in 1981 were arrested for incorrigibility or injurious behavior. This was not true, by the way, of males whose arrests fell within this category; only 35.6% of these males were arrested for status offenses. Arrests of female youth for liquor, drug offenses, and curfew violations accounted for another 15.1%.

A comparison of the arrest patterns of both male and female juveniles reveals that although most delinquent behavior is relatively trivial, it is obvious that this is a much more accurate characterization of female than male delinquency. Moreover, if a change is occurring in adolescent female behavior, it appears from official data that the change is occurring in the area of these trivial offenses. A careful analysis of arrest data over time, executed by Steffensmeier and Steffensmeier (1980), shows this very clearly. The researchers weighted youthful arrest data to account for changes in population and then examined changes in male and female arrest rates over a 12-year period, 1965–1977. The authors also examined the changes, if any, in the gap between the two arrest rates with an eye toward whether the relative gap between the two sexes had narrowed or widened.

They initially noted that female rates rose in the majority of offense categories, with large increases occurring in the categories of larceny, liquor law violations, narcotic drug laws, and runaway. They did, however, also note declines in female arrests for gambling, curfew, sex offenses, vagrancy, and suspicion. Moreover, male arrest rates during the same period showed patterns of change similar to those of their female counterparts, with the exception of a decline in male rates for auto theft and disorderly conduct while there was an increase in the number of arrests of girls for these offenses.

With respect to the arrest of young women for specific violent so-called masculine crimes (murder, aggravated assault, other assaults, weapons and robbery) there was a slight narrowing of the gap between male and female rates. However, much of this apparent female gain arouse from an increase in arrests of girls for other assaults, which are "relatively non-serious in nature and tend to consist of being bystanders or companions to males involved in skirmishes, fights, and so on" (Steffensmeier & Steffensmeier, 1980). In general, the authors note that those offenses that have accounted for large increases in female arrests are "traditionally" female; secondly, they are in areas in which changes in enforcement practices have also been occurring.

For example, arrests of youth for drug offenses rose more quickly than any other offense category from 1965 to 1973 and then dropped off, suggesting that changes in police practice were at least partially involved in that change. Dramatic increases in the number of arrests of males and females for larceny may be due to increased willingness of store owners to prosecute shoplifters. Finally, a decrease in the number of male arrests for disorderly conduct compared to an increase in the arrests of young women for this offense may point to decreasing use of this statute to control public drunkenness or to apprehend males suspected of crimes but the continued use of this statute to arrest girls suspected of prostitution.

In short, the authors suggested there is no evidence in the official statistics to conclude that young women were engaging in more "serious crimes" in 1977 than were their counterparts in 1965. Almost all of the apparent support for that contention came from increases in the number of women arrested for shoplifting, under-age drinking, and marijuana use.

The authors also reviewed data on court referrals for roughly the same period. Here, again, they suggest that much of the increase observed in the number of females referred to court was due to increases in court referrals for shoplifting, marijuana and drug use, and status offenses such as running away or violating curfew. Finally, the authors note that many of these increases in both female arrest and referral rates have leveled off since 1970.

As this research effort suggests, there are problems with using arrest data as the only source of information about the extent and character of either male or female misbehavior. Potential biases in police detection and referral of delinquent youth may make these data somewhat suspect (Chesney-Lind, 1978), and to this reservation must be added a concern about parental bias because parents constitute a major source of referrals of youth into the juvenile justice system (Teilmann & Landry, 1981).

Fortunately, there are a number of studies that solicit from young people themselves accounts of the volume and frequency of illegal activity. These self-report studies have been conducted with some uniformity since the mid-1950s and several have utilized nationwide samples of adolescents. Because of this, these studies constitute a rich source of information about the actual dimensions of the gender gap in serious delinquent behavior.

SEX DIFFERENCES IN SELF-REPORT DATA

Self-report studies reveal that the volume of unreported delinquency is substantial, and this is especially true of female delinquency. Cernkovich and

Table 2
Comparison of Sex Difference in Self-reported and Official
Delinquency Involvement for Violent Offenses

Delinquent act	Percent engaging in act 1 or more times			Official rates
	Male	Female	Ratio	
Attack someone with fists[a] (other assaults)[b]	47.8	25.1	1.9	3.9
Use weapon to attack someone[a] (aggravated assault)[b]	11.6	6.6	1.8	5.8
Gang fight[a] (other assaults)[b]	38.9	14.5	2.7	3.9
Robbery[a] (robbery)[b]	5.0	0.9	5.6	13.5
Carry weapon[a] (weapons: carrying, possessing, etc.)[b]	34.3	17.1	2.0	5.1

[a]self-report item.
[b]F.B.I. crime category.
Note. Compiled from data provided in Cernkovich & Giordano, 1979.

Giordano (1979), for example, note that while the ratio of female to male arrestees is approximately 1:5, this figure was approximately twice as large as the mean ratio of 1:2.18 that they found in self-reported delinquent behavior. Similar figures have been reported in earlier studies. These studies also reveal that female misbehavior is far more versatile than one would assume from the popular conception of female delinquency, which stresses the trivial and non-criminal nature of female misbehavior. Essentially, these studies have consistently revealed that young women engage in a wide variety of delinquent behavior, including violent and aggressive behavior, far in excess of their representation in arrest statistics or juvenile court populations.

For example, looking at the violent and aggressive offenses surveyed by Cernkovich and Giordano (1979), the male to female ratios for those youth who have ever reported certain violent offenses is far narrower than those found in official statistics (see Table 2). Take, for example, the percentage of males and females who reported that they had on at least one occasion ever "attacked someone with fists." The self-report ratio on this item is 1.9:1 whereas ratios found in arrest data for the comparable year are 5.8:1 for aggravated assault and 3.9:1 for other assaults (Criminal Justice Research Center, 1982). Self-report ratios of similarly low magnitude can be found for the whole range of violent offenses.

Indeed, one of the remarkable observations that can be made about the self-report data collected by these researchers is the fact that male delinquency specialization appears more pronounced in such activities as vandalism (M:F ratio of 3.4), car theft (M:F ratio of 5.0), theft of car parts (M:F ratio of 6.4), and burglary (M:F ratio of 4.2), than in the violent or aggressive behaviors shown in Table 2. The one exception to this statement, and a significant exception, is the crime of robbery, which shows a self-report ratio of 5:1, but even this figure reflects far more female participation in the offense than the official statistics, which reveal a ratio of 13.5:1.

Significant, too, when one examines the self-report data, are the large numbers of males reporting status or sexual offenses. Indeed, nearly equal numbers of males and females in the study reported truancy (M:F ratio of 1:0), incorrigibility (with M:F ratio of .96 for "disobeying parents" and .99 for "defying parental authority"), running away from home (M:F ratio of .99), and sex with the opposite sex (M:F ratio of 1.25), while larger numbers of males reported "sex for money" (M:F ratio of 4.8). The later figure appears to confirm a growing suspicion that significant numbers of young boys may be entering the ranks of prostitution; but this is not reflected in official statistics, where the official arrest ratio for prostitution is .54:1 (M:F) (Cernkovich & Giordano, 1979).

Before concluding that females are nearly as violent as males, it should be noted that statistically significant differences were consistently found between the mean number of acts reported by males and the mean number reported by females in all of the violent offenses covered in the study. For example, differences in the means for all violent offenses reported in Table 2 were significant at the .01 level. Indeed, males committed significantly more delinquent acts than females on 25 of the 36 items on the scale with the only exceptions to this being nonviolent status and decorum (drug and alcohol) offenses. Consistently, other studies have also reported that once one examines the frequency of serious delinquency, the males in every self-report sample tend to pull away from the females (Williams & Gold, 1978; Elliot & Voss, 1974). Nonetheless, even mean differences found in recent self-report data do not reflect the dramatic sex differences found in official arrest data.

Of course, these data could be seen as support for the notion that women have become more violent in recent years. However, several thorough reviews of different self-report studies over time have failed to confirm this suspicion. For example, Weis (1976), in his comparison of four self-report studies conducted between 1960 and 1971, was particularly interested in exploring differences over time in the character and volume of self-reported delinquency in order to determine whether, in fact, the women's movement had had any impact on the actual volume of female misbehavior. Comparing the findings of self-report studies conducted during 1960, 1964, 1968, and 1971, he showed that "the mean sex ratios across all delinquent acts and for theft and aggression items have not changed in the direction predicted by the 'liberation' theories for this time period." He also noted that sex ratios across all offenses were "relatively stable" for the decade, contrary to the prediction that they would become more narrow. Indeed, rates of violent behavior actually showed boys becoming more violent while girls were becoming less violent.

Specifically, Weis reported that the aggression ratios showed little change from 1964 to 1968 but substantial change between 1968 and 1971; but here the data indicated a pattern antithetical to those suggesting that the women's movement was causing young women to become more aggressive. The data, he reported, "suggest that boys became more violent and/or girls became less violent during this period" (Weis, 1976).

Gold and Reimer (1975) compared two national self-report studies for the periods 1967 and 1972 and confirmed Weis's general findings regarding the lack of any apparent increase in the frequency of serious offenses among young women during the interval between their two surveys. They did, however, note other changes in female delinquency. The comparison found that although girls in 1972 were reporting less larceny, property destruction, and breaking and entering, "they reported greater use of marijuana and alcohol which increased their overall amount of reported delinquency." Steffensmeier and Steffensmeier (1980) have conducted the most ambitious review of self-reports by reviewing the results of twelve surveys. They note that although male and female delinquency showed some increase during the 20-year period covered by the studies, the increases were far less than those suggested by official statistics. Moreover, the studies show that "young women have always committed illegal acts which have been viewed as masculine offenses" and that there is little evidence that the female violation rate has increased at a faster pace than that of the males.

Specifically, there were "no discernable trends" noted for violent offenses such as fist fighting, gang fighting, carrying a weapon, and strong-arm theft. Moreover, a comparison of male–female differences found in three studies conducted during the years 1972–1977 showed a remarkable stability in self-reported female offenses when, in their words, "the Women's movement should have been having its greatest impact." In short, though there may have been a slight increase in "deportment" offenses among young women, there is no support in these studies for the notion that dramatic changes in the type and level of female criminality have occurred as a result of the women's movement. If anything, these studies point to a leveling off of changes in both unofficial and official rates of female delinquent activity during the 1970s, precisely the period during which one would expect to see the greatest change if the women's movement had in fact caused a change in the level of female deviance.

When examining the self-report data, one comes to the incontrovertible conclusion that although official statistics seem to present a considerable underestimation of the involvement of girls in serious delinquent behavior, there remains even in these data a rather substantial and apparently stable sex difference. Clearly, there is a need for a systematic examination of the sources of this remarkably persistent finding.

SOURCES OF THE GENDER GAP IN DELINQUENT BEHAVIOR

The notion that delinquency is essentially a male problem has been, until recently, so widespread that there have been very few works that have systematically applied theories of juvenile delinquency to adolescent female misbehavior. Instead, the female delinquent has been viewed as almost exclusively a sexual offender and her behavior discussed largely within this paradigm.

A good example of what was to become the standard approach to the subject of young women in trouble with the law and one that supplied academic legitimacy to the assumption that female deviance was predominantly sexual may be found in W. I. Thomas's *The Unadjusted Girl* (1928). Based on his evaluation of case records drawn from the Girls' Protective Bureau and the Cook County Juvenile Court, the book represents one of the first scholarly attempts to explore the source of female delinquent behavior. Since most of these cases involved young women taken into a custody as a result of the ''wholesale arrests of girls and women on the suspicion of venereal disease'' (Thomas, 1928) during World War I, it is not surprising that Thomas determined that nearly all female delinquency was an expression of sexual problems.

Initially, Thomas (1928) noted that the definition of young women as sexual property is culturally determined:

> The role which a girl is expected to play in life is indicated to her by her family in a series of aesthetic-moral definitions of the situation. Civilized societies have endowed the young girl with a character of social sacredness. She is the subject of far-going idealization. ''Virginity'' and ''purity'' have an almost magical value. (p. 98)

This awareness of the arbitrary emphasis placed on a young woman's sexuality sets Thomas apart from his contemporaries. He also determined that young women were not involved in sexual activity out of curiosity but rather, he felt, were encouraged to use sex as their ''capital'' to obtain other valued goods (clothing, money). Thomas did not condemn this arrangement but rather condemned a social class system that enabled higher-status women to sell themselves only once (for marriage) whereas poor women were forced to settle for less (''entertainment, affection and perhaps gifts'').

Thomas repeatedly debunked the notion that women are being punished for simple sexual experimentation:

> The cases which I have examined . . . show that sexual passion does not play an important role, for the girls usually become "wild" before the development of sexual desire, and their casual sexual relations do not usually awaken sex feeling. (p. 109)

Nor was he hesitant about the source of the problem ("bad family" and "demoralization") and its solution—the family court:

> During the past decade some of these (family) courts have reached a high degree of elaboration and perfection. Their service has been very great in checking the beginnings of demoralization. The court is much wiser than the parents of children and incidently does much to influence home life. (p. 119)

Thomas hoped that the family court would remedy the problems he detailed as being in the reformatories, and he placed great hope in sensitive and enlightened casework.

Thomas's work in many ways set the tone for the prevailing approach to family delinquency in the next half of the century. Subsequent researchers (Cowie, Cowie, & Slater, 1968; Konopka, 1966; Pollack & Friedman, 1969; Vedder & Somerville, 1970) consistently echoed the themes found in *The Unadjusted Girl*, albeit in less stilted language. That is to say, the authors made two critical assumptions: first, they assumed that most female delinquency was either "sexual" or "rational" rather than criminal in nature; and second, they expressed the certainty that social intervention, administered by sensitive and informed individuals, could help young women with their problems.

Basing their conclusions almost without exception on labeled and/or incarcerated juvenile females (roughly three-quarters of whom were charged either directly or indirectly for sexual offenses), such authors rarely questioned the equity of the family court's exclusive preoccupation with female sexuality. Indeed, most were anxious to justify the situation:

> On first examination it would appear from these data that the court discriminates heavily against the female sex offender, even though the offense that brings her to court is seldom, if ever, bizarre sex behavior characteristic of the male offender. Such an interpretation is, in our opinion, totally at variance with the facts. Training schools are more frequently needed for the promiscuous female for her own protection. (Acheson & Williams, 1954)
>
> [The] sexually delinquent girl violates the caring and protective attributes of her maternal role in a way which will harm her and her offspring for the remainder of her life. (Blos, 1962)

One early author did comment critically about this situation noting: "Most girls find themselves confused because of the still prevailing double standard for boys and girls, and because of conflicting precepts which pronounce sex as healthy and good on the one hand and as base and sinful on the other" (Konopka, 1966).

However, none of these authors recommended withdrawal of social service agencies from involvement in the noncriminal but sexual behavior of young women. In fact, some scholars in their national review of female training schools are enthusiastic about the intervention: "While studying delinquent girls, we should keep this in mind; when you train a man you train one individual; when you train a woman, you train a family."

The consistent theme in these works is how best to diagnose, treat, and confine young women, thereby protecting them from environments that might lure them back into sexual activity.

From these basic sources, it is accurate to say that the remaining literature on female delinquency falls into one of two general categories. The first category is comprised of numerous descriptive articles on the characteristics of labeled and/or incarcerated female youth, suggestions about treatment strategies for female delinquency, and literature on the social organization of female institutions. The second category includes a small but growing number of sociological attempts to develop a coherent theory of female delinquency.

Since so few researchers had paid serious attention to female delinquents, the early literature in this area was flawed by its intellectual isolation. In brief, those who have elected to study female delinquency or criminality confronted an enormous task of theory building, since the vast bulk of the available theoretical literature was seen as inapplicable to women. Moreover, when research on female delinquency was conducted it was largely ignored; it is remarkable, for example, that although Cohen (1955) and others have acknowledged a deep intellectual debt to G. H. Grosser (1952) for his work, *Juvenile Delinquency and Contemporary American Sex Roles,* it remains today an unpublished Ph.D. dissertation, as does Ruth Rittenhouse Morris's (1963) dissertation, *A Theory and Comparison of Female and Male Delinquency.*

These early works assumed that young women in juvenile court populations across the country (most of whom were charged with sexual or relational offenses) were representative of the actual character of female delinquency, and all attempted to generate theories to explain this phenomenon. Grosser basically contended, and Cohen agreed, that the differential sex role socialization of males and females pushed women to achieve success through affiliation (marriage) while males were encouraged to achieve success through achievement. Female delinquency, then, was both an extension and violation of the female subculture, in the same way that aggressive and criminal behavior was a product of the male subculture.

Morris's work provides a number of important insights into the sources of the gender gap in delinquent behavior. Although Morris accepted the notion that female delinquency was deeply influenced by male and female socialization, she designed rigorous studies to explore differences between female and male delinquents. She also explored differences between these delinquents and their nondelinquent counterparts and, finally, she probed differences in the societal reaction to boys' and girls' delinquencies. Morris attempted in her dissertation (1963) and two published papers (1964, 1965) to develop a comprehensive theory of female delinquency that would explain both its sexual character and, in comparison to male delinquency, its lower figures.

To explain the smaller number of female delinquents, Morris argued that women experience both less access to illegitimate means and greater social disapproval of their delinquent acts than do their male counterparts. To explain the predominance of relational offenses among women, she suggested that since "factors which interfere with reaching culturally defined success goals by legitimate means are most likely to lead to deviancy" (1964) and since these goals are different for males and females, the sources and character of delinquent behavior would, of necessity, be different. Obstacles to attaining economic power and status would be most likely to lead to delinquency in males, whereas obstacles to maintaining positive affective relationships would most likely produce delinquency in females. In testing this hypothesis, Morris found that female delinquents were more likely than a matched sample of nondelinquents to come from broken homes or from families with many family tensions and to be rated low in personal appearance and grooming skills.

Other theorists have also argued that female delinquents are more sensitive to family disruption than either female nondelinquents or males, but the research on this is, by and large, unconvincing. As Shover and Norland (1978) observe in their review of the evidence on this point, "usually this assertion has been supported by research on officially adjudicated delinquents." Since it is now known that young women are more often reported to the police by their parents than are young men, this might make it appear that family discord is a more important factor for females, even in the absence of any relationship between family problems and female delinquency.

Indeed, a related hypothesis, that girls would report significantly stronger family bonds and therefore significantly lower delinquency, was tested by Cantner (1981) using a national probability sample of 1,725 adolescents. She did find significantly higher rates of male delinquency but "the expected sex differences in family bonds were not observed." Indeed, although the lack of family bonds was modestly correlated with delinquency in both sexes, there was "evidence of their greater association among males in many cases" (unnumbered abstract page). Another study of self-reported adolescent marijuana use (Anderson, 1977) did, however, find a stronger relationship for young women than for young men between "attachment" to family and extensiveness of youthful marijuana use. The author attributed this finding to the "over-socialization" of female youth.

Yet another study (Norland, Shover, Thornton, & James, 1979), based on a self-report sample of high school youth in the Southeast, examined family dynamics (particularly family conflict) and found them to be important predictors of both male and female delinquency. Although the study found that the total effect of family conflict on delinquency was stronger for females than males, the relationship was largely indirect through reduced identification with parents, adoption of more relativistic beliefs about law, reduced parental supervision, and increased exposure to social support for delinquency. Examinining the direct effects of family conflict on property and aggressive offenses, the researchers found these to be greater for males than for females; only for the status offenses did the effects of family conflict appear to be slightly greater for females.

Another of Morris's notions—that female delinquents experience frustration in the legitimate realization of female goals (i.e., dating and marriage)—has also not been confirmed or disproved. For example, Sandhu and Allen (1969) concluded in their study of delinquent and nondelinquent girls that "delinquent girls showed significantly less commitment to marital goals, expressed less desire to marry, and perceived fewer obstacles in the fulfillment of their marital goals as compared to nondelinquent girls."

Morris, in her dissertation (1963), also had problems with this portion of her argument, reporting that her data failed to provide conclusive support for the notion that male delinquency is caused by "status" frustration whereas female delinquency is caused by "relational frustration," in part because delinquent females seemed to report low concern for both status and relational goals.

On the other hand, in another examination of differential opportunity theory, Datesman, Scarpitti, and Stephenson (1975) found some evidence that girls arrested for "public policy offenses" did have the lowest perception of opportunities among both nondelinquent and delinquent women. However, they cautioned that causality is difficult to establish since sexual activity among young women, in a society that condemns such behavior, may cause girls to experience less success in obtaining dates. Finally, both Morris and Datesman and her associates found strong evidence that the female delinquent enjoys significantly less subcultural support than her male counterpart, with both males and females being less tolerant of female delinquency.

In general, though, it can be seen that these approaches to the study of female delinquency, and particularly the early efforts, were hampered by stereotypical assumptions about the nature of youthful female misbehavior. They tended to assume that virtually all female delinquency is sexual or interpersonal in nature, in contrast to male delinquency, that was presumed more likely to be aggressive and criminal. Second, they assumed that differential socialization of male and female children plays a significant though unspecified role in the generation of basic personality characteristics which, in turn, make it less likely for women to consider illegal behavior.

Because of the widespread acceptance of these two points, it was also assumed that young women who deviate from stereotypical feminine characteristics might become "more delinquent." This contention, which supplied the basis for the notion that the women's movement would increase female delinquency, was widely believed despite the fact that there were virtually no empirical efforts to test it. Recently, however, a number of studies have attempted to evaluate what might be called this "masculinity" hypothesis with decidedly mixed results.

Cullen, Golden, and Cullen (1979), using a university student sample ($N=182$) and "masculinity scale" utilizing six "stereotypically masculine traits," found that in their group male traits increased the likelihood that the youth would be involved in delinquency. They found, however, a residual affect called "being male" which had an incremental effect on the rate of delinquent behavior. Their study also showed that possession of male traits was no more predictive of violent offenses than property offenses and had no relationship with drug offenses. Finally, they concluded that "while male traits increase the likelihood that members of both sexes will engage in delinquency, their effects are greater for males than for females" (1979, p. 307).

Another series of studies found less support for the masculinity hypothesis. Norland, Wessel, and Shover (1979), using a larger high school population ($N=1,002$) and a 15-item semantic differential scale, found that for males masculinity was directly related only to status offenses (i.e., not related to male participation in either property or aggressive offenses). The authors also found, surprisingly, that females with more masculine characteristics were "less involved" in delinquency than those reporting fewer masculine traits, because such young women were more likely to exhibit attachment to conventional others.

Thornton and James (1979) surveyed the same group of youth but utilized yet another five-item scale, this one based on sex-typed behavior. They, too, found that sex "remains related to delinquency when masculine self-expectations are controlled." Indeed, by controlling for sex the authors found that the 14 delinquent acts they examined were not related to masculine identification for either males or females. Unfortunately, the authors did not examine different types of delinquency separately.

The most intriguing of this group of studies is the one by Loy and Norland (1981) on the same self-report data in which a far more complex and multidimensional conceptualization of masculinity was employed. The authors developed two Likert-type measures of gender role expectations, one for traditional masculinity and another for traditional feminity. They then scored people as androgynous when they scored above the midpoint on *both* scales. Traditional males and females were those who scored significantly higher on their respective scale. Finally, the authors developed an "undifferentiated" category for youth who scored below the midpoint on both scales. (See Table 3.)

Dividing the self-reported delinquency of both sexes into property, status, and aggressive behavior, the authors found that undifferentiated females were far more delinquent in all areas than their traditional or androgynous counterparts.

Table 3
Mean Delinquent Behavior by Offense, Sex and Gender

	X status	X property	X aggressive
Androgynous females	9.3 (57)	0.7 (56)	1.0 (57)
Androgynous males	36.2 (212)	5.7 (213)	4.0 (215)
Difference score	26.9	5.0	3.0
Traditional females	16.4 (344)	2.4 (348)	0.7 (352)
Traditional males	58.0 (178)	14.2 (180)	14.2 (182)
Difference score	41.6	11.8	13.5
Undifferentiated females	34.7 (78)	4.0 (81)	5.6 (81)
Undifferentiated males	38.4 (17)	2.5 (19)	1.7 (19)
Difference score	3.7	−1.5	−3.9

Note. From Loy & Norland, 1981, p. 279.

Indeed, the mean number of aggressive acts for undifferentiated females was roughly six times larger than that for either of the other two groups of girls. For males, a different pattern is found, with traditional males reporting the greatest amount of delinquency; this difference was particularly marked for aggressive behavior.

Another set of studies that directly addresses the question of young women's attitudes toward women's rights and the traditional female sex role also confounds the notion that as women begin to approve of traditionally male behavior, they will become increasingly delinquent. James and Thornton (1980) questioned 287 young women about their attitudes toward feminism and the extensiveness of their delinquent behavior. They found that attitudes toward feminism had little direct effect on social delinquency but did have slight direct effects on property and aggressive delinquency. However, in the latter case, this influence was found to be negative, which clearly does not support the notion that the women's movement is providing attitudinal support for female entry into the criminal world. Indeed, this negative relationship held even when the young women were encountering such delinquency-producing forces as "high degrees of delinquency opportunity," "social support for delinquency," and "low levels of parental control."

This finding was also confirmed by Giordiano and Cernkovich (1979), who examined the attitudes of girls in three high schools and two state institutions regarding the acceptability of nontraditional female behavior. In general, there was a lack of significant associations as well as some negative associations, indicating, in the authors' words, that "the more delinquent girls were actually less liberated in those respects." They also noted, like earlier authors, that delinquent girls were also less attached to marriage and children as goals, but they quickly added that "it did not appear that they were reaching for male-dominated occupations as an alternative" (p. 479).

In general, these studies reveal that popular notions about the relationship between masculinity or masculine characteristics as conventionally defined and delinquency must be explored more carefully. It is not so much that there is no relationship between gender and delinquency; rather, it is the case that the complexity of both the variables and the relationship is only beginning to be understood.

Increasingly, explanations of this delinquency gender gap that rely solely on differential socialization (which is assumed to produce different attitudes and/or personality characteristics) are giving way to more complicated efforts that also include considerations of the differences in the everyday life of young men and young women in our society.

Studies that explore differences in the routine activities of male and female youth as well as differences in male and female perceptions of conformity and deviance, though few, have produced some intriguing findings. Jensen and Eve (1976) examined the effects of "relationship with parents," "attachment to law," "academic performance," and "participation in youth culture" and concluded that even controlling for all of these the "direct" contribution of sex to delinquency is significant.

Looking at attitudes toward both education and educational performance, Rankin (1980) did find sex differences in the relationship of these variables to delinquency. Rankin expected to find that these factors would have a greater effect on male than on female delinquency, since males have traditionally been seen as more directly affected by occupational achievement (or surrogates for this, such as educational success). He found, instead, that although negative attitudes toward school and poor school performance were both significant in predicting delinquency in both sexes, this relationship was stronger for girls than for boys.

Other major theoretical perspectives in delinquency stress the delinquents' ability to neutralize negative or delinquent acts and the availability of opportunities to behave in a delinquent manner. On the former, Ball and Lilly (1976, p. 281) note that in their research among female sixth-grade students there was "an untapped reservoir of attitudinal predispositions toward delinquency." Indeed, they found no significant difference in attitudes toward delinquency between their sample and another sample of institutionalized male delinquents.

Shover, Norland, James, & Thornton (1979) examined the masculinity hypothesis (already discussed) against the "opportunity" and "attachment to conventional others" theories with their self-report sample and concluded that "the criminogenic importance of the traditional masculine role, itself, proved to be much less important than the traditional feminine role as a predictor of the extent of involvement in both types of delinquency (property offenses and aggressive offenses).''

In the case of the female role, it appears that the observed effects are largely indirect; young women perceive less access to delinquent opportunities and express more attachment to conventional others than do males. This conclusion was particularly true for property offenses, however: for aggressive behavior the authors found evidence that for both males and females opportunity does not appear to play a strong role and that even with increased opportunity there has been no increase in aggressive female criminality.

A British self-report study (Mawby, 1980), which attempted to examine the utility of five theoretical approaches to delinquency, including the masculinity–femininity hypothesis, also concluded that the effects of the social role are indirect. For example, girls were found to hold more positive attitudes toward the police, and they were less likely to report criminal victimization.

Most interestingly, however, were the author's findings regarding differences in male and female behavior that would have an indirect effect on both the visibility of female misbehavior and the likelihood that the setting would provide criminal opportunities. The author noted that the data indicated that girls' movements were more "controlled." Young women were more likely to "play or muck about" the home while boys would "play or muck about" on deserted land (Mawby, 1980, p. 540). Girls, when they did steal, would steal from homes or school; boys would also steal from building sites or by breaking into empty buildings.

Norms such as these may play another role in the generation of the gender gap in serious delinquency: it may be that they could contribute to a sex differential in vulnerability to arrest. For example, it is known that young women are now using drugs, particularly marijuana, in large amounts, but they are less vulnerable to arrest for this activity. Studies of illegal drug use among college students show that whereas males tended to buy drugs, females were far more likely to have been given their drugs (Bowker, 1976). Another study (Johnson, Peterson, & Wells, 1977) combined questionnaire data on the extent of marijuana use with arrest statistics in three metropolitan areas to estimate arrest probabilities. The researchers discovered that differences in male and female drug use were exaggerated by official statistics and concluded that this pattern was explained almost entirely by the fact that males are far more likely than females to be arrested.

The data on this study of the circumstances of arrest suggest that males tended to use marijuana in settings that made them more vulnerable to arrest. Since men were using marijuana "on the streets," they were more likely than women to be arrested by general patrolmen, more often arrested in vehicles, and more often arrested alone.

On the other hand, women were more likely to be arrested as a result of raids on private residences. Since use of marijuana in private locations is, generally speaking, less visible than public use or transport, and since police raids into private domiciles are more strictly regulated by statute, fewer women are arrested. In essence, the restrictions on female mobility (Mawby, 1980), as well as social norms that encourage women to rely on men to procure marijuana for them (Bowker, 1976), may cushion both girls and women from drug arrests.

While not dealing specifically with violent offenses, these findings are suggestive. Essentially, young women could enjoy a lessened vulnerability to arrest because of the settings within which they commit their offenses and because of a possible reluctance on the part of victims, particularly other females (Hindelang, 1979), to report the offense.

Another study confirming the notion that young women, even those who report serious and frequent delinquency, are less vulnerable to arrest comes from Hindelang's analysis of the proportion of youth in his 1976 self-report study who reported that they had been picked up by the police. He found that, in general, females reported being picked up less frequently in both rural and urban areas. Moreover, unlike males (who were more vulnerable to arrest when in groups), girls, particularly in urban areas, were more vulnerable to arrest when alone (Hindelang, 1976). Clearly, norms that prohibit or discourage female mobility play a role in both the lower rate of serious crime committed by women and in the generation of even lower official measures of that misbehavior.

A study by Richards and Tittle (1981) provides yet another approach to the question of differential incidence of male and female misbehavior by focusing on the respondents' perceived chances of arrest. A national sample of adults (age 15 and above) was questioned about their estimates of arrest if they committed an illegal act. A variety of other orientations toward misbehavior were also solicited, including such things as ''stakes in conformity,'' ''desire to break the law,'' ''visibility'' (the notion that one's activities are closely monitored), ''conventionality'' (a commitment to conventional views of crime and deviance), and ''information about the sanction.'' Because of this extensive list, this study was able to explore more thoroughly the notion that the female sex role (the feminization hypothesis) provides women with attitudes which encourage conformity.

The authors found that women systematically give higher estimates of arrest probability than males, feel more visible than men, and have greater stakes in conformity (meaning that they anticipate more negative consequences if they deviate). The authors suggest that women ''may think that legal sanction is relatively certain because they are more likely to think of themselves as subject to surveillance and general social reaction than men'' (Richards & Tittle, 1981, p. 1196). Like Morris (1965), these researchers suspect that women's greater relative stakes in conformity may make deviance more threatening for them, and this, in turn, may lead to their high sanction–risk estimates. These variables, which the authors linked to women's recognition of their "structural position" in a sexually stratified society, were found to be more important than those which are related to personality characteristics.

VIOLENCE AND TRADITIONAL FEMALE DELINQUENCY

Although young women are less likely than males to act out aggressively, this does not mean that violence and aggression do not play a substantial though indirect role in the generation of female delinquency. There is a growing awareness among those who work with female status offenders that a substantial number are the victims of both physical and sexual abuse. A study of females in detention in Washington, for example, found that upwards of 40% were victims of physical and/or sexual abuse and that 17% were incest victims (National Institute of Mental Health, 1977).

Another and more recent sample survey of 192 female youth in the juvenile justice system in Wisconsin (Phelps, McIntosh, Jesudason, Warner, & Pohlkamp, 1982) revealed that 79% of the young women, most of whom were in the system for petty larceny and status offenses, had been subjected, previous to arrest, to physical abuse that resulted in some form of injury. The extent of injury ranged from bruises, welts, and severe pain to "being knocked unconscious" (21%) or having a broken bone (12%).

Additionally, 32% had been sexually abused by parents or other persons who were closely connected to their families, and 50% had been sexually assaulted (raped or forced to participate in sexual acts) (Phelps *et al.,* 1982). These young women ran away from homes that bear little resemblance to the stereotypical intact family, and once on the streets they are forced further into crime in order to survive. In this study, 54% of the girls who ran away found it necessary to steal money, food, or clothing in order to survive. A few exchanged sexual contact for money, food, and/or shelter.

My own research (Chesney-Lind & Rodriquez, 1983) on the backgrounds of adult women in prison revealed that virtually all of the sample were the victims of physical and/or sexual abuse as youngsters; over 60% had been sexually abused and about half had been raped as young women. This situation prompted these women to run away from home, and once on the streets they began engaging in prostitution and other forms of petty property crime. As adults, these women continue in these activities, having truncated educational backgrounds and virtually no marketable occupational skills. Three-quarters had been arrested for status offenses. There may be a profound link, then, between the victimization of young women and their subsequent involvement in such noncriminal status offenses as running away from home and being "a person in need of supervision," at least for those women who go to prison as adults.

CONCLUSION

It is obvious that young women have always been more aggressive than official arrest statistics would indicate. However, young women, even according to self-report data, engage in substantially less aggressive behavior than their male counterparts. Moreover, if changes have been occurring in delinquent female behavior, it does not appear that these shifts signal greater involvement of young women in aggressive behavior.

The delinquency theorist is then confronted with a dilemma. What accounts for the persistent gender gap in both self-reported and official acts of aggressive delinquency? Criminologists have long supposed, without adequate research on the point, that differential socialization (broadly defined) results in the specialization of young women in traditionally female offenses (status offenses) and young men in a broader array of misbehavior, including aggressive delinquency. Rigorous examination of this masculinity hypothesis, however, exposes the need for a more systematic investigation.

Essentially what is emerging is that female behavior and misbehavior are as complex as the male counterpart, and unicausal theories (for instance, that femininity induces conformity) are no more adequate in predicting delinquency among young women than in predicting male delinquency. This does not mean, however, that specific theories to explain female delinquency need to be generated. What seems to be necessary, instead, is the rigorous examination of the phenomenon of female delinquency, using the conceptual tools that have been used in the past to understand better the dynamics of male delinquency. Some of this work is already underway, as this chapter shows, and it has revealed that *both* sex differences in personality and sex differences in the structural position of women must be considered in a discussion of the gender gap in serious delinquency.

Concluding any discussion of aggression and female delinquency without mention of the role that violence plays in the generation of "traditional" female delinquency would be inappropriate. Recent research indicates that many of the young women who find their way into the juvenile justice system as status offenders (as runaways, "incorrigible," "in need of supervision," truants, etc.) are actually victims of physical and sexual abuse. Clearly, those interested in the prevention of traditional female delinquency should also attend to the long neglected problem of child abuse and neglect.

As to preventing aggression in young men, one could consider differences in the socialization process and ponder the role that the cultural legitimization of male violence plays in this regard (see Eron, 1980, for an exploration of the role of the media in this regard). It is certainly clear that simply giving women leave to consider some masculine attributes has not made them more violent. Indeed, it may be that possession of some so-called masculine attributes may actually reduce their delinquency.

It is also clear that some of the traditionally male perogatives also create a greater likelihood for delinquency. It may be, for example, that expecting boys to "sow wild oats" could create less concern among young men about the consequences of this behavior if they are apprehended. It may also be that males are freed from parental and societal supervision to such an extent that they can freely frequent settings where certain forms of delinquency are more likely to occur. This access to opportunity for delinquent behavior, without the buffering of either traditionally female attributes or the restrictions that accompany being female, may contribute to greater amounts of serious delinquency in males.

Finally, there is evidence that androgyny might be the key to lower delinquency for both males and females. On this point, this chapter has presented evidence that possession of some traditionally masculine traits lowers female delinquency potential as well as evidence that possession of some traditionally female traits lowers the likelihood that males will engage in delinquency, particularly aggressive delinquency. Contrary to popular mythology, then, freeing the sexes from the confines of narrow stereotyped roles may actually prove to be an effective approach to delinquency prevention.

REFERENCES

Acheson, J. D., & Williams, D. C. (1954). A study of juvenile sex offenders. *American Journal of Psychiatry, 3*, 366–370.

Adler, F. (1975). *Sisters in crime.* New York: McGraw-Hill.

Anderson, E. (1977). A comparison of male and female adolescents' attachment to parents and differential involvement with marijuana. *International Review of Modern Society, 7*, 213–223.

Ball, R. A., & Lilly, R. (1976). Female delinquency in an urban county. *Criminology, 14*, 279–281.

Blos, P. (1962). *On adolescence: A psycho-analytic interpretation.* New York: Free Press.

Bowker, L. (1976). *Drug use at a small liberal arts college.* Palo Alto, CA: R. and E. Research Associates.

Cantner, R. (1981). *Family correlates of male and female delinquency.* Boulder, CO: Behavioral Research Institute.

Cernkovich, A., & Giordano, C. (1979). A comparative analysis of male and female delinquency. *Sociological Quarterly, 20*, 131–145.

Chesney-Lind, M. (1978). Young women in the arms of the law. In L. H. Bowker (Ed.), *Women, crime, and the criminal justice system.* Lexington, MA: Lexington Books.

Chesney-Lind, M., & Rodriquez, N. M. (1983). Women under lock and key: A view from the inside. *Prison Journal, 63*, 47–65.

Cohen, A. K. (1955). *Delinquent boys.* Glencoe, IL: Free Press.

Cowie, J., Cowie, V., & Slater, E. (1968). *Delinquency in girls.* Chicago: Aldine Press.

Criminal Justice Research Center. (1978). *Sourcebook of criminal justice statistics—1977.* Washington, D.C.: U.S. Government Printing Office.

Criminal Justice Research Center. (1980). *Sourcebook of criminal justice statistics—1979.* Washington, D.C.: U.S. Government Printing Office.

Criminal Justice Research Center. (1982). *Sourcebook of criminal justice statistics—1981.* Washington, D.C.: U.S. Government Printing Office.

Cullem, F. T., Golden, K. M., & Cullen, J. B. (1979). Sex and delinquency. *Criminology, 7*, 301–310.

Datesman, S. K., Scarpitti, F. R., & Stephenson, R. M. (1975). Female delinquency: An application of self and opportunity theories. *Journal of Research in Crime and Delinquency*, July, 107–132.

Deming, R. (1977). *Women: The new criminals*. New York: Dell.

Elliot, D., & Voss, H. (1974). *Delinquency and dropout*. Lexington, MA: Lexington Books.

Eron, L. (1980). Prescription for reduction of aggression. *American Psychologist, 35*, 244–252.

Federal Bureau of Investigation. (1974). *Uniform crime reports for the United States*. Washington, D.C.: U.S. Government Printing Office.

Giordano, P. C., & Cernkovich, S. A. (1979). On complicating the relationship between liberation and delinquency. *Social Problems, 26*, 467–481.

Gold, M., & Reimer, D. J. (1975). Changing patterns of delinquency behavior among Americans 13 through 16 years old. *Crime and Delinquency literature, 7*, 483–517.

Grosser, G. H. (1952). *Juvenile delinquency and contemporary American sex roles*. Unpublished doctoral dissertation, Harvard University.

Heindensohn, F. (1968). The deviance of women: A critique and an enquiry. *British Journal of Sociology*, June, 160–176.

Hindelang, M. J. (1979). Sex differences in criminal activity. *Social Problems, 27*, 143–156.

Hindelang, M. J. (1976). With a little help from their friends: Group participation in reported delinquent behavior. *British Journal of Crimmology, 16*, 109–125.

Hoffman-Bustamante, D. (1973). The nature of female criminality. *Issues in Criminology, 8*, 117–136.

James, J., & Thornton, W. (1980). Women's liberation and the female delinquent. *Journal of Research in Crime and Delinquency*, 230–244.

Jensen, G. J., & Eve, R. (1976). Sex differences in delinquency: An examination of popular sociological explanations. *Criminology, 13*, 427–448.

Johnson, W. T., Peterson, R. E., & Wells, L. E. (1977). Arrest probabilities for marijuana users as indicators of selective law enforcement. *American Journal of Sociology, 83*, 681–699.

Konopka, G. (1966). *The adolescent girl in conflict*. Englewood Cliffs, NJ: Prentice-Hall.

Lov, P., & Norland, S. (1981). Gender convergence and delinquency. *Sociological Quarterly, 22*, 275–283.

Mawby, B. (1980). Sex and crime: The results of a self-report study. *British Journal of Sociology, 31:4*, 526–543.

Morris, R. R. (1963). *Comparison of female and male delinquency*. Unpublished doctoral dissertation, University of Michigan.

Morris, R. R. (1964). Female delinquency and relational problems. *Social Forces, 43*, 82–89.

Morris, R. R. (1965). Attitudes toward delinquency by delinquents, non-delinquents, and their friends. *British Journal of Criminology, 5*, 249–265.

National Institute of Mental Health. (1977). Study of females in detention in King County, VA. Washington, DC: U.S. Government Printing Office.

Norland, S., Shover, N., Thornton, W., & James, J. (1979). Intrafamily conflict and delinquency. *Pacific Sociological Review, 22*, 233–237.

Norland, S., Wessel, R. C., & Shover, N. (1979). *Masculinity and delinquency*. Paper read at the annual meeting of the Society for the Study of Social Problems, Boston, MA.

Phelps, R. J., McIntosh, M., Jesudason, V., Warner, P., & Pohlkamp, J. (1982). *Wisconsin female juvenile offender study project*. Youth policy and Law Center, Wisconsin Council on Juvenile Justice.

Pollak, O., & Friedman, A. S. (Eds.), (1969). *Family dynamics and female sexual delinquency*. Palo Alto, CA: Science and Behavior Books.

Rankin, J. H. (1980). School factors and delinquency: Interaction by age and sex. *Sociology and Social Research, 64(3)*, 420–434.

Richards, P., & Tittle, C. R. (1981). Gender and perceived chances of arrest. *Social Forces, 51*, 1182–1199.

Sandhu, H. S., & Allen, D. E. (1969). Female delinquency: Goal obstruction and anomie. *Canadian Review of Sociology and Anthropology, 5,* 107–110.

Shover, N., & Norland, S. (1978). Sex roles and criminality: Science or conventional wisdom. *Sex Roles, 4,* 111–125.

Shover, N., Norland, S., James, J., & Thornton, W. (1979). Gender roles and delinquency. *Social Forces, 58,* 162–175.

Steffensmeier, D. J., & Steffensmeier, R. H. (1980). Trends in female delinquency. *Criminology, 18,* 62–85.

Teilmann, K. S., & Landry, P. H., Jr. (1981). Gender bias in the juvenile justice system. *Journal of Research in Crime and Delinquency, 18,* 47–80.

Thomas, W. I. (1928). *The unadjusted girl.* Boston: Little, Brown.

Thornton, W. E., & James, J. (1979). Masculinity and delinquency revisited. *British Journal of Criminology, 19,* 225–241.

Vedeer, C. B., & Sommerville, D. B. (1970). *The delinquent girl.* Springfield, IL: Charles C Thomas.

Weis, J. G. (1976). Liberation and crime: The invention of the new female criminal. *Crime and Social Justice, 6,* 17–27.

Williams, J. R., & Gold, M. (1978). From delinquent behavior to official delinquency. In B. Krisberg & J. Austin (Eds.), *The children of Ishmael.* Palo Alto, CA: Mayfield.

CHAPTER 9

Familial, Peer, and Television Influences on Aggressive and Violent Behavior

DAVID PEARL

I intend in this presentation to discuss general aspects of the problems of child-hood aggression and violence and to consider briefly what research has to tell us about the source and development of the child's aggressive behavior, violence, and delinquency. I intend also to give an overview of behavioral and social science research on television viewing as it relates to aggressive and violent behavior and attitudes of children and youth.

Heightened concern has been felt by the general public, as well as others who are professionally involved, that aggressive and violent behavior of children and youth has increased in recent years. Fears have been expressed that juvenile or adolescent delinquency today is more pervasive, is being committed at earlier ages, and has changed in quality, becoming more violent. The scope of the problem is dramatically illustrated by a recent conclusion (Morris & Hawkins, 1977) that an American boy born in 1974 is more likely to be murdered than an American soldier was likely to die in combat during World War II.

DEMOGRAPHIES OF AGGRESSIVE BEHAVIOR

What are some of the normative aspects of the development and charac-teristics of aggressive behavior in children and youth? Early on, ages 1 and 2, half of children's interactions can be considered aggressive (Cairns, 1979). As they grow older, children's aggressiveness decreases. By 2 ½ years, only about 20% of interactions with peers are aggressive. Such behaviors tend to be hitting,

DAVID PEARL • Chief, Behavioral Sciences Research Branch, Alcohol, Drug Abuse, and Mental Health Administration, Rockville, Maryland 20857.

punching, pushing, and pulling. The nature of aggressiveness also changes with age. The majority of such behaviors become instrumental, intended to accomplish or to gain something. As little as 5% is then meant to be hostile, deliberately to hurt or injure another. A number of studies in the United States and in other cultures show that there is a consistent tendency in home and school for there to be reductions in antisocial behavior with the increasing age of the child. One can conclude that a continued high level of aggressive or coercive behavior of the child represents a failure of adequate socialization.

From an early age boys are consistently more aggressive physically than girls, although girls often exceed them in verbal aggressiveness. In part, there is a biological basis for this, but there also is cultural encouragement and the shaping of behavior for girls to become more conforming and physically less expressive.

Socioeconomic class generally has been assumed to be a factor for higher aggressive or coercive behavior. While early research has shown that working-class youth has higher official delinquency rates, the data has often been confounded and the assumption has been questioned. A 1970 analysis of studies in the scientific literature (Hood & Sparks, 1979) showed a differential ratio of 1 ½ to 1 when lower-class and middle-class youth were compared on the basis of self-reports of behavior. Also, a recent national youth survey (Elliot & Huizenga, 1982) reported that middle-class adolescents generally had lower delinquent behavior rates on the basis of self-report. However, this was more the case for males than females and for serious and violent offenses than for nonserious and nonviolent events. Also, parental and teacher reports of offensive behavior were not found to relate consistently to class membership (Feshbach, 1970). And a recent study of bullies in a Swedish school system did not confirm the importance of class when peer ratings for aggressiveness were considered (Olweus, 1980).

Two major demographic studies have given valuable information about the presence or absence and progression or cessation of delinquent offensive acts. Wolfgang and Tracy (1982) initially studied an entire male cohort born during 1945 in Philadelphia for delinquent offenses during the age span of 10–18 years. Wolfgang followed up with a similar study of a second cohort including girls born during 1958 in Philadelphia. Although his analyses of this second cohort are not fully completed, Wolfgang has examined cohort differences between those growing up mostly in the 1950s and those who were adolescents in th 1970s. Approximately one-third of each cohort has had a history of one or more delinquent offenses. For both cohorts, those who have been chronic offenders constituted approximately 20% of the entire delinquent population, yet committed 52% and 61% respectively of all offenses. Chronic offenders in both cohorts have been highly involved in serious delinquencies, committing two-thirds or more of all murders, rapes, robberies, or aggravated assaults. When delinquencies for both cohorts are scored for seriousness, it appears evident that the second cohorts, born in 1958 and growing up 18 years later, have committed more offenses and more serious crimes than youth born in 1945.

The other major study to be cited is by Elliot and Huizenga (1982). This involves a national youth panel on deviant or delinquent behavior first held in 1976. Over 1,700 persons age 11–17 were interviewed yearly until the end of 1981. As part of the yearly procedure, the young people were given a self-report global delinquency scale. Analyses revealed that annual incidences regularly increased over the years, but this was attributable primarily to an increasing rate in relatively nonserious or nonviolent offenses, whereas a considerable reduction in serious and violent crimes took place. Chronic offenders committing serious criminal offenses including assault, theft, or property damage involved only 8% of the youth sample. This small group, however, committed 44% of all offenses. Those responsible for less serious criminal offenses made up an additional 7% of the cohort. Combined, these groups involved only 15% of the youth sample but committed two-thirds of all offenses, including 87% of crimes against persons and 85% of all thefts. These data also suggest that these criminal offenders escalated both the frequency and range of delinquencies over time, diversifying the kinds of acts involved.

All in all, these studies reveal that a relatively small portion of the adolescent population is responsible for performing a sizable majority of the more serious, offensive, and antisocial acts committed by adolescents.

PREDICTION OF ANTISOCIAL BEHAVIOR

This fact suggests several questions. First, is it possible to identify those children early in childhood who are at risk for joining the small adolescent group of serious criminal offenders? Second, what are the factors and influences that turn or shape children and youth into aggressive and delinquent persons? Third, can we use knowledge gained in attempts to answer these questions to concentrate efforts and scarce resources more effectively on high-risk children so as to influence developmental, family, and environmental processes and thereby reduce the number of serious offenders?

A variety of studies have shown that certain aggressive or deviant acts in childhood or early adolescence are related to later antisocial behavior. Such behavior has been differentiated into overt versus covert acts and most studies have been with boys. The proportion of young boys with confrontational, overt antisocial behavior such as aggression, excessive quarreling, disobedience, and fighting decreases as they become older. By age 16 only a small percentage of antisocial boys continue to be overtly aggressive. On the other hand, several covert antisocial behaviors such as stealing, vandalism, truancy from school, association with "bad" friends, and alcohol or drug use have been reported to increase until about 16 or 17, when a decline sets in. The proportion of children who frequently lie apparently stays fairly constant over the range of these years. We can judge from such data that there is a large percentage of children who probably are only temporarily antisocial, but there is also a small group whose antisocial behaviors remain fairly consistent over the years.

The continuity of antisocial behavior appears to hold particularly for those children or youths who early show a high frequency of misdeeds. Rolf Loeber (1982) has recently summarized the relevant scientific literature. He concludes that there are certain behavioral characteristics that are predictive of the small group who later are severe antisocial and violent offenders, that is, children who rate at the extremes of certain dimensions of antisocial behaviors are at risk for continuing with their deviant or criminal acts over time.

What are these characteristics? First, children who show high rates of antisocial behavior early, as compared to those with lower rates, are more likely to continue to be seriously antisocial later in life. Second, children who show significant antisocial behavior in more than one setting—the family home, others' homes, the school, or in the community—are at greatest risk for becoming chronic offenders. Third, the earlier the onset of deviant behavior in the elementary school years, the greater the risk for a chronic delinquent career. These characteristics point to risk not only for later chronicity but also for the commission of more serious crimes.

There is reasonable likelihood, then, that the calibration and weighted combination of these potential predictors may prove empirically to be a good method for identifying potentially serious chronic antisocial actors.

It is probable that a number of different stages occur in the development of antisocial behavior. Various factors are involved in such stage transitions. Some youth may not progress beyond early stages and then offensive behavior may remain trivial and sporadic. A decidedly smaller proportion may progress to more serious stages and accordingly manifest more severe and frequent chronic delinquent behavior.

Theoretical views of stages and factors which presumably incubate and encourage serious delinquencies generally have been of two types. The first gives primary consideration to the social environment of the child or youth, particularly his social bonding to his reference groups and acceptance of their norms and values. The second broad approach stresses the importance of intraindividual factors and internal controls. These are largely in the context of parent–child emotional relationships, child-rearing patterns, and parental regulation of the child's behavior.

The social bonding emphasis gives consideration to the changing influences of the child's reference groups as their relevance change for him. The family is the primary group in childhood and early adolescence. From about 13 years on, the school context assumes more salience and the peer group begins to replace the family in influence on the teenager. The attenuation of bonding to the family is accompanied increasingly by a weakening of and less conformity to the conventional norms of behavior which earlier were fostered by the family. For those youngsters who, early within the home setting, were already showing serious conduct or antisocial problems, the drift to the peer group provides incentives or reinforcements to keep and perhaps even to intensify offensive behavior.

The longitudinal studies of behavior and psychosocial development of youth by the Jessors (1977) are consistent with other data in highlighting the effect of peers on adolescents' problems. They found that youth who became marijuana users had been increasingly influenced by delinquent peers while sloughing off conventional parental controls. Nonusers failed to show a similar turning to delinquent peers or a detachment from parents. To summarize, if peer groups with which a growing adolescent identifies hold conventional values and behavioral norms, it is unlikely that the adolescent will become a serious chronic delinquent. But if his peers are delinquent, offensive antisocial behavior and values are more likely.

Educational adequacy also has been found to be important for youthful self-esteem in the earlier adolescent years. Adolescents with low school achievement and learning problems form the majority of school dropouts. Several studies have agreed that the highest dropout rates occur for nonachieving adolescents, who, frustrated in school and estranged or isolated from the social networks of the school, are instead tied socially to a network of delinquent friends. Typically, the antisocial behavior of such youth increase after they have dropped out (Elliot & Huizenga, 1974). According to various estimates, over 75% of juvenile delinquents have a prior history of a learning disability and academic failure, and many also are dropouts.

The second approach to the study of the development of serious delinquencies emphasizes the role of the family and home in the shaping of children, the precursors of serious antisocial behavior in the family and home setting, and the conditions controlling the occurrence of such behavior. Research has frequently emphasized the key role of parental attitudes and emotional relationships between child and parent, particularly the mother, and the kind and consistency of child-rearing practices in the home that influence conduct development.

Many studies provide clear indications of how necessary warm parental and consistent affectional attitudes, as well as consistency in child-rearing practices, are for the optimum development of the child. For example, Lee Robins's well-known studies (1966) have stressed the importance of love-oriented parental discipline. Michael Rutter (1971) has conducted a number of valuable studies of psychiatric disturbance and delinquency in English children in London and on the Isle of Wight. He has concluded that parental discord and the absence of a warm and stable relationship with parents, together with erratic and deviant child-rearing methods, are linked to an antisocial outcome. Langner (1979) has also found from the data of the Manhattan longitudinal study that antisocial children were less delinquent and offensive in their behavior when parents became less rejecting of them than they had been previously. Olweus (1980) who studied the development of aggressive reaction patterns in Swedish boys, reports four major variables as having causal influence: (1) the mother's permissiveness for aggression, (2) the mother's negativism, (3) the boy's temperament, and (4) the mother's and father's methods for power assertion.

Patterson (1982), who is one of the most tireless and productive researchers studying children's antisocial behavior and family processes, has reported that disobedience is an early precursor of both overt and covert antisocial traits in the child. Parents often permit such children to disobey. Patterson's analysis of the antisocial acts of clinic-referred children has lead him to postulate a development sequence in which frequent lying precedes stealing, and these also precede school truancy and drug taking. Patterson views covert behavior as tending to occur in children whose parents do not monitor the child's whereabouts or associations with peers. Overtly antisocial children, on the other hand, are seen as associated with early hyperactivity as well as the failure of parents to use discipline to control the child's behavior. Ineffectual problem solving in the family also appears to be a factor in antisocial behavior. Overall, the children are at risk for offensive behavior when there are poor family management practices or when family disruptions occur.

Patterson, along with a number of other investigators in this area, has attempted to integrate the social environmental and the intraindividual and internal control perspectives. These integrations are often placed within a social learning framework that posits learning on the basis of observation of models (for example, the parents or peers with whom the child identifies), on attitude formation, and on the positive and negative reinforcements the child receives for his behavior.

One key socializing influence to which developmental psychology has not yet given adequate attention in regard to the shaping of behavior and attitudes is television. Television provides a wide range of models for the viewer, and it can be very potent with respect to its symbolic reinforcements. We shall now consider television as it relates to aggressive and violent behavior of viewers and associated concerns.

TELEVISION AND AGGRESSIVENESS

From its early days, television has increasingly become an important part of the life of the viewing public, including children. Television is now a socializing agent almost comparable in importance to the home, school, and neighborhood in influencing children's development and behavior. The medium is a formidable educator the effects of which are both pervasive and cumulative. Research findings have long since destroyed any illusion that television is merely innocuous entertainment: it can no longer be considered to be simply a casual part of daily life.

Surveys have indicated that each person in the United States, on the average, watches television for approximately 25 to 30 hours per week. Some, of course, watch much more. Viewing times for individuals may range from one or two to many hours daily and some keep the set on all day long. Children, women, older persons, and those in the lower socioeconomic strata of society view the most. One survey has found that for large numbers of people, television ranks third among all activities, after sleep and work, in the number of hours devoted to it. By the time an average child graduates from high school, he has devoted a significantly larger number of hours to the television screen than he has spent in the classroom.

Public interest and concern about televised violence began to be manifested in the 1950s, and two governmental commissions considered this problem in the late 1960s. The first, the National Commission on the Causes and Prevention of Violence, concluded that the viewing of televised violence increased the likelihood that a viewer might behave violently; this conclusion was reached on the basis of a relatively small number of laboratory studies. The second commission was the Surgeon General's Scientific Advisory Committee, set up in 1969, which decided that there were gaps in the knowledge needed and therefore commissioned 25 new research projects. Its 1972 report confirmed the pervasiveness of television, and the major conclusion was that there was fairly substantial experimental evidence for a short-run causation of aggression among some children viewing televised violence but less evidence from field studies regarding long-term causal effects (Surgeon General's Scientific Advisory Committee, 1972).

Since then, numerous studies of the medium's influence have been conducted over a broad range of behavioral topics. Over 80% of all publications of research on television influences have appeared in the last decade—over 2,500 titles. Because of this outpouring of research, leading investigators in 1979 suggested the timeliness of an update of the 1972 Surgeon General's Report through an assessment and integration of this burgeoning literature. The Surgeon General and the National Institute of Mental Health agreed, and the project was initiated in late 1979. The update was conducted by key NIMH staff together with a small distinguished advisory group of consultants. These included child development experts, behavioral scientists, mental health researchers, and communication media specialists. Comprehensive and critical evaluations of the scientific literature were commissioned from leading researchers. The update group assessed and integrated these contributions as well as additional pertinent data. The import of the group's evaluations as well as the commissioned state-of-knowledge articles were incorporated in a two-volume report published in 1982 (Pearl, Bouthilet, & Lazar, 1982; NIMH, 1982).

The unanimous consensus of the update team was that there is a general learning effect from television viewing that is important in the development and functioning of many viewers, particularly children. The learning and expression of aggressive behavior is one aspect of this. This convergence of findings from a large body of literature supported the influence of a causal connection between televised violence and later aggressive behavior. The conclusions reached in the 1972 Surgeon General's Report thus were strengthened by the more recent research.

Such empirical support for the link does not mean, of course, that all aggressive or violent behavior in the real world relates to or is caused exclusively by television viewing. The causes of behavior are complex and are determined by multiple factors, and the viewing of televised violence is only one in a constellation of determinants or precipitating factors involved in antisocial or aggressive behavior. Probably no single factor by itself makes a child or anyone else seriously aggressive or antisocial. Certainly, in some psychological, social, or environmental circumstances television may exert little or no easily discernible influence on behavior. But under other conditions it may play a significant role in shaping behavioral style, in determining when and how violence, aggressiveness, or other antisocial behavior is expressed. Television viewing also may function as a triggering or releasing mechanism for overt behavior that otherwise might be inhibited.

An additional consequence of televised violence may be desensitization, particularly for those who are heavy viewers of violent programs. What is of concern is the insidious effect on attitudes and expectations, particularly for children. They may begin to accept a higher level of violence or aggressiveness as being normal and thus become more willing to accept aggressive behavior by other children and adults. And there may therefore be lessened compassion for or empathy with the objects of aggression and the victims of violence.

In general, the reliability of results from basic laboratory studies of television or audiovisual influences are well established and provide more readily acceptable causal inferences than do data from outside the laboratory. But laboratory studies have been questioned regarding their generalizability to real-life aggression and violence. Field studies, on the other hand, are more naturalistic and realistic, although they are less precise and less readily interpretable regarding causal relationships. The majority of observational or experimental field studies and surveys so far do indicate that there is a significant positive correlation between television viewing and aggressive behavior. The strength of this relationship differs among various field studies on the basis of differences in samples and in procedures for assessing both viewing and aggressive or anti-social behavior.

One can conclude, therefore, that there is a body of experimental and field findings that coalesce and are mutually supportive in a broad sense. Two compilations, which combined reported studies involving as many as up to 100,000 persons as subjects (Andison, 1977; Hearold, 1979), summarize the strong evidence for a positive relationship between the viewing of televised violence and subsequent aggressive behavior. The possibility that there is a bidirectional causal effect must be considered. The path analyses of data from recent longitudinal coordinated studies in the United States and in Finland, as reported by Huesmann, Lagerspetz, and Eron (1984), do support such an interaction. The authors conclude that extensive viewing of televised violence by children instigates greater aggressiveness, and this effect does indeed occur not only for those children who are initially highly aggressive. Reciprocally, then, for children who thus become more aggressive an increased attentiveness to and preference for programs with violence and high action are engendered.

Huesmann et al's data from their large sample of American children indicates, too, that a positive link holds for primary school girls as well as for boys, contrary to earlier findings in the literature that such a relationship holds only for boys. Also, considering the research of the past decade in this country, it is clear that the link holds for the entire childhood age spectrum, having been reported for study samples ranging from preschool through the adolescent years.

Eron (1982) has linked heavier television viewing and aggressive behavior for some children to their unpopularity with schoolmates and to low school achievement. Those with difficult interpeer relations often turn to television, which provides them with more satisfaction. Those who have learning problems or who otherwise do not succeed in school also may spend more time in front of the television set than do their scholastically successful classmates. These heavier viewers have more opportunity to observe the many aggressive models to be found in television programs and to identify more with them than do their peers. Accordingly, they more readily employ the aggressive problem-solving tactics of their models and became more coercive in their interpersonal behavior. This behavior, in turn, tends to isolate the heavier viewers even more, and circularly this maintains heavier television viewing and its effects.

Some critics have discounted the antisocial effects of television shown by past research on the grounds that such effects, although statistically significant, nevertheless are not large enough to be meaningful in a practical sense. But even if this were so and the extensive viewing of televised violence has only a comparatively small effect on children, youth, and other viewers, such an effect could still be of major social significance. Consider, for instance, that if only one out of a thousand viewers were affected, a given prime-time national program with an audience of 15 million would generate a group of 15,000 viewers who had been influenced. Consider also the cumulative effects for viewers who watch such programs throughout the year. Even if only a small number of violent antisocial incidents are precipitated in any community, these often are sufficient to be disruptive and to impair the quality of social life for the whole community.

Furthermore, we know that television presentations of various newsworthy antisocial or violent acts have instigated imitations. This has occurred in regard to airplane hijacking and, more recently, in an increase of poison threats through tampering with over-the-counter drugs. Other documentary or semifictional presentations as well as fictional dramatic programs have stimulated replications of violence or threats of violence. A number of months ago, a teenager in the South shot his grandparents, and according to the media (a reporter in that community called me), this occurred after he had watched a similar incident in the fictionalized documentary "The Executioner's Song" shown on national television. Recently, too, a motorist was charged for running down a motorcycle police officer on the shoulder of the highway. Witness testimony described the motorist's car as rapidly crossing three traffic lanes before entering the shoulder and smashing into the motorcycle. Laboratory tests indicated that the man had taken PCP (angel dust) and, according to his wife, had, a scant six hours before, seen a televised late night movie, "Gauntlet," starring Clint Eastwood, which portrays Eastwood in his car smashing through a road barrier and running down a motorcycle police officer. Also, numerous self-inflicted deaths and woundings involving both adults and adolescents have been reported all over the country at different times following the showing on television of the movie "Deerhunter," which features a "Russian roulette" episode. And Bandura has documented (1973) the fact that airlines in various cities and countries have reported imitative extortion threats to blow up aircraft through implanted pressure-sensitive bombs following the showing of the television play "Doomsday Flight" in these cities.

Three kinds of television-related effects can be identified. The first involves the direct imitation of observed violence. This is the effect that first springs to mind when one thinks about television violence. There are many examples of the learning and overt imitation of viewed violent or aggressive actions. The medium often has provided graphic tutoring or training on how to do it—how to burglarize, physically manhandle an opponent, and so forth. One example reported in a newspaper involved the arrest of a youth in his first attempt to break open a telephone coin box. He had learned the technique from a television crime show, which, however, had failed to explain that such telephones also have a built-in silent alarm system. The outcome of this episode was the criminal labeling and incarceration of the youth with possible long-lasting consequences.

A second type of effect occurs when the television violence serves to instigate or trigger overt acts which are not imitations of what has been immediately observed but rather relate to earlier learned aggressive or violent tactics.

Viewer habituation or desensitization to the occurrence of violence is yet a third potential outcome of a heavy diet of televised violence. The child especially, but youth and adults too, may conclude that violent behavior or aggressive tactics are appropriate in many circumstances. Such viewers would learn gradually to accept a higher level of violent behavior as being normal. There are a number of studies suggesting that the development over time of this frame of mind may result in a greater tolerance of violence when it occurs, a decrease of empathy toward others in distress, or an increase in apathy relative to the helping of victims.

A number of studies, mostly experimental, have delineated those viewing circumstances wherein televised violence was most likely to influence behavior. Aggressiveness is most likely to be emulated when: (1) it pays off: that is, the actor or model solves his problem, achieves his goal, or satisfies his need; (2) it is not punished: there is no retribution, censure, or unfavorable consequence to the actor as a result of the use of violence; (3) it is shown in a justifying context: that is, the violence, threat, or injury meted out is justified by the events and the victim is shown to have merited such treatment (this typically occurs in police shows); (4) it is socially acceptable; the aggressive behavior is presented as acceptable to the characters portrayed in the context of the social practices and attitudes characterizing the setting and plot of the program, as in the hanging of a rustler in a "Wild West" program; (5) it appears realistic rather than as a segment of a fictitious program; (6) it appears motivated by a deliberate intent to injure the victim; (7) it is expressed in conditions, cues, or circumstances similar to those experienced or lived in by the viewer; and (8) it is perpetrated by a model whom the viewer perceives as similar to himself.

Just as media influence facilitates acting out behavior there are also, of course, media "messages" which for older youths and adult viewers can serve to inhibit acting out. These include (1) retribution and punishment following violence—a clear indicator that crime does not pay; (2) a sequential showing of the destructive and painful consequences of aggression; and (3) reminders that such behavior is contrary to ethical or moral principles. But research has disclosed that these messages probably are not very effective with younger children. There are age-related links between what is viewed and what is comprehended as well as what is acted out. Young children particularly have difficulty in understanding or remembering plots and sequences. They may have difficulty in understanding the context of behavior and therefore may interpret events differently than would older viewers. One can, therefore, question the contention that depicting motives and consequences for antisocial acts nullifies their potential impact on children. Presentation characteristics like subtlety or the separation in time of important plot elements may militate against the drawing of intended inferences by the child.

A number of field studies of the last decade deserve special attention. The longitudinal study initially reported by Lefkowitz, Eron, Walder, and Huesmann in 1972 and later in 1977 found that preferences of 8-year-old children for watching television violence assessed in 1960 contributed to the development of aggressive habits as measured a decade and more later.

Singer and Singer (1980), in two short-term longitudinal studies, followed middle-class and lower-socioeconomic class 3- and 4-year-olds and assessed both their television viewing and behavior at four different times. They concluded in both studies that watching violence on television was a cause of heightened aggressiveness.

McCarthy and colleagues (1975) came to the same conclusion as a result of a five-year study of 732 children. Several kinds of aggressive behavior including conflict with parents, fighting, and delinquency proved to be positively associated with amount of television viewing. In a recent Canadian study, aggressive behavior of primary school children in a small community was assessed before and after television was introduced. These data were compared with those for children of two other towns which already had access to television. Increases in both verbal and physical aggression occurred after television was introduced and were significantly greater here than in the two comparison communities (Joy, Kimball, & Zabrack, 1977).

A similar Canadian study (Granzberg & Steinbring, 1980) compared a Cree Indian community into which television had been introduced with a control Indian community and a control Euro-Canadian community which already had television. Significant increases were found for children who became heavy viewers of the newly introduced medium. Adolescents were the subjects of a study reported by Hartnagel, Teevan, and McIntyre (1975). They found a significant though low correlation between violence viewing and aggressive behavior.

Huesmann *et al.* (1982) collected data on 758 first- and third-graders for each of three years through an overlapping longitudinal design which then provided data for grades 2 to 5. Similar data were collected on 220 children in Finland. Analyses revealed that viewing of violence was related to concurrent aggression and significantly predicted future changes in aggression for boys in both countries and for girls in the United States. Both the frequency with which violence was viewed and the extent of violence contributed to the causal relationship.

Another field study reported by Parke, Berkowitz, Leyens, and Sebastian (1977) involved three studies of adolescent males in the United States and Belgium. These juveniles were selectively exposed to five viewing days of either violent or neutral control films. In both countries, those who saw the more violent films were characterized as acting more aggressively during the five days. There was some tendency for boys initially more aggressive to show the greatest increase in aggression.

A noteworthy study in England by Belson (1978) concerned 1,650 boys 13–16 years of age. These boys were evaluated for violent behavior, attitudes, sociocultural background, and exposure to television violence. After being divided into two groups on the basis of exposure to televised violence, the lighter and heavier exposees were equated on the basis of personal characteristics and background variables. The data strongly supported the conclusion that long-term exposure increased the degree to which boys engaged in serious misbehavior such as burglary, destruction of property, infliction of personal injuries, or attempted rape. Boys with heavy exposure to televised violence were 47% more likely than boys with light exposure to commit the above acts and were 11% more likely to commit violent acts in general. Belson also reported that the viewing of certain program types seemed more likely than others to lead to serious behavioral offenses. These included programs involving physical or visual violence in close personal relationships, programs with gratuitous violence not germane to the plot, realistic fictional violence, violence in a good cause, and violent Westerns.

In a striking contrast, Milavsky and his colleagues (Milavsky, Kessler, Stipp, & Rubens, 1982) in a National Broadcasting Company panel study concluded differently. They collected data at several points of time over a three-year period for 2,400 elementary school children and for 800 teenage high school boys in two cities. Peer nominations of aggression were collected for the elementary school children while the teenagers gave self-reports. The results obtained through the use of a recently developed model for causal analysis (Lisrel IV computer program) showed that there were short-term small positive correlations between viewing measures and aggressive behavior taken at the same point of time. They did not find any long-term effects, and they concluded that short-term effects did not cumulate and produce stable patterns of aggressive behavior in the real world.

The seeming excellence of this study's data and analysis might appear to pose a serious challenge to the conclusions of the NIMH report regarding causal influence. But the full appropriateness of the analytic model has been questioned. A reanalysis by Cook, Kendzierski, & Thomas (1982) led them to conclude that the NBC study analysis was faulty and that a more tenable conclusion was that television violence may well increase aggression in children from 7 to 16 years of age.

Since the publication of the NIMH report (1982), another study has appeared (Hennigan et al., 1982) which is consistent with the view of television as a potent influence on viewer behavior. This study used interrupted time series data to examine how the introduction of television into American cities at different times affected FBI indicators of larceny and auto theft. The research was possible because television reception by communities throughout the country began at different times. This artificial staggering resulted from a Federal Communications Commission freeze on new broadcasting licenses between late 1949 and mid-1950s. Areas receiving television before the freeze could then be compared at different times for levels of crime with communities provided with television only after the freeze. Sophisticated analyses did not reveal a consistent effect for all crimes but did show that the introduction of television conclusively increased larcenies and, less definitively, auto thefts. The authors believed that these increases were probably largely due to attitudinal and motivational changes. Their analysis of early television programming indicated that these most likely were due to the arousal of consumption appetites in many young viewers by the portrayal of middle-class life-styles and the heavy advertising of consumption goods.

THE MEASUREMENT OF VIOLENCE ON TELEVISION

Despite some argument over how to measure the amount of television violence, the level of violence on commercial television has remained relatively stable over the past decade. According to the yearly Violence Profile reports issued by the Annenberg School of Communications in Philadelphia, there has been no overall decrease, although some aspects have changed. This measurement employs an index of violence that combines several measures such as the prevalence of violence on programs and among characters and its rate per program and per hour. The analysis includes clear-cut and unambiguous violence in any context, including fantasy, humor, and cartoons. This yearly profile has pointed up the shocking fact that over recent years, weekend daytime children's programs have exceeded adult prime-time dramatic programming in overall violence. Gerbner, testifying before a congressional committee in 1981 (Gerbner, 1981), reported that the most recent assessment showed that children's programs continued to rise in violence on all three major networks, especially for the rate of violent incidents per hour: "Violence strikes at the rate of almost six times per hour in prime time and 25 times an hour during weekend daytime children's programming" (p. 155). Some have dismissed such data as ridiculous because cartoon violence is included in the assessment. Cartoons are often considered by adults as harmless fantasy. Yet there are a number of studies indicating that preschool and young school children who often watch cartoons with a great deal of violence are the most aggressive.

PREVENTION AND INTERVENTION

This chapter has made it evident that there can be harmful consequences to children from extensive viewing of televised violence. Is there anything that can be done to prevent or minimize such harm? Direct governmental intervention with respect to broadcast programming is in violation of constitutional First

Amendment rights. Experience and research suggest, however, that parents, teachers, and older brothers and sisters are important in determining television effects on children.

Parental control of the amount and kind of viewing is a major factor in minimizing effects. An early study suggested that parents were relatively apathetic about their children's television viewing. More recently, parental concern has risen. Surveys also have previously indicated that parents significantly underestimated their children's viewing times and were not adequately aware of the kinds of programs watched. There are two major ways in which parents can assume a more active role in intervening with and controlling television viewing: they can help their children obtain critical viewing skills, and they can plan parent–child activities other than television viewing.

For some years now, attention has been given to the moderating influence of critical viewing skills. The idea here is that if children learn how to watch television, understand broadcasting goals regarding audience and advertising, and have some awareness of the reality–fantasy aspects of programs and realize how the content and program attributes may influence their feelings, ideas, and behaviors, the medium's potential adverse influences may be minimized.

Research has shown that adult's comments affected the child's later aggressive behavior. If the adult made favorable comments regarding the television-displayed aggression, the child became more aggressive than if the adult made unfavorable remarks. Adult involvement has also been found in other studies to influence attitudinal change and to increase children's learning from television programming.

Six specific ways have been suggested in which parents can help their children to obtain critical viewing skills (O'Bryant & Corder-Bolz, 1978):

1. Limited viewing. Parents can limit the amount of time children view television.
2. Content control. Parents can encourage or discourage viewing particular programs.
3. Purposeful viewing.
4. Direct mediation. Parents can provide explanatory comments.
5. Indirect mediation. Parents can model critical viewing skills by discussing programs with others in the presence of the child.
6. Springboard techniques. Parents can show children how television information can be applied to and have implications for many events in everyday life.

Whether such efforts to prevent or mitigate possible undesirable influences of the medium are more than bandaids is debatable. These may very well need supplementation by pressure on broadcasters from citizen's groups and periodic public discussion. We shall await further developments.

REFERENCES

Andison, F. S. (1977). TV violence and viewer aggression: A cumulation of study results 1956 to 1976. *Public Opinion Quarterly, 41,* 314–331.

Bandura, A. (1973). *Aggression: A social learning analysis.* Englewood Cliffs, NJ: Prentice-Hall.

Belson, W. (1978). *Television violence and the adolescent boy.* Lexington, MA: Lexington Books.

Cairns, R. B. (1979). *Social development: The origins and plasticity of interchanges.* San Francisco: W. H. Freeman.

Cook, T. D., Kendzierski, D. A., & Thomas, S. F. (1982, December). *Television research for science and policy: An alien perspective on the NIMH report on television and behavior.* A report for a committee of the National Research Council, Washington, D.C.

Elliott, D. S., & Voss, H. L. (1974). *Delinquency and dropout.* Lexington, MA: Lexington Books.

Elliot, D. S., & Huizenga, D. (1980, November). *Defining pattern delinquency: A conceptual typology of delinquent offenders.* Paper presented at the annual meeting of the American Society of Criminology, San Francisco.

Elliot, D. S., & Huizenga, D. (1982). *Social class and delinquent behavior in a national youth panel.* Unpublished monograph. Boulder, CO: Behavioral Research Institute.

Eron, L. D. (1982). Parent–child interaction, television violence and aggression of children. *American Psychologist, 37,* 197–211.

Feshbach, S. (1970). Aggression. In P. H. Mussen (Eds.), *Carmichael's manual of child psychology* (Vol. 2). New York: Wiley.

Gerbner, G. (1981, October). Statement on violence on television before the U.S. House Subcommittee on Telecommunications, Consumer Protection and Finance, 97th Congress. *Congressional Record,* serial no. 97-84, p. 155.

Granzberg, G., & Steinbring, J. (1980). *Television and the Canadian Indian* (Technical Report). Winnipeg: Department of Anthropology, University of Winnipeg.

Hartnagel, T. F., Teevan, J. J., Jr., & McIntyre, J. J. (1975). Television violence and violent behavior. *Social Forces, 54,* 341–351.

Hearold, S. L. (1979). *Meta-analysis of the effects of television on social behavior.* Unpublished doctoral dissertation, University of Colorado.

Hennigan, K. M., DelRosario, M. L., Heath, L., Cook, T. D., Wharton, J. D., & Calder, B. J. (1982). The impact of the introduction of television on crime in the United States: Empirical findings and theoretical implications. *Journal of Personality and Social Psychology, 42,* 461–477.

Hood, R., & Sparks, R. (1979). *Key issues in criminology.* London: Weidenfeld and Nicholson.

Huesmann, L. R., Lagerspetz, K., & Eron, L. D. (1984). Intervening variables in the television–aggression relation: Evidence from two countries. *Developmental Psychology, 20,* 746–775.

Jessor, R., & Jessor, S. L. (1977). *Problem behavior and psychological development: A longitudinal study of youth.* New York: Academic Press.

Joy, L. A., Kimball, M., & Zabrack, M. L. (1977, June). Television exposure and children's aggressive behavior. In T. M. Williams (Chair), *The impact of television: A natural experiment involving three communities.* A symposium presented at the annual meeting of the Canadian Psychological Association, Vancouver.

Langner, T. S. (1979). Predictors of child behavior and their implications for social policy. In R. G. Simmons (Ed.), *Research in community and mental health: An annual compilation of research.* Greenwich, CT: JAI.

Lefkowitz, M. M., Eron, L. D., Walder, L. O., & Huesmann, L. R. (1977). *Growing up to be violent.* New York: Pergamon.

Lefkowitz, M. M., Eron, L. D., Walder, L., & Huesmann, L. R. (1972). Television violence and child aggression: A follow-up study. In G. A. Comstock & E. A. Rubinstein (Eds.), *Television and social behavior: Television and adolescent aggressiveness* (Vol. 3). Washington, D.C.: U.S. Government Printing Office.

Loeber, R. (1982). The stability of antisocial and delinquent child behavior: A review. *Child Development, 53,* 1431–1446.

McCarthy, E. D., Langren, T. S., Gersten, J. C., Eisenberg, J. G., & Orzeck, L. (1975). Violence and behavior disorders. *Journal of Communication, 25,* 71–85.

Milavsky, J. R., Kessler, P., Stipp, H., & Rubens, W. (1982). Television and aggression: Results of a panel study. In D. Pearl, L. Bouthelet, & J. B. Lazar (Eds.), *Television and behavior: Ten years of scientific progress and implications for the eighties* (Vol. 2). *Technical reviews.* Washington, D.C.: U.S. Government Printing Office.

Morris, N., & Hawkins, G. (1977). *Letter to the President on crime control.* Chicago, IL: University of Chicago Press.

O'Bryant, S. L., & Corder-Bolz, C. R. (1978). Tackling the tube with family teamwork. *Children Today, 7,* 21–24.

Olweus, D. (1980). Familial and temperamental determinants of aggressive behavior in adolescent boys: A causal analysis. *Developmental Psychology, 16,* 644–660.

Parke, R. D., Berkowitz, L., Leyens, J. P., & Sebastian, R. J. (1977). Some effects of violent and nonviolent movies on the behavior of juvenile delinquents. In L. Berkowitz (Ed.), *Advances in experimental social psychology* (Vol. 10, pp. 135–172). New York: Academic Press.

Patterson, G. R. (1982). Coercive family process. Eugene, OR: Castalia.

Pearl, D., Bouthilet, L., & Lazar, J. B. (Eds.) (1982) *Television and behavior: Ten years of scientific progress and implications for the eighties* (Vol. 2). *Technical reviews.* Washington, D.C.: U.S. Government Printing Office.

Robins, L. N. (1966). *Deviant children grow up: A sociological and psychiatric study of sociopathic personality.* Baltimore: Williams & Wilkins.

Rutter, M. (1971). Parent–child separation: Psychological effecs on the children. *Journal of Child Psychiatry, 12,* 233–260.

Singer, J. L., & Singer, D. G. (1980). *Television imagination and aggression: A study of preschoolers play.* Hillsdale, NJ: Erlbaum.

Surgeon General's Scientific Advisory Committee on Television and Behavior. (1972). *Television and growing up: The impact of televised violence.* Washington, D.C.: U.S. Government Printing Office.

National Institute of Mental Health. (1982). *Television and behavior: Ten years of scientific progress and implications for eighties: Summary Report,* (Vol. 1). Washington, D.C.: U.S. Government Printing Office.

Wolfgang, M. E., & Tracy, P. E. (1982, February). *The 1945 and 1958 birth cohorts: A comparison of the prevalence, incidence and severity of delinquent behavior.* Paper presented at the Conference on Public Danger, Dangerous Offenders and the Criminal Justice System, Harvard University, Cambridge, MA.

CHAPTER 10

Aggression and Its Correlates over 22 Years

LEONARD D. ERON, L. ROWELL HUESMANN,
ERIC DUBOW, RICHARD ROMANOFF,
AND PATTY WARNICK YARMEL

It is apparent from the varied substance of the chapters in this book that aggression is an overdetermined behavior. There are genetic, constitutional, and environmental factors as well as individual learning history and specific situational events which go into determining whether a person will act in an aggressive manner at any specific time. However, the large number of possible determinants does not mean that aggressive behavior cannot be predicted or explained. Research that my colleagues and I have been doing indicates, in fact, that aggressive behavior is consistent over time and across situations despite the fact that a number of factors contribute to the behavior in varying degrees.

In 1960, we completed a survey of all the third-grade school children in a semi-rural county in New York State. This included approximately 870 youngsters whose modal age at the time was 8 years. We also interviewed 80% of their mothers and fathers. The focus of our procedures was the aggressive behavior of the subjects as manifested in school. Our purpose was to delineate the learning conditions for aggression, and therefore we collected information about the presumed psychological and social antecedents and correlates of aggressive behavior. Most of the findings of this phase of the study have been published, and they indicate that many children learn to be more or less aggressive from interactions with the environment (Eron, Walder, & Lefkowitz, 1971).

LEONARD D. ERON, L. ROWELL HUESMANN, ERIC DUBOW, RICHARD ROMANOFF, AND PATTY WARNICK YARMEL • Department of Psychology, University of Illinois at Chicago, Chicago, Illinois 60637. The research reported here has been supported by Grant No. MH 34410 from the National Institute of Mental Health.

Ten years later, we reinterviewed 427 of the original subjects (modal age, 19). One of the most impressive findings, using a variety of measurement operations, was the stability of aggressive behavior over time and across situations (Lefkowitz, Eron, Walder, & Huesmann, 1977). The relation of aggression to psychopathology became manifest as well as the role of prosocial behaviors in inhibiting the development and expression of aggressive behavior. Further, it was apparent that the youngsters' intellectual ability was negatively related to aggressive behavior both contemporaneously and over time, and that intellectual competence itself showed a remarkable constancy over time and across measures.

In 1981, we again interviewed approximately 295 of the original subjects in person and another 114 by mail (modal age, 30). In addition, we obtained data about these subjects and 223 other original subjects from the New York State Division of Criminal Justice Services, the Division of Motor Vehicles, and the Departments of Mental Hygiene and Health. These data include criminal offenses, traffic violations, state hospital admissions, and particulars about perinatal events.

We also were successful in obtaining interviews with the spouses of 165 subjects and 82 of the subjects' own children, who at the time were approximately the same age as the subjects had been when first seen. Thus, there are data from three generations of informants—the subjects, their parents, and their children. In this paper, however, we will be concerned mainly with the early measures of aggression and intellectual competence of the subjects and how they relate to each other and to later indicators of aggression and competency.

EARLY MEASURES

Child aggression in our study in 1960 was measured by a peer nomination technique (Walder, Abelson, Eron, Banta, & Laulicht, 1961). In this procedure, every child in a class rates every other child on a series of ten specific items of aggressive behavior. The child's aggression score is the percentage of times he was nominated by his peers on the ten items out of the total number of times he could have been nominated. The reliability and validity of this measure have been extensively documented (Eron *et al.*, 1971; Lefkowitz *et al.*, 1977; Eron, Huesmann, Brice, Fisher, & Mermelstein, 1983). Intelligence in our study in 1960 was measured by the California Mental Maturity Scale, Short Form (Sullivan, Clark, & Tiegs, 1957).

LATER MEASURES

Indications of the subjects' aggression 22 years later, at age 30, were derived from self-ratings, ratings of the subject by the spouse, and citations of offenses by the New York State Divisions of Criminal Justice and Traffic. Self-ratings included the sum of MMPI scales 4, 9, and F, which previous research (Huesmann, Lefkowitz, & Eron, 1978) has indicated is a reliable and valid measure of overt aggression. Ratings by the spouse of the subject's aggression included behavior directed toward him or her by the subject. The items came from the Straus Home Violence Questionnaire (Straus, Gilles, & Steinmetz, 1979). The criminal justice scores were the total number of convictions in New York State in the previous ten years and a rating of the seriousness of the corresponding offenses. The latter is a system used by the New York State Criminal Justice Division, in which each type of offense is assigned a specific seriousness score (Rossi, Bose, & Berk, 1974).

For those subjects who had children, there were also ratings of how severely the subject punished the child as well as self-ratings of aggression by the child. We will also be referring to another punishment score reflecting how severely the subjects themselves were punished by their own parents. This of course is not a later measure but was obtained concurrently with the peer nomination measure in the first wave of the study. For comparison purposes we will also be referring to a peer nomination measure of aggression obtained in the second wave, when the subjects were 19 years old.

Indications of intellectual and social competency at age 30 included achieved educational and occupational status of subject, level of ego development as measured by the Loevinger Sentence Completion Test (Loevinger & Wessler, 1970), Wide Range Achievement Test (WRAT) Spelling, Reading and Arithmetic (Jastak & Jastak, 1978), and scores of social incompetency as measured by the Ullmann–Giovannoni Scale (1964). The last scale, ordinarily used to tap premorbid adjustment of schizophrenics, measures a broad range of competency behaviors including adolescent socialization and occupational stability.

DATA ACQUISITION

Subjects were contacted by mail and telephone. Addresses were obtained from local directories, a network of informants, newspaper stories, and newspaper advertisements. Subjects were paid $40 for an interview lasting one to two hours. The interview was administered in our field office on a microcomputer. The questions were displayed on a video monitor and answered by the respondent typing into the computer keyboard. With this procedure the subjects' responses were immediately punched into the computer and stored on floppy disks which were then read by more powerful computers. This was an efficient, time-saving, and relatively error-free procedure. Respondents learned the procedure quickly, enjoyed the novelty, and were reassured of the confidentiality of their responses. It is very likely that using the computerized interview added to the validity of the information obtained.

At the close of the interview, the subject was asked for permission to contact the spouse for an interview; and if the subject had a child age 6 to 12, permission was sought to interview the child, or the oldest such child if there were more than one. Spouses were also paid $40 per interview, and children were paid $20. Those subjects who were unable to come to the field office for interviews were asked to fill out a mailed questionnaire and were paid $40 if it was sent back within two weeks. Certain of the measures which required personal interaction, for example, the WRAT, were omitted in the postal sample. However, for those measures that could be obtained through the mail, the results were merged with those obtained in the interview procedure. This accounts for the differences in the numbers of subjects in various procedures. Spouses and children were not interviewed by mail.

RESULTS AND DISCUSSION

The effect of attrition over 22 years on the composition of the sample was evaluated by comparing the mean 1960 peer-nominated aggression scores for those subjects who were interviewed at all in 1981. It is apparent from Table 1 that male subjects who were not interviewed in 1981 had a significantly higher mean aggression score in 1960 than those male subjects who were interviewed. However, there was no difference between the personal and postal interview groups. As for the female subjects, there were no significant differences in 1960 aggression scores among any of the groups. Male subjects, as might be expected, had significantly higher aggression scores than females in each group.

The same analysis was done for IQ scores of those subjects interviewed and those not interviewed. These results are contained in Table 2. Those subjects, both male and female, who were not interviewed had significantly lower IQ

Table 1

Mean 1960 Peer-nominated Aggression Scores of
Subjects in 1981 sample by Gender and Interview Status

1980 Interview	Males		Females	
	M	N	M	N
No interview	17.5	160	8.9	63
Personal interview	12.9	136	8.3	159
Postal interview	12.1	62	9.2	52
	14.8	358	8.6	274
	$F_{2,355} = 4.54$		n.s.	
	$p < .05$			

Table 2
Mean 1960 IQ Scores of Subjects in 1980 Sample by
Gender and Interview Status

1980 Interview	Males		Females	
	M	N	M	N
No interview	99.1	160	98.7	63
Personal interview	104.4	136	103.9	159
Postal interview	105.9	62	106.0	52
	102.4	358	103.1	274
	$F\ 2,355 = 8.24$		$F\ 2,271 = 5.66$	
	$p < .001$		$p < .01$	

scores than those who were interviewed, but again there was no difference between those who had personal interviews or postal interviews; nor was there a difference in IQ between males and females in any group.

Correlations between the early measures of aggression and later measures of aggression, IQ, and competency are shown in Table 3. Early aggression and

Table 3
Correlations of Peer-nominated Aggression and IQ at Age 8 with Aggression and
Competence at Age 30

Age 30 measures	Age 8 Aggression		Age 8 IQ	
	Males	Females	Males	Females
Aggression measures:				
MMPI Scales F + 4 + 9	.30***	.16*	−.19**	—
Rating of subject by spouse	.27**	—	—	—
Punishment of child by subject	.24*	.24*	—	−.21*
Criminal justice convictions	.24***	—	−.15*	—
Seriousness of criminal offense	.21***	—	−.14*	—
Moving traffic violations	.21***	—	—	—
Driving while intoxicated	.29***	—	—	—
Competence measures:				
WRAT Spelling	−.30***	−.35***	.54***	.44***
WRAT Reading	−.20*	−.37***	.56***	.47***
WRAT Arithmetic	−.19*	−.35***	.55***	.42***
Education	−.25***	−.25***	.33***	.29***
Occupational status	.17*	.28***	−.36***	—
Social incompetence	.15*	.28***	−.24**	−.27***
Ego development	−.15*	−.21**	.30**	.24***

***$p < .001$. **$p < .01$. *$p < .05$.

Table 4
Mean Scores on Later Measures of Aggression (1981) According to Level of Earlier
Aggression (1960)

Level of aggression in 1960:		Low (0–25%)	Medium (26–75%)	High (76–100%)	F
Measure of later aggression					
MMPI 4 + 9 + F	N				
Males	135	162.14	174.27	186.23	9.60***
Females	158	165.54	176.45	174.94	5.17**
Aggression toward spouse					
Males	135	27.30	46.85	83.29	1.71
Females	158	46.86	77.57	50.93	.72
Punishiment of child					
Males	63	44.00	48.27	77.14	2.94+
Females	96	35.00	54.90	64.14	2.33+
Moving violations					
Males	335	.24	.40	.64	4.23*
Females	207	.12	.15	.05	1.22
Driving while impaired					
Males	335	.06	.10	.39	10.39***
Females	207	.02	.00	.05	1.18
Criminal justice convictions					
Males	335	.22	.26	.76	4.87**
Females	207	.00	.03	.36	1.81
Seriousness of offenses					
Males	335	15.19	18.32	46.99	4.13**
Females	207	.00	2.17	34.77	2.06

Note. The low aggressive group includes those subjects in the lowest 25% of the distribution of peer nomination scores at age 8 and the high aggressive groups, those subjects in the highest 25%.
***p < .001. **p < .01. *p < .05. +p < .10.

early IQ are themselves moderately correlated negatively ($-.27$ for boys and $-.32$ for girls), and on each variable IQ and aggression relate in opposite directions. It is apparent that over 22 years there is still some predictability from early aggression to later aggression, at least in the case of males. Although the stabilities are not as high for aggression as they are for intellectual competence, they are still noteworthy and hold up across method, informant, and situation as well as time. Especially impressive is the correlation for males between aggression at age 8 and later encounters with the law as indicated by driving and criminal offenses (.21 to .29). Since a disproportionate number of the original subjects who moved out of the state subsequent to the original testing were in the highly aggressive groups (Lefkowitz *et al.*, 1977), the range of aggression scores has been truncated and the correlations are probably a minimal estimate of the

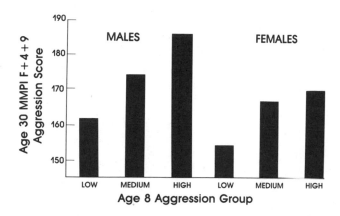

Figure 1. Relation of peer-nominated aggression at age 8 to self-rated aggression (MMPI) at age 30.

relation between aggression at age 8 and later antisocial behavior which brings individuals into contact with the law. Further, as we saw in Table 1, the 1960 aggression score of males not interviewed was significantly higher than the aggression score for those males who were interviewed.

Another reason why the Pearson r may be an underestimation of the true relation among variables presented here is that the distributions of many of the measures are skewed (e.g., peer-nominated aggression has a pileup of scores at the low end of the scale). A more representative demonstration of the relations can be obtained by dividing the subjects into low, medium, and high groups according to the original peer-nomination measure and then calculating mean scores on each of the criterion variables separately for each of the three groups. These mean scores are presented in Table 4. However, the relations among the

Table 5

Proportion of Subjects Convicted for a Crime in New York State before Age 30 According to Gender and Peer-nominated Aggression at Age 8

	Age 8 peer-nominated aggression		
Gender	Low	Medium	High
Males	$\frac{8}{89} = 9.0\%$	$\frac{24}{161} = 15\%$	$\frac{19}{82} = 23\%$
Females	$\frac{0}{49} = 0.0\%$	$\frac{2}{110} = 1.8\%$	$\frac{3}{48} = 6.3\%$

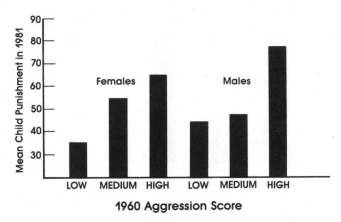

Figure 2. Relation of peer-nominated aggression at age 8 to punishment of child at age 30.

variables for which substantial correlations were found are seen much more graphically in Figures 1 to 5. When tested by analysis of variance, the differences among the means for each of the criterion variables in these figures are highly significant, again at least in the case of males. The actual number of subjects from each of the high, low, and medium groups who were subsequently convicted of crimes is presented in Table 5.

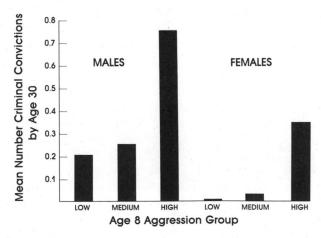

Figure 3. Relation of peer-nominated aggression at age 8 to record of criminal behavior at age 30.

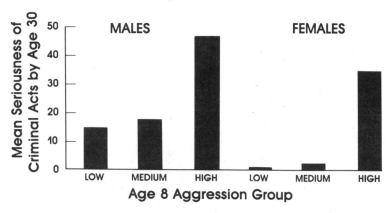

Figure 4. Relation of peer-nominated aggression at age 8 to seriousness of criminal acts by age 30.

Lisrel analysis, which takes into account the unreliability of the measures of any specific behavior or other characteristics and provides a more realistic estimate of stability over time and across measures, indicates a stability coefficient of .50 for boys for these data over a period of 22 years (Huesmann, Eron, Lefkowitz, & Walder, 1984). The comparable coefficient for girls is .35 and for all subjects .46. This compares very favorably with the stability of other personality and intellectual variables over similar lengths of time.

There are more significant predictions from 1960 aggression to 1981 aggression for males than for females (7 versus 2), as seen in Table 3. Also, in predicting later aggression from early IQ level, there is only one significant relation for females whereas there are three for males. It is interesting that the one aggression area at the later period that is predicted successfully for females *both* from early aggression and early IQ is punishment of the subject's child. Child punishment may be the only area in which a female can express aggression without fear of social censure or retaliation. In the other areas—aggression toward spouse, criminal offenses, and moving traffic violations—there is such a low frequency for females that successful prediction from earlier indications of aggression is very unlikely. On the other hand, predictability of competency from early IQ scores is surprisingly high, given the variety of measures and situations covered (as indicated in Table 3). There are significant correlations for seven out of seven criteria for males and six out of seven criteria for females. The intellectual competency was measured over 22 years, at each point by a paper-and-pencil test consuming less than 50 minutes of time.

Since IQ and aggression were significantly related to begin with, as noted previously, it is fair to ask how much of the stability of either variable results

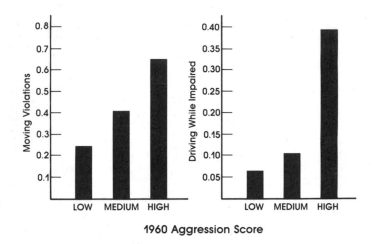

1960 Aggression Score

Figure 5. Relation of peer-nominated aggression at age 8 to record of traffic offenses at age 30.

from its correlation with the other. In Table 3, it can be seen that although there is good stability over time for both aggression and intellectual competency, later social and intellectual competency is better predicted from early aggression than later aggression is from earlier intellectual competence.

The relative contribution of earlier aggression and IQ to later aggression and competence can be evaluated more precisely by multiple regression analysis. A number of multiple regressions were done in which both early aggression and early intellectual competence were related to 1981 aggression criteria. For example, as indicated in Table 6, in predicting MMPI aggression scores, the standardized regression coefficient for aggression was significant but the standardized coefficient for IQ was nonsignificant; therefore IQ has little to do with that relation. Similarly, in predicting criminal justice convictions, the standardized regression coefficient for aggression was significant for males while the standardized coefficient for IQ was nonsignificant. In the prediction of driving while intoxicated, the standardized coefficient for aggression was significant for males and for IQ nonsignificant. The same pattern is present for the other four aggression measures for males. Thus, although IQ and aggression are indeed related at age 8, the relation of early aggression to later aggression is independent of the relation between IQ and aggression, at least for males. Whatever effect IQ has on aggression, it has already taken place before age 8, because subsequent change in aggression is no longer affected by IQ to any appreciable extent for males.

It would not seem likely that early aggression could account for a significant proportion of the variance in the relation between early IQ and later measures of competency. However, the same type of regression analysis was done predicting

Table 6

Regression of Age 8 Aggression and IQ Scores on Age 30 Aggression and Competency Measures

| | Standardized coefficients | | | |
| | 1960 Aggression | | 1960 IQ | |
Age 30 measures	Males	Females	Males	Females
Aggression measures:				
MMPI Scales F + 4 + 9	.27***	.16*	NS	NS
Rating of subject by spouse	.26*		NS	
Punishment of child by subject	.25*	.19*	NS	NS
Criminal justice convictions	.22***		NS	
Seriousness of criminal offense	.19***		NS	
Moving traffic violations	.17***		NS	
Driving while intoxicated	.31***		NS	
Competence measures				
WRAT Spelling	−.23**	−.21**	.50***	.36***
WRAT Reading	NS	−.22**	.54***	.38***
WRAT Arithmetic	NS	−.23**	.53***	.33***
Education	−.19**	−.17*	.29***	.23**
Occupational Status	NS	.27***	−.34***	NS
Social incompetence	NS	.22**	−.21**	−.19**
Ego development	NS	−.14*	.28***	.19**

***$p < .001$. **$p < .01$. *$p < .05$. +$p < .10$.

the 1981 social and intellectual competency scores from 1960 IQ and aggression scores. Only in predicting educational attainment did both 1960 IQ and aggression scores have significant standardized regression coefficients for both males and females. For males, early aggression had no other relation to later competency. For females, however, both 1960 IQ and aggression scores had significant predictive relations to later social incompetency and ego development. It is interesting that for females, aggression and not IQ had a significant standardized coefficient with occupation status, with less aggressive females achieving higher status, regardless of IQ level. For males *only,* IQ and *not* aggression predicted to occupational status, as well as to social incompetency and ego development. Thus, aggression and IQ are both interdependently predictive of later social and occupational competency for females, but for males primarily IQ is involved in such prediction.

A somewhat similar pattern has been noted in predicting intellectual competency as measured by scores on the WRAT. For females, both early IQ and aggression accounted for significant portions of the variance; for males, only IQ was a significant predictor of later WRAT scores. It would appear that for females, aggression is as incapacitating as low IQ, so that females who characteristically engage in aggressive behavior are impaired in many areas. For males, perhaps because aggression is more socially acceptable than it is for females, the effect on competency, either social or intellectual, is only minimal and intelligence is the primary determinant of later intellectual competency.

INTERGENERATIONAL EFFECTS

Our data, collected over three generations, indicate that aggression, as a characteristic behavior, is transmitted from parent to child. It should be noted that genetic transmission is not necessarily implied here. Beyond whatever equipment and tendencies the child is born with, there are many ways in which parents can teach children aggression, which we have earlier reviewed (Eron, Walder, & Lefkowitz, 1971; Lefkowitz, Eron, Walder, & Huesmann, 1977). Now we are interested in examining the total effect of these learning interactions across generations.

In the 1960 study, there was a relation between how aggressive the subjects were in school, as nominated by their peers, and how severely they were punished for aggression by their parents at home (.23, $p < .0001$). When the subjects were 19 years of age, they were asked to imagine how they would respond to their child's aggression if they had an 8-year-old. The correlation was .24 between their peer-nominated aggression score in 1960 and their hypothetical response in 1970, and .31 between their hypothetical response in 1970 and their own parents' actual responses in 1960.

In 1981, those subjects who now had children between 6 and 12 years were asked the same questions and the correlation between their earlier peer-nominated aggression score and how severely they reported punishing their own child for aggression was similar (.24). Furthermore, the subjects' peer-nominated aggression score obtained in 1960 correlated moderately with their children's self-rated aggression in 1981 (.34). This is especially interesting since the self-rating items used for the children were the same ten items that had comprised the peer nominations on which their parents had been rated 20 years earlier. Further, the subjects' 1960 aggression score is correlated even more highly (.44) with the extent to which the subjects' own children tend to fantasize about aggression.

In chapter 7, Belsky and Vondra warn us about being too facile in attributing causality to the circumstance that abusing parents had themselves been abused as children; but the dramatic findings we have uncovered over three generations cannot be ignored. Certainly, there are many things going on; the correlations are only in the range of .20 to .35, and the univariate correlations cannot account for more than a small portion of the variance. However, many of the variables and processes can be specified, and together they may account for a major portion of the variance. With our recent advances in computer technology, this multiplicity of variables can be synthesized into complex, comprehensive process models which can then describe specific children at risk for developing the kind of behavior we have been discussing. Thus, we are not limited to aggregate statistics that tell us very little about individual children. Finally, the whole process can be simulated. And in two or three years, perhaps, once we have submitted this mass of data to such treatment, we will be able to describe this complex process.

In summary, then, the degree of stability we have seen in aggressive behavior of individuals over a 22-year span, reaching back as well to a previous generation and ahead to a future one, is impressive. The stability holds up across situations, measures, and informants as well as time.

One possible implication of this consistency is that aggression is not situation-specific or determined solely by the contingencies, that the individual carries around something inside that impels him or her to act in a characteristically aggressive or nonaggressive way. This is not to say that this is genetic or constitutional, although there may be some such basis for this type of behavior. Much of this behavior is learned, and it may be the memory traces in the brain (or well-rehearsed scripts, if you will) that are activated when the individual is in a situation with some similarities to the one in which an aggressive sequence was originally encoded. It must be noted that the stability in aggressive behavior could also be attributed to situational consistency over time, but over 22 years this is unlikely.

CONCLUSION

The chapters in this book present some attempts to break up the self-perpetuating loops formed by aggression, its antecedents, and its reinforcements. However, we all know it will not be easy—it will take all the knowledge, ingenuity, talent, and persistence we can muster. We have to know specifically which variables require change and concentrate on them. As Belsky points out, until we know the causes of behavior deviance, we cannot institute appropriate change. And the cause is a process involving many variables, each impinging on the other in reciprocal loops. If we are lucky, we can break into these loops by identifying specific processes and attempting to change them. But we must start early in the lives of developing youngsters. By the time a child is 8 years old, characteristic ways of behaving aggressively or nonaggressively have already been established. Aggression as a problem-solving behavior is learned very early in life, and it is learned very well; the payoff is tremendous. The inducement to change must be made equally attractive.

ACKNOWLEDGMENTS

Thanks are due to Drs. Monroe Lefkowitz and Leopold O. Walder for their help in mounting this project and their expert consultation throughout.

REFERENCES

Eron, L. D., Huesmann, L. R., Brice, P., Fischer, P., & Mermelstein, R. (1983). Age trends in the development of aggression, sex typing, and related television habits. *Developmental Psychology, 19,* 71–77.

Eron, L. D., Walder, L. O., & Lefkowitz, M. M. (1971). *Learning of aggression in children.* Boston: Little, Brown.

Huesmann, L. R., Eron, L. D., Lefkowitz, M. M., & Walder, L. O. (1984). The stability of aggression over time and generations. *Developmental Psychology.*

Huesmann, L. R., Lefkowitz, M. M., & Eron, L. D. (1978). Sum of MMPI Scales F, 4 and 9 as a measure of aggression. *Journal of Consulting and Clinical Psychology, 46,* 1071–1078.

Jastak, J. F., & Jastak, S. (1978). *Wide Range Achievement Test: Manual of instructions* (rev. ed.). Wilmington, Delaware: Jastak.

Lefkowitz, M. M., Eron, L. D., Walder, L. O., & Huesmann, L. R. (1977). *Growing up to be violent: A longitudinal study of the development of aggression.* New York: Pergamon.

Loevinger, J., & Wessler, R. (1970). *Measuring ego development. I: Construction and use of a sentence completion test.* San Francisco: Jossey-Bass.

Rossi, P., Bose, C., & Berk, R. (1974). The seriousness of crime, normative structure and individual differences. *American Sociological Review. 39,* 224–237.

Straus, M. A., Gilles, R. J., & Steinmetz, S. K. (1979). *Behind closed doors: Violence in the American family.* New York: Doubleday/Anchor.

Sullivan, E. T., Clark, W. W., & Tiegs, E. W. (1957). *California short form test of mental maturity.* Los Angeles: California Test Bureau.

Ullmann, L. P., & Giovannoni, J. M. (1964). The development of a self-report measure of the process-reactive continuum. *Journal of Nervous and Mental Disease. 138,* 38–42.

Walder, L. O., Abelson, R., Eron, L. D., Banta, T. J., & Laulicht, J. H. (1961). Development of a peer-rating measure of aggression. *Psychological Reports, 9,* 497–556 (monograph supplement 4–19).

CHAPTER 11

Etiology and Prevention of Antisocial Behavior in Children and Adolescents

J. DAVID HAWKINS AND DENISE LISHNER

This chapter reviews the existing evidence on childhood predictors and correlates of antisocial behavior, presents a theory integrating these factors, and describes a prevention project based on a theory that has demonstrated positive effect on youngsters at risk of involvement in delinquent behavior.

The prevention approach described here is based on the assumption that prevention effects must address the causes of the problem they are attempting to prevent if they are to be effective (Hawkins, Pastor, Bell, & Morrison, 1980). This assumption implies that prevention interventions should be designed to address the risk factors or predictors of antisocial behavior identified in etiological and epidemiological research on antisocial behavior.

Research has revealed consistent results regarding some of the early risk factors for conduct disorders and delinquency (Hawkins, Lishner, & Catalano, 1985; Loeber & Dishion, 1983). In the next section, these major risk factors will be described.

Points of view or opinions in this document are those of the authors and do not represent the official position or policies of the U.S. Department of Justice.

J. DAVID HAWKINS AND DENISE LISHNER • School of Social Work, University of Washington, Seattle, Washington 98195. Preparation of this chapter was supported in part by grant No. 80-JS-AX-0052 from the National Institute for Juvenile Justice and Delinquency Prevention, Office of Juvenile Justice and Delinquency Prevention, U.S. Department of Justice.

EARLY PREDICTORS OF ANTISOCIAL BEHAVIOR AND DELINQUENCY

Conduct Disorders and Antisocial Behavior

A number of studies have shown that antisocial conduct early in life continues into later life for certain groups of children (Gersten, Langer, Eisenberg, Simcha-Fagan, & McCarthy, 1976; Ghodsian, Fogelman, Lambert, & Tibbenham, 1980; Loeber & Dishion, 1983; Patterson, 1982; Robins, 1966; Werner & Smith, 1977; West & Farrington, 1973). As part of a constellation of antisocial behavior problems, delinquency is predicted by previous patterns of antisocial behavior.

Robins (1966) found that the greater the variety, frequency, and seriousness of childhood antisocial behavior, the more likely later delinquent behavior became. Jessor and Jessor (1978) found that one could predict transitions of specific antisocial behaviors of school-age children into drinking, loss of virginity, marijuana use, and delinquency about equally well; they also concluded that similar antecedents foster a wide range of problem behavior. They posited that certain youths were prone to various problem behaviors, which they called a "deviance syndrome." A longitudinal study of high-risk early signs of delinquency by Spivack, Rapsher, Cohen, and Gross (1978) also revealed that conduct disturbances ten years later could be predicted from kindergarten and first-grade signs of acting out, overinvolvement in socially disturbing behavior, impatience, impulsivity, and deviant and negative activity.

However, several limitations should be noted regarding predictions based on early childhood behavior. First, the age at which childhood conduct disorders can be reliably identified is not clear. Typically, stable predictions have been noted from the age of school entry, but not before (Robins, 1979; Rutter & Giller, 1983). Secondly, although serious conduct disorders in childhood appear to be virtually a prerequisite for serious antisocial behavior in later life, fewer than half of those with behavior problems in childhood will manifest serious behavior problems later (Robins, 1978). Loeber and Dishion (1983) report that 30%–43% of children engaging in maladaptive behavior at ages 4 through 11 continue the same behavior 4 to 9 years later (Farrington, 1978; Ghodsian et al., 1980; Glavin, 1972; Werner & Smith, 1977.) Therefore there is a risk of false positive prediction associated with the early identification of "predelinquent" individuals. This risk suggests that great caution must be exercised in selecting target groups for prevention programs if the risk of incorrectly identifying and treating particular young people as predelinquents is to be avoided.

Family Factors

Among the most important childhood predictors of delinquency are composite measures of family functioning (Loeber & Dishion, 1983), parental family management techniques (Baumrind, 1983), and parental criminality or antisocial behavior (Langner, Gersten, Wills, & Simcha-Fagan, 1983; Loeber & Dishion, 1983). Disruptions in family behavior management are a major mediating variable for antisocial behavior in children (Patterson, 1982). Variables associated with antisocial behavior in children include household disorganization, poorly defined rules, and inconsistent, ineffective family management techniques (Loeber & Dishion, 1983).

Although some researchers have found that nonintact families predict subsequent delinquency (Robins, 1980), there is disagreement on this point. Family structure appears to be less important as a predictor of delinquency than attachment to parents (Nye, 1958; Sederstrom, 1978; Weis et al., 1980; Wilkinson, 1974).

Little research has been conducted on the effects of familial violence and abuse on adolescent involvement in delinquency. Several studies have suggested a relationship between child abuse and delinquency (Garbarino, 1981; Pfouts, Scholpler, & Henley, 1981; Steele, 1976; Timberlake, 1981). When case records of abused and neglected children were checked over 12 years later, 30% were discovered to be delinquent or in need of supervision (Alfaro, 1976). Some researchers have found that excessively severe, physically threatening, and physically violent parental discipline has been associated with aggressive and destructive acts of delinquency (Deykin, 1971; Haskell & Yablonsky, 1974; Shore, 1971). However, recent research by Brown (1984) suggests that emotional abuse and neglect are related to delinquency but that physical abuse is not a predictor of delinquent behavior.

School Factors

There is considerable evidence that male delinquency is related to academic performance in junior and senior high school (Brooks, Linkoff, & Whiteman, 1977; Elliott & Voss, 1974; Jensen, 1976; Johnson, 1979; Kelly & Balch, 1971; Linden, 1974; Noblit, 1976; Polk & Shafer, 1972). Juvenile delinquents appear to perform more poorly in school than do nondelinquents (Anhalt & Klein, 1976; Frease, 1973; Jessor, 1976; Kelly & Balch, 1971; Polk, Frease, & Richmond, 1974; Senna, Rathus, & Siegel, 1974; Simon, 1974).

What is not clear from the existing research is when, developmentally, low school achievement becomes salient as a possible predictor of delinquency.

Spivack *et al.* (1978) determined that initial signs of low academic achievement in the first grade were not predictive of subsequent conduct or delinquent disturbances. Other studies indicate, however, that by the end of elementary school, low achievement, low vocabulary, and poor verbal reasoning are predictors of delinquency (Farrington, 1979; Rutter, Maughan, Moretimore, & Ouston, 1979). Academic performance appears to emerge in importance as a delinquency predictor sometime after the first grade.

It is possible that early antisocial behavior in school predicts both academic underachievement in later grades and later delinquent behavior. Theorists have also interpreted the association between school failure and delinquency as a function of dislike of school and consequent rejection of authority (Hirschi, 1969) and as a search for reinforcements from delinquent peers; this search in turn results from school failure and low self-esteem (Catalano, 1982; Cohen & Short, 1961; Gold, 1978; Kaplan, Martin, & Robbins, 1982).

There is also evidence that a low degree of commitment to education is related to delinquency. Students who are not committed to educational pursuits are more likely to engage in delinquent behavior (Brooks *et al.,* 1977; Elliott & Voss, 1974; Friedman, 1983; Galli & Stone, 1975; Hirschi, 1969; Kim, 1979; Robbins, 1980). Factors such as how much students like school (Kelly & Balch, 1971), how much time they spend on homework, and the nature of their perception of the relevance of coursework are also related to delinquency (Friedman, 1983). Czikszentmihalyi and Larson (1978) suggest that involvement in antisocial behavior may be perceived by some students as offering the opportunity for challenges and rewards not experienced in the school setting.

Peer Factors

Association with delinquent peers during adolescence is among the strongest predictors of delinquent behavior (Akers, 1977; Akers, Krohn, Lanza-Kaduce, & Radosevich, 1979; Catalano, 1982; Elliott, Huizinga, & Ageton, 1982; Ginsberg & Greenly, 1978; Goldstein, 1975; Hirschi, 1969; Huba, Wingard, & Bentler, 1979; Jensen, 1972; Jessor, Chase, & Donovan, 1980; Jessor & Jessor, 1977; Meier & Johnson, 1977; O'Donnell & Clayton, 1979; O'Donnell, Voss, Clayton, & Room, 1976; Orcutt, 1978; Smart, Gray, & Bennett, 1978; Winfree, Theis, & Griffiths, 1981).

In their longitudinal study of the National Youth Panel, Elliott *et al.* (1982) found direct effects of delinquent peer association on delinquency and only indirect effects on delinquency of social bonds to family and school mediated by involvement with delinquent peers. Elliott *et al.* suggest that these findings reflect the time-ordering of experiences by youth in the social contexts they encounter.

Attitudes, Beliefs, and Personality Traits

Individual personality traits, attitudes, and beliefs are variously related to delinquency. Generally, a constellation of attitudes and beliefs indicating a social bond between the individual and conventional society has been shown to inhibit delinquency (Hindelang, 1973; Hirschi, 1969).

The elements of this bond that have been shown to be most consistently inversely related to delinquency are attachment to parents (Adler & Lutecka, 1973; Chassin *et al.*, 1981; Jessor & Jessor, 1977; Kim, 1979; Krohn, Massey, Laner, & Skinner, 1983; Shibuya, 1974; Wechsler & Thum, 1973; Wohlford & Giammona, 1969), commitment to school and education (Elliott & Voss, 1974; Friedman, 1983; Hirschi, 1979; Johnston, Bachman, & O'Malley, 1981; Kim, 1979; Krohn *et al.*, 1983), and belief in the generalized expectations, norms, and values of society (Akers.*et al.*, 1979; Hindelang, 1973; Krohn *et al.*, 1983).

Alienation from the dominant values of society (Jessor & Jessor, 1978; Kandel, 1982; Kandel, Kessler, & Margulies, 1978; Smith & Fogg, 1978) and low religiosity (Jessor *et al.*, 1980; Kandel, 1982; Robins, 1980) have been shown to be positively related to drug use and delinquent behavior.

AN INTEGRATED THEORY OF DELINQUENCY

A developmental view that incorporates the etiological risk factors for delinquency reviewed above has been integrated into a theory of delinquency and its prevention called the "social development model" (Hawkins & Weis, 1985; Weis & Hawkins, 1981). The theory integrates social control and social learning theories, as has the work of others (Braukman, Kirigin, & Wolf, 1980; Conger, 1976; Elliott *et al.*, 1982; Johnson, 1979; Johnston *et al.*, 1981; Linden & Hackler, 1973; Meade & Marsden, 1981). In contrast to the others, however, this theoretical model seeks explicitly to serve as a basis for delinquency-prevention planning. It describes general stages of development and identifies intervention approaches that would appear appropriate at each stage, on the basis of etiological research (Hawkins & Weis, 1985).

The social development model posits that social bonds to prosocial others inhibit delinquent involvements; it also identifies three general conditions that appear to be necessary in the formation of a social bond in each context of socialization. These conditions are opportunities for involvement, skills, and reinforcements (see Figure 1). The model posits that social bonds are formed in families, in school, or among peers when youths have the opportunity to be involved with others in activities and interactions in these social units, when they have the skills necessary to perform competently in the social units, and when they experience consistent rewards or reinforcement for their involvement.

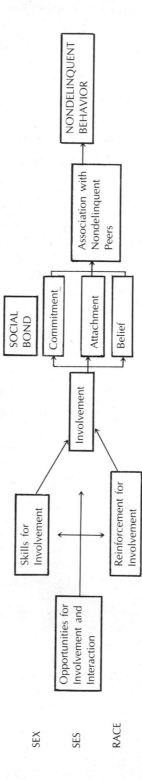

Figure 1. The social development model.

The process of social bonding begins in the family. When youths experience opportunities for involvement in the family, when they develop the requisite social, cognitive, and behavioral skills to perform as expected in family activities and interactions, and when they are rewarded consistently by parents for adequate performance in the family, it is hypothesized that they will develop a bond of attachment, commitment, and belief in the family. When these three conditions are not present in the family, a bond to family is not likely to develop.

Bonding to school is conditioned by the extent to which social bonds to the family have developed by the time the child enters school as well as by the extent to which the child experiences opportunities for involvement, develops skills, and is rewarded for skillful performance at school. Similarly, social bonds to peers, whether prosocial or delinquent, should develop to the extent that youths have opportunities for involvement with those peers, the skills to perform as expected by those peers, and the rewards that are forthcoming from interaction with those peers. The model does not suggest that strong bonds of attachment to family and school will preclude the development of strong bonds of attachment to peers so long as the norms of family members, school personnel, and peers regarding appropriate performance or behavior do not conflict. However, it is hypothesized that the formation of social bonds to family and school will decrease the likelihood that youths will develop attachments to delinquent peers in adolescence, since the behaviors rewarded in family and school and the behaviors likely to be rewarded by delinquent youths are generally not compatible.

As a foundation for delinquency prevention, the social development model implies that families, schools, and peer groups are appropriate objects for intervention, depending on the developmental stage of the child. Interventions that seek to increase the likelihood of social bonding to the family are appropriate from early childhood through early adolescence. Interventions that seek to increase the likelihood of social bonding to school are appropriate throughout the years of school attendance. Interventions that seek to increase social bonding to prosocial peers and to inhibit association with delinquent peers are particularly important as youths approach and enter adolescence.

PREVENTION PROJECT

Currently, in a field experiment in Seattle, we are testing the combined effect of a set of developmentally sequenced interventions that are based on the social development model and that seek to address the early risk factors for antisocial behavior previously discussed. We are seeking to identify the combined and, where possible, individual effects of the interventions to see whether they increase the opportunities, skills, and rewards available to youths in the primary socializing institutions they encounter; to determine the extent to which the interventions generate increased social bonding to family, school, and pro-social peers; and to learn the extent to which the interventions are successful in reducing antisocial and delinquent behavior.

The test is being conducted using an experimental and quasi-experimental longitudinal design involving students in seven elementary schools and five middle schools in Seattle. The first cohort includes 551 students who entered the first grade in September 1981 and were randomly assigned to experimental or control classrooms in seven elementary schools. The second cohort includes 1,166 students who entered the seventh grade in September 1981 and were assigned to experimental or control classrooms in five Seattle middle schools. New students entering the target grades in participating schools are assigned on a random basis to experimental or control classes and are included in the cohorts with date of entry noted. Thus the total number of elementary students in the research project currently is 992 (493 experimentals and 499 controls) and the total number of secondary students is 1,630 (861 experimentals and 769 controls).

The prevention approaches included in the experimental project are outlined below. All of the interventions are based in the schools although they intervene in all of the major areas of socialization.

School-based, Family-focused Prevention Services

Family-focused prevention services implemented through the schools have been included in the project. We have previously noted the importance of family management practices in predicting antisocial behavior in children. Social learning approaches to improving family management skills have demonstrated successful outcomes in treating aggressive behavior of children (Fraser & Hawkins, in press; Patterson, 1982; Reid, 1975) and have been adapted for use here as a prevention strategy.

The family component of the longitudinal experimental prevention project has been successfully implemented with experimental students and their families in 11 participating Seattle schools. Three family-focused interventions have been offered to the experimental elementary school cohort, starting in the first grade. Home–school liaison specialists were assigned to visit schools and homes of experimental students in order to increase positive communication and cooperation between parents and school personnel. The home visits sought to communicate teachers' expectations to parents and to initiate positive communication from school to home. Home–school liaison specialists also arranged with teachers to hold small group coffees at the school during school days so that visiting parents could see their children in the classroom and could get to know teachers in a supportive atmosphere.

The second family-focused service consisted of a series of parent-training classes held at the school over a three-year period. These classes taught parents family management skills as well as ways in which to help their children do well in school and to achieve to the best of their abilities.

Conflict resolution is the third family-focused intervention. This service is provided to experimental students experiencing academic or behavioral problems in school, including aggression or misconduct, and to their families. The goals of the intervention are to facilitate parent–teacher communication and collaboration in the child's education and socialization and to promote more effective family management practices in order to create a supportive and consistent family environment for the child's development.

Preliminary results from teacher ratings using the Child Behavior Checklist (Achenbach & Edelbrock, 1983) indicate reduced levels of aggressive behavior among experimental elementary students as compared with controls.

Both parent-training classes, which focused on helping parents to improve their parenting skills and increase the consistency of home and school in interacting with students, and conflict resolution services have been offered to the parents of secondary cohort experimental students as well.

Classroom-focused Prevention Service

We have noted the association between school factors and student antisocial and delinquent behavior. A set of classroom-focused strategies have been implemented in the project to address these factors. Three classroom-focused instructional interventions have been undertaken in experimental classrooms in grades 2–3 and 7–8. These are proactive classroom management, interactive teaching, and student team or cooperative learning techniques. These interventions seek to introduce systematic changes in classroom instructional practices in order to increase the proportion of students who experience academic success, to increase the likelihood that students will develop commitments to educational goals, increase students' attachments to teachers and nondeviant peers, and students' belief in the fairness of the school environment (see Hawkins & Lam, in press).

Proactive classroom management is aimed at establishing an environment that is conducive to learning and promotes appropriate student behavior, minimizing disruption to classroom activities. Such an environment increases opportunities for skill development for all students and should therefore increase student commitment to learning. Teachers are taught to give clear and explicit instructions for student behavior and to recognize and reward attempts to cooperate. Classroom routines are to be established by the teacher at the beginning of the school year. These set up a consistent pattern of expectations between the teacher and students. Clear directions and consistent expectations should result in effective use of classroom time for skill development and should prevent discipline problems (Emmer & Evertson, 1980).

Teachers are also taught methods for preventing minor classroom disruptions from interrupting instruction and decreasing opportunities for learning (Cummings, 1983). The teacher learns to take immediate and brief action to restore the learning environment while simultaneously downplaying the incident. Also integral to effective management of the classroom is the frequent appropriate use of encouragement and praise. Praise should specify exactly what student behavior is being rewarded so that desired behaviors are reinforced (Martin, 1977). The contingent use of praise should increase social bonding of student to teacher and classroom. Together, these strategies should create a positive climate for learning and deter incidents of disruption, affording students a more productive classroom experience, which in turn should contribute to greater academic achievement and social bonding to school.

Interactive teaching is a method based on the premise that virtually all students under appropriate instructional conditions can and will develop the skills necessary to succeed in the classroom (Bloom, 1976). This approach has resulted in improved learning in a variety of classroom situations (Block, 1971, 1974; Peterson, 1972; Stalling, 1980). The components of interactive teaching used in this project are mental set, objectives, input, modeling, checking for understanding, remediation, and assessment. Interactive teaching requires that students master clearly specified learning objectives before proceeding to more advanced work. Grades are determined by demonstration of mastery and improvement over past performance rather than by comparison with other students. Interactive teaching expands opportunities for students to attain success while reducing the risk of failure. This should enhance students' perceptions of their own competence as well as their commitment to educational pursuits. The use of clear and explicit objective standards in grading should promote students' belief in the fairness of the educational system.

Cooperative learning involves small heterogeneous groups of students as learning partners. Students of differing abilities and backgrounds work together in teams to master curriculum material and receive recognition as a team for their group's academic performance. Cooperative learning makes students dependent on one another for positive rewards (Slavin, 1980). Team scores are based on the individual student's academic improvement over past performance, allowing each student to contribute to the team's overall achievement. The cooperative learning techniques used in the project are Student Teams Achievement Divisions (STAD) (Slavin, 1980), Teams–Games–Tournaments (TGT) (DeVries & Slavin, 1978), and Jigsaw (Aronson, 1978).

Cooperative learning creates a classroom norm favoring learning and academic performance (Slavin, 1979). Mastery of learning tasks, motivation, positive student attitudes toward teachers and schools, and positive self-concept are greater in cooperative classrooms than in competitive or individualistic ones (Johnson & Johnson, 1980; Slavin, 1979). Research has shown that cooperative learning methods are more effective than traditional methods in increasing student achievement and in developing mutual concern among students across racial groups (Slavin, 1982). In combination with training in basic cooperative skills, this approach reinforces students' efforts to help each other succeed in classroom endeavors. Positive student interaction should reduce alienation in the classroom and promote attachment among students based on the pursuit of accepted academic goals (Slavin, 1980). This should, in turn, reduce the likelihood that students will form alternative attachments with delinquent peers that will lead to delinquent behavior (Hawkins, 1981).

Peer-focused Strategies

Peer-focused interventions have been implemented in the elementary and middle-school classrooms to address peer factors associated with antisocial behavior. To help students to interact successfully with their teachers and peers and to promote cooperative efforts among students in the classroom, social skills training has been provided. A cognitive approach to social skills development (Shure & Spivack, 1979) was offered to first-graders to help them develop communication, conflict resolution, decision-making and self-discipline skills. In the second grade, the Classroom Learning to Attain Social Skills (CLASS) curriculum, consisting of 36 scripted lessons in the areas of friendship, cooperation, and communication, was used by experimental teachers (Hoagland, Eyler, & Vacha, 1981). It is hypothesized that social skills training, in combination with student team learning, will promote positive peer relationships among more students and increase the attachment between students and teachers.

Community-focused Strategies

Two community-focused interventions for middle-school students have been implemented. These are experience-based career education and the community mentorship program. In the first program, teachers were trained to integrate work-related examples and problems into the curriculum. Students were exposed to a range of future career options through presentations by outside speakers from various occupations and through field trips to work settings in areas of occupational interest selected by students. The mentorship program paired students, especially those experiencing problems in school, with adult role models from the community who volunteered to meet with the student weekly, usually in the workplace.

These programs sought to relate what was being learned in the classroom to opportunities in the community, thereby increasing the relevance of education and the students' commitment to school. It is also hypothesized that involving marginal and high-risk students in meaningful prosocial activities while providing them with support, prosocial role models, and individualized attention will lessen the likelihood of involvement in antisocial behavior.

Project Effects

Experimental and control students have been compared in a series of surveys that measured student perceptions; achievement; bonding to family, school, and peers; and antisocial behavior. Additional measures of project effects include classroom observation data, test scores from the California Achievement Test, grades, classroom sociometric data, and parent reports from mail and telephone surveys. Results have been analyzed for the secondary cohort as a whole and for a subsample of low achievers in math (77 students in the experimental condition and 83 students in the control condition) at the end of the first academic year of the project. These findings have been reported elsewhere (Hawkins & Lam, in press; Hawkins, Doueck, & Lishner, unpublished). The preliminary outcomes from the seventh grade as related to antisocial behavior and its predictors are summarized below.

Student Academic Achievement. Teachers' use of the project teaching methods as measured by summary implementation scores from classroom observations was related to student behavior in class. Greater use of the teaching practices was associated with more student time spent in learning or "on task" activities ($r = 0.38$; $p \leq .001$). Conversely, use of the project teaching practices was negatively related to disruptive and "off task" behavior in the classroom ($r = -0.60$; $p \leq .001$).

These relationships suggest that when teachers use the teaching methods advocated by the project, students are more likely to engage in behavior associated with academic success. Regression analyses controlling for spring 1981 scores on the California Achievement Test (CAT) were conducted at the teacher level to assess the relationship between teacher implementation scores and CAT scores for spring 1982. There was no relationship between language-arts teacher scores and CAT reading or language-arts scores, but there was a relationship in the predicted direction between math teacher implementation scores and CAT math scores (semipartial $r = 0.30$). The relationship between grades and teacher implementation scores was assessed and also found to be strongest in the predicted direction for math teacher implementation scores and math grades ($r = 0.46$). When a subsample of low math achievers was examined, no significant achievement differences were found between experimental and control groups, suggesting that during the first academic year participation in the project did not significantly affect achievement rates of low achievers.

Student Bonding to School and Peers. A positive relationship was found between teacher use of project practices and student attitudes toward math ($r = 0.54$), but this relationship was not found for language arts and social studies classes. Use of project practices was positively correlated with student educational aspirations, expectations, and interest in continuing their education. However, it does not appear that use of teaching practices or participation in the experimental cohort was associated with overall student attachment to school or teachers after one year of implementation. It also does not appear that use of project teaching practices has led the general population of experimental students to choose new "best friends" who are better students or in trouble less frequently, although use of the practices is accompanied by a greater total number of close friends in school, as reported by students.

In contrast, however, a positive effect was found on attachment and commitment to school among low achievers in math. Experimental low math achievers demonstrated more positive attitudes toward their classes, especially math classes, than did their counterparts in control classes. This was paralleled among experimental low math achievers by increasing expectations for continuing their education whereas low-achieving control students' expectations for education dropped during the same period.

Student Antisocial Behavior and Delinquency. During the first project year, no relationships were found between use of teaching practices and student self-reports of truancy, theft from desks or lockers, and getting into trouble in school for drugs or alcohol. More promising results were found for suspensions and expulsions, with greater use of project teaching practices associated with lower rates of disciplinary action and fewer days of student suspensions from school, as measured by official disciplinary reports and student self-reports ($r = -0.44$; $p = .006$; semipartial $r = 0.28$; $p = .05$).

Although it is impossible to separate the extent to which these results reflect changes in teacher versus student behavior, the results suggest that use of project teaching practices is associated with greater retention and participation in school. A modest negative relationship also was found between project teaching practices and student self-reports of getting high on drugs at school.

In regard to low math achievers, no significant differences were found between experimental and control groups for delinquency or drug-use items. However, a significant difference was found in rates of suspension and expulsion from school. Prior to the project, experimental low achievers had been suspended from school slightly (though not significantly) more often than control low achievers. But by the spring of the first project year, control low achievers were suspended significantly more often ($x = .89$ suspensions) than were experimental low achievers ($x = .48$ suspensions; $F = 4.67$; $p<.05$).

In the elementary school, experimental first- and second-grade students were reported by their teachers as less aggressive, using the Child Behavior Checklist (Achenbach & Edelbrock, 1983), than were their counterparts in control classrooms. These gains appeared in the first year of student participation. The data suggest that one of the early predictors of antisocial behavior, childhood aggression, may be affected by the project interventions.

DISCUSSION AND CONCLUSION

The social development model postulates that the process of becoming delinquent is a developmental one and that the process of developing social bonds capable of preventing delinquency also takes place over time (Hawkins & Weis, 1985; Weis & Hawkins, 1981). Therefore the absence of project effects on delinquency and drug use at the end of one academic year of intervention with seventh graders is not inconsistent with the model hypotheses.

However, project effects on intervening variables in the model during this time period had also been hypothesized. We had expected to observe effects on academic achievement, social bonding to school, and school misbehavior. Furthermore, we had expected these effects to be most readily observed among low achievers who should, according to previous research, have higher rates of alienation and misbehavior. However, in regard to academic achievement, the results reported here are not consistent with our hypotheses. The grades and standardized achievement test scores of experimental seventh-grade students did not differ significantly from those of controls at the end of the first project year, even when examining results for low achievers only.

Results from other analyses we have conducted suggest that these outcomes may be related, in part, to problems of implementation of the interventions. In-depth analyses of the use of project teaching methods by experimental and control teachers have revealed that experimental teachers used the methods significantly more than did control teachers. However, variability has been found in the use of the methods across teachers, suggesting that attention must be given to level of teacher implementation of the practices in seeking to assess the effects of the project teaching practices on student achievement. Promising project effects have been found, in fact, for math achievement when the level of teacher implementation is included as a predictor in analysis (Hawkins & Lam, 1983).

In contrast to the above-mentioned finding, the results regarding social bonding to school and school misbehavior as measured by suspensions and expulsions are as hypothesized. Participation in the experimental project appears to have resulted in greater social bonding to school and in greater educational expectations among experimental subjects (including low achievers) when compared with controls. It is possible that these changes in student attitudes reflect changes in teachers' classroom behavior, including the introduction of opportunities for exploration of the community and the world of work and also including improved methods of classroom management and instruction.

Similarly, project participation appears to have held down the rates of suspension and expulsion from school among experimental students (including low achievers) when compared with controls. This is an important finding, as low-achieving students had been disproportionately suspended and expelled as compared with their more highly achieving peers.

It is impossible to determine from these results the extent to which differences in rates of suspensions and expulsions reflect changes in experimental teacher behavior as opposed to changes in experimental students' behavior. The results may reflect an interaction between changes in behavior of both teacher and students. Regardless of the specific dynamic, the data suggest that the project intervention is resulting in greater retention of low-achieving and general-population seventh-graders in school. In this way, the project may be providing low achievers with continuing opportunities for school participation while reducing the likelihood of alienation from school as a consequence of forcible removal through suspension or expulsion.

These preliminary results regarding the suspension and expulsion of experimental students and especially of low achievers are encouraging, as they suggest possible future differences in rates of more serious delinquent behavior. It appears that the project may be addressing some of the early risk factors associated with antisocial behavior and may be having some impact on those students who are at high risk of involvement in delinquency. However, definitive conclusions regarding the effects of the interventions of antisocial behavior await analysis of subsequent data from this longitudinal study.

REFERENCES

Achenbach, T. M., & Edelbrock, C. S. (1983). Taxonomic issues in child psychopathology. In T. H. Ollendick & M. Hersen (Eds.), *Handbook of child psychopathology*. New York: Plenum Press.

Adler, P. T., & Lutecka, L. (1973). Drug use among high school students: Patterns and correlates. *International Journal of Addictions, 8,* 537–548.

Akers, R. L. (1977). *Deviant behavior: A social learning approach* (2nd ed.). Belmont, CA: Wadsworth Press.

Akers, R. L., Krohn, M. D., Lanza-Kaduce, L., & Radosevich, M. (1979). Social learning and deviant behavior: A specific testing of a general theory. *American Sociological Review, 44* (4), 636–655.

Alfaro, J. (1976). Report of the New York State Assembly Select Committee on Child Abuse. *Child Protection, 2* (1).

Anhalt, H., & Klein, M. (1976). Drug abuse in junior high school populations. *American Journal of Drug and Alcohol Abuse, 3,* 589–603.

Aronson, E. (1978). *The jigsaw classroom.* Beverly Hills, CA: Sage.

Baumrind, D. (1983, October). *Why adolescents take chances and why they don't.* Presentation at the National Institute for Child Health and Human Development, Washington, D.C.

Block, J. H. (1971). *Mastery learning: Theory and practice.* New York: Holt, Rinehart, Winston.

Block, J. H. (1974). *Schools, society, and mastery learning.* New York: Holt, Rinehart, and Winston.

Bloom, B. S. (1976). *Human characteristics and school learning.* New York: McGraw-Hill.

Braukman, C. J., Kirigin, K. A., & Wolf, M. M. (1980). Group home treatment research: Social learning and social control perspectives. In T. Hirschi & M. Gottfredson (Eds.), *Understanding crime.* Beverly Hills, CA: Sage.

Brooks, J. S., Linkoff, I. F., & Whiteman, M. (1977). Peer, family, and personality domains as related to adolescents' drug behavior. *Psychological Report, 41,* 1095–1102.

Brown, S. E. (1984). Social class, child maltreatment, and delinquent behavior. *Criminology, 22* (2), 259–278.

Catalano, R. F. (1982). *Relative reward deprivation and delinquency causation.* Unpublished doctoral dissertation, University of Washington.

Chassin, L., Presson, C. C., Bensenberg, M., Corty, E., Olshavsky, R. W., & Sherman, S. J. (1981). Predicting adolescents' intentions to smoke cigarettes. *Journal of Health and Social Behavior, 22,* 445–55.

Cohen, A. K., & Short, J. F., Jr. (1961). Juvenile delinquency. In R. K. Merton & R. A. Nisbet (Eds.), *Contemporary social problems.* New York: Harcourt, Brace, and World.

Conger, R. O. (1976). Social control and social learning models of delinquent behavior: A synthesis. *Criminology, 15,* 117–126.

Conger, R. O. (1976). Social control and social learning models of delinquent behavior: A synthesis. *Criminology, 14,* 17–40.

Cummings, C. (1983). *Managing to teach.* Snohomish, WA: Snohomish Publishing Company.

Czikszentmihalyi, M., & Larson, R. (1978). Intrinsic rewards in school crime. *Crime and Delinquency, 24,* 322–335.

DeVries, D. L., & Slavin, R. E. (1978). Teams–games–tournament: A research review. *Journal of Research and Development in Education, 12,* 28–38.

Deykin, E. V. (1971). Life functioning in families of delinquent boys: An assessment model. *Social Services Review, 46* (1), 90–91.

Elliott, D. S., & Voss, H. L. (1974). *Delinquency and dropout.* Lexington, MA: Heath.

Elliot, D. S., Huizinga, D., & Ageton, S. S. (1982). *Explaining delinquency and drug use* (Report No. 21). Boulder, CO: Behavioral Research Institute.

Emmer, E. T., & Evertson, C. M. (1980). *Effective management at the beginning of the school year in junior high classes* (R & D Report #6107). Austin, TX: University of Texas at Austin, Research and Development Center for Teacher Education.

Farrington, D. P. (1979). Longitudinal research on crime and delinquency. In N. Morris, & M. Tonry (Eds.), *Crime and justice: An annual review of research* (Vol. 1, pp. 289–348). Chicago: University of Chicago Press.

Farrington, D. P. (1978). The family background of aggressive youths. In L. A. Hensor, M. Berger, & D. Shaffer (Eds.), *Aggression and anti-social behavior in childhood and adolescents.* Oxford: Pergamon Press.

Fraser, M. W., & Hawkins, J. D. (In press). Parent training for delinquency prevention: A review. *Child and youth services.*

Frease, D. E. (1973). Schools and delinquency: Some intervening processes. *Pacific Sociological Review, 16,* 426–448.

Friedman, A. S. (1983). High school drug abuse clients. In *clinical research notes, Division of clinical research.* Rockville, MD: National Institute on Drug Abuse.

Galli, N., & Stone, D. B. (1975). Psychological status of student drug users. *Journal of Drug Education, 5* (4), 327–333.

Garbarino, J. (1981). Child abuse and juvenile delinquency: The developmental impact of social isolation. In R. Hunner & Y. Walker (Eds.), *Exploring the relationship between child abuse and delinquency.* Montclair, NJ: Allanheld.

Gersten, J. C., Langner, T. S., Eisenberg, J. S., Simcha-Fagan, D. J., & McCarthy, E. D. (1976). Stability and change in types of behavioral disturbance of children and adolescents. *Journal of Abnormal Child Psychology, 4,* 111–127.

Ghodsian, M., Fogelman, K., Lambert, L., & Tibbenham, A. (1980). Changes in behavior ratings of a national sample of children. *British Journal of Social and Clinical Psychology, 19,* 247–256.

Ginsberg, I. J., & Greenley, J. R. (1978). Competing theories of marijuana use: A longitudinal study. *Journal of Health and Social Behavior, 19,* 22–34.

Glavin, J. P. (1972). Persistence of behavior disorders in children. *Exceptional children, 38,* 367–376.

Gold, M. (1978). Scholastic experiences, self-esteem and delinquent behaviors: A theory for alternative school. *Crime and Delinquency, (3),* 290–308.

Goldstein, J. W. (1975). Assessing the interpersonal determinants of adolescent drug use. In D. J. Lettieri (ed.), *Predicting adolescent drug abuse: A review of the issues, methods, and correlates.* Rockville, MD: National Institue on Drug Abuse.

Haskell, M. R., & Yablonsky, L. (1974). *Crime and delinquency* (2nd ed.). Chicago: Rand-McNally.

Hawkins, J. D. (1981). Student team learning: Preventing the flocking and feathering of delinquents. *Journal of Primary Prevention, 2* (1), 50–55.

Hawkins, J. D., Doveck, H., & Lishner, D. M. (unpublished). Changing teaching practices in mainstream classrooms to reduce discipline problems among low achievers. Seattle: University of Washington, Center for Social Welfare Research.

Hawkins, J. D., & Lam, T. (in press). Teacher practices, social development and delinquency. In J. Burchard (Ed.), *The prevention of delinquent behavior.* Beverly Hills, CA: Sage.

Hawkins, J. D., & Weis, J. G. (1985). The social development model: An integrated approach to delinquency prevention. *Journal of Primary Prevention, 6 (2)* 73–97.

Hawkins, J. D., Pastor, P. A., Jr., Bell, M., & Morrison, S. (1980). *A typology of cause-focused strategies of delinquency prevention.* (19810-341-233-1841), National Institute for Juvenile Justice and Delinquency Prevention, Office of Juvenile Justice and Delinquency Prevention. Washington, D.C.: U.S. Government Printing Office.

Hawkins, J. D., Lishner, D. M., & Catalano, R. F., Jr. (1985, April). Child predictors and the prevention of adolescent substance abuse. In C. L. Jones & R. J. Battjes (Eds.), *Etiology of drug abuse: Implications for prevention.* Washington D.C.: National Institute on Drug Abuse, ADM 85–1385.

Hindelang, M. (1973). Causes of delinquency: A partial replication and extension. *Social Problems, 20,* 471–487.

Hirschi, T. (1969). *Causes of delinquency.* Berkeley, CA: University of California Press.

Hoagland, C., Eyler, S., & Vacha, E. (1981). *Classroom learning to attain social skills: Teacher's handbook.* Orcutt, CA: Orcutt Union School District.

Huba, G. J., Wingard, J. A., & Bentler, P. M. (1979). Beginning adolescent drug use and peer and adult interactions. *Journal of Consulting and Clinical Psychology, 47,* 265–276.

Jensen, G. F. (1972). Parents, peers, and delinquent action: A test of the differential association perspective. *American Journal of Sociology, 78*, 562–575.

Jensen, G. F. (1976). Race, achievement, and delinquency: A further look at delinquency in a birth cohort. *American Journal of Sociology, 82*, 379–387.

Jessor, R. (1976). Predicting time of onset of marijuana use: A developmental study of high school youth. *Journal of Consulting and Clinical Psychology, 44*, 125–134.

Jessor, R., & Jessor, S. L. (1977). *Problem behavior and psychosocial development: A longitudinal study of youth.* New York: Academic Press.

Jessor, R., & Jessor, S. L. (1978). Theory testing in longitudinal research on marijuana use: In D. Kandel (Ed.), *Longitudinal research on drug use.* Washington, D.C.: Hemisphere.

Jessor, R., Chase, J. A., & Donovan, J. E. (1980). Psychosocial correlates of marijuana use and problem drinking in a national sample of adolescents. *American Journal of Public Health, 70*, 604–613.

Johnson, D. W., & Johnson, R. W. (1980). Cooperative learning: The power of positive goal interdependence. In V. M. Lyons (Ed.), *Structuring cooperative experiences in the classroom: The 1980 handbook.* Minneapolis, MN: Cooperation Network.

Johnson, R. E. (1979). *Juvenile delinquency and its origins: An integrated theoretical approach.* New York: Cambridge University Press.

Johnston, L. D., Bachman, J. G., & O'Malley, P. M. (1981). *Student drug use in America 1975–1981.* National Institute on Drug Abuse (DHHS. No. (ADM) 82-1208). Rockville, MD: National Institute on Drug Abuse.

Kandel, D. B. (1982). Epidemiological and psychosocial perspectives on adolescent drug use. *Journal of American Academic Clinical Psychiatry, 21*, 328–347.

Kandel, D. B., Kessler, R., & Margulies, R. (1978). Antecedents of adolescents' initiation into stages of drug use: A developmental analysis. In D. B. Kandel (Ed.), *Longitudinal research in drug use: Empirical findings and methodological issues* Washington, D.C.: Hemisphere-Wiley.

Kaplan, H. B., Martin, S. S., & Robbins, C. (1982). Applications of a general theory of deviant behavior: Self-derogation and adolescent drug use. *Journal of Health and Social Behavior, 23*, 274–294.

Kelly, D. H., & Balch, R. W. (1971). Social origins and school failure: A re-examination of Cohen's theory of working-class delinquency. *Pacific Sociological Review, 14*, 413–430.

Kim, S. (1979). *An evaluation of ombudsman primary prevention program on student drug abuse.* Charlotte, NC: Charlotte Drug Education Center, Inc.

Krohn, M. D., Massey, J. L., Laner, R. M., & Skinner, W. F. (1983, December). Social bonding theory and adolescent cigarette smoking: A longitudinal analysis. *Journal of Health and Social Behavior, 24*, 337–349.

Langner, T. S., Gersten, J. C., Wills, T. A., & Simcha-Fagan, O. (1983). The relative roles of early environment and early behavior as predictors of later child behavior. In D. F. Ricks & B. S. Dohrenwend (Eds.), *Origins of psychopathology.* New York: Cambridge University Press.

Linden, R., & Hacklee, J. C. (1973). Affective ties and delinquency. *Pacific Sociology Review, 16 (1)*, 27–46.

Loeber, R., & Dishion, T. (1983). Early predictors of male delinquency: A review. *Psychological Bulletin, 93*, 68–99.

Martin, D. L. (1977). Your praise can smother learning. *Learning, 5* (6), 42–51.

Meade, A. C., & Marsden, M. E. (1981). An integration of classic theories of delinquency. In A. C. Meade (Ed.), *Youth and society: Studies of adolescent deviance.* Chicago: Institute for Juvenile Research.

Meier, R. F., & Johnson, W. T. (1977). Deterrence as social control: The legal and extra-legal production of conformity. *American Sociological Review, 42* (2), 292–304.

Noblit, G. W. (1976). The adolescent experience and delinquency: School versus subculture effects. *Youth and Society, 8*, 27–44.

Nye, F. I. (1958). *Family relationships and delinquent behavior.* New York: Wiley.

O'Donnell, J. A., & Clayton, R. R. (1979). Determinants of early marijuana use. In G. M. Beschner & A. S. Friedman (Eds.), *Youth drug abuse: Problems, issues, and treatment.* Lexington, MA: Lexington Books.

O'Donnell, J. A., Voss, H. L., Clayton, R. R., & Room, R. (1976). *Young men and drugs: A nationwide survey:* NIDA Monograph 5. Washington, D.C.: U.S. Government Printing Office.

Orcutt, J. (1978). Normative definitions of intoxicated state: A test of several sociological theories. *Social Problems, 4,* 385–396.

Patterson, G. R. (1982). The management and disruption of families. In *A social learning approach, Vol. 3: Coercive family process.* Eugene, OR: Castalia Publishing.

Peterson, P. (1972). *A review of research on mastery learning strategies.* Unpublished manuscript. Stockholm: International Association for the Evaluation of Educational Achievement.

Pfouts, J. H., Scholpler, J. H., & Henley, H. C., Jr. (1981). Deviant behavior of child victims and bystanders in violent families. In J. Hunner & Y. E. Walker (Eds.), *Exploring the relationship between child abuse and delinquency.* Montclair, NJ: Allanheld, Osmun.

Polk, K., & Schafer, W. E. (1972). *School and delinquency.* Englewood Cliffs, NJ: Prentice-Hall.

Polk, K., Frease, D., & Richmond, F. L. (1974). Social class, school experience, and delinquency. *Criminology, 12,* 84–96.

Reid, J. (1975, April). *A social learning approach to family therapy: Outcome and process data.* Paper presented at the Symposium on Behavior Modification: Methodology and Psychotherapy, Monterey, NC, Mexico.

Robins, L. N. (1966). *Deviant children grown up: A sociological and psychiatric study of sociopathic personality.* Baltimore, MD: Williams & Wilkins.

Robins, L. N. (1978). Sturdy childhood predictors of adult anti-social behavior: Replications from longitudinal studies. *Psychological Medicine, 8,* 611–622.

Robins, L. N. (1979). Longitudinal methods in the study of normal and pathological development. *Psychiatrie der Gegenwart, Vol. 1: Grundlagen und Methoden der Psychiatrie* (2nd ed.). Heildelberg: Springer-Verlag.

Robins, L. N. (1980). The natural history of drug abuse. In *Evaluation of treatment of drug abusers. Acta Psychologica Scandinavia, Supplement 284,* 62.

Rutter, M., & Giller, H. (1983). *Juvenile delinquency: Trends and perspectives.* New York: Penguin Books.

Rutter, M., Maughan, B., Mortimore, P., & Ouston, J. (1979). *Fifteen thousand hours: Secondary school and their effects on children.* Cambridge, MA: Harvard University Press.

Sederstrom, J. (1978). *Family structure and juvenile delinquency.* Unpublished masters's thesis, University of Washington, Seattle.

Senna, J., Rathus, S. A., & Siegel, L. (1974). Delinquent behavior and academic investment among suburban youth. *Adolescence, 9,* 481–494.

Shibuya, R. R. (1974). Categorizing drug users and nonusers in selected social and personality variables. *Journal of School Health, 44,* 442–444.

Shore, M. F. (1971). Psychological theories of the causes of antisocial behavior. *Crime and Delinquency, 17,* 456–468.

Shure, M. B., & Spivack, G. (1979). Interpersonal problem solving in young children: A cognitive approach to prevention. *Journal of Clinical and Child Psychology, 8,* 89–94.

Simon, W. (1974). Psychological needs, academic achievement, and marijuana consumption. *Journal of Clinical Psychology, 30,* 496–498.

Slavin, R. E. (1979). *Using student team learning.* Baltimore, MD: Center for social organization of schools, Johns Hopkins University.

Slavin, R. E. (1980). Cooperative learning in teams: State of the art. *Educational Psychologist, 15,* 93–111.

Slavin, R. E. (1982). *Cooperative learning groups: Student teams. What the research says to the teacher.* Washington, D.C.: National Education Association.

Smart, R. G., Gray, G., & Bennett, C. (1978). Predictors of drinking and signs of heavy drinking among high school students. *International Journal of Addiction, 13,* 1079–1094.

Smith, G. M., & Fogg, C. P. (1978). Psychological predictors of early use, late use and non-use of marijuana among teenage students. In D. B. Kandel (Ed.), *Longitudinal research on drug use: Empirical findings and methodological issues.* Washington, D.C.: Hemisphere-Wiley.

Spivack, G., Rapsher, L., Cohen, A., & Gross, R. (1978). *High risk early signs for delinquency and related behavioral difficulties: The first nine years of a longitudinal study.* National Institute for Juvenile Justice and Delinquency Prevention, Office of Juvenile Justice and Delinquency Prevention, Law Enforcement Assistance Administration. Washington, D.C.: U.S. Department of Justice.

Stalling, J. (1980). Allocated academic learning time revisited, or beyond time on task. *Educational Researcher, 9* (11), 11–16.

Steele, B. (1976). Violence in the family. In R. Helfer & C. H. Kempe (Eds.), *Child abuse and neglect: The family and the community.* Cambridge, MA: Ballinger.

Timberlake, E. M. (1981). Child abuse and externalized aggression: Preventing a delinquent lifestyle. In R. J. Hunner & Y. E. Walker (Ed.), *Exploring the relationship between child abuse and delinquency.* Montclair, NJ: Allanheld, Osmun.

Wechsler, H., & Thum, D. (1973). Teenage drinking, drug use, and social correlates. *Quarterly Journal of Studies on Alcohol, 34,* 1220–1227.

Weis, J. G., & Hawkins, J. D. (1981). *Prevention delinquency: The social development approach.* National Institute for Juvenile Justice and Delinquency Prevention, Office of Juvenile Justice and Delinquency Prevention, Law Enforcement Assistance Administration, United States Department of Justice. Seattle, WA: University of Washington, Center for Law and Justice.

Weis, J. G., Hall, J. D., Henney, J. S., Sederstrom, J., Worsley, K., & Zeiss, C. (1980). *Peer influence and delinquency: An evaluation of theory and practices* (Part I and Part II). National Institute for Juvenile Justice and Delinquency Prevention, Office of Juvenile Justice and Delinquency Prevention, Law Enforcement Assistance Administration. Washington, D.C.: U.S. Department of Justice.

Werner, E. E., & Smith, R. S. (1977). *Kauai's children come of age.* Honolulu, HI: University Press of Hawaii.

West, D. J., & Farrington, D. P. (1973). *Who becomes delinquent?* London: Heinemann.

Wilkinson, R. (1974). *Prevention of drinking problems: Alcohol control and cultural influences.* New York: Oxford University Press.

Winfree, L. T., Theis, H. E., & Griffiths, C. T. (1981). Drug use in rural America: A cross-cultural examination of complementary social deviance theories. *Youth and Society, 12* (4), 465–489.

Wohlford, P., & Giammona, S. T. (1969). Personality and social variables related to the initiation of smoking cigarettes. *Journal of School Health, 39,* 544–552.

PART IV

OVERVIEW

CHAPTER 12

Childhood Aggression and Violence
Individual and System Approaches

CLIFFORD R. O'DONNELL

In his introductory chapter, Deane Neubauer offered some caveats for our consideration, noting that in American culture and society violence and aggression are framed as a social problem and that "we are led by our values, beliefs, and professional training to seek resolution of the problem by locating it within the individual and searching for means of effective individual intervention." The effects, he warned, "of articulating individual-focused behavior changes as the *primary* vehicle for intervention" are to shift responsibility onto individuals, to suggest that little "can be done to affect these problems at the level of social causation," to medicalize, professionalize, and depoliticize the issue, and to provide intervention in a form most likely to benefit "those groups predisposed by education and other SES-related attributes to change in a self-interested direction." He then concluded that although an individual focus is vitally important it is also insufficient and hoped that we would not pursue it "to the extent that efforts to expand the social understanding and treatment of violence and aggression are shunted aside as important but somehow insufficiently demanding problems for our attention."

The purpose of this final chapter is to consider the contributions to this volume in light of these caveats. First the approach that locates childhood aggression and violence within the individual is considered. It is followed by a presentation of a *systems* approach that is being developed as an alternative. For each approach, the relevant material from the preceding chapters is briefly considered and an assessment is made of the contribution of the approach and its potential for the future.

CLIFFORD R. O'DONNELL • Department of Psychology, University of Hawaii at Manoa, Honolulu, Hawaii 96822.

CHILDHOOD AGGRESSION AND VIOLENCE WITHIN THE INDIVIDUAL

Efforts have been made to locate aggression and violence within the individual by means of both biological and psychological variables. Much of the evidence using biological variables was reviewed in chapter 2. Genetics, hormones, and hyperactivity were emphasized. Overall, the evidence linking biological variables to childhood aggression and violence has been weak, except in the case of a small minority of individuals.

In reviewing the findings on genetic variables, Crowell noted that the best evidence for genetic influence is among chronic criminals. Although chronic criminals are a relatively small percentage of those who engage in crime, they are nevertheless important because of their multiple offenses. It is possible that in these individuals there is some biological factor that is transmitted genetically (Mednick, Gabrielli, & Hutchings, 1983). Overall, however, Crowell concluded that although "there is suggestive evidence that antisocial behavior might be attributed to polygenic factors" the effect, if any, is of low magnitude and "none of the evidence currently appears likely to define specific genetic factors that directly or indirectly influence aggressive behavior."

Hormonal variables have been most extensively investigated in gender studies. There is agreement that males and females differ in overt aggressive activity, but whether this difference can be attributed to biological differences is the subject of much debate. On the basis of Crowell's review, the evidence for a hormonal base underlying gender differences in aggressive activity is inconclusive. To date, however, it suggests that a hormonal influence, if any, is small.

Finally, there is some evidence that those hyperactive children with the highest rates of activity across many situations are also most likely to be involved in aggressive acts (Prinz, Connor, & Wilson, 1981; Schleifer et al., 1975). Whether this relationship is an artifact, with higher rates of activity increasing the rates of all active behaviors, or a precursor of adolescent or adult criminal behavior is unknown at this time. The identification of this subgroup of hyperactive children does, however, offer opportunities for further research.

The studies reviewed by Crowell of the use of biological variables to locate aggression and violence within the individual indicate that, at best, there may be a relationship sufficient to explain the behavior in a limited number of individuals. In chapter 3, Pincus also stated that the same is true with neurological variables. He presented evidence suggesting "the importance of considering the presence of organic brain dysfunction in extremely violent children" but noted that this evidence applies to only a small number of children. The identification of these individuals and the specific biological or neurological variables is nevertheless important, especially if chronic criminal or violent behavior is involved. At the present time, however, the possibility that biological or neurological variables could account for most childhood aggression and violence appears remote.

Psychosocial variables are the other means by which aggression and violence may be located within the individual. Of course, psychosocial variables may also be used to locate aggression and violence within the behavioral systems, such as the family, in which the individual participates. To focus on the individual, it is necessary to show how aggressive and violent behavior can be acquired, and the specific psychosocial conditions associated with their acquisition, and to demonstrate that they occur in other circumstances and that they are maintained over time. Overall, the available evidence presented throughout the chapters in this volume indicates that these requirements have been met in the case of some individuals. For example, in Chapter 4 Evans and Scheuer used the theory of social behaviorism (Staats, 1975) to show how aggressive and violent behaviors can be acquired as part of a repertoire of responses, with examples of aggressive and violent behaviors in relationship to other parts of a repertoire such as overactivity, intellectual handicap and other developmental disabilities, social skills, and internalized social prohibitions. In addition, some specific psychosocial family characteristics such as negative, punitive, coercive family patterns, marital hostility, and child abuse have been associated with highly aggressive children. Furthermore, aggressive behavior has often come to the attention of authorities precisely because it did occur outside of the family and was maintained over time.

Indeed, stability is often a characteristic of male aggressive behavior. Crowell reviewed studies of aggression and antisocial behavior among boys and found moderate correlations in aggressive patterns over 18 years. The younger the age at which the behavior began and the greater the number of settings in which it occurred, the more likely it was to continue. Fighting, conflict with parents, and delinquency appeared particularly stable. Eron *et al.* (Chapter 10) also found some stability in aggression over 22 years for males. They correlated peer-nominated aggression at age 8 with a variety of adult-aggression measures at age 30. Although there was little evidence for continuity of aggression for females, there was modest evidence for males (correlations of .21 to .30, Table 3 in Chapter 10). Since the continuity extends from childhood to adult status, these data indicate that there are individuals, mostly male, for whom aggressive behavior is stable. These data do not address the questions of the cause of the stability of aggression among some individuals, of the instability among others, or of the gender difference. Studies reviewed by Olweus (1984) show that aggressive behavior is more stable over shorter durations, even among females, and that the lower stability among females may occur because there are "far fewer highly aggressive girls than boys."

Research on efforts to locate childhood aggression and violence within the individual using either biological or psychosocial variables has resulted in knowledge of how these behaviors may be acquired and in some cases continue over many years. In addition, progress has been made on the early identification of these individuals.

Many have suggested that this knowledge be used to develop screening methods for early identification and intervention. There are two reasons why any procedures to implement these suggestions should be critically examined. First, as Evans and Scheuer point out, there are many problems inherent in the use of the rating scales that are often used in the assessment of aggression and even with the best of these early predictors the rate of false predictions is high. For example, in the studies reviewed by Crowell, predictions were far better for stealers than for those considered aggressive, of whom only 15% later became delinquent (Moore, Chamberlain, & Mukai, 1979); of those who were delinquent before the age of 14, 59% were no longer committing crimes by their 17th year and most of the offenses were nonviolent (Hamparian, Schuster, Dinitz, & Conrad, 1978); and even with the three-stage screening assessment proposed by Loeber, Dishion, and Patterson (1984) there was a 44% false positive error rate. If the procedures developed by Eron *et al.* were used to predict conviction of a crime by age 30, the false positive error rate would be 77% for males and 93.7% for females nominated as highest in aggression at age 8 (see Table 5 in Chapter 10).

The second reason is that intervention is often ineffective or of short-term benefit (O'Donnell, 1977). Intervention programs may even exacerbate the problem for some participants (e.g., O'Donnell, Lydgate, & Fo, 1979). In this volume, Belsky and Vondra (Chapter 7) also warned against relying solely on treatment. They pointed out that remedial efforts can often suffer from lack of client motivation, social stigma, excessive cost in time, energy, and money, and limitations on the number of people who can be served. They also noted the "notoriously poor success rates" of parental remediation for child maltreatment. Pincus (Chapter 3) also noted the limited use of medication, psychosurgery, and psychotherapy. In addition, his suggestion "to separate very violent individuals from society in some manner until their thirties or until some truly effective therapeutic measure is developed" is also limited to those individuals convicted of a crime that justifies such a sentence.

Since early identification and intervention procedures may identify many youngsters for whom intervention is inappropriate, and intervention may be ineffective, costly, and sometimes harmful, it is necessary to attempt to reduce these possibilities. One means to reduce at least the possibility of harm is to ensure that neither the identification nor the intervention procedures result in the labeling of youngsters. Although it will often be necessary to select and identify individual youths to implement and evaluate the program, this information can frequently be restricted so that those in a position to affect the youths, such as peers, teachers, and parents, would not label the selected youngsters. Another safeguard is to avoid increasing contact among youths who are at higher risk for antisocial or delinquent behavior. All too often programs intended to prevent or treat antisocial behavior provide the activities and occasions for contact among the participants and thus counteract any beneficial program effects (O'Donnell, Manos, & Chesney-Lind, in press).

Overall, the efforts to locate childhood aggression and violence within the individual have resulted in some worthwhile progress. It currently appears that there are individuals, much more likely to be male, who engage in antisocial or aggressive behavior at a young age, in a variety of settings, and continue to do so over many years. Additional research may result in much greater accuracy in the identification of these individuals. If so, then intervention programs will have fewer misidentified participants at risk, and more effective intervention strategies may be developed.

However, the available evidence also suggests that the individual-focused approach is limited because many individuals do not fit the pattern and because, as Evans and Scheuer noted, in cases of crime many criminals are not apprehended. For them, it may be that the occurrence of aggressive or antisocial behavior is strongly influenced by their social context. In this view the social context is important not only in regard to how behavior may be acquired but also in regard to the probability, timing, location, and form of occurrence. Several of the chapters in this volume used a systems approach to incorporate social context. This approach considers the individual as an essential part of the social context; together they form a unit, and neither can be completely understood separately.

TOWARD A SYSTEMS ALTERNATIVE

Although many sources of influence have been addressed in these chapters, the major emphasis has been on the family. Teru Morton (Chapter 6) discussed a family systems approach in detail. She presented the family as an arena of conflict with finite resources to meet the competing needs and desires of its members. Aggression was seen as one of an array of social influence strategies learned by children in this competitive process. The quality of the marital relationship was the most important factor in the regulation of this inherent conflict. A good relationship helped to balance competing interests and supported positive child development. Correspondingly, marital problems were associated with disruptions in family functioning. In one type of disfunction, negative, punitive, coercive family patterns were linked to the rearing of highly aggressive children.

Morton also provided examples of how problem family patterns could develop. She reviewed studies of the coercive trap in which parents reinforce aversive behavior by complying with the child's demands. In this process parents are negatively reinforced by the termination of the aversive behavior. This can then develop into a contagion process in which other children in the family learn to use coercion, often with the mother as victim, and dyadic relationships within the family become increasingly negative. In these families the mother is often the link between the aggressive behavior of the children and the marital problems with her husband. The strain this places on the role of the mother–wife may well exacerbate the problems.

This connection between parental and child functioning was also supported by Belsky and Vondra (Chapter 7). The studies they reviewed showed that parental psychological problems can undermine child development. Most notably, the aggression of adolescent sons was associated with the marital hostility of their parents. In contrast, marital harmony promoted their social competence.

The most direct evidence of parental behavior's causing childhood aggression came from the literature on child abuse. Pincus (Chapter 3) noted that a factor strongly distinguishing the small number of extremely violent children "was a history of extreme physical abuse by parents or parent substitutes" and that for these children neurological factors "are interactive with environmental factors and perhaps particularly with abuse." Belsky and Vondra documented childhood aggression as a "primary pattern of response to abuse" and concluded that violence "seems to be a consistent pattern displayed by abused children, many of whom are otherwise characterized by an emotional unresponsiveness." In addition, Crowell reviewed studies concluding that "parental assaultive behavior increases the probability of childhood assaultiveness" and that the common factor in the etiology of violent sex offenses was the significant role of the family (Knight, Prentky, Schneider, & Rosenberg, 1983). This evidence was supported by Chesney-Lind (Chapter 8), who reported the high rates of physical and sexual abuse adult women in prison had received as children.

Chapter 7 extended the family systems approach into an ecological model based on the family. Developed from earlier work by Bronfenbrenner (1979) and Belsky (1980), it analyzes child maltreatment as a function of many interrelated processes. These include the developmental history of the parents (ontogenic development), the interaction of child characteristics with the other factors of family functioning (microsystem), extrafamilial factors that can affect family life such as a restricted social network, unemployment, and social isolation (ecosystem), and the cultural values by which childrearing practices are evaluated (macrosystem). The comprehensiveness of this model provides a context for all the familial sources of influence on childhood aggression. This allows for the assessment of how each factor may itself be influenced by related processes and contribute to the perpetuation of aggression across generations.

Another contribution toward a systems alternative is provided by Hawkins and Lishner (Chapter 11). According to their theory of social development, the prevention of antisocial behavior is a function of the social bonding of youth to family, school, and prosocial peers. Bonds form when there are opportunities, necessary skills, and reinforcement for involvement in familial, educational, and prosocial-peer activities. In their study of low-achieving seventh-graders, they encouraged the development of these bonds by the use of skills-training for parents, conflict resolution services for students and their families, improvement of teaching methods, and experience-based career education activities. The preliminary results of this longitudinal experiment show that those in the experimental group liked school more, had higher expectations for future education, and were suspended less often than those in the control group.

A contribution of this theory is the inclusion of family, school, and peers within one system. This contribution allows a study of how one part of the system may affect the others. For example, one possibility is to examine the degree of influence parents exert over the school and peer activities of their children. Parents may exert this influence by their choice of schools, their own involvement in school and neighborhood activities, and the opportunities and reinforcement they provide for skill development and activities at home, in school, and with prosocial peers.

The concept of the degree of parental influence may also be extended to help account for the traditional difference in arrest rates between boys and girls. Chesney-Lind presented an intriguing account of how girls might come to have lower official rates of serious delinquency and violence. Noting that there is considerably less disparity between genders in self-report studies of serious delinquency than in official rates, especially in the percentage of individuals committing delinquent acts, she reviewed evidence that females engage in the delinquent behavior in more private settings and therefore are usually less vulnerable to arrest. Those who are arrested are more likely to have frequented public settings, often as a result of less parental supervision, family conflicts, and abuse. Some run away from problem homes and thereby receive increased exposure to crime and greater support for delinquent behavior, and become more susceptible to arrest. In this analysis, what had been typically understood as a gender difference became more of a setting phenomenon.

This suggests that an important key to arrest rates for both girls and boys is the combination of association with delinquent peers and participation in public settings. The effect of family ties is based on the potential to influence these associations and settings. Traditionally most families have exercised this influence less with boys than with girls and therefore arrest rates have been higher for boys. However, when family problems lower the parental supervision of girls, their arrest rates also become higher.

Suggestions for intervention in childhood aggression based on this evolving systems approach were offered in several of the chapters. Pearl (Chapter 9), who summarized familial, peer, and especially television influences, focused on parental control. He cited methods parents could use to help their children develop critical viewing skills: limit the amount of time children watch television, control the programs children view, provide explanatory comments and discuss programs with their children and others, and relate television information to events in everyday life.

Morton recommended child management training, marriage therapy, and family systems therapy. She noted that training parents in child management can be effective when inadequate parenting skill is the primary problem but that marital therapy may be necessary if the parents of an aggressive child have a troubled marriage. More complex family problems may require family systems therapy to enhance communication, achieve supportive relationships, and improve family problem solving.

Direct-treatment forms of intervention are, of course, also consistent with the individual-focused approach. The unique potential of a systems approach lies in the development of prevention efforts within the organized systems of everyday life. Belsky and Vondra offered specific suggestions for doing so. They suggested that preventive efforts be directed through target settings rather than specific, identified individuals. By making services available to everyone within the setting, they hope to avoid the difficulties associated with labeling individuals as people with problems requiring special help. They also offered examples of services for family development. Suggested were formal training for parenthood in school, family-planning services accessible to teenagers, parenthood-training in childbirth classes, support services and information for parents through health care, day-care, and workplace personnel, and an integrated community service network designed for early intervention. In each, the use of geographic and setting propinquity was encouraged to extend the social networks of the participants.

These suggestions are consistent with the family and school-based program of Hawkins and Lishner and could also be extended to place a greater emphasis on peers. Peer influence is especially important during adolescence. As the studies of Turiel (Chapter 5) pointed out, developing social organization concepts can produce strong group commitments among adolescents. Adolescents whose parents exercise little influence, those who live in problem homes with few resources, family conflict, or abuse, and those who attend schools in which their opportunities and participation are restricted, are particularly vulnerable to antisocial peer influence. The development of their moral judgments is then stimulated by reciprocal social interaction with antisocial peers (Turiel). We need to know more about peer settings and networks, about the roles of youth within these settings, about the activities performed by youths in these roles, and about how peer settings and networks vary with degree and types of participation in family and school settings (O'Donnell, 1984).

We do know that delinquency rates are higher among youths in peer-controlled settings (Schwendinger & Schwendinger, 1982) and that settings which bring antisocial, aggressive, or delinquent youth together are counterproductive.

In a review of neighborhood and diversion delinquency programs, O'Donnell *et al.* (in press) found the social network to be the common factor which best explained the results. Programs which provided activities which brought participants in contact with each other were ineffective or harmful, while the few which discouraged contact among participants produced some positive outcomes.

CONCLUSION

In summary, both individual and system approaches have contributed to our understanding of childhood aggression and violence. The potential of a strict individual-focused approach may be best developed by a focus on those who repeatedly engage in aggression and violence. An understanding of these individuals is important, since their rates of aggressive and violent acts exceed their proportion in numbers. A systems approach, based on the family but developing to include school and peer influences, offers the promise of a more complete understanding of childhood aggression and violence with the potential for effective prevention.

As Evans and Scheuer noted, the linking of individual and system approaches is no contradiction. A system is comprised of settings, which form the link to individuals. Obviously, all individual behavior occurs in some setting and is thereby part of a larger system; and all human settings, by definition, include individuals whose behavior contributes to the operation of the setting. The evaluation of referred individuals can often benefit from the assessment of others in the setting of interest (e.g., Melahn & O'Donnell, 1978). Indeed, the *occurrence* of a behavior in a specific setting may depend on its relationship to the response repertoires of others in the setting; skills and deficiencies are, of course, always relative to the competencies of others and the demands of the setting. In turn, a detailed assessment of a setting requires knowledge of the response repertoires of individuals and of how well they match the response required by their roles and the activities of the setting.

It is the potential of the developing systems approach to provide the context for individual behavior that is responsive to the concern expressed by Neubauer in his introductory chapter: that the recognition of the vital importance of an individual focus not shunt aside efforts to expand the social understanding of aggression and violence. That our understanding of these problems requires knowledge of individuals and their social systems is illustrated by the sources of influence, prevention, and control presented in this volume.

REFERENCES

Belsky, J. (1980). Child maltreatment: An ecological integration. *American Psychologist, 35,* 320–335.

Bronfenbrenner, U. (1979). *The ecology of human development: Experiments by nature and design*. Cambridge, MA: Harvard University Press.

Hamparian, D. M., Schuster, R., Dinitz, S., & Conrad, J. P. (1978). *The violent few*. Lexington: Heath.

Knight, R., Prentky, R., Schneider, B., & Rosenberg, R. (1983). Linear causal modeling of adaptation and criminal history in sexual offenses. In K. T. Van Dusen & S. A. Mednick (Eds.), *Prospective studies of crime and delinquency*. Boston: Kluwer-Nijhoff.

Loeber, R., Dishion, T. J., & Patterson, G. R. (1984). Multiple gating: A multistage assessment procedure for identifying youths at risk for delinquency. *Journal of Research in Crime and Delinquency, 21*, 7–32.

Mednick, S. A., Gabrielli, W. F., & Hutchings, B. (1983). Genetic influence in criminal behavior: Evidence from an adaptation cohort. In K. T. Van Dusen & S. A. Mednick (Eds.), *Prospective studies of crime and delinquency* (pp. 39–56). Boston: Kluwer-Nijhoff.

Melahn, C. L., & O'Donnell, C. R. (1978). Norm-based behavioral consulting. *Behavior Modification, 2*, 309–338.

Moore, D. R., Chamberlain, P., & Mukai, L. (1979). A follow-up comparison of stealing and aggression. *Journal of Abnormal Child Psychology, 7*, 345–355.

O'Donnell, C. R. (1977). Behavior modification in community settings. In M. Hersen, R. M. Eisler, & P. M. Miller (Eds.), *Progress in behavior modification* (Vol. 4). New York: Academic Press.

O'Donnell, C. R. (1984). Behavioral community psychology and the natural environment. In C. M. Franks & C. Diament (Eds.), *New developments in practical behavior therapy: From research to clinical applications* (pp. 495–524). New York: Haworth Press.

O'Donnell, C. R., Lydgate, T., & Fo, W. S. O. (1979). The buddy system: Review and follow-up. *Child and Family Behavior Therapy, 1*, 161–169.

O'Donnell, C. R., Manos, M. J., & Chesney-Lind, M. (In press). Diversion and neighborhood delinquency programs in open settings: A social network interpretation. In E. K. Morris & C. J. Braukmann (Eds.), *Behavioral approaches to crime and delinquency: Application, research, and theory*. New York: Plenum Press.

Olweus, D. (1984). Stability in aggressive and withdrawn inhibited behavior patterns. In R. M. Kaplan, V. J. Konecni, & R. W. Novaco (Eds.), *Aggression in children and youth* (pp. 104–137). Boston: M. Nijhoff.

Prinz, R., Connor, P., & Wilson, C. (1981). Hyperactive and aggressive behaviors in childhood: Intertwined dimensions. *Journal of Abnormal Psychology, 9*, 191–202.

Schleifer, M., Weiss, G., Cohen, N. J., Elman, M., Cvejic, H., & Kruger, E. (1975). Hyperactivity in preschoolers and the effect of methylphenidate. *American Journal of Orthopsychiatry, 45*, 38–50.

Schwendinger, H., & Schwendinger, J. (1982). The paradigmatic crisis in delinquency theory. *Crime and Social Justice, 17*, 70–78.

Staats, A. W. (1975). *Social behaviorism*. Homewood, IL: Dorsey Press.

Index